Ancestry

**Portrait of Mrs Ellen Lloyd of Tŷ Newydd
painted by Hugh Hughes in 1845**

Second Stages in
RESEARCHING
WELSH
ANCESTRY

Edited by
John & Sheila Rowlands

FFHS/UWA
1999

Published by
The Federation of Family History Societies (Publications) Ltd
in conjunction with
**The Department of Continuing Education,
University of Wales, Aberystwyth**

Distributed by:
      The Federation of Family History Societies (Publications) Ltd,
      2-4 Killer Street, Ramsbottom, Bury, Lancs BL0 9BZ

Copies also available from:
      John and Sheila Rowlands
      PO Box 37, Aberystwyth, Ceredigion SY23 2WL

Cover design by Elgan Davies of The Welsh Books Council

Typeset by the Editors
Printed and bound by Biddles Ltd of Guildford

CONTENTS

LIST OF FIGURES
(including Tables and Appendices)

ACKNOWLEDGEMENTS

Unless otherwise stated, illustrations come from private collections and are reproduced by kind permission of the owners. Maps, tables and pedigree charts with the exception of those listed below have been drawn and compiled by the individual authors or by the editors. The map in Fig. 5-2 was drawn with the assistance of Antony Smith. Unfortunately we have been unable to ascertain who drew the map in Fig. 22-2.

Permission to reproduce the following is gratefully acknowledged:
Frontispiece: Mrs C.J. Jones (photograph by Gerallt Llewelyn, Caernarfon).
The National Library of Wales, Aberystwyth, for Figs 3-2 and 5-1, Figs. 9-3 and 9-4, reproduced from P.C. Bartrum, *Welsh Genealogies AD 1400-1500* (Aberystwyth, 1983), and Figure 22-1 (Parliament House of Owain Glyndwr, Dolgelley by A. Le Petit, *c*.1820).
The University of Wales Press for Figs. 9-1 and 9-2, reproduced from P.C. Bartrum, *Welsh Genealogies AD 300-1400* (Cardiff, 1974).
Merthyr Tydfil Borough Library and Museum for Fig. 5-3.
Figs. 15-1 and 15-2 are © Crown copyright, 1998, from copies in the possession of RCAHM (Wales).
Mr and Mrs W. Ll. Jones for Fig. 19-1 (photograph by Gerallt Llewelyn, Caernarfon).
Carmarthenshire Archive Service for Fig. 21-2.

NOTES ON CONTRIBUTING AUTHORS

Emeritus Professor Ieuan Gwynedd Jones was born in the Rhondda and educated at Bridgend Grammar School, University of Wales, Swansea, and Peterhouse, Cambridge. Appointed to a lectureship in History at Swansea in 1953, he then held the Sir John Williams Chair of Welsh History at the University of Wales, Aberystwyth, from 1970 until retirement in 1984. He is an Honorary Fellow of the University of Wales, Swansea.

Michael Gandy, FSG, is Chairman of the Catholic Family History Society and a former member of the Council of the Catholic Record Society. He is the author of *Catholic Missions and Registers 1700-1800*; *Catholic Family History: a bibliography* and many articles on aspects of tracing Catholic ancestry in England and Wales since the Reformation.

Sheila Rowlands, FSG, a native of Pembrokeshire, is a History graduate and teacher. The founding Director of Family History in Wales courses in 1986, she has helped to organise them and given talks on varied subjects ever since. She has edited several family history society journals and is co-editor of *Welsh Family History: A Guide to Research* and co-author of *The Surnames of Wales*.

John Rowlands, FSG, is a Chartered Civil Engineer and is the Chairman of the Cardiganshire FHS. He has been a Director of the Family History in Wales courses since 1989. He has lectured extensively in Britain and abroad on aspects of Welsh research. He is co-editor of *Welsh Family History: A Guide to Research* and co-author of *The Surnames of Wales*.

Dr Sandra Wheatley helped found the original Family History in Wales course and is an Associate Director. She has lectured widely on aspects of family and local history, including talks on the use of illustrations for family historians. Her research interests include the 18th and 19th century historical geography of Wales and cartographic history; she has contributed to the *Cardiganshire County History*.

Dr Malcolm Symons, a Civil Engineer specialising in the field of Geotechnics, has worked in industry and lectured at the University of Wales, Cardiff. He acts as a mining consultant to civil engineering companies and as expert witness in legal cases. He has researched the history of the coal mining industry in the Llanelli area of Carmarthenshire for many years, lecturing and publishing regularly on the topic.

Dr Susan Davies has taught palaeography and archive studies to trainee archivists at the University of Wales, Aberystwyth, for many years, as well as providing short courses for others. She has run palaeography workshops during several Family History in Wales courses, and has a personal interest in local and family history.

Dr Michael Siddons, Hon. D.Litt. (Wales), FSA, FSG, is Herodr Arbennig Cymru/Wales Herald Extraordinary. He is author of the three-volume work, *The Development of Welsh Heraldry* (1991-3), of *Visitations by the Heralds in Wales* (1996), and is working on the continuation of Peter Bartrum's *Welsh Genealogies, AD 1400-1500*.

Murray Chapman, FICE, has had an interest in the Court of Great Sessions records since his study of the history of his home county of Montgomeryshire led to the discovery that little work had been done on these records. In 1996, the National Library of Wales jointly with the Powysland Club published the first of a series of transcripts of Montgomeryshire Gaol Files.

Graham C.G. Thomas is Senior Assistant Archivist in the Department of Manuscripts and Records, National Library of Wales. Born and educated in Cardiff, he has been on the staff of NLW since 1974, previously working as an Assistant Librarian in Liverpool University. He is the author of *The Charters of the Abbey of Ystrad Marchell* (Aberystwyth, 1997), and has contributed many articles on Welsh literature to learned journals.

Hilary Malaws B.Lib., MIFA, is Head of Library and Reader Services at the RCAHM (Wales), for which she has worked since 1977. With a keen interest in local and heritage studies, she is a Past President of the Association for Industrial Archaeology, a former Chairman of the Wales/Cymru Group of the Institute of Field Archaeologists and currently Secretary of the Welsh Mills Society.

Gerald Morgan has spent his career in Welsh education, working as a secondary school teacher and headteacher, and for the past ten years in the University of Wales, Aberystwyth. He has written and published extensively on a variety of subjects, most recently on the history of Ceredigion.

Dr Lewis Lloyd (1939-1997), after lecturing in Law at universities in Britain and Australia, taught Politics at Coleg Harlech until his retirement in 1992. Local, family and maritime history were spare-time interests, but he was a prolific author and speaker. He was a founding editor of *Maritime Wales/Cymru a'r Môr*.

J. Dilwyn Williams is a qualified archivist and teacher who now works as a free-lance researcher and lecturer, based mainly at the University of Wales, Bangor. He has taught for the WEA and the Centre for Continuing Education, Bangor, for a number of years, specialising in the history of the landed estates of Llŷn.

Helen Hughes Kaznowski comes of a loyal but long-exiled Welsh family. London-born but Norfolk-bred, she has a B.A. Honours degree in Geography (London, 1947). After many years of various teaching jobs, her large family and a life-long interest in History and writing now keeps her busy.

Marion Martin, a piano teacher from Dorset and member of the Incorporated Society of Musicians, has been researching her Welsh ancestry since 1993 and attended courses at the University of Wales from that year to 1997. She began studying 'Family and Community History' with the Open University in February 1999.

Dr E. Mary Hartley, MBE (1923-1998), was educated at Newnham College, Cambridge, obtaining a Ph.D. in Mathematics in 1951. After teaching at the University of London, she worked in Africa, teaching at universities in Ghana for many years. In retirement she pursued her researches into her family history, attending the very first, and several subsequent, Family History in Wales courses, and also taught the subject for the University of the Third Age.

FOREWORD

The origins of this book lie in courses on family history which have been run annually as residential summer schools at the University of Wales, Aberystwyth, since 1986. From the outset the main course on offer was a basic 'Family History in Wales' course, the content of which has remained broadly the same over the years. The high quality of presentations on this course has been regularly commented on by those who have attended and it has certainly been a cause for regret for us as directors that they have had to be confined to a maximum of thirty participants each year. In an effort to overcome this the core of those presentations formed the basis for *Welsh Family History: a Guide to Research*, which was published by the Federation of Family History Societies in 1991. A second edition was produced in 1996 following major local government re-organisation in Wales.

In time we came under pressure to offer a more advanced course and from 1991 a series of courses under the title 'Second Stages in Researching Welsh Ancestry' have been run – initially they were week-long courses but more recently they have been held over long weekends. These courses have focused on specific themes, which have included: 'Sources for Family History in Wales 1660-1830', 'Occupations and the Records Relating to them', 'People, Places and Pedigrees', and, essentially at the same level but in conjunction with the Society of Genealogists, 'Genealogy on the Wales-England Border'.

Typical courses have been attended by people from all over Britain and also from Australia, Canada, New Zealand and the United States. They were expected to have completed a basic 'Family History in Wales' course or an equivalent elsewhere. This became particularly relevant when, in 1995, it was decided that these courses should offer the opportunity for credits as part of the formal teaching programme of the University. As we have always tried to give personal attention to course-members, once again there was a limit on the numbers which could attend; this time it was set at twenty-four. The only exception to this was 'Genealogy on the Wales-England Border' which, being more of a conference (which did not offer credits) than a course, had an attendance of just under a hundred.

On these second stage courses we have been privileged to listen to so many valuable talks that we felt it very unsatisfactory that they should be heard once and for all by only a small number of people. For economic reasons it is rarely practicable to re-run a course and so we decided to approach our many lecturers to contribute to a book which might be seen as a companion volume to *Welsh Family History: a Guide to Research*. It is in this way that this book has come about.

If every lecturer had been in a position to contribute, the book would have become unwieldy, so we selected themes and chose our speakers (now our contributing authors), around those themes. This book may, therefore, be seen as having six parts, the first five of which have the following themes:

- Religion and Society
- Industry and Occupations
- Documents and Specialist Studies
- People and Places
- The Welsh at Home and in the Professions

The sixth and final part arose out of the fact that, when the system of accreditation of courses came in, participants had to complete assignments both during and (voluntarily) after their course. As the general standard of post-course essays was very good it seemed eminently sensible to us to include a small number of them in this book, not least as a means of encouraging others to set down on paper the product of their researches. In the event we chose three to include here. Although there were many worthy candidates for inclusion, we chose these particular ones chiefly for the contribution they make to our understanding of Welsh family and social life. We should mention that these assignments were illustrated with relevant pictures and copies of documents which, for reasons of copyright and space, could not be reproduced here.

With the exception of the final three chapters, this book is, therefore, largely based on talks which have been given over several years, with all the variety of approach we might expect from many individual lecturers, all of whom have been encouraged to retain their personal approach. No author was required to update a talk for the book but, not surprisingly, some chose to introduce newer material, and this is particularly noticeable (and useful) in the select bibliographies and endnotes. Many lecturers on the courses used large numbers of illustrations and, of course, once again we could only reproduce a small number here.

Unfortunately, the concomitant of running the courses for a long period has been the loss of some (both speakers and participants) who have become very good friends. One such loss occurred in April 1997, with the death of Dr Lewis Lloyd. Lewis had spoken on maritime matters on both the basic and the second stage courses over the years. He always combined his visits with research at the National Library of Wales and frequently joined us for the traditional end-of-course supper, appearing several times in our souvenir group photographs. We were delighted when he agreed both to speak on the Pugh family of Llanfair to the September 1996 course and to write up his talk for this book. His sudden death left us with a personal sense of loss, which will be shared by all who met him. We are most fortunate to have had permission to adapt a paper he had already had published which contains much of the material covered in his talk. However, this was considerably longer than we could include here and, in the end, we adopted the compromise of producing a shortened version, concentrating on the aspects covered during the course. With regret we had to omit his endnotes.

The full version, 'The Pugh Family of Llanfair and Llanbedr, 1775-1900', which includes copious references, was published in the *Journal of the Merioneth Historical Society* in 1990. We wish to thank the Society and the Executors of Lewis's estate for permission to include this chapter.

Another sad loss has been Mary Hartley, who attended the very first course in 1986 and several after that, culminating in the 1996 Second Stages course, for which she submitted the essay which appears as Chapter 23 of this book. No-one could know Mary without remarking on her considerable intellect and down-to-earth manner. She had a doctorate and remarked wryly that she would not let the prospect of the ten credits on offer change her life: nevertheless, we are so glad that she took the time to write up part of the story of her descent from 'Baron' Lewis Owen. We met her a couple of times in the year following the end of the 1996 course, discussing minor modifications and practicalities, and then suddenly Mary was gravely ill and she died in Cambridge in January 1998. We hope that we have – with consultation no longer possible – interpreted her thoughts as she would have wished. We thank her family for agreeing to her work appearing here.

Mention should also be made of the presence of two 'Family History in Wales' talks in this book. When *Welsh Family History: a Guide to Research* was first produced, its contents were decided by a committee. In the democratic process some subjects were thought better suited to separate publication (though this has not happened). We are very pleased to publish here the essence of talks by Dr Sandra Wheatley on maps which have been given to every 'Family History in Wales' Course. Sandra has been a director of the basic courses since their inception, speaking not only on maps, but also on the census, other nineteenth-century sources such as trade directories, rate books, etc, and on a wide range of illustrative material such as pictures and prints. A talk she gave to second stage courses is also published here.

John Dilwyn Williams came to give his talk on the Lloyds of Tŷ Newydd to the 'Family History in Wales' Course in 1991, when *Welsh Family History: a Guide to Research* was already in production. This talk was so greatly enjoyed that we have continued to invite him back over the years. It is not often that the story of a single family is supported by such a vast variety of sources, and it is with great pleasure that we share it, and so much more, with a wider public.

In addition we should mention that, when Gerald Morgan spoke to the 1996 course, his book, *The Vaughans of Trawsgoed,* was still some months away from publication. Because of this, there seemed little point (either to Gerald or to us) in repeating his talk on the subject. Instead he has written about the background research which went into his book.

We want to thank all the authors who have contributed to this volume, not only for their hard work during courses but also in preparing these chapters for publication. We also want to thank them for their patience in waiting for the book to appear. We always maintained that we would be as quick as our slowest author, but in the final analysis it has been health considerations for us as editors which have been the deciding factor.

Finally we want to record our thanks for the support we have been given within the Department of Continuing Education at the University of Wales, Aberystwyth, both for the courses and for the preparation of this book. The residential nature of the courses has been an important aspect in their success and we want to record our thanks for the contribution which has been made to that success initially from Steve Lawrence and latterly from Jim Wallace, as well as the staff at various halls of residence at the University.

John and Sheila Rowlands
Aberystwyth, July 1999

1. RELIGION AND SOCIETY IN NINETEENTH CENTURY WALES

Ieuan Gwynedd Jones

The single most striking feature about society in Wales during the last century (and for much of this present century) was the importance of organised religion in it.[*] Visitors to the country often came away with the impression that the Welsh people were an extraordinarily religious people, far more so than the English, or even the Scots. In 1834, for example, an American thought that Wales was more religious than his native New England, and that 'there is perhaps no other Christian people in the world who manifest so much religious susceptibility, or who can, as a body, be brought so much under its power'.[1]

The phrase, 'brought under its power', was particularly apt, for the first half of the century was experiencing a country-wide series of evangelical revivals which fuelled a phenomenal expansion in the provision of the means for public worship. Welsh men, women and children deduced from what was happening that they had been chosen by God for his peculiar blessings, and that as a nation they were destined to become instruments of the divine purpose to bring peoples everywhere into his kingdom. This was a joyous period in the history of the churches in Wales, and helps to explain why, despite the often desperate condition of the people at large, they continued to devote a high proportion of their disposable income to the building of chapels, to support for the work of the Bible Society, both locally and nationally, and the various missionary societies, and to the restoration of churches. It was also one of the most creative periods in the people's history: there was an outpouring of praise, expressed in hymns and anthems and music of extraordinary richness and profundity and beauty. A total culture based on religious values was being created, and it was inconceivable for the generations most affected that any counter-culture

---

[*] This chapter is based on a talk given to the Second Stages Course, 'Conformity and Dissent', in September 1994.

could possibly make headway against such hegemonic power. 'O Gymru, pa le mae dy debyg wlad dan y nef? A pha genedl dan haul sydd a chymaint o ôl crefydd arni, ag sydd ar genedl y Cymry'. (O Wales, where is thy like under the heavens? What nation under the sun has so many of the marks of religion as the Welsh?)[2] A few years later, the chemist and literary historian, Thomas Stephens of Merthyr Tydfil, pointed to their religiosity as the unique feature in their culture. 'Mae crefydd ac ordinhadau crefyddol yn un o brif neullduolion Cymru: ac oddieithr trigolion Sgotland, y Cymry yn ddiamheuol yw y bobl fwyaf grefyddol o fewn cyffiniau Ewrop'. (Religion and the maintenance of religious ordinances is one of the chief characteristics of Wales; with the exception of Scotland the Welsh are undoubtedly the most religious people within the boundaries of Europe).[3]

These were impressions based upon what people could see happening around them, the unceasing building of places of worship, the astonishing growth in the numbers of members of individual churches, and ministers and preachers to serve in them. It was based also on information published in the denominational periodicals, and on the constant pursuit of literacy and things of the mind so evident in all corners of the land. But no one could be entirely certain as to the reliability of what little statistical evidence existed, and there was no body of objective statistics regarding the country as a whole. Reliable statistics first became available in 1853, when the Census of Religious Worship of 1851 was published.[4] The civil servant responsible for its preparation and publication, Horace Mann, prefaced the Report with a long and detailed analysis of its contents and an estimate of its importance in understanding the true situation concerning the success or otherwise of the churches and their relation to the varying types of society in England and Wales. In a lecture before the Royal Statistical Society in 1854 he drew attention to the curious and puzzling fact that the geographical distribution of the various denominations and sects suggested that different parts of the country favoured particular denominations and were adverse to others.[5] The Calvinistic Methodists, for example, were highly successful in Wales but relatively weak in England, and the success or popularity of the large denominations varied enormously in different parts of the country. Clearly, these geographical contrasts in the spread of the denominations pointed to differences in the nature of society in different parts of the country, for example, between urban and rural society, and the different kinds of urbanity and rurality which were developing under the stress of population change, internal migration, and the industrial revolution.[6]

The Religious Census also revealed that nearly one and a half million persons in England and Wales appeared to have no affiliation whatever with any of the main denominations. Religious leaders and politicians were shocked and alarmed by this conclusion, and readily accepted Mann's conclusion – based on a calculation that 58% of the population were theoretically free to attend religious worship – that there was a shortage of over a million sittings, or about two thousand places of worship, and that the deficiency was greatest in the large towns. But this was not the case in Wales: here there was no shortage of places and sittings. Horace Mann calculated that there were 4,006 separate places in Wales, containing a total of 1,005,410 sittings for a total population of 1,188,914. Mann's formula for calculating the numbers of persons able to attend public worship (58% of the whole), gave a notional 700,000 worshippers in Wales, but there were over a million sittings available. In the two countries together there was a deficiency of one million sittings, but in Wales a surplus of over a quarter of a million. Mann noted this remarkable difference in his Report. 'It will be noticed, indeed, how favourably Wales in general is circumstanced – nearly all the registration districts having a surplus of provision', 'fortunately basking', as he put it, 'in excess of spiritual privileges'.[7] Mann thought that the deficiencies in provision, as we have observed, were all in industrial areas, in large towns and cities where the millions dwelt who did not attend religious worship, 'who every Sunday neglect religious ordinances ... of their own free will'.[8] He calculated that only about one in ten attended services in church or chapel on census day in the large provincial towns of the Midlands. Or, as Edward Miall, editor of the influential *The Nonconformist* newspaper, put it, 'The bulk of our manufacturing population stand aloof from our Christian institutions ... and must be described as living beyond occasional contacts with the institutions of Christian faith and practice'.[9]

Putting aside for the moment the over-arching question of why the whole of Wales should have been so markedly different from England, one conclusion is inescapable. As in England, so in Wales, differences in the provision of facilities for religious worship did somehow correspond to differences in local economies and societies. Provision was greatest in rural counties, and lowest in industrial and heavily urbanised places, such as Merthyr Tydfil. In Machynlleth Registration District provision was made for 24% more than the total population, in Merthyr for 42% less than the total. The same was true of the proportions of their populations which made use of the available provision. Higher proportions of rural populations attended services than of industrial populations. It is difficult to obtain reliable figures, but it is probably safe to conclude that more than a third of the total population had some connection with religious institutions. In some rural

Districts (Aberystwyth, Machynlleth, Cardigan, Bangor) more than half their populations attended one or more services, but in Newport, Swansea and Neath Districts slightly less than one-third were present on Census Sunday. The proportion was higher in Merthyr Tydfil and Pontypool, but still significantly lower than in the rural Districts.

One can therefore conclude that, in comparison with England, Wales was extraordinarily successful both in its provision for religious worship and in the use made of it. But it is equally clear that, like England, Wales was subject to those same social forces that were shaping the pattern of religious worship in both countries alike, and that there was an organic relation between the external evidence of religious behaviour and the society of which that religion was an essential part. In particular, the relative success of organised religion depended very largely, first, on the nature and extent of industrialisation, and, second, on the amount and type of urbanisation which accompanied industrialisation.

It is important to distinguish between the nature and magnitude of industrialisation on the one hand, and the extent of urbanisation on the other. From the point of view of provision, it was not industrialisation as such that was necessarily antipathetic to religious growth: on the contrary, industry created wealth which could be invested in places of worship, in support of the ministry, to finance schools, academies and colleges, etc. This was as true of the rural areas as of the manufacturing and mining areas, for industry benefited agriculture by providing an expanding market for the food it produced, and a refuge of sorts for the surplus population that would otherwise be a drain on their resources. It was the social consequences of industrialisation in the large towns that were so antipathetic to the religious lives of their inhabitants. By mid-century in Britain, the population of large towns (i.e. towns of more than 20,000 inhabitants) was growing at a faster rate than that of the county as a whole. By 1861 a total of about 5.5 millions lived in seventy-two towns with populations of 10,000 and over.[10] Religious deprivation was but one aspect of their more general social deprivation: indeed, as Charles Booth and other social investigators were to discover later in the century, the spiritual needs of their inhabitants were commensurate with their physical needs. High birth-rates and the flood of new immigrants from surrounding rural areas and from further afield had the malign effect of overwhelming all religious and cultural resources that the town may have provided before the onset of rapid growth.

The basic pattern of industrial growth in Wales was similar to that in England, but there were profound differences also which determined that the social consequences should be different. Of fundamental importance was the fact that there were great differences of scale. Nowhere in Wales were there towns to compare in size with the great provincial cities of England. In the 1850s there were only three 'great towns', namely, Merthyr Tydfil, Newport and Swansea. Their socio-economic structures were very different from those of Liverpool or Manchester or the wool towns of the Midlands. They were rather conglomerations of industrial villages nucleated around iron and non-ferrous works, iron mines and coal mines, and quarries. This applies to the old commercial towns, such as Swansea and Neath and Aberafan, which were rapidly being transformed at the same time.[11] These also, in effect, were collections of industrial villages or small towns, and in their social life they were very different from the great provincial towns. What many of them had in common with the latter were the terrible social problems which followed in the wake of haphazard and too-rapid growth. There were slums of classical character in all of them, places of appalling living conditions, of cruelty, inhumanity and despair, where crime flourished and the forces of law and order feared to go. Swansea had its Dyfatty, and Merthyr Tydfil its China.[12] 'By common consent, this district (China) was as bad, if not worse than the "Little Sodom" areas of Liverpool. Nottingham and Derby'.[13] But, as Jones and Bainbridge show in their study, 'China' was not Merthyr, and social reformers, including evangelical ministers and clergy and the advocates of 'town improvement', were becoming increasingly sensitive to the evil reputation which such places could give to an otherwise well-behaved and respectable town.

While it is important, therefore, to mark the unplanned nature of the new industrial towns, their lack of efficient systems of sewage disposal and of adequate supplies of clean water, their lack of amenity buildings, the gross overcrowding that was so characteristic of them, and the universal lack of good governance, it is also necessary to stress their small size and the fact that their individuality bred community and practical co-operation, both in their places of work and in the streets of homes. In the anthracite coalfield many of the emerging industrial towns were forming around existing agricultural villages, and the new developments were taking place at such a relatively slow pace as not to destroy completely their ancient character. Almost anywhere on the coalfield town and country seemed to be in balance, and the quality of the interpenetration was such as to create a new culture rather than to produce conflict between the old and the new.

There were differences of social structure, also, between the Welsh and English industrial towns, especially in their class structure. It was often remarked that the Welsh towns were working-class towns. This was certainly the opinion of English visitors, and it was the opinion of their inhabitants when they chose to think in such categories. Between the ironmaster or the coal proprietor and their workmen, it was said, there was no middle class of any substance: there were very few men of private means, professional men, tradesmen and large shopkeepers. That state of affairs corresponded to the distribution of wealth in society. The master owned the capital, and the worker (sometimes) his tools. His value lay in his skills and his physical strength. So there was no strong, visible middle class to carry the responsibilities of government, to invest capital in cultural overheads, to secure and defend an official form of religious culture, a middle class into which members of the lower classes could aspire to ascend. It was this lack of a thrusting, competitive middle class which enabled the capitalists to exercise an almost total control over the administration of justice and of local government. Where, as in Swansea, there were prestigious town corporations and wealthy middle class families to serve them, the advance of industrialisation did not entirely negate the possibility of social advancement for all but the very lowest in the community.[14]

These considerations are important. At the time in England there was a great deal of discussion about the causes of the irreligion of the working classes. 'All the writers of the bourgeoisie are unanimous on this point', wrote Engels, 'that the workers are not religious and do not attend church'.[15] Round about the same time, in 1847, one of Engels's bourgeois writers, Edward Miall, editor of *The Nonconformist* newspaper, was expressing his conviction that one of the obstacles that Christianity had to face in its efforts to convert the people was what he called 'the spirit of aristocracy', by which he meant precisely those narrow, hard class divisions in society. The middle classes shaped religion in their own image and in such a way as to express their own snobbery – their own version of aristocratic exclusiveness – but at the cost of excluding from their places of worship the poor among the working classes. Mann's five and a half million irreligious were not to be found among the middle classes, for membership of church or chapel was an essential part of their mode of living and an essential indicator of respectability.[16] Rather it was to be found among the millions of workers, whom Mann called 'unconscious Secularists', or, more realistically, 'non-believers'. It was safe to assume, he thought, that many of these would have received some little instruction in the elements of Christianity in Sunday school or in day schools, 'but no sooner do they mingle in the active world of labour ... than they soon become strangers to religious ordinances as the people of a heathen country ... as ignorant of Christianity as were heathen Saxons at Augustine's landing'.[17]

Almost certainly these explanations do not apply strictly to Wales. Developments were following different paths in the middle decades of the century, though they more closely paralleled those of England later in the century. We have already noted that Wales lacked that middle class which was the engine of social change in England. But in any case, that amplitude of religious provision that was the main characteristic of Welsh religious growth had not been provided by the middle classes. It had not been middle-class people who had directed the vast expansion of the previous half century, but the ordinary people themselves. Hence, it was the shape and structure of society which partly accounted for the outstanding success of religion in Wales, and that at a time when organised religion could scarcely be expected to flourish at all.

The different patterns in the growth and spread of the various denominations in the two countries help to explain why there was such an amplitude of provision in Wales as compared with England. In England and Wales as a whole 41% of all places of worship belonged to the Anglican church – a fact which was seized upon as illustrating the extent to which the Established Church has lost its ascendancy in the religious life of the country. But measured by the numbers of sittings the Church was by far the largest provider, having no less than 52% of the total available. The Church was also ahead in the ratio of seats to population, for every 100 persons the Church providing thirty sittings to the nonconformists' twenty-eight. In Wales alone, however, the differences were much wider and favoured the Nonconformists. Of the total number of places of all kinds, 29% belonged to the Church and 71% to the other denominations. For each 100 persons, the Church provided twenty-six sittings, and others, between them, 58%. Of the total of 983,653 sittings, 30.5% belonged to the Church and 69.5% to the Nonconformists.

Differences in the patterns of denominational adherence were even greater. In England and Wales together almost as many worshippers attended the Anglican services as attended Nonconformist services. But in Wales alone only 9% were present in Anglican churches, and 87% in Nonconformist chapels. There were variations in these proportions, the established Church being strongest in rural, anglicised Districts, especially in the border counties, and weakest in the industrial, Welsh-speaking Districts. The problem for the Church was that it was weakest in the Welsh-speaking parts of the country.

Clearly, the masses had rejected the established church, and the measure of that rejection was the astonishing success of the people in providing themselves with places devoted to alternative forms of worship. Wales was a

Nonconformist country. There are two aspects of this which need to be emphasised. First, and crucially, its doctrinal orthodoxy. The religion of Wales was massively Evangelical Protestantism, and although a substantial number of Anglicans subscribed to the same moderate Calvinistic theology, it was the Nonconformist majority which determined that this should be the form of Christianity which should be the dominant religion. The main denominations were the Congregationalists (or Independents), and the Baptists, denominations which traced their beginnings back to the reign of Queen Elizabeth, and which shared not only a common theology but also a common form of church government. The other major denomination, the Calvinistic Methodists, were likewise, as their name indicates, Calvinist, but by the middle of the century the strict predestinarianism of their eighteenth-century leaders had been modified to the extent that they believed, and acted on the belief, that all men were free to accept salvation through Jesus Christ. In church government they adopted a modified form of Presbyterianism. The Wesleyan Methodist denomination, which had begun to be established in the first decade of the nineteenth century, were Arminian in theology, but to all intents and purposes, except in political matters, were closely identified with the other Nonconformist denominations. The Roman Catholics had scarcely begun to expand significantly: they had only twenty-one churches in the whole of the Principality. The only sects were the Mormons, or Latter-day Saints, who had thirty-one congregations, mainly in south Wales. Orthodox Protestantism was the religion of the Welsh people.

It is the simplicity rather than, as in England, the complexity of this pattern which is striking. Among the old dissenters, the Independents, with over 700 churches, were the most numerous, followed by the Baptists, with 528, and the Unitarians, who had twenty-five congregations, coming third. Membership in all these denominations, was confined to those who accepted the particular theological standpoint of the congregation, but it is clear that all the churches expected to recruit new members from among the children of members, and from among the 'hearers', persons who attended services but did not take part in the formal life of the church. In these ways, the family and the local community were the natural, creative organisms which gave life and purpose to the individual churches.

The Calvinistic Methodists were the most powerful denomination of all. With over 806 churches, they were considerably larger than the Wesleyan Methodists, who had 626. What is remarkable about the Wesleyans is how negligible were the numbers of the secessionist churches, such as the Methodist New Connexion, the Wesleyan Association, the Bible Christians, and the Primitive Methodists.[18] Of these, only the Primitive Methodists, with

100 congregations, seemed to register much success, but most of them were very small and insecure congregations, using rented accommodation, or meeting in private houses, located only along the English border, and probably finding the main support among English immigrants.[19]

This still left the Anglican Church, judged by the number of its places of worship, as the most powerful denomination of all.[20] It had a total of 1,110 churches and chapels, and was present in every parish and divided parish in the country. In 1851, under the leadership of a number of reforming bishops, it was beginning the huge task of reconstruction and expansion which was not to be complete until the end of the century. Like the other main denominations, the Established Church was Evangelical in its theology, and only a small proportion of its clergy and adherents propagated High Church doctrines and liturgical practices. Even so, these 'Romish churches' so feared and detested by the other denominations were growing in numbers and influence, and the nature of the wealthy patronage they enjoyed increased the alarm they provoked in the communities at large. Anglo-Catholicism was restricted, more or less, to the coastal plain of north Wales, to a few coastal parishes in south Wales, and a few in Cardiganshire and Breconshire. More significantly, Aberdare became strongly tractarian in the early 1860, and remained so throughout the century. Their presence did not, however, affect the massive orthodoxy of the majority of Welsh people.

Within the body of belief there was plenty of room for doctrinal variations and differing emphases; the denominational periodicals thrived on controversy and theological arguments, but the consensus held.[21] There was a community of belief which made it possible for denominational differences to be overcome, and for co-operation at a practical level to be the norm in the behaviour of the competing denominations. It is possible to exaggerate denominational differences at the expense of the fundamental community which existed throughout the country, which, on the whole, enabled men of different persuasions to rejoice in the success of the whole.

It is a striking fact that, despite the enormous differences between rural and urban society, between farming communities and industrial communities, between small scattered townships and heavily populated streets of houses, between an agriculture dependent upon man-power and horse-power, and industries increasingly dependent upon steam and engineering, that there should have been no substantial differences between the religion of the one and the other. Town chapels were larger and often more magnificent and impressive as buildings than the chapels of the countryside, but no-one going from one to the other would feel alienated: the religious culture was the same. This was attested to by the fact that it was the custom for people moving from the country to industrial towns to take with them letters of recommendation by which their membership was transferred to a new chapel of the same denomination. Transfers of membership which this system facilitated were a powerful instrument in the maintenance of community between rural and urban churches. Thus it came about that the social role of religion in the mining and manufacturing areas was fundamentally not so very different from its role in the rural areas. In the latter, religion had developed in and through the relations of kith and kin, working organically within, and as part of, the inescapable facts of life for farmers, craftsmen and labourers. When one considers the stupendous changes that took place in rural society as a result of the growth of population it is difficult to see how those ancient societies could have adapted themselves relatively peacefully were it not for the influence of religion. In this context, its role was precisely to defend the communities against the forces that threatened to destroy or enslave them, providing families which were tied to the soil and locked into deferential societies with areas of freedom beyond the reach of landlord or proprietor. In this sense only can one accept the notion that Methodism saved society against revolution. Calvinistic Methodism was a profoundly conservative force in society because it believed the communities in which it was the most important element to be its own creation, which it had a primary duty to defend against attacks from without and anarchy from within.

In the mining and manufacturing areas in north and south Wales the challenge was not so much the preserving of the old as the creation of new communities in entirely novel and unprecedented situations. All denominations, church as well as chapel, faced the same basic social problems even though they might differ one from another in the quality of their apprehension of it, namely, the problem of maintaining their integrity and of extending their moral influence in the wild and lawless communities in which they found themselves. These were culturally 'frontier societies', and because, by reason of their geographical situation and the nature of their growth, they were subject to only the most elementary forms of control from without or, indeed, from within, their inhabitants themselves had to order them in accordance with their own notions of social good.[22] Hence the important role of friendly societies and other popular movements. It is in this context that the role of religion in industrial society must be understood: religion was one instrument in the hands of people who were seeking to adapt creatively to an environment over which they had little or no control, and, in doing so, shaping as much of it as was practicable in accordance with their own highest cultural aspirations.

This goes some way towards understanding why religious bodies, in particular the Nonconformists, insisted on a strict adherence to the values of temperance and sobriety, why they should have expected that individuals and families should live according to narrow and puritanical codes of behaviour, why Sabbatarianism should have occupied such an important place in the hierarchy of virtues, why prudence and self-denial should be so admired, why respectability should have become the outward significator of chapel membership, and why education and literacy should occupy a central role in the life of the churches. If patterns of behaviour in society generally were to be raised then the churches felt obliged to emphasise the gulf that existed between them and the brutal, ignorant and violent communities in which they were planted.

Until well into the second half of the century the industrial communities of the iron and coal fields were left alone to take care of themselves: the industrialists for whom they laboured did little to alleviate the degrading conditions under which they lived and worked: Anthony Hill of the Penydarren Ironworks thought that local government in Merthyr should be confined to 'two only objects – to tax and to punish':[23] and it was left to the churches to make good the deficiencies as best they could. So the chapels preached a morality higher than that of the brutalising culture of 'the Works', opened up possibilities for gifted, ambitious men to occupy positions of trust and responsibility in the chapels, provided an education in literacy in the Sunday schools, and kept before the communities at large the ideal of a better, culturally richer and more meaningful life. Of course, this religious culture was likely to produce bigoted and hypocritical creatures: this, perhaps, was the greatest danger, and the frequency of exhortations to avoid such sins showed how sensitive religious leaders were to this danger.

Finally, these considerations explain why the Nonconformist denominations should have been more popular than the Anglican church. The clergy were seen to be identified with the ruling classes of landowners and industrialists, and their places of worship no longer, as once they had been, organically a part of the communities in which they were planted.[24] This was strange when we consider that a majority of the lower clergy were drawn from the same farming and industrial classes as the people among whom they worked. But the hierarchy, the bishops and archdeacons, the men who possessed and exercised ecclesiastical authority, and often magisterial powers as well, were closely identified by class and interest with the ruling classes. Incumbents of livings obtained part of their income from tithes, could exercise the right to demand that their parishioners pay rates for the upkeep of the church buildings and cemeteries, and had the power to turn away the funerals of people who requested burials according to their own denominational rites. It was for reasons such as these that clergymen were commonly believed to be out of sympathy with the common man. But in fact, there were clergymen who were deeply involved in working-class self-help associations, such as friendly societies and even trade unions,[25] in sporting and other forms of recreation.[26] Some, like the Reverend John Griffith, Rector of Merthyr and later archdeacon of Llandaff, were deeply sympathetic to the grievances of Nonconformists, and every bit as radical in their political and social attitudes as the more advanced Nonconformists.[27] But the tone of the established Church was set by its hierarchy, and it was difficult, if not impossible, to eliminate from the minds of the Nonconformist majority feelings of distrust and alienation which had been generated over many decades of persecution and injustice.

There were other factors which disadvantaged the Anglicans in their endeavours to attract more people into their churches. The divisions between Church and Chapel were not only over constitutional or political matters, and theological doctrines concerning the nature of the Christian church, but they also involved different sensibilities. In the matter of public worship, for example, Nonconformists thought that Anglicans were boxed into a narrow interpretation of the legitimate requirements of 'the beauty of holiness', while Anglicans were repelled by the familiarity with the Almighty assumed by Nonconformists in their public prayers. More seriously, the Established church was felt to be, against all the evidence, an 'alien church', in particular in its attitude to the Welsh language. Until 1870, the bishops of the four Welsh dioceses were Englishmen who had little or no grasp of the Welsh language and, in some cases, apparently no sympathy with it.[28] A new sensitivity to the Welsh language in the services of the church in Welsh-speaking areas was a major element in the reforms being slowly carried out from the middle decades of the century, but Nonconformists claimed the high ground, and made the Welsh language the touchstone of nationality, the surest indicator of the cultural uniqueness of Wales. The campaign to disestablish the church thus came to have powerful nationalistic overtones, and Welsh Nonconformity came to provide Welsh people with a body, a special kind of institutionalised religion, around which a nascent nationalism could cohere, and through which a new kind of democratic politics could form.

NOTES TO CHAPTER 1

[1] Calvin Cotton in the *New York Observer*, 7 March 1835. Quoted in Richard Cawardine, 'The Welsh Evangelical Community and Finney's Revival', *Journal of Ecclesiastical History* 29, no. 4 (October 1978), p. 463.

[2] *Yr Adolygydd* III (1850), p. 19.

[3] Thomas Stephens, 'Sefyllfa wareiddiol y Cymry', *Y Traethodydd*, XIII (1857), p. 397.

[4] Census of Great Britain 1851: Religious Worship: England and Wales (London, 1853). I.G. Jones & D. Williams, *The Religious Census of 1851: A Calendar of the Returns relating to Wales: Vol. 1, South Wales* (Cardiff, 1976); and I.G. Jones, *The Religious Census of 1851: A Calendar of the Returns relating to Wales: Vol. 2, North Wales* (Cardiff, 1981).

[5] Horace Mann, 'On the Statistical Position of Religious Bodies in England and Wales', *Journal of the Royal Statistical Society*, XVIII (1855), p. 155.

[6] See 'The religious frontier in nineteenth century Wales', in Ieuan Gwynedd Jones, *Communities. Essays in the Social History of Victorian Wales* (Llandysul, 1987), pp. 211-36.

[7] Report, op. cit., p. cxxvii.

[8] ibid., p. cliii.

[9] Edward Miall, *The British Churches in Relation to the British People* (1849), pp. 222-3.

[10] Census of 1851. Report, pp. 10-11.

[11] For Swansea, see Ieuan Gwynedd Jones, 'The City and its Villages', in Ralph Griffiths (ed), *The City of Swansea. Challenges and Change* (1990), pp. 79-97, and Jones, 'The making of an industrial community' in Glanmor Williams (ed), *Swansea. An Illustrated History* (Swansea, 1990), pp. 115-144.

[12] For Dyfatty see Jones in Griffiths (ed), *City of Swansea*, pp. 119-20, and for 'China', see Keith Strange, 'In Search of the Celestial Empire', *Llafur*, 3, no. 1 (Spring 1980), pp. 44-6, and David Jones and Alan Bainbridge, 'The 'Conquering of China': Crime in an Industrial Community 1842-64', *Llafur* 2 no. 4 (Spring 1979), pp. 7-37, esp. pp. 25-7.

[13] Jones and Bainbridge, op. cit., p. 7.

[14] See Glanmor Williams, *Swansea*, op. cit., *passim.*

[15] F. Engels, *The Condition of the Working Class in England in 1844* (Moscow, 1953), pp. 158-9.

[16] Miall, *British Churches*, op. cit.

[17] Mann, *Religious Census*, op. cit., pp. clviii ff.

[18] On these see, R. Currie, *Methodism Divided* (London, 1968).

[19] For the history of the Primitive Methodists see H.B. Kendall, *The Origin and History of the Primitive Methodist Church*, 2 vols. (London, 1906), and the brief but penetrating account in Owen Chadwick, *The Victorian Church*, vol. 2 (2nd ed, 1970), pp. 386-91.

For some of the salient characteristics of the Primitive Methodists see the pioneering K.S. Inglis, *Churches and the Working Classes in Victorian England* (London, 1963) pp. 12f. and 328f., and H. McLeod, *Religion and the Working Classes in Victorian England* (London, 1963), passim. Very little has been written about their Welsh churches.

[20] For the established Church see, in general, Chadwick, *Victorian Church*, op. cit., and David Walker, *A History of the Church in Wales* (Church in Wales Publications, 1976).

[21] Welsh periodicals are listed and described in Huw Walters, *Llyfryddiaeth Cylchgronau Cymreig 1735-1850. A Bibliography of Welsh Periodicals 1735-1850* (Aberystwyth, 1993). The same author's *Yr Adolygydd a'r Beirniad: eu Cynnwys a'u Cyfranwyr* (Aberystwyth, 1996). This latter work gives a history of the publication of these two periodicals and provides a list of the individual essays, and an index to, and brief biographies of, their authors.

[22] The best sustained analysis of the nature of these societies is in David J.V. Jones, *The Last Rising. The Newport Insurrection of 1839* (Oxford, 1985), and idem., *Rebecca's Children. A Study of Rural Society, Crime, and Protest* (Oxford, 1989).

[23] Quoted in Jones, *Communities*, p. 257.

[24] For a useful discussion of this see W.R. Lambert, 'Some working class attitudes towards organised religion in nineteenth-century Wales', *Llafur* 2, no. 1 (Spring, 1976), pp. 4-17.

[25] For example, Canon John David Jenkins, Tractarian Vicar of Aberdare 1870-6, who was known as the 'Railmen's Apostle'. See his obituary in the *Merthyr Telegraph*, 1 December 1876.

[26] For examples, see David Smith and Gareth Williams, *Fields of Praise. The Official History of the Welsh Rugby Union 1881-1981* (Cardiff, 1980), pp. 6-8.

[27] For Griffith, see Wilton D. Wills, 'The Revd John Griffith and the revival of the established church in nineteenth century Glamorgan'. *Morgannwg* XIII (1969), pp. 75-102.

[28] See Eryn M. White, 'The Established Church, Dissent and the Welsh Language *c.*1660-1811' in Geraint H. Jenkins (ed), *The Welsh Language before the Industrial Revolution* (Cardiff, 1997), pp. 235-287.

2. CATHOLICS IN WALES

Michael Gandy

Throughout its history as an independent nation, Wales was a Catholic country.* Those who valued the Welsh heritage in the sixteenth century felt they saw clearly that the English church was the main method by which Welshness was being destroyed. If most of the Welsh upper classes had not co-operated with anglicisation or even emigrated to make their careers in England, then Celtic Wales might have remained as fervently Catholic and anti-Saxon as Celtic Ireland and the Highlands of Scotland. The departure of the most influential and educated class was increasingly compounded by the impossibility of finding enough priests who could speak Welsh and produce more work, such as that of the martyr Richard Gwyn who declared uncompromisingly:

> *Y Beibl Seisnig sydd chwym chwam*
> (The Saxon Bible is a load of rubbish)[1]

In 1587 Welsh-speaking Jesuits were discovered operating a secret printing-press in a cave on the Little Orme, above Llandudno. They published part of *Y Drych Cristionogawl*, the first book to be printed in Wales. However they had to flee and there was no further work of this sort.

As in England many people held on to the religion of their childhood until the early 1600s. Others were brought back to Catholicism by the new priests who had trained on the continent after the reforms of the Council of Trent. Government repression was increasingly severe and from 1581 it was illegal for a priest to breathe the air of England. Over the next 100 years, sixty-four men, both priests and laymen, were executed, technically for treason but actually for practising their religion. These are listed in Fig. 2-1.

Many others escaped death and Bellenger lists 194 priests of Welsh origin before 1800.[2] Most of these men were from families of the lower gentry or upper yeomanry and many could claim descent from the princely

---

* This chapter is based on a talk given to the Second Stages Course, 'Conformity and Dissent', in September 1994.

families. For example, John Roberts, a Benedictine who was martyred in 1610, was descended from Rhodri Mawr on at least four lines, and David (Anselm) Baker, another Benedictine, was a direct descendant of Owain Glyndwr.[3] The books listed in the bibliography give a good deal of information on the parentage of the other priests.

Thomas Andrews	William Guy	Charles Parry
Roger Cadwaladr	David Gwynn	John Phillips
Francis Cotton	Richard Gwynn	John Plessington
Arthur Crowther	Roger Gwynn	Edward Powell
Thomas Crowther	James Humphreys	Philip Powell
John Davies	John Ingram	Ignatius Price
William Davies	John Jetter	Charles Pritchard
Robert Edmonds	David Jones	Humphrey Pritchard
Edward Edwards	Edward Jones	Robert Pugh
Edward Ellis	John Jones	Robert ap Rhys
George Ellis	Walter Jones	John Roberts
William Ellis	John Kemble	Nicholas Spenser
Humphrey Evans	David Joseph Kemeys	John Thomas (1)
Philip Evans	David Lewis	John Thomas (2)
John Eynon	John Lloyd	James Turberville
Richard Fetherston	Richard Lloyd	Lewis Turberville
— Glynn	William Lloyd	Thomas Vaughan
John Goodman	Charles Meehan	Nicholas Wheeler
John Griffith	Edward Morgan	George Williams
William Griffith	John Owen	John Williams
William Gunter	Nicholas Owen	Richard Williams

Fig. 2-1: Priests executed for practising their religion, 1581 on[4]

Numbers declined slowly but surely, however. In some counties Catholicism died out almost completely but throughout the seventeenth century there were pockets at Holywell and Talacre in north Wales, Powis Castle and Brecon in central Wales, and in Monmouthshire. The surviving Catholic gentry all supported the King during the Civil War and Catholicism gained some ground during the short reign of James II. A few men and women continued to go abroad to the great Catholic colleges and convents. Most were of gentry background but they included Catherine Powel, whose father was a poor labouring man who worked for the Marquis of Worcester. She joined the Carmelites in 1644 with her mistress, Lady Anne Somerset, and spent the next forty years in the Spanish Netherlands as Sister Alexia of St Winefrede.

By 1700 very few aristocratic families of Welsh origin were still based primarily in Wales and this itself affected the survival of Catholicism in the Principality. In a national list of *c.*1705 only the 'Duke of Powis' (William, 2nd Marquess of Powis) and the 'Lady Dowager Abergeny' (née Belasyse, widow of the 12th Baron Bergavenny) represent their class.[5] However quite a few of the provincial gentry and the upper yeomanry remained Catholic and the following families supported missions in their area, even when the Catholic flame flickered lowest in the eighteenth century:

Croft of Llanfair Cilgoed, Monmouthshire
Fowler of Bettisfield, Flintshire
Gunter of Abergavenny and Chepstow Grange, Monmouthshire
Havard of Devynock, Breconshire
Herbert of Clytha, Monmouthshire
Jones of Dingestow, Monmouthshire
Jones of Llanarth, Monmouthshire
Lorimer and Powel of Perthir, Monmouthshire
Milborne of Wonastow, Monmouthshire
Mostyn of Talacre, Flintshire
Needham of Skenfrith, Monmouthshire
Parry of Tŷ Tywisog, Denbighshire
Lord Powis of Powis Castle, Montgomeryshire
Price of Buttington Hall, Montgomeryshire
Prichard of Y Graig, Monmouthshire
Roberts and Gifford of Nerquis, Flintshire
Turberville of Pyle, Glamorgan
Vaughan of Courtfield, Monmouthshire

By 1773 there were estimated to be only 750 Catholics and nine priests in the entire Principality. From 1744 to 1797 the whole of south Wales was served from Bristol and, as late as about 1815, it is said that the only Catholic family in Pembrokeshire were persuaded to move to Swansea to make life easier. However even in such an un-Catholic county as Cardiganshire folk memories lingered on and Canon Cunnane has recently shown that as late as the mid-nineteenth century Welsh hymns in honour of Mary were still being handed down from mother to daughter.[6]

In the nineteenth century the poor Irish flocked into the new industrial areas. By 1838 there were 6,250 Catholics in Wales, of whom over half were in Monmouthshire and by 1850 there were 10,000 distributed in the larger towns as follows:

Abergavenny	400
Bangor	250
Brecon	220
Cardiff	1800
Chepstow	100
Dowlais	1200
Holywell and Talacre	60
Llanarth	170
Milford and Haverfordwest	100
Mold	100
Monmouth	300
Newport	2300
Pembroke Dock and Tenby	150
Pontypool	1000
Swansea	500
Usk	70
Wrexham	300

Numbers continued to grow quickly and for nearly 150 years Catholics have constituted about 10% of the population of Wales (and far more in Glamorgan and Monmouthshire). The family historian must therefore expect to find Catholic connections (amongst the cousins if not in the direct line) in any family tree based on urban South Wales and to be aware that, once you are working before 1700, the chances of Catholic ancestry become steadily more rather than less likely. As for the great bardic genealogies and the princely families, from Rhodri Mawr and Hywel Dda to Llywelyn Fawr and Owain Glyndŵr, every Welshman, great and small, followed the religion of St David.

The records

This chapter is aimed at the family historian who knows in general how family history research is carried on in England and Wales but is less aware of sources for specifically Catholic families since the Reformation.

Unfortunately there has been no systematic publication of material relating to Welsh Catholicism, though a great deal of material has appeared in the volumes of the Catholic Record Society (CRS). However, many articles relating to sources for English Catholics apply to Wales without qualification since the two countries have been administratively united throughout the post-Reformation period. This also applies wholesale to the political and social background works, the State Records (especially those in the Public Record Office) and the Anglican Records listed in *Catholic family history: a bibliography of general sources* (M.J. Gandy, 1996). Fr Cronin in the 1920s published a large number of articles on the Irish in

South Wales, but they were based more on anecdote and oral tradition than on archival sources.

A full analysis of printed material will be found in *Catholic family history: a bibliography for Wales* (M.J. Gandy, 1996).

State sources

In the last years of the sixteenth century Catholics were thought of as almost certain to be traitors and there is a great deal of information on them in the State Papers Domestic. At local level, recusants (those who refused to go to church) were first cited before the Quarter Sessions and, in due course, fined. If they continued to refuse, the fines mounted up and eventually their lands were subject to sequestration, two-thirds going to the Crown. From 1581-1592 details are recorded in the Pipe Rolls (CRS 71). From 1592-1691 convictions were recorded in separate Recusant Rolls. Those for 1592-1596 have been published (CRS 18, 57, 61); later rolls remain more or less unresearched.

The Proceedings of the Committee for Compounding with Delinquents 1643-1660 relate to Royalists in the aftermath of the Civil War but recusancy is always stated. Unfortunately the Protestation Returns of 1641/2, which were expressly intended to identify Catholics, do not survive for Wales. Foreigners and Catholics (because they are foreigners at heart) were required to pay double in the Lay Subsidies and, later, in the eighteenth century, were required to pay double Land Tax, so they are easily recognisable.

In the aftermath of the 1715 Jacobite Rebellion further laws were passed against Catholics. First, they were required to register their wills in the Close Rolls; second, they were required to register full details of their property. Registration of Estates was the law from 1717 to 1778 but the majority of entries refer to the beginning of that period. A simple abstract of the returns was published in 1885 (see bibliography) and the Welsh counties are included. In Breconshire, for example, Joseph Philips of Ludlow, Salop, gent, and Catherine, his wife, registered a farm, called 'Mayes-Cletter', and tithes of the chapel of Gwenddwr, in right of Catherine, the widow of Thomas Bradford – a reminder that many Catholic gentry were impropriators of Anglican tithes or had the right to appoint to Anglican livings.

Many of those registering were quite small property-owners and many others lived away from the area where they owned property; in addition the returns give details of occupiers, so very many non-Catholics are included.

All the above material except the Land Tax and some Registration of Estates is in the Public Record Office, London.

Anglican records

In practice most Catholics were married and buried in the Church of England and our problem in tracing them may not be their Catholicity but the comparatively poor survival of early Anglican registers in Wales. Catholics also took out marriage licences and proved their wills in the local bishop's court in the same way as anyone else. Since there were very few poor Catholics the percentage of them in these sources is quite high.

Conviction of recusancy carried a number of legal disabilities and many Catholics eventually went through the process of conformity, certifying officially to the local bishop that they had received the Anglican communion. The names of seventy-four men and women who produced Conformity Certificates in Wales between 1590 and 1620 have been published in *Catholic Ancestor* Vol. 5, No 5 (June 1995).

In the 1630s Catholics might be cited before the local bishop's court but this was a period when pressure was on the Puritans rather than the Catholics.

Over the years a number of censuses of Catholics were taken, usually through the Anglican administrative structure but at the wish of Parliament. The Compton Census of 1676 shows 218 papists in the Diocese of St David's, all but twenty-one in the Archdeaconry of Brecon; nineteen in the Diocese of Bangor; 274 in the Diocese of St Asaph and 551 in the Diocese of Llandaff.[7] Unfortunately names are not given.

Four years later in 1680 a list of the names of Catholics in Breconshire shows 177, of whom the largest number are in Devynock.[8]

There are later lists for 1705 and 1767. The latter gives full details of family groups but omits the names; there were 362 Catholics in the Diocese of St Asaph, sixteen in the Diocese of Bangor; 114 in the Diocese of St David's and 434 in the Diocese of Llandaff. Of these 428 were in Monmouthshire and only six in Glamorgan![9]

In addition, Monmouth itself, which came in the Diocese of Hereford, had 102 Catholics.

Catholic records

Since Catholicism was illegal and for many years priests lived in fear of their lives, or at least imprisonment, it is not surprising that there are very few early registers. We know of a notebook kept by Father Ignatius Thorpe, SJ, when he was at Monmouth, 1685-9, and Holywell 1698-9, and another kept by Father Monox Harvey when he was at Buttington Hall, near Welshpool, 1747-1752. Otherwise only the following registers are known from before 1850:

Breconshire:	Brecon	1799
Carmarthenshire:	Carmarthen	1850
Flintshire:	Holywell	1730
	St Asaph	1849
Glamorgan:	Swansea	1805
	Cardiff	1836
	Dowlais	1836
Monmouthshire:	Abergavenny	1740
	Perthir	1751-1818
	Courtfield	1773
	Llanarth	1781
	Monmouth	1791
	Newport	1836
	Pontypool	1836
	Chepstow	1836
	Coedanghred	1846
Pembrokeshire:	Pembroke Dock	1850

Over the next twenty years, however, there was enormous Catholic expansion in the industrial towns of the south. There were substantial efforts to extend Catholicism in north and central Wales but they foundered on the insoluble problem of providing Welsh-speaking priests. Some Breton-speaking priests attempted to found a mission at Aberystwyth in the 1840s but they were not successful. In practice, apart from magnificent exceptions such as the life of the Marquis of Bute in Cardiff, the history of Catholicism from the 1840s is almost co-terminous with the history of the Irish in South Wales. They should appear in the standard Anglican and state sources for the poor (and can be identified easily from Workhouse Creed Registers), but there are also a number of specifically Catholic sources. In many industrial towns the parish became the social centre and heart of the Irish community. Irishness and Catholicism went together and, whether in the second or third generation, as they lost one they usually lost the other. In practice as genealogists we are initially interested in the basic acts of baptism and marriage which may be recorded for the family of even the least committed Catholics. By the 1840s Catholicism had been legal for many years and a trained priesthood was keeping proper records.

In many areas the Catholics were far too poor to build a proper chapel and the mission began when the priest hired a warehouse for Sunday mornings, or when the first few Catholics in the place met in someone's parlour. When, in the 1860s, Government began to pay grants towards the building of schools, the overstretched finances of many priests went into providing a school, part of which could be used as a chapel and there are many examples of Catholic missions which had a school for thirty years before they had a separate chapel. Many applications from local Catholic schools are in the Public Record Office (in Class ED 7) and these contain useful information on the teachers.

Any standard mission should have the following registers:

Baptism

These give the name of the child and of both its parents (including the maiden name of the mother), date of baptism and birth, and the names of the sponsors. Indications of residence or occupation are very rare.

By the late nineteenth century the printed form for Catholic baptisms has a space to record the marriages of the child in later life.

Marriage

The basic form required the names of the bride and groom, the date and the names of the witnesses. Often the names of all four parents are given, including the mothers' maiden names. Age and occupation are rare, but birthplace is sometimes recorded, or even the place of residence of both the couple and their parents. This can give a firm link back to Ireland.

Where pre-nuptial enquiries survive they should contain the date and place of birth and a copy of the baptism certificate. This is a standard twentieth-century record but is rare in the nineteenth century.

Deaths

Most Catholic churches did not keep burial registers as such. However by the mid-nineteenth century most priests were keeping death registers and the printed form has a space to record where the body was buried. Otherwise the only information usually given is the name and age of the deceased.

Confirmation

In the larger parishes the Bishop came round every year to administer confirmation, and the list of boys and girls is more or less a census of children of the right age (about seven to nine until the early twentieth century). Name, surname and religious name are recorded. However the confirmation name usually has no genealogical significance.

Other parish records.

Apart from the standard sacramental registers which should exist in every parish there are a number of records which are found fairly frequently. However a lot of the older material is still in the bottom of some cupboard in the presbytery and even the priest doesn't know he's got it.

Obits

Every parish has a list of the anniversaries from which names are read out each Sunday '... and also for those whose anniversaries occur about this time.' There have always been lists of those for whom Masses must be said.

Status Animarum

Every priest was required from time to time to send in an account of his congregation. Nowadays these are purely statistical but many of the older lists go into detail about particular families, especially the doubtful cases, the ones who were lapsing, the mixed marriages, the ones whose children were in school but who were never seen on Sundays. On the whole these are likely to be more complete for the smaller, rural congregations and a number of them appear in the old mission registers published by the Catholic Record Society.

Parish Census

Many urban parishes have compiled these from time to time, and they are usually up-dated for a few years afterwards (not necessarily systematically).

Easter Communions

Again, these annual lists are more frequently found in smaller parishes.

Sick calls

Many priests noted who they had visited, especially when they were called out to give the Last Rites. These books occasionally survive.

Guilds and Fraternities

Most Catholic parishes had a number of organisations to which active people could belong. Most of the best-known had a religious content, though many big urban parishes in their heyday ran their own billiards competitions, football teams, boy scouts and girl guides, etc, and, of course, both the dances and the temperance movement. There were frequent collections and subscription lists and, where there was a proper parish magazine, such as in Cardiff, hundreds of people may be mentioned in the course of a year. As the nineteenth century drew to a close many Catholics were respectably working-class, rather than destitute, and perfectly able to find the right clothes for their children's First Communion, or the annual processions, for which there were often printed programmes giving the names of those representing each organisation. There were the annual outings (whether for children or grown-ups) and, by the twentieth century, the diocesan pilgrimages. Many of these events were also reported in the local newspaper.

Naturally much of this material consists simply of names with only a little extra information. Some sources are particularly valuable, however.

Bona Mors (The Confraternity of a Happy Death)

This was a little like a burial society, but was more concerned with the spiritual duties than the money. The members all attended each other's funerals and anniversaries and the membership lists are therefore all annotated with the eventual date of the member's death. The same applied to the Rosary Confraternity. Catholics lay great emphasis on making a good death and the Irish like a good turn-out from the community for their funerals – and the wake!

Society of St Vincent de Paul

This was founded in France in 1838. The aim was practical, and charitable people took a few families under their wing and saw them through hard times, or helped them get on. When a family was recommended, a couple of the Brothers went round to do, basically, a social-work report and see if the family were deserving. Their reports sometimes give addresses, names, ages, occupations, details of relatives living nearby, some background (e.g. what regiment the man had been in, where the widow's husband had worked). They were sympathetic but they wanted to do lasting good and were not prepared to waste their limited funds on the undeserving. They were also well aware what was available from the Board of Guardians and did not want to duplicate.

By the late nineteenth century some branches of the SVP had a printed form which included spaces for date and place of marriage, and details of baptism, not only of the children but of the parents.

Non-parish sources

By 1900 there were many orders of religious men and women working in Wales, most of them working directly for the Catholic (Irish) poor. They ran schools, hospitals and old people's homes. Some of the early admission books even give the date and place of birth of the old people being admitted.

The records of Catholic children's homes are usually excellent, though information may be limited to dates. Every children's home was listed in the *Catholic Directory*. Although many of the religious orders have now withdrawn from this kind of work the successor organisations in each Catholic diocese are happy to help enquirers, though of course they are social workers not family historians. For modern contact addresses refer to the current *Catholic Directory*.

Lastly the clergy and religious themselves. Records of them are excellent (see bibliography). The Catholic Family History Society has an index of about 14,000 nineteenth-century nuns working in England and Wales; for almost all of them a birth-place is given, and for a very large number the names of the father and mother. The addresses of the religious orders are also published in the *Catholic Directory*. These days there is usually an archivist very willing to pass on what she knows. If you cannot find a statement of Grandpa's birthplace, then that of his sister is the next best thing.

BIBLIOGRAPHY

NB: Although some of these books only refer to England, national developments include developments in Wales.

Background

Aveling, J.C.H., *The Handle and the Axe* (Blond and Briggs, 1976).

Beck, G.A. (ed), *The English Catholics 1850-1950* (Burns Oates, 1950).

Leys, M.D.R., *Catholics in England: a social history 1559-1829* (Longman, 1961).

Norman, E., *Roman Catholicism in England from the Elizabethan Settlement to the Second Vatican Council* (OUP, 1986).

Tracing a family

Gandy, M., 'Catholic Ancestors' in *Family History News and Digest* Vol. 8 No. 1 (April 1991), pp. 26-29.

Gandy, M., 'Catholics in your One-Name Study' in *The Journal of One-Name Studies* Vol. 3 No. 11 (July 1990), pp. 327-331.

Non-Catholic records

Steel, D.J., *Sources for Roman Catholic ... Family History*. National Index of Parish Registers Vol. 3 (Society of Genealogists, London, 1974, reprinted 1986).

Williams, J.A., 'Sources for Recusant History (1559-1791) in English Official Archives' in *Recusant History* Vol. 16, No. 4 (CRS, October 1983).

Mission Registers

Gandy, M., *Catholic Missions and Registers 1700-1880: Volume 3: Wales and the West of England* (1993).

Gandy, M., *Catholic Parishes in England, Wales and Scotland: an atlas* (1994). Up to 1950

Kelly, B.W., *Historical Notes on English Catholic Missions* (Kegan Paul, Trench, Trubner and Co, 1907. Reprinted M. Gandy, 1995). Includes Monmouthshire.

There are many individual mission histories.

Monumental Inscriptions
There were no specifically Catholic graveyards until the nineteenth century and Catholics were buried in Anglican churchyards, often with no indication of their Catholicity.

Wills and Estates
Catholic wills appear in the usual sources but in the eighteenth century they were also supposed to be enrolled in the Close Rolls.

Anon, 'Wills Enrolled in the Close Rolls' in *The Genealogist* (NS) Vol. 1, p. 267, and Vol. 2, pp. 59-60, 279-282.

Anstruther, G., 'Abstracts of Wills', *London Recusant* Vol. 3, No. 2 (May 1973) – *London Recusant* (NS) No. 1 (1980), *passim*. Mostly of priests and their relations.

Estcourt, E.E. and Payne, J.O., *The English Catholic Nonjurors of 1715* (Burns and Oates, 1885). Details of those who registered their estates in the eighteenth century.

Payne, J.O., *Records of the English Catholics of 1715* (Burns and Oates, 1889, republished 1970). Abstracts of over 400 wills and administrations relating to known Catholics of the eighteenth century.

Biography and Family History
Catholics appear in all the standard sources and many histories of the older missions are, in practice, histories of the gentry families which protected them. The prime Catholic work is:

Gillow, J., *A Bibliographical Dictionary of the English Catholics* (Burns and Oates, 5 vols, 1887-1902, republished *c.*1968). Concerned with Catholics who wrote, so many people of social importance are not included.

Kirk, J., *Biographies of English Catholics in the Eighteenth Century* (Burns and Oates, 1909, reprinted 1969).

Bence-Jones, M., *The Catholic Families* (Constable, 1992). The great aristocratic families of the nineteenth century.

Gordon-Gorman, W., *Converts to Rome: a list of over 3000 Protestants who have become Roman Catholics since the commencement of the nineteenth century.* (W. Swan Sonnenschein and Co, 1884). Arranged by occupation; later, expanded editions to 1910 were arranged alphabetically.

Various, *The Catholic Who's Who* (34th edition, 1941; 35th edition, 1952). Catholics of standing in Great Britain and the British Empire.

The Clergy and Religious

During the seventeenth and eighteenth centuries all clergy and religious, male and female, were trained abroad and there were about forty institutions specifically for English and Welsh Catholics, many of them also providing an education for Catholic children. For a general history see:

Guilday, P., *The English Catholic Refugees on the Continent 1558-1795* (Longmans, Green and Co, 1914).

The following general works should be consulted first.

Male: The following handlists are as complete as the present stage of research allows:

Bellenger, D.A., *English and Welsh Priests 1558-1800* (Downside Abbey, 1984).

Fitzgerald-Lombard, C., *English and Welsh Priests 1801-1914* (Downside Abbey, 1993).

For biographies of individuals:

Anstruther, G., *The Seminary Priests: A Dictionary of the Secular Clergy of England and Wales 1558-1850* (Mayhew-McCrimmon, 4 vols to 1800 Vol. 5 not published, 1969-1977).

Birt, H.N., *Obit Book of the English Benedictines 1600-1912* (Edinburgh, 1913. Republished, Gregg International, 1970).

Foley, H., *Records of the English Province of the Society of Jesus* (Burns and Oates, 8 vols, 1877-1883).

Gumbley, W., *Obituary Notices of the English Dominicans from 1555 to 1952* (Blackfriars Publications, 1955).

Fr Thaddeus OFM, *The Franciscans in England 1600-1850* (1898).

Zimmerman, B., *Carmel in England: a history of the English Mission of the Discalced Carmelites 1615-1849* (Burns and Oates, 1899).

For a general history of the other Orders working in Wales see:

Steele, F.M., *Monasteries and Religious House of Great Britain and Ireland* (R. and T. Washbourne, 1903).

Female: The records of many of the recusant convents (including detailed biographies of the nuns and their families) have been published by CRS. By 1900 thirteen Orders of women were working in Wales. The best general surveys are:

Whelan, B., *Historic English Convents of Today* (Burns Oates and Washbourne, 1936).

Steele, F.M., *The Convents of Great Britain* (Sands and Co, 1902).

See later under Education.

Martyrs and Prisoners

Anon, *The Martyrs of England and Wales 1535-1680* (CTS, 1985).

Challoner, R., *Memoirs of Missionary Priests* (Burns Oates and Washbourne, 1924).

Ellis, T.P., *The Catholic Martyrs of Wales* (1933).

Ellis, T.P., *Welsh Benedictines of the Terror* (1936).

There are no lists of Catholic prisoners in Wales, though various Welshmen appear in the London prison lists which have been published in CRS and there is a great deal of information in standard local sources. There is a lot of mythology about priests' hiding places. For a serious expert account, also discussing those in Wales, see:

Hodgetts, M., *Secret Hiding Places* (Veritas Publications, 1989).

Civil War

Anon, *Calendar of the Proceedings of the Committee for Compounding with Delinquents 1643-1660* (HMSO, 5 vols). Recusants noted.

Jacobites

Jacobites too were not necessarily Catholics. See in particular:

Lart, C.E., *Jacobite extracts from the Parish Registers of St-Germain-en-Laye, 1689-1720,* 2 vols (The St Catherine Press Ltd, 1910-1912).

Anon, *The Records of the Forfeited Estates Commission* (HMSO, 1965). Includes rentals, leases, wills and estate papers.

Education

For two centuries Catholic education was illegal and many children were sent abroad, though that was illegal as well. Many school lists have been published by CRS. See:

Beales, A.C.F., *Education under Penalty: English Catholic Education from the Reformation to the Fall of James II* (The Athlone Press, 1963).

The appendix lists thirty-five boys' schools on the Continent (including Irish and Scots) of which the most important were Douai, Rome, Valladolid, Seville, St Omer, Dieulouard, Madrid, Lisbon and Bornhem. The records of most of these have been published by CRS. In the 1790s the surviving colleges returned to England and are represented by St Edmund's College, Ware, Ushaw, Downside, Stonyhurst and Ampleforth. They joined Sedgley Park and the Bar Convent, York, which had both been functioning for many years. All the above have published lists of students in which pupils of Welsh origin may appear. For nineteenth century developments see Beck,

G.A., (ed), *The English Catholics 1850-1950* (Burns Oates, 1950), especially the following articles:

Battersby, W.J., 'Secondary Education for Boys'.
Battersby, W.J., 'Educational Work of the Religious Orders of Women'.
Evenett, H.O., 'Catholics and the Universities'.

The most important early work for the urban Catholic poor in Wales was done by the Rosminians.

Journals and Periodicals

Dwyer, J.J., 'The Catholic Press' in G.A. Beck (ed.), *The English Catholics 1850-1950* (Burns Oates, 1950).

Fletcher, J.R., 'Early Catholic Periodicals in England' in *Dublin Review* Vol. 198, No. 397 (April 1936), pp. 284-310.

Other Material

For an analysis of other available material in print see:

Gandy, M., *1. Catholic family history: a bibliography of general sources* (1996).

— *2. Catholic family history: a bibliography of local sources* (1996).

— *3. Catholic family history: a bibliography for Scotland* (1996).

— *4. Catholic family history: a bibliography for Wales* (1996).

Numbers 1 and 4 are essential for research on Catholic families in Wales.

Catholic Family History Society

This Society covers all aspects of Catholic ancestry (including Irish) in England, Scotland Wales (but not Ireland). The address of the current Secretary is available through *Family History News and Digest*.

NOTES TO CHAPTER 2

[1] *Catholic Record Society,* Vol. 5 (1908) p. 94.
[2] D.A. Bellenger, *English and Welsh Priests 1558-1800* (1984).
[3] T.P. Ellis, *The Welsh Benedictines of the Terror* (1936).
[4] Compiled from T.P. Ellis, *The Catholic Martyrs of Wales* (1932).
[5] *Recusant History,* Vol. 12 No. 1 (January 1973).
[6] J. Cunnane, 'Ceredigion and the Old Faith' in *Ceredigion,* Vol. 12 No 2 (1994) pp. 3-34.
[7] A. Whiteman (ed.),*The Compton Census of 1676: a critical edition,* (1986).
[8] 'Papists in the counties of Brecon and Flint, 1680' in *Catholic Ancestor,* Vol. 6, No. 3 (November 1999), pp. 108-111.
[9] *Return of Papists 1767*, CRS Occasional Publications, No. 2 (1989).

3. A CLERGYMAN IN THE FAMILY

Sheila Rowlands

Researching Anglican clergymen can be very satisfying: one does not have to be descended from one – when they appear on the family tree, the sources related to them can lead to much extra family history information.[*] Many people, aware of the largely nonconformist character of modern Wales, may assume that this subject has little relevance to family history research. I hope to show that, in a certain type of Welsh family, quite significant in Welsh history, individuals did join the ranks of the Anglican clergy, and that the divide between Anglicans and nonconformists was not so clear-cut as is often assumed.

My examples and case-studies are taken from one extended family, the Albans, a freeholding family from mid-Cardiganshire, and those who intermarried with them, which has been the subject of much personal research and so allows for the connecting thread which runs through this chapter.[1] However, similar examples have been found for many individuals whose ancestry has a similar background in rural Wales.

Background

The subject of the numerous small freeholders of Wales has been well covered by Dr Evan James.[2] These men held their land usually by the inheritance of small estates which had been sub-divided over many generations by partible inheritance; in other words, their ancestors (who are sometimes to be traced in the manuscript pedigrees[3]) had split their land amongst their sons in the traditional Welsh way. By 1873, Wales had over 17,000 'small proprietors', that is, owners of anything from one to 100 acres.[4] Above them in the hierarchy were the lesser yeomen, with 100 to 300 acres, the greater yeomen, squires, great landowners and peers. Cardiganshire, the focus of the present study, still had over 1,500 small proprietors and over 300 lesser yeomen in 1873. By virtue of their long

---

[*] This chapter is based on a talk given to the 'Second Stages in Researching Welsh Ancestry' course in September 1992.

connection with the land, their known descent and the paucity of social superiors (Cardiganshire had but one peer and eight great landowners in 1873), the freeholders and small yeomen had considerable status in many parishes. They tended to marry women of similar background, from their own and other nearby parishes. Sometimes these alliances were the subject of marriage settlements, and the actual marriage might be by licence (though by no means always). From their numbers came churchwardens and other parish officers, and they sat on juries, in Quarter Sessions and Great Sessions. They tended to leave wills and to feature in financial transactions such as mortgages. The descriptions of this class in documents vary a great deal, but the same individual might be called freeholder, yeoman or even gentleman in records – and often more than one of these at a time. Eighteenth-century marriage registers in the county sometimes have numerous references to 'yeoman' against the names of bridegrooms, not because this gave some artificial social boost, but because many of the adult males of the parish came into the freeholding category.

Such glimpses as we get of the life of the freeholding families in earlier centuries give the impression of a fairly rustic existence, but they became more sophisticated in the later seventeenth and eighteenth centuries. The prosperous ones took a greater lead in community life and developed ambitions, if not for themselves then for the next generation through education and entry to the professions.[5] By the eighteenth century, too, many were developing a greater piety and interest in religion. Many of the early leaders of Methodism came from this small freeholder background. The Methodist movement was, throughout the eighteenth century, one of reform from within the Church: 'At the beginning methodism was not a movement but an attitude to religion'.[6] However, not all who were increasingly inclined to a religious awakening were drawn to Methodist reform, and ordination was one of the options for a son of a parish gentleman.

The Sources
Sources for the Anglican clergy may include any or many of the following:
- records of the Church in Wales,[7] including episcopal registers, ordination papers, appointments to benefices, etc
- Clergy Institution Books[8]
- clergy lists and directories
- censuses, especially the 1851 religious census
- diocesan histories
- denominational yearbooks
- Parliamentary Papers
- biographical works, including biographical dictionaries

- newspapers and periodicals, including denominational periodicals
- the writings of the clergy themselves, including the registers of their parishes
- monumental inscriptions
- probate records

A selection of these sources is reflected in the remainder of this chapter.

Alban Thomas, Gentleman of this Parish

Alban Thomas (*c.*1685-1742) was a significant parishioner in Llansantffraid, Cardiganshire. Little is known of his life and origins, but he married Catherine, the daughter of a freeholder, Evan Lewis, and probably thereby obtained the freehold of Tŷ Mawr in the parish. A shadowy figure, Alban Thomas is chiefly represented by his educated signature, when he witnessed neighbours' wills, and by his fine tombstone, now on the outside wall of Llansantffraid church. The latter tells of the death of Alban Thomas, gentleman of this parish, of his wife Catherine (who had, in her widowhood, married another freeholder of an adjoining parish), and of their infant children, Elizabeth, Diana, Evan, and Mary *Thomas*. The small children are given a 'surname' and not their father's forename – a rare thing in mid-Cardiganshire in the first half of the eighteenth century and an indicator of status. Alban Thomas's death in his fifty-seventh year may have been sudden and unexpected, for no will or other probate document has been found.

The Alban Family of Llansantffraid

There was also a long-established family called Alban in the parish of Llansantffraid. John and David Alban featured in surviving parish registers of the eighteenth century; they and Alban Alban, of the next generation, lie beneath an impressive group of tombs in the churchyard, and the latter's son, another John, by his marriage to a freeholder's daughter, began a dynasty at Hafod Peris in the parish which has lasted to the present day.[9] Taking into account the rarity of the name Alban, it was reasonable to consider the possibility that the Albans might be descended from Alban Thomas, yet the tombstone evidence suggested that a surname was in use by his children. The parish registers of Llansantffraid are not good for the eighteenth century (far from uncommon in Wales) and though parties with the second name Alban appeared in the 1754 marriage register, the baptismal and burial registers survive only from 1796.[10] Proof of the connection was likely to be elusive.

As Alban was a fairly unusual surname (and first name), it was a candidate for a one-name study.[11] The latter soon revealed a quantity of clergymen bearing the name from the eighteenth to the twentieth centuries (see Fig. 3-1) and some of these are the subject of case-studies below. The first clergyman to be noted was the Reverend Thomas Alban, whose will was proved in 1776, and it was this document, in conjunction with his ordination papers, which proved to be the key to the structure of his wider family in the eighteenth century.

Thomas Alban (1730-1776)

The will of the Reverend Thomas Alban, of Frome Bishop in the county of Hereford, was proved in the Archdeaconry of Carmarthen in St David's diocese on 16 April 1776. It is a holograph will – that is, in his own handwriting – and unsigned and unwitnessed. That the fine handwriting was that of Thomas Alban was attested to by William Higgs Barker of St Peter's, Carmarthen. In his will, Thomas Alban mentioned his brothers, John Alban and David Alban of the parish of Llansantffraid, Cardiganshire, and so an important link was found. Bequests made in the will throw light on Thomas Alban's standard of living, for John was to have his silver watch, his knee and shoe buckles, his stock buckle and his best hat, a bureau and pewter dishes and plates. David received wearing-apparel, beds and bed-clothes. John inherited Thomas's real estate in the parish, while David was to have money, apart from a bequest to the poor of Pendine and Llandawke, Carmarthenshire, where Thomas had been Rector. We know the location of Thomas's real estate, Tŷ Mawr, from a 1760 list of freeholders.[12]

A picture of a civilised lifestyle emerges from Thomas's will, but perhaps the most significant clause in the present context was this: 'If either of my brothers shall have a son which he shall bring up to be a Clergyman … my books … and my written papers to be carefully laid up for that son.' This was perhaps the inspiration for the long succession of clergymen in the family thereafter.

To discover more about Thomas Alban, his ordination papers were sought. Ordination papers for the Welsh dioceses are listed in the National Library of Wales, but there are gaps, especially in the eighteenth century, in most dioceses.[13] Nevertheless, hundreds of names are listed and Thomas Alban, who was ordained deacon in 1753 and priest in 1754, is among them.[14] A set of such papers should, with luck, contain a record of the ordinand's name and place of abode, proof of age (normally a certificate of baptism), a certificate of the publication in his parish church of the candidate's intention to take Holy Orders (the document which is known as *si quis*), testimonials as to the character and conduct of the ordinand, and a nomination to a curacy.[15] Among those for Thomas Alban was a transcript of his baptism from the lost parish register of Llansantffraid, for 12 April

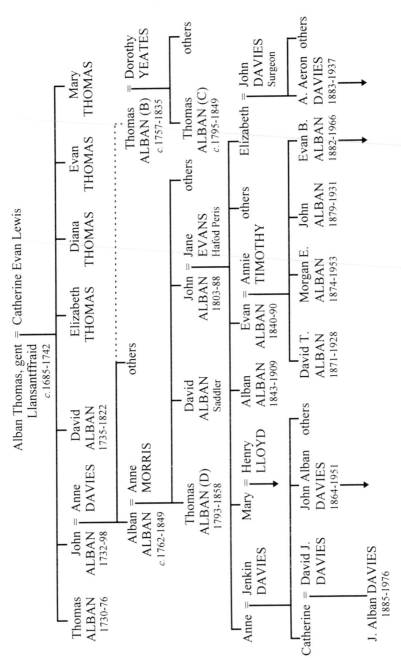

Fig. 3-1: Selective pedigree: Members of the Alban Family named in the chapter

1730, which described him as the son of Alban Thomas and Catherine his wife.

Apart from its obvious value in establishing part of the family pedigree, this evidence points to the instability of surnames at this time, even among the freeholding class, particularly in special circumstances. Alban Thomas, may, at the time of his death, have been thought of as having the 'surname' Thomas, but his sons who grew up (they were only five, seven and nine at his death) had no difficulty in taking their late father's first name in accordance with the older practice.

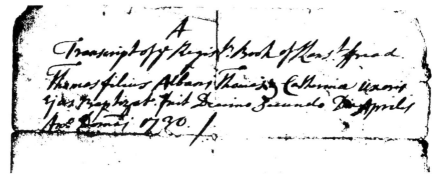

Fig 3-2: Transcript of the Baptism of Thomas Alban

The Reverend Thomas Alban was not a graduate and so does not appear in the University *alumni*. When his ordination as priest was listed in the bishop's register[16] he was described as a 'literate person', one of those non-graduate clergy 'ordained in large numbers in the diocese of St David's', without whom the Church's structure would have collapsed.[17,18] We do not know where he received his education or training, but he may have attended the Grammar School in Carmarthen or in Cardigan.[19]

The brothers of Thomas Alban, John and Dafîd, spent their lives as yeoman farmers in their native parish and left no clues to the fate of Thomas's books and papers. John (Siôn Penlan), in particular, was active in parish administration. Although he was not a clergyman, we should spare time to consider him, for his influence on the religious life of the Alban family was considerable. He was a follower of Daniel Rowland, the great Methodist, going regularly to Llangeitho and attending meetings held in a farmhouse in Llansantffraid.[20] When the latter became too small for the congregation in 1762, he built at his own expense the Calvinistic Methodist chapel in Llanon. When he died in 1798, the break with the Anglicans was still in the future. His descendants through his second marriage retained their connection with the chapel, yet, like many nonconformists throughout the nineteenth century, were interred in the churchyard at Llansantffraid.

Thomas Alban (*c.* 1757-1835)

In contrast to the first Revd Thomas Alban (1730-76), the man I shall call Thomas Alban (B) has an enigmatic background, though it is possible that he was the nephew to whom the former's books and papers went.[21] On 3 September 1780, Thomas Alban of Llansantffraid was ordained deacon at Abergwili; he became priest two years later. These events are recorded in the bishop's register,[22] but are not supplemented by a set of surviving ordination papers, so that proof of his parentage is not readily available. He was certainly in the parish of Llansantffraid before his ordination, appearing as a witness to marriages from 1778; from 1780 to 1782 he officiated at marriages locally. We have, therefore, several examples of his signature. In 1782, Thomas Alban (B) was curate of nearby Llanddeiniol.

In 1785 Thomas Alban, Clerk, of Hitchin in Hertfordshire, married Dorothy Yeates, of a prosperous family, in Leominster, Herefordshire. The following year he entered Peterhouse College, Cambridge, as a sizar.[23] His age was given as twenty-four, though if he were the man ordained in 1780 he would have been older than this in reality. After graduation, he embarked on a career in the church which gave him livings in Ludlow, Culmington and Snead, all on the Wales-England border; but mostly he lived a comfortable life at his wife's home, Broadward in Leominster, becoming a JP. His three surviving sons were, respectively, a gentleman, a lawyer and a clergyman, and his grandchildren and great-grandchildren went to English public schools and entered the professions, none counting Wales as their home.

What reason is there, other than the coincidence of an unusual name in a small Welsh parish, to connect this upwardly mobile Thomas Alban with the Albans of Llansantffraid? The parish register gaps ensure that there is no helpful baptismal record, and he was not mentioned by name in family wills. Nevertheless, in later years he wrote several letters concerning property transactions in Cardiganshire, as well as expressing his opinion about such local matters as orchards in the county. In 1824 his name was in a list of subscribers, most of whom had attended the school run by David Davis at Castell Hywel, an establishment with a fine reputation which, though its founder was a Unitarian minister, was attended by many Anglican ordinands.[24] We have, once more, several examples of the signature of this Thomas Alban, and they bear a close resemblance to that of the man ordained in 1780, who (if he was a different person altogether) disappeared without trace after 1782.

If Thomas Alban (B) was a grandson of Alban Thomas, as seems likely, from which son did he descend? There is little evidence: most of his children were named for his wife's family, but he called two of the later ones John and Anne, and none of them David and Margaret,[25] and that is about all, except that a man of his ambition fits better into what is known of John Alban's family. This paucity of evidence highlights the problem when ordination papers have been lost.

The clergyman son of Thomas Alban (B) bore the same name and we shall call him Thomas Alban (C). He was born about 1795, obtained degrees at Oxford,[26] and succeeded his father as rector of Snead, where he was buried in 1849, aged fifty-five; he had no issue.

Thomas Alban (1793-1858)

Thomas Alban (D), eldest son of Alban Alban, son of John,[27] was born in Llansantffraid in 1793. His absence from the *Alumni* suggests that he was a literate person when he was ordained. No record of his ordination has been found, but because he lived to the mid-nineteenth century we are able to locate him in the clergy lists which began to be produced in that century. In the 1847 *Clergy List* he is rector of Llanelian, Denbighshire, admitted to that benefice in 1831. It was then easy to locate him in the 1851 census and later to find the grant of administration to his next-of-kin, his brother David (a master saddler of Aberystwyth who was also referred to as 'gentleman' and 'esquire' in documents). We should not omit reference to the religious census of 1851, which provides much information about the living of Llanelian, including the size of congregation and the income it brought. The incumbent was resident (and we know had Welsh as his first language), but the two Sunday services in Welsh were taken by the curate.

Thomas Alban (D) appears in Joseph Foster's *Index Ecclesiasticus, 1800-1840,* where we find that he had been curate of other North Wales parishes. However – as so often in published lists – there is an error in Foster's work, for under the single heading 'Thomas Alban' the careers of Thomas Alban B, C and D are conflated. Although Alban is an unusual name, relations bearing the same forename are easily confusable in any family and it was only the steady collection of widespread occurrences of the name which has permitted them to be distinguished from each other. Quite probably, other confusions are hidden in these and similar lists for more common names such as Davies and Jones.

Thomas Alban (D) was unmarried, but the line of clergy continued with the sons of his eldest married brother.

Evan Alban (1840-1890)

Evan Alban was a graduate of Jesus College, Oxford, where he matriculated in 1864, aged 24, took his BA in 1867, and MA in 1871. In *Alumni Oxonienses 1715-1886*, he is described as the third son of John, 'of Havod, near Aberystwyth, co. Cardigan, gent.' His father, John Alban (1803-1888), a younger son of Alban Alban, could more realistically have been described as yeoman farmer of Hafod Peris, Llansantffraid,[28] but, again, he was a freeholder of good family and 'gentleman' was, as we have seen, often applied to that class. Evan, born and brought up in a Methodist environment – his maternal grandfather, another freeholder, having been one of the founders of Capel Rhiwbwys, Llanrhystud – nevertheless wished to become an Anglican priest, much to the dismay of his parents.[29] In spite of burgeoning ambition among such families by this time, it is unclear whether he went to Oxford for a general education and was there influenced by Anglican ideas, or went, as many men did, with ordination in mind. He was already twenty-four when he arrived at Oxford, and the latter seems, on balance, more likely.

After graduating, Evan Alban was ordained in the diocese of St David's.[30] Through Crockford's we may trace his career, from curacies in Llangendeirne, and in Llanwenog with Llanybyther, to becoming vicar of Llanfihangel Lledrod, Cardiganshire, in 1880, when his net income was £300. By the 1881 census, he was settled in the parish at Blaengader, with his wife, Annie (née Timothy), and four children aged one to nine.[31] The rest of the household consisted of a student-boarder, a nurse, a dairymaid and a farm servant, indicating that clerical duties (and stipend) were augmented by teaching and farming – the tie to the land still held, though fate intended it to last little longer in this line. When Evan Alban died on 3 December 1890 at the age of fifty, a significant change came about, as we shall see.

Alban Alban (1843-1909)

First, however, we should compare the career of Evan's younger brother, Alban. He too met parental opposition to his vocation and was not ordained deacon until the mature age of thirty-one. He had received his early education at Ystrad Meurig school, then went to St David's College, Lampeter, where he took his BA in 1874. When he was ordained his father, who had the custody of the chapel register, certified that Alban was born on 13 June 1843 and baptised on 23 July that year at Capel Rhiwbwys.[32] He became curate of St Dogmaels and then of Llangoedmor, and then curate and later rector of Bridell in north Pembrokeshire. In 1885 he married Alice Bowen, who, in 1881, had been farming Plasnewydd, Bridell, when the new rector was lodging there.[33] The couple lived at Plasnewydd, where Alban was also able to retain his contact with the land. He is buried in the parish he served for thirty years and, like most but not all of his relatives, is commemorated by a fine monument in a prominent position. His funeral, with an immense turnout of family and clergy, was covered fully by the local newspaper.[34]

The Sons of Evan Alban (1840-1890)

By the time of his death in 1890, Evan Alban had six children, of whom all four sons entered the church. The education of the two eldest, David Timothy Alban (1871-1928) and Morgan Evans Alban (1874-1953), was well advanced when their father died. David Timothy Alban became a distinguished West Wales churchman, vicar of the important parish of Lampeter (Llanbedr Pont Stephan) and rural dean. His obituary in *Yr Haul*, the publication of the Church in Wales, bears his photograph – like many other Albans who lived in the era of photography he has a distinctive bald head and a kindly face.[35] From another obituary we learn that he attended Lampeter School, then St David's College, after which he spent some time teaching in Yorkshire.[36] The account of his funeral in a local newspaper gives the names of numerous relations, including clergy, and lists no fewer than forty-seven other clergymen, including the bishop of St David's, who attended.[37]

Morgan Evans Alban, the second son, went to St David's College, Lampeter, soon after his father's death. Testimonials from the Principal and his tutor, in recommending him for a schoolmaster's position, mentioned his athletic ability. He went to a curacy in Denbighshire and later spent much of his career in England.

The two younger sons, John Alban (1879-1931) and Evan Basil Alban (1882-1966), were barely eleven and eight on their father's death, and steps were taken to ensure that their education did not suffer: they went to the Clergy Orphan School, by that time in Canterbury, Kent.[38] An essentially English education removed them some distance from their roots and their careers were spent almost wholly in England. John, after St David's College, Lampeter, was ordained in Lichfield diocese, and held benefices in Birmingham, Wiltshire, Herefordshire and London, where he ended his days. Evan Basil took a degree at Durham University and was ordained in the diocese of Birmingham. Though he was briefly a curate in Swansea, the rest of his life was also spent in England.

John Alban Davies (1864-1951)

John Alban Davies was another grandson of John Alban (1803-1888), his mother being the latter's daughter, Anne, who married Jenkin Davies, master mariner (also a descendant of freeholders). Both of John's parents were baptised in Rhiwbwys Calvinistic Methodist Chapel, Llanrhystud, Cardiganshire, yet the Anglican influence somehow prevailed in his own life. Among his ordination papers are an affidavit by his mother that her son John Davies, then of St David's College, Lampeter, had been baptised at home (Hafod Newydd, Llansantffraid) by the Reverend Morgan James, minister of Rhiwbwys, and a copy of his birth certificate, in which he is again named simply as John. [39] Welshmen with common names entering the professions were frequently urged by this time to add a middle, distinguishing name – very often, of course, the name chosen was the mother's maiden name. From the point that he was ordained in 1890, John Davies was known as John Alban Davies.

He is to be found in many printed works. Crockford's allows us to follow his career in detail, his education, the dates that he took Holy Orders, his curacies at Rhymney, Monmouthshire and Cockett, Swansea. He became vicar of Talley, Carmarthenshire, during which time he married Catherine Matthews. There is a joking reference in the *Western Mail* of the time to the fact that he had called his own banns, one of his colleagues, who didn't, being teased about his 'lack of albanium daviesio pluck'. [40] We may wonder at how gossip columns have changed, but also take advantage of the interest in everyday matters of clerical life which was shown in newspapers. Next he became vicar of Llannerchaeron, then rector of Llanddewi Aberarth, Cardiganshire, and Rural Dean.

These moves, and his involvement in parish and county life, sitting on boards and councils, can also be traced through entries in such biographical works as *Who's Who in Wales.* The various editions of this work, in 1920, 1933 and 1937, are an excellent source for the clergy (as well as for many worthy but ordinary people who would not have made the English equivalent).

John Alban Davies was often called upon to baptise new additions to the family, who were brought from far-off parts of Wales from time to time during his later career in Cardiganshire. Sometimes he himself travelled long distances to perform the ceremony, and not only for the immediate family: in 1911 he baptised the illegitimate child of a sister's servant, involving travelling from Talley to Llansantffraid (a difficult journey of over thirty miles). [41] Not all families treated illegitimacy harshly.

His long and useful life is commemorated with a reredos in the church of Llannerchaeron, where he is buried in the peaceful churchyard.

Jenkin Alban Davies (1885-1976)
Every so often national and local newspapers in Wales write about Welsh rugby's 'Terrible Eight', the Welsh pack of 1914 which built up a 'fearsome

reputation'. From the accompanying photograph looms the impressive figure of their captain and prop forward, the Reverend J. Alban Davies – commentaries always mention his profession, for the contrast of 'a highly respected member of the clergy' with the acknowledged hard play of his team caused a frisson.

Jenkin Alban Davies (known as Alban) was born at Hafod Newydd in Llansantffraid, the home of his mother, Catherine (sister of John Alban Davies, above) and her husband, David Davies – of a different Davies family.

If we consider briefly his father, David Davies was at that time himself preparing to take Holy Orders at St David's College, Lampeter, and was ordained deacon in 1885 at the age of thirty-five and priest in 1887. There were other examples of student sons-in-law in the family; for example, Mary Alban of Hafod Peris married Henry Lloyd, a Carmarthen man, and was supported at home by the family while her husband studied at St Bee's in Cumbria.[42] The parents in the related households of Hafod Peris and Hafod Newydd were faithful in their support of Capel Rhiwbwys, as we have seen, yet, whatever their deepest thoughts may have been, maintained good relations with their children and in-laws who were drawn to the Anglican Church. David Davies's ordination papers mention his baptism with the single forename, once more in a Calvinistic Methodist chapel;[43] but he too took an additional name, becoming known as David John Davies. At his ordination he had the nomination to the curacy of Ystradgynlais in the Swansea Valley, then became vicar of Llanddeusant, finally returning to his native county when he became vicar of Llandysiliogogo.

Returning to our main subject, (Jenkin) Alban Davies was the eldest child. He went to St John's School in Leatherhead, for the sons of the clergy, and then to Llandovery College, where many sons of this generation and later ones were educated.[44] He was an Exhibitioner of Jesus College, Oxford, but took only a third class honours degree in Theology, perhaps because rugby had become an important part of his life. After graduating he went to St Michael's Theological College, Llandaff, and was ordained deacon in 1909 and priest in 1910. His first appointment was to the curacy of Christ Church, Swansea, and around this time he played rugby for Swansea, Llanelli, Cardiff and London Welsh. He played in seven International matches for Wales, but the Great War put an end to this phase of his life and he spent most of the war as a temporary Chaplain to the Forces. After the war he turned to teaching, taking up appointments in schools overseas, then at Wellington College and Epsom College. He returned to parish life when he became vicar of St Paul's, Hook, in Surrey,[45] followed by livings in Kent. Perhaps his early schoolmastering experiences had given him a taste for warmer climes, for he emigrated to South Africa in the 1950s, becoming a prison chaplain. Later still, he went to California, where he died in 1976.

Alban Aeron Davies (1883-1937)

Alban Aeron Davies was another grandson of John Alban (1803-1888), being the son of Elizabeth Alban and John Davies, surgeon of Aberaeron, Cardiganshire (of yet another separate Cardiganshire Davies family). He was one of sixteen children of the couple, of whom there were eleven sons who at one point formed a football team to play against the town. Many of the sons had distinguished careers in the professions, including two others in the clergy, and the daughters who married wed a clergyman and a doctor. Though we can, as usual, follow him through his ordination papers and in the pages of Crockford's, as so often with the clergy, his obituary and the account of his funeral add much to our knowledge of his life and beliefs.

At the time of his death in a London nursing-home, Aeron Davies, as he was known, was vicar of All Saints, Penarth, Glamorgan. The newspaper account tells us that he was educated at St David's College, Lampeter, and Wycliff Hall, Oxford, and ordained in the diocese of Llandaff in 1909, after which he became curate of Mountain Ash. Like many of his age-group, he was affected by the First World War, when he became a Chaplain to the Forces in France. During the War, he was mentioned in dispatches, another source of information for the family historian.[46] A family photograph exists of him in his chaplain's uniform. Aeron Davies's funeral, the account of which is illustrated with a later photograph, took place in his native county of Cardiganshire, at Henfynyw. The funeral was private but was attended not only by his widow (though not by the two children mentioned in his obituary) but by numerous Albans, Davieses and Alban Davieses, many of them, of course, clergy themselves – one can nearly always expect a grand turnout for a clergyman's funeral.

There are two reasons for selecting the Reverend Aeron Davies to finish this chapter, when one could have chosen from many, brothers and cousins, in the same generation. First, newspapers, though an excellent source for the modern clergy, are often difficult to search, even when one has a precise date. The accounts mentioned here were found in an alphabetical biographical index of cuttings compiled by W.W. Price, which has much to offer those researching Welsh people of local or national significance.[47] Second, there is a sense of the wheel turning full circle with Aeron Davies, as he was brought back to lie close to his roots, when one reads in his obituary, 'Mr Davies had often expressed the opinion that a vicar could not claim to be different from a Nonconformist minister. He had often taken an active interest in meetings of Nonconformist churches held in the town.' In the tradition of his forebears, his religion was deeply felt, but charitable and tolerant.

BIBLIOGRAPHY

General and Background

Walker, David (ed.), *A History of the Church in Wales* (Church in Wales Publications, 1976; reprinted 1990). This and the following work have useful bibliographies.

Williams, Glanmor, *The Welsh Church from Conquest to Reformation* (Cardiff, 1962; 2nd ed. 1976).

— *Wales and the Reformation* (Cardiff, 1997).

Bevan, A., *Tracing your Ancestors in the Public Record Office* (London, HMSO, 5th ed., 1999).

Bourne, S. & Chicken, A.H., *Records of the Church of England* (2nd revised ed., 1991).

Guy, J.R., *The Diocese of Llandaff in 1763* (Cardiff, 1991).

Jones, O.W. & Walker, D., *Links with the Past: Swansea and Brecon Historical Essays* (Llandybïe, 1974).

Owen, D.M., *The Records of the Established Church in England.* Archives and the User No. 1. (British Records Association, 1970; reprinted 1996).

Published Sources

The Clerical Guide (first published 1817).

Clergy List (first published 1841).

Clerical Directory (from 1858; from 1876-present as Crockford's).

Ecclesiastical Directory (1829).

Foster, J., *Index Ecclesiasticus, 1800-1840.*

Foster, J., *Alumni Oxonienses 1500-1714* (Oxford & London 1891-2).

Foster, J., *Alumni Oxonienses 1715-1886* (Oxford & London 1887-8).

Jenkins, R.T. (ed.), *The Dictionary of Welsh Biography down to 1940* (London, 1959).

Jones, I.G., & Williams, D., *The Religious Census of 1851: a Calendar of the Returns relating to Wales,* Volume I, South Wales (Cardiff, 1976); Volume II, North Wales (Cardiff, 1981).

Le Neve, J., *Fasti Ecclesiae Anglicanae* (Oxford, 1854; revised London, various dates).

Venn, J. & J.A., *Alumni Cantabrigienses, from the Earliest Times to 1900* (Cambridge, 1922-54).

NOTES TO CHAPTER 3

[1] More than thirty descendants of Alban Thomas and the husbands of daughters of the family are known to have been Anglican clergymen – it is quite probable that more are to be found, especially where the surname changed at marriage. Those discussed in this chapter are necessarily a selection. The number has dwindled by the late twentieth century, with a noticeable decline after World War I, not least because of the attractions of other professions.

[2] Evan L. James, 'The Freeholders' in John & Sheila Rowlands, *Welsh Family History: A Guide to Research* (FFHS, 2nd ed., 1998).

[3] See, for example, Francis Jones, 'Aspects of Welsh Genealogy' in *Transactions of the Honourable Society of* Cymmrodorion (1948), p. 394ff.

[4] *Return of Owners of Land 1873* (HMSO, 1875), quoted in Evan L. James (Note 2).

[5] Confirmation can be found in Evan L. James (Note 2), and in the chapters in the present book by Dr Lewis Lloyd and John Dilwyn Williams.

[6] Owain W. Jones, 'The Welsh Church in the Eighteenth Century' in Walker (1976, 1990) p. 110.

[7] During most of the period covered by this chapter, the established church in Wales was the Church of England, the disestablishment of the Welsh church to form the present Church in Wales taking place in 1920. References here are therefore to the Church of England but the relevant records, at the National Library of Wales, Aberystwyth, are under the heading of Church in Wales.

[8] PRO: E331.

[9] Family information. For background to Hafod Peris, see also Spencer Thomas, 'The Enumerator's Returns as a source for a period picture of the parish of Llansantffraid, 1841-1851' in *Ceredigion*, iv, 408-21. The same author's 'Land occupation, ownership and utilisation in the parish of Llansantffraid' in *Ceredigion*, iii, 124-55, contains useful information.

[10] C.J. Williams & J. Watts-Williams, *Cofrestri Plwyf Cymru/Parish registers of Wales* (Aberystwyth, 1986) says that diocesan records suggest that *c.*1790 Llansantffraid parish registers went back to 1696.

[11] Alban is registered with the Guild of One-Name Studies, Box G, 14 Charterhouse Buildings, Goswell Road, London EC1M 7BA. Website: <www.one-name.org>.

[12] J.H. Davies, 'Cardiganshire Freeholders in 1760' in *West Wales Historical Records*, iii (1913), pp. 73-116.

[13] Lists of men ordained deacon and priest are in the bishops' registers for the Welsh dioceses (NLW, Church in Wales records), but do not give details of parentage.

[14] NLW: SD/O/642 (Deacon); SD/O/679 (Priest).

[15] For fuller details see D.M. Owen (1970, 1996) and Bourne & Chicken (1991).

[16] NLW: SD/BR/4. Twenty-three was the usual age for taking holy orders.

[17] O.W. Jones, 'The Mountain clergyman: his education and training' in Jones & Walker (1974), p. 165ff.

[18] In 1754, of seventeen men ordained deacon, six were literates; of thirty-four ordained priest, including Thomas Alban, twenty-nine were literates and only five

had degrees or were of an Oxford or Cambridge college. Details of educational background are not always given in the ordination lists.

[19] O.W. Jones, op. cit.

[20] *Hanes Methodistiaeth De Aberteifi*, p. 135ff.

[21] New evidence came to light during the preparation of this chapter and has yet to be followed up fully.

[22] NLW: SD/BR/5, pp. 102, 110.

[23] *Alumni Cantab.* 'Sizar' is defined as an undergraduate receiving financial help from the college, formerly one having certain menial duties.

[24] *Dictionary of Welsh Biography, sub* David Davis.

[25] NLW: SD/PR Llansantffraid: 1755 John Alban married Anne Davies; 1757 David Alban married Margaret David.

[26] *Alumni Oxon.*

[27] NLW: E.T. Price Papers.

[28] Hafod Peris was affected by a boundary change and, though in Llansantffraid for most of the period under discussion, is now in Llanrhystud.

[29] Family information from Elizabeth Alban, his niece (1891-1979).

[30] NLW: SD/O/1473 (Deacon); SD/O/1495 (Priest).

[31] PRO: RG 11/5444 f.8.

[32] NLW: SD/O/1613/B.

[33] PRO: RG 11/5428 f.5.

[34] *Cardigan & Tivyside Advertiser*, 5 Feb 1919. There is a useful index to this newspaper at the Ceredigion Record Office and the County Library, Aberystwyth.

[35] *Yr Haul* (1835-) can be seen on open shelves in the Department of Printed Books at NLW. It is always worth consulting for the lives of the Anglican clergy.

[36] *Cardigan & Tivyside Advertiser*, 6 April 1928.

[37] *Cardigan & Tivyside Advertiser*, 13 April 1928.

[38] M.J. Simmonds (ed.), *Register of the Clergy Orphan School for Boys 1751-1896*. This and other school registers were consulted in the Library of the Society of Genealogists, London, which has an extensive collection of such works.

[39] NLW: LL/O/2032.

[40] *Western Mail*, 7 Aug 1905, 'Wales Day by Day'. Mr D. Emrys Williams, Aberystwyth, kindly brought this to my attention.

[41] NLW: SD/PR Llansantffraid; family information.

[42] St Bee's College Entry Registers (1816-1895) are in Cumbria Record Office, Whitehaven. Mr J.H. Jones of Beckermet, Cumbria, kindly provided details of the entry relating to Henry Lloyd (later vicar of Aberdaron, Caernarfonshire).

[43] NLW: SD/O/1918. The baptism took place in Dyffryn CM Chapel, Llanbadarn Fawr, Cardiganshire; the father was William Davies.

[44] St John's, Leatherhead, School Register 1852-1937, is also in the Library of the Society of Genealogists (see note 38 above); where school and college registers have not been published, the search is harder, depending on response to enquiries by individual schools and colleges.

[45] His period at Hook was only eight years (1924-32) but he was thereafter known as 'Alban Hook' in the family.

[46] *London Gazette,* in large libraries.

[47] W.W. Price, Aberdâr, *Biographical Index* [NLW 1981].

4. INDICATORS OF NONCONFORMIST ANCESTRY

John Rowlands

The knowledge that a long-dead ancestor was (or was not) a nonconformist can be of considerable help in the pursuit of family history research.* It can, for example, help to explain why an ancestor does not come to prominence in a community – as a churchwarden, magistrate, etc – despite having a clear status within it.

Unfortunately, the written records relating to individuals which family historians rely on in their researches seldom include the simple and unambiguous statement: '… is a nonconformist' (be it Baptist, Independent, Methodist or whatever). Indeed, many of those living in the nineteenth century would have considered this to be a wholly superfluous statement, living as they were in a society which was predominantly nonconformist. For those living in less tolerant centuries, such a statement would have been avoided like the plague as it would have been seen as an admission of treasonable association. To confuse the situation further, over the centuries the majority of nonconformists have had some involvement with the Established (or Anglican) Church, and that involvement, being recorded, can lead to the conclusion that they held allegiance to the Church.

Because of this, contrary evidence identifying them as nonconformists, which is often far less clear-cut but which establishes their true allegiance, assumes an increased importance. It may, for example, lead a researcher to pay greater attention to local chapel histories or year books than he, or she, might otherwise have done. This can be especially so for a non Welsh-speaker as a significant proportion of those histories or year books are likely to be in Welsh. Furthermore, it should not be forgotten that allegiances could change (and frequently did) in response to changing religious attitudes and opportunities, or the influence of a particularly powerful preacher.

---

* This chapter is based on a talk given to the Second Stages Course, 'Conformity and Dissent', in September 1994.

Finally (in introduction), when pursuing ancestors who might have been nonconformists, it is necessary to have some knowledge not only of the growth of nonconformity over time, but also the different areas in which the main denominations became dominant.

The Value of Indicators

Indicators of possible nonconformist allegiances may be used in two separate ways as an aid to research. First, the actual existence of commonly accepted indicators in an individual's life may be used *in combination* to establish the likelihood of a nonconformist allegiance. Second, those indicators may be used to test the hypothesis that a particularly shadowy ancestor might have been a nonconformist. When testing such a hypothesis it is essential only to accept it as evidence when those indicators exist *in suitable combination*.

I have given emphasis above to the need to use indicators *in combination* as any one indicator could well have a perfectly reasonable explanation in the life of an individual which is totally unrelated to nonconformity. For example, I describe later how marriage by licence in the parish church can, in the right circumstances, be an indicator of nonconformity. However, marriage by licence was also the common choice of the higher echelons of Welsh society who were, in the main, firmly wedded to (as well as in) the Established Church.

The nature of a particular denomination being followed can also have a profound bearing on the significance of an indicator, as, for example, would be the case when consulting records of baptism in parish registers. These may (for reasons explained later) include children from many denominational backgrounds, but would most probably not include those from Baptist families.

Firmly held religious convictions can, of course, not only colour an individual's attitude towards commonplace activities such as baptism, marriage and burial, but it can also colour the Established Church's attitude towards the individual in these matters; matters in which it has long held a dominant role. This is most evident in burials at the parish church where the appropriate nonconformist minister might well be excluded from active involvement in the burial ceremony.

The Growth of Nonconformity

Of particular importance for research, however, is the fact that the likelihood of an ancestor being a nonconformist varies substantially over time. In Wales it can vary from being a totally exceptional activity to one which would have been very much the rule. Unfortunately, few records exist which allow us to identify the growth and spread of nonconformity in Wales in the

200 years after 1577 when conventicles were first reported to exist.[1] It was not until the latter part of the eighteenth century that anything approaching a significant body of information became available to allow us to build up a picture of the place which nonconformity was assuming in the religious life of Wales. And it was not until the Religious Census of 1851 that data became available to enable us to do so with reasonable certainty.

Taking information from a variety of sources, it would appear that the growth of nonconformity in Wales is likely to have been broadly in line with the figures set out in Fig. 4-1. However, the significance of these figures needs to be viewed in the context that there were 1,180 Anglican places of worship in Wales by 1851; a figure which is unlikely to have varied a great deal since the Reformation.

From Fig. 4-1 it can be seen that, initially, the number of nonconformist congregations was relatively small, and it was not until the nineteenth century that the nonconformist denominations (collectively) had achieved comparable strength to that of the Established Church in terms of the number of congregations and the number of adherents.

Year	No of Congregations	Percentage of the worshipping population
1630	Not known	Minimal
1676	Not known	1+
1689	Not known	2
1716	70	15
1745	110	16
1775	171	17
1816	993	35
1851	2826	80

Fig. 4-1: The growth of Nonconformity in Wales, 1630-1851[2]

It is interesting to note, however, that the significant expansion in the number of congregations during the eighteenth century is not matched by a comparable increase in the proportion of nonconformists in the worshipping population, and a number of possible explanations might be put forward for this.

For example, there was a general upsurge in religious activity throughout Wales at this time and nonconformity might have been making its greatest inroads amongst those who had not previously been part of the worshipping population. In addition, there is every likelihood that while Methodist congregations (both Calvinistic and Wesleyan) were being formed, their adherents were still considered to be part of the Established Church.

From the beginning of the nineteenth century the picture began to change dramatically, with the number of nonconformist congregations and adherents totally outstripping figures for the Established Church. Indeed, the Religious Census of 1851 showed that, by the middle of the century, 80% of the worshipping population of Wales held an allegiance to one of the nonconformist denominations.[3] At the local level, however, there was considerable variation about this figure and in the Merthyr Tydfil Registration District, for example, the figure was as high as 93%, while at Chepstow it was as low as 40%.[4]

The nature of Nonconformity in Wales
The above figures relating to the growth of nonconformity in Wales give no indication of its nature at different periods, or the thinking and attitudes (especially towards the Established Church) which lie behind them.

I do not intend to describe here the nature of nonconformity in Wales at different periods at any length or in any detail, as this has been more than adequately covered elsewhere (see Bibliography). However, it would not be inappropriate to remind the reader of the changing nature of the whole religious scene in Wales from the Reformation to modern times, as, for many, this will be the context in which they will be searching for evidence of their ancestors.

There is plenty of evidence to suggest that, after the Reformation, Wales was a backward country with a very low level of religious observance, and that this situation remained largely unchanged for some considerable time. As a result, Catholicism and Catholic practices were able to linger on in many parts due in large measure to the poverty and inaccessibility of the country, where Welsh was the main language of the ordinary people. When a religious awakening did come about, it would have been (initially at least) towards the Established Church, which had retained many of the ceremonies of its predecessor. This probably explains why, perhaps surprisingly, many parts of Wales were for the King during the Civil War.

The fact that no significant measure of nonconformity was to be found in Wales until well on into the seventeenth century tends to confirm the basic conservatism of Welsh society.

Early nonconformists in Wales were largely Congregational Baptists and this led, in 1649, to the formation of the famous Baptist Church at Ilston on Gower under John Miles. With the Restoration of the Monarchy, persecution of the Baptists and other religious minorities such as the Quakers became so intense that some congregations emigrated to America *en masse*. The congregation at Ilston was one such, and the original Ilston register, containing 261 baptisms, which went with them to America (probably in 1663), survives to this day.[5] However, remnants of Baptist, Independent and other denominations survived to form the basis for later congregations in the more tolerant climate under William and Mary.

Throughout the eighteenth century those congregations grew and increased in number alongside the development of Methodism within the framework of the Established Church. Eventually, of course, Wesleyan Methodism broke away from the Church in 1784, and Calvinistic Methodism (far and away the dominant denomination in Wales) did so in 1811.

By the middle of the nineteenth century the relative strengths of all the religious denominations in Wales, as derived from the Religious Census of 1851, was as follows:

Denomination	Places of worship	Attendance (as % of total)
Church of England	1180	20.0
Independents	700	21.8
Baptists	533	17.4
Wesleyan Methodists	659	12.4
Calvinistic Methodists	808	25.7
Other	126	2.6
Total	**4006**	**100**

Fig. 4-2: Places of worship and attendance by denomination

Within this overall picture, while all the main denominations are to be found throughout Wales:

- the Independents and the Baptists were the dominant forces across South Wales
- the Calvinistic Methodists were particularly strong in West and North-west Wales, and
- the Wesleyan Methodists were, largely speaking, only found in significant numbers along the English border, although there were pockets in lead mining and slate quarrying areas as a result of in-migration (see also Chapter 7).

A Nonconformist in the Family

With nonconformity taking such a hold on the religious life of Wales, it would not be too far-fetched to state that no-one with a significant measure of Welsh ancestry over the past 150 years can avoid having a nonconformist ancestor somewhere in their family tree, no matter how 'church' they might feel themselves to be. The writer's father, for example, had four uncles on his mother's side (out of six) who were Anglican clergymen and he would have considered himself to be very much a part of a church family. Yet the construction of his religious pedigree (based on the vital events, of baptism, marriage and burial, in the lives of his ancestors) shows that in his recent ancestry this was anything but the case. It also suggests that, when one takes into account the requirement to be married in the Established Church (between 1754 and 1837) in order to contract a legal marriage, an involvement with nonconformity could well have been a longer-term aspect of his ancestry.

However, single events such as a baptism, a marriage or a burial are not certain indicators that an individual was (or was not) a nonconformist. It merely indicates that they (or their parents) thought in a particular way at a particular point in time in relation to that specific event. Furthermore, a duality of thinking could often be involved. This point was very well illustrated recently in a written assignment by a participant on the 1998 'Family History in Wales' Course held in Aberystwyth. In that assignment she quoted from the memoirs of an elderly relation (born in 1910) who had written:

> We were all christened into the Church of England, for although the village boasted Methodist, Baptist and Congregational Chapels, and we children attended the last, these were not considered important enough by many for the sacraments. So, when old Adam had been expelled by the Rector in the Parish Church, we later attended the Welsh Congregational Sunday School – 'to learn a bit of Welsh, not too much', as my father put it.[6]

This example not only gives a clear insight into the relaxed relationship which existed between church and chapel in many areas, but also (and interestingly) an insight into social attitudes towards the Welsh language in the early-to-middle part of this century. In recent years it has been recognised that the antagonism which is supposed to have existed between church and chapel was often something of a myth, and there is plenty of other evidence to show that individuals often moved between the churches in response to changing personal beliefs, or the particular appeal of a powerful preacher. As Ieuan Gwynedd Jones records, it was not until 1849 that the members of one Calvinistic Methodist Chapel in north Cardiganshire (Tabor, Llangwyryfon) ceased attending the parish church after their own morning service, and it was not uncommon for a father to educate one son for the Church and another for the nonconformist ministry.[7]

THE INDICATORS THEMSELVES

There are seven main indicators of likely nonconformist allegiance which may be borne in mind when searching in any part of Wales (there could well be several more of significance in more local areas). They are:

- an unexpected absence of baptisms in parish registers
- marriage by licence
- the lack of an official position where one would normally expect to find it
- an affidavit confirming conformity
- the lack of a University education in a profession in which it might be expected
- the choice of given names for children
- the use of land to build a chapel or the leaving of land for that purpose in a will

An absence of baptisms in parish registers: Prior to July 1837 this can be an indicator of nonconformity, especially where the family features in the records of burial within those registers. This is especially the case for those with an allegiance to the Baptists, but less so for the Independents and Methodists.

For the period 1754-1837 the existence of a marriage record cannot be used as a contrary indicator as it was necessary to be married in the parish church to contract a legally recognised marriage during this period following the implementation of the Hardwicke Act of 1753.

Clearly, the Baptists, for whom the baptism of believers (and not infants) is a central tenet of faith, would have a particular aversion to infant baptism in the parish church, despite the fact that there were important civil advantages in doing so.

Prior to July 1837 a record of baptism in a particular parish church could be used as a form of 'civil' registration quite separate from its obvious religious connotations. As a result, an individual could claim a settlement in that parish and hence qualify for parish relief if they were unfortunate enough to fall on hard times. Any religious aversion is unlikely to be strong enough in the case of the Independents or the Methodists (who were in any case still part of the Anglican Church for much of the period from their formation to 1837) to overcome the civil advantages.

Burial in the parish churchyard was also an accepted part of community life which was acceptable to most denominations, especially as it need not involve going into the church itself.

Marriage by licence: This is commonly supposed to be an form of marriage which is confined to the upper levels of society who sought to avoid the need to publish banns (and hence, in theory at least, potential challenge). However, the publishing of banns in the parish church was often an anathema to many nonconformists, the bulk of whom, being minor freeholders, tradespeople, labourers or industrial workers, would not normally be expected to use this device. As a result, we find, for example, in the parish of Llanelli (Carmarthenshire) that the proportion of marriages by licence doubles in the ten years after 1826 compared to the preceding ten years. This was a twenty-year period when the town of Llanelli was experiencing an exceptional increase in its population (mainly through an influx of industrial workers).

The lack of an 'official' position: This lack in a person of substance who might be expected to hold a position such as churchwarden, portreeve or even magistrate within a community, can often be an indication of nonconformist beliefs, as only practising members of the Anglican Church were permitted, by law, to hold official positions of this sort.

An affidavit: Where this testifies to the fact that someone in an 'official' position was a practising Anglican, it is usually clear evidence that there was considerable doubt in the matter. The qualifying act is normally taken as evidence of them having attended the Communion Service on Easter Day which, if that is the sum total of their religious involvement with the church, would make them only nominal Anglicans – albeit sufficiently so. However, this does not prove that they were nonconformists as it could equally well mean that they had no religious beliefs.

Lack of a University education: Where a person without an university education follows a profession which normally requires a degree, it should be a reasonable cause for asking 'why?' This is especially the case where the family has the substance to fund such an education.

The simple answer could be that that person might have been a nonconformist, as access to university was denied to other than practising Anglicans prior to the University Test Acts of 1871, although there had been a degree of relaxation in this at Oxford from 1854. However, University College, London (now London University) was founded in 1828 with the express purpose of providing university opportunities for nonconformists.

The choice of given names for children: Within nonconformist families the choice of given names is often very different to that within Anglican families. Whereas the latter has a heavy emphasis towards the names of Kings of England and the Saints of the Christian Church, the former – and in particular the Independents and the Baptists (the older forms of Dissent) – often involves the use of Old Testament names and sometimes names expressing piety or good works. Thus we find men with the given names

Aaron, Benjamin, Enoch, Gabriel, Habakkuk, Isaac, Mordecai, Salathiel, etc, and women with given names such as Prudence, Patience, Grace, Sage, Faith, Hope, Charity, etc. All of the given names for men (and many more besides) have become surnames which have survived to the present day.

In *The Surnames of Wales for Family Historians and Others* we list fifty-five surnames which had been derived from Old Testament given names.[8] Anyone with a Welsh background holding one of those surnames today can be virtually certain of having a nonconformist ancestor in their family tree.

The leaving of land in a Will for the construction of a chapel or the establishment of a nonconformist burial ground displays (at the very least) a very great sympathy towards a dissenting cause. In all probability it shows a direct allegiance to that cause.

The granting of permission to build a chapel on one's land is likely to be one stage less conclusive than the above. Nevertheless, it could again be an indication of active nonconformist allegiance.

In conclusion

So, if you are descended from a somewhat shadowy eighteenth-century ancestor:

- by the name of David Mordecai
- who was the first of a local, and much respected, family of solicitors
- who, although he was both married (by Licence) and buried in the parish church, you cannot find any record of his baptism or that for any of his children
- he does not feature in any University records or the incidental records of the parish (such as vestry records, churchwarden's accounts, etc), although several of his children do, and
- the local Baptist Chapel was built on land which is on the edge of farmland believed to have been owned by the family at one time.

What might you conclude about his religious upbringing and the beliefs of his parents? In what new places might you look for further clues about him and his parents?

BIBLIOGRAPHY

A substantial bibliography relating to nonconformity is given in Chapter 23 in *Welsh Family History: A Guide to Research* (FFHS, 2nd ed, 1998) and I do not propose to repeat it all here. However, new books continue to be published, while certain others have a particular relevance to this chapter. In addition, the chapters in this book by Ieuan Gwynedd Jones and Michael Gandy make frequent reference to books and articles which are of value.

The bibliography which follows is, therefore, highly selective and the reader is advised to consult these other works for reference to books, etc, giving information about nonconformity on a broader front.

Barnes, David Russell, *People of Seion* (Llandysul, 1995). Describes patterns of Nonconformity in Cardiganshire and Carmarthenshire in the century preceding the Religious Census of 1851.

Bassett, T.M., *The Welsh Baptists* (Swansea, 1977).

Davies, D. Elwyn, *They Thought for Themselves*, (Llandysul, 1982). A brief look at the story of Unitarianism and the liberal tradition in Wales and beyond its borders.

Evans, M.B., 'Nonconformity' in John & Sheila Rowlands (eds), *Welsh Family History: A Guide to Research* (2nd ed., FFHS, 1998).

Ifans, Dafydd (ed.), *Cofrestri Anghydffurfiol Cymru/Nonconformist Registers of Wales* (NLW, Aberystwyth, 1994).

Jones, Ieuan Gwynedd & Williams, David, *The Religious Census of 1851: A Calendar of the Returns relating to Wales*, Vol. I, South Wales (Cardiff 1976), also Jones, I.G., Vol. II, North Wales (Cardiff, 1981).

Rees, Thomas *The History of Protestant Nonconformity in Wales* (London, 1883).

Richards, Thomas *Wales under the Penal Code* (London, 1925).

Shorney, David *Protestant Nonconformity and Roman Catholicism: A guide to sources in the Public Record Office*. PRO Readers' Guide No. 13 (PRO, 1996). Has an excellent general history of Nonconformity and (at long last) is a book which is very precise in its references to England, Wales, and England and Wales.

Also (all published by the Society of Genealogists):

Breed, G.R., *My ancestors were Baptists*.

Clifford, D.J.H., *My ancestors were Congregationalists in England & Wales*. Has a list of registers.

Leary, W., *My ancestors were Methodists*.

Milligan, E.H. & Thomas, N.J., *My ancestors were Quakers.*

Mordy, Isobel, *My ancestors were Jewish.*

Steel, D.J., *Sources for Nonconformist Genealogy and Family History*, National Index of Parish Registers.

Wiggins, Ray, *My ancestors were in the Salvation Army.*

NOTES TO CHAPTER 4

[1] David Shorney, *Protestant Nonconformity and Roman Catholicism: A Guide to Sources at the Public Record Office*, PRO Readers' Guide No. 13 (PRO Publications, 1996). Chapter 1 is an excellent historical introduction to the emergence of the Protestant dissenting tradition.

[2] The sources used for this table include, 'The Compton Census of 1676', and Dot Jones, *Statistical Evidence relating to the Welsh Language, 1801-1911*. (Cardiff, 1998). Table: Religion 1.1 on p. 425.

[3] Ibid.

[4] Ibid. Table: Religion 1.2, p. 430 and p. 431.

[5] For a full description of the history and contents of the Ilston Book, see B.G. Owens, *The Ilston Book* (Aberystwyth, 1996)

[6] I am grateful to Mrs Pam Reynolds of Clayhidon in Devon for providing this information as part of her post-course written assignment on the 1998 'Family History in Wales' Course.

[7] See Chapter 21, 'Church and Chapel in Cardiganshire, 1811-1914' in Geraint H. Jenkins, and Ieuan Gwynedd Jones, (eds.) *Cardiganshire County History*, Volume 3 (Cardiff, 1998).

[8] Those surnames were: Aaron, Abednego, Abel, Abraham, Absolom, Amos, Benjamin, Caleb, Elias, Elisha, Emmanuel, Enoch, Enos, Ephraim, Esaias, Esau, Ezekiel, Gabriel, Habakkuk, Hoseah, Isaac, Ishmael, Israel, Jacob, Japheth, Jehu, Jehosophat, Jeremiah, Jesse, Job, Joel, Jonah, Jonathan, Joseph, Joshua, Josiah, Levi, Lot, Meshach, Methusalem, Micah, Mordecai, Moses, Nathan, Nathaniel, Rachel, Salathiel, Samuel, Samson, Shadrach, Sim(e)on, Solomon, Tobias, Zacharias, Zacchaeus.

Note the existence in this list of the surname Rachel. Also note that the surname Daniel has not been included as there is a body of opinion which believes its popularity stems from its closeness to the Welsh saint's name of Deiniol. It is certainly very common throughout Wales (0.25% overall) and has a distinctively different distribution to the surnames in the main list.

5. URBAN GROWTH AND INDUSTRIALISATION IN WALES

Sandra Wheatley

The general aim of this chapter is to bring to the attention of family historians how diverse and complex were the urban communities of Wales, especially following the great changes associated with the Industrial Revolution.* Some mention will also be made of matters which were of vital concern to our ancestors, such as housing and health. Family historians will gain a better appreciation of the lives of their ancestors and the history of their everyday surroundings by becoming aware of this historical background and thus acquiring a fuller sense of the past, with some understanding of how the lives of our ancestors were shaped by the types of communities in which they lived. This chapter divides into three main parts: firstly, the towns of Wales before the industrial revolution, secondly, the changes which occurred in the urban structure of Wales with the rise of industry in the late eighteenth century and during the nineteenth century and finally, examining one town, Merthyr Tydfil, in more detail, with mention of a number of useful sources.

Urban Growth

Modern urban life in Wales[1] can be traced back to the Anglo-Norman conquest of the twelfth and thirteenth centuries, when some ninety bastide or fortified towns were founded as administrative and economic centres to complement the military installations of the castles. Edward I's eight castles were built between 1277 and 1330 as an attempt to solve his 'Welsh Problem' and, in the case of Aberystwyth, Flint, Rhuddlan, Conwy, Caernarfon and Beaumaris, the castle and town were built as one unit, with borough charters being granted at the time of construction. With many of the earlier Norman castles, the associated settlement was only given a charter when control of the local population was secured. In Pembrokeshire, for

---

* This chapter is based on talks given to the 'Second Stages in Researching Welsh Ancestry' courses held in September 1991 and September 1992.

example, at Haverfordwest, Tenby, Pembroke, and Newport, there are significant gaps between the dates of building the castles and the first charter.

In general, these Edwardian towns were imposed upon a Welsh society, which had been largely characterised by scattered rural settlement. The towns had legal rights, defined by charters, allowing certain privileges, such as giving burgesses the right to hold markets, establishing trading codes of practice, and possibly the right to hold courts, although frequently the native Welsh were excluded from these privileges. Lists of burgesses do exist for this mediaeval period, but generally indicate that, initially, mainly non-Welsh people were granted burgess status, but as time passed the Welsh element grew stronger. The imposition of these planted towns, coupled with political uncertainties of the period, meant that centuries passed before they became truly urban, in the sense of being integrated into the life of the countryside and independent of a need for a military presence to support their economic and administrative role. Chepstow and Aberystwyth, for example, may be regarded as examples of planted boroughs, but in other cases development was more gradual, such that natural integration into the surrounding area occurred, as at Carmarthen, Swansea and Cardiff. In further places, such as Lampeter and Nefyn, the boroughs had connections with earlier Welsh market centres. Therefore, mediaeval boroughs within Wales could have fairly diverse origins, and would have been modest commercial centres for fairs and markets and would have also supported craftsmen and exercised a basic legal jurisdiction. However, a poor transport network, with difficult long-distance trading routes, tended to keep Welsh towns very modest in size in comparison with their English counterparts, with populations of less than 2,000. Commercial activities were largely centred on the chief border towns of Chester, Shrewsbury, Ludlow, Hereford and Gloucester during the middle ages.

By the early seventeenth century, some changes had occurred in the distribution of towns within Wales, since certain boroughs had failed, perhaps because too many were founded within a small area or perhaps because of poor siting. Kenfig in Glamorgan, for example, was overtaken by advancing sand-dunes and further places are worthy of note. Camden in 1610 wrote:

> Newborough having bin a long time greatly annoyed with heaps of sand, driven in by the sea, complaineth that it hath lost much of its former state that had.[2]

Some newer towns had appeared since the foundation of the mediaeval bastides, including Fishguard, Tregaron, Wrexham and Bangor. Others replaced failed mediaeval boroughs: Machynlleth, for example, grew instead of the one planned at Bere, and Harlech, on the coastal fringe, was superseded by a more accessible market town at Dolgellau. However, during the late mediaeval and into the early modern period, the Welsh population was still predominantly rural and scattered, but with greater concentrations on the north and south coastal lowlands and in the eastern borderlands, these being the areas where good quality farming land existed. Town such as Carmarthen and Caernarfon served relatively rich country areas and prospered during sixteenth and seventeenth centuries, whilst those towns which had a mainly defensive function in earlier centuries decayed. Tudor legislation had provided important administrative functions for some towns as centres for the Courts of Great Sessions; these were Brecon, Denbigh, Caernarfon and Carmarthen, all established market centres. Yet these four regional capitals, despite the addition of the Courts, remained relatively small in scale; Elizabethan Brecon or Carmarthen, for example, had populations of only around 2,000. Contemporary comments confirm their high status. George Owen called Carmarthen '... the largest towne in Wales, faire and in good state', and he described Brecon as '... a bigge towne faire built'.[3] Speed called Denbigh '... the greatest Market-Towne of North-Wales',[4] while Pennant described Caernarfon as '... justly the boast of North Wales'.[5] Other towns of importance, such as Haverfordwest, Swansea and Cardiff, were ports and also served fairly prosperous agricultural areas. In contrast, a series of smaller market towns existed, serving only local areas. Dolgellau and Machynlleth, already mentioned, were two of these; many others existed, including Hay-on-Wye and Bala.

The size of the main pre-industrial towns in Wales has been calculated from the 1670 Hearth Tax.[6] Carmarthen, Brecon and Haverfordwest had just 2,000 people in the late seventeenth century and Caernarfon an even smaller population. Wrexham was identified as the largest town with a population of just over 3,000; an eighteenth century visitor wrote that '... Wrexham seemed to be the capital of North Wales, larger and more prosperous than Caernarvon'.[7] Apart from this group of more important centres, an average market town such as Welshpool contained only some 913 persons in 1670. Many travellers reported that, in general, Welsh towns were small and unimportant. According to Malkin, '... Welsh towns are universally censured by strangers for the inelegance and inconvenience of their houses'.[8] Welsh towns, although having something of a 'village' character, provided an urban role for the surrounding countryside, with posting-inns and whatever shops existed sited at the town centres, although until the nineteenth century, shops as we know them were few and far between. Most selling was carried out in market halls or in temporary stalls erected for weekly markets or regular fairs, probably occupying the high street for the day. Craft industry, which provided for most immediate needs, was scattered throughout the town. In general, the wealthy and professional people lived nearer the centres of towns, thus having convenient access to what services the towns had on offer in times of primitive transport. The poor were distributed throughout the town, but often collected in peripheral groups, showing similarity to the mediaeval situation where the native Welsh population were often kept outside the town walls. Towns in this early modern period may studied through such records as the hearth tax figures, together with rate books, burgess rolls and court leet documents, and in the reports of visitors, although the latter could be somewhat partial. Perhaps a comment about Builth Wells at the very beginning of the nineteenth century summarises the nature of these small towns:

> The town in general exhibits that air of impoverished and dilapidated antiquity which so universally bespeaks the negligent and unambitious character of a thinly peopled country. The trade of Builth Wells extends no further than supplying necessaries to the neighbouring farmers and peasantry who flock there on market days.[9]

Three towns, where early industrial growth had already brought about considerable change, will now be introduced. The first of these is Swansea, which combined in an unexpected way, towards the end of the eighteenth century, the early attributes of a seaside resort with those of a rapidly growing metallurgical industry, in particular its copper works. A contemporary visitor noted:

> Swansea in its extent, the width of its streets and aspect of its buildings, far exceeds all the towns in South Wales ... all the resources of polished society are here at times to be found amidst the noise of manufacture, and the buzz of incessant commerce.[10]

At the 1670 Hearth Tax, the population estimate was 1,733, so that great expansion had taken place in the eighteenth century, after the beginning of copper and lead smelting in 1717, bringing it to the second largest town in Wales by the 1801 census, with a population of 6,099. Holywell in the north was to some extent similar to Swansea, with a copper industry but also brass works and cotton mills, and probably achieving the peak of its prosperity at the end of the eighteenth century, when it was recorded that:

> ... flourishing mines, that were for some time discovered in the neighbourhood, made a great change in the appearance and introduced the effects of wealth. The town ... contains more than 2,000 souls.[11]

However, it was in Merthyr Tydfil that the most rapid growth of all had taken place; in the second half of the eighteenth century it had increased so extensively with the development of the iron industry, that in 1801, having a population of 7,705, it was already the largest town in Wales, a position it was to hold until 1881. The ten most populous towns in Wales at all censuses between 1801 and 1841 were headed by Merthyr Tydfil, with Swansea second. At 1801, all the other eight towns were the traditional regional market centres in the south and the north, which had functioned as such since late mediaeval times. Other figures worth noting are those of Cardiff and Newport which began to merit mention in 1831 and rise in rank in 1841; these were becoming major ports and they gradually made their way up the table, with Cardiff eventually becoming the largest Welsh town in 1881 and staying there right to the present day. Its initial rapid expansion is attributed to its being the major port for the iron manufacturing and coal mining areas of south Wales.

By the late eighteenth and into the early nineteenth century, both industrialisation and commercial development had made their impact on Welsh society. Towns were becoming the main distribution points for a range of manufactured goods and centres of local society as well as business activities. A regular system of coaches and carriers connected the main towns by 1820, and in addition an important water-borne trade was carried by coastal vessels and by canal. Improvements in transport technology most particularly included the growth of a rail network from around 1840. Other major transformations occurred in both industry and in retailing. With industry, up to the middle of the eighteenth century, the situation had been one of small-scale craft industries, based on workshops scattered throughout the towns and producing for local markets. These gradually declined from the second part of the eighteenth century and large-scale, factory-based industry came into being, demanding large areas of land and encouraging the growth of new specialist industrial towns such as Merthyr Tydfil and Holywell. In retailing, a series of changes took place. Temporary stalls were slowly replaced by permanent shops, the first stage of which was often the building of a market hall. Specialist retailers appeared, selling manufactured goods, instead of the workshop-related establishments which had existed from the middle ages.

Professor Ieuan Gwynedd Jones has written:

The years between 1820 and 1895 – the life-span of an oldish person as the expectation of life was then measured – were the most momentous in the history of modern Wales. It was during that short period that the social consequences of the first stage of the industrialization of Wales became apparent and would be worked out in the transformation of Welsh society.[12]

The new society was growing rapidly in numbers, with a considerable alteration in the geographic balance over the counties within Wales, best illustrated with a few statistics. At the first census of 1801, the total population was just under 600,000, with about 43% in north Wales and 57% in south Wales. The Welsh population grew to just over two million by 1901 and with it the balance not only between north and south but also between rural and urban underwent considerable modification. At the end of the eighteenth century, for example, about four-fifths of the Welsh population lived in rural areas, while four-fifths lived in urban-industrial areas by the beginning of the twentieth century. Between 1851 and 1901 Glamorgan's population increased from just over 70,000 to nearly one-and-a-quarter million, a five-fold expansion and representing over half the population of all of Wales. In contrast, rural counties such as Cardiganshire and Montgomeryshire declined, especially after 1851 with movement of labour to the coalfields. Within some communities, the scale of growth was enormous: in the first part of the nineteenth century, this was especially obvious in the iron-manufacturing towns such as Merthyr Tydfil, while in the second part in the coal mining valley settlements, such as Rhondda, which grew from 1,636 in 1831 to 128,000 in 1891. The predominant cause for this revolutionary change was industrialisation.

The Impact of Industrialisation

The significance of industrialisation to Wales cannot be over-stated, transforming what was, in essence, a fairly poor country into a much richer one. This, in consequence, changed the social structure and generated finance, some of which helped to feed a revitalised Welsh culture. With regard to the development of major industry in Wales, only that which had any urban impact will be considered here. The coalfield areas will be examined firstly, including iron-manufacturing, non-ferrous metal production, and also coal-mining itself. This will be followed by a consideration of two industries located outside the coal fields, slate quarrying and woollen manufacturing.

By the mid-eighteenth century, industry was well-established although small in scale, but the potential for development was present on both the south Wales and north Wales coalfields. Crucial to this industrial growth around the coalfields were cheap, local supplies of iron ore and limestone, coal in variety and abundant water. Technological change was provided by power sources from Watt's steam engine (used, for example, to pump water out of mines, to crush ore and to power blast furnaces) and by the puddling process for making wrought iron. In the late 1790s, canals solved the transport problem of taking the manufactured product to the coast. In North

Wales, ironworks were centred on Brymbo, Holywell and Bersham. From the end of the eighteenth century, the most obvious evidence of industrialisation was the ironworks across the heads of the south Wales valleys. Most prominent were Hirwaun, Dowlais, Plymouth, Cyfarthfa, Sirhowy, Nantyglo and Blaenavon. Almost all ironworks were created on the South Wales or Flintshire coalfields and the industry involved much capital, extensive works, expensive equipment and a large labour force. The iron industry will be considered again later when dealing with Merthyr Tydfil.

The copper smelting industry was also centred on the coalfields. In north Wales, the copper industry was located at Holywell and at Bagillt, while the chief centres in the south were around Swansea and at Neath, with its works built up by Sir Humphrey Mackworth. From the mid-eighteenth to the mid-nineteenth century, copper works dominated the lower Swansea valley. Ore came from Cornwall until the 1770s, when Parys Mountain on Anglesey became the main supplier for several decades. However, by 1844 the north Wales mines had closed and supplies were by then coming entirely from abroad. In the nineteenth century, Welsh copper smelting was of world importance with some 90% of copper smelted in Britain coming from south Wales, mainly from an area between Kidwelly and Neath, where it remained a significant industry up to the Great War. Sea access was very necessary for the import of copper ore; Swansea had long been the largest port for this area and by the mid-nineteenth century was a major industrial and commercial centre in own right. The Swansea area was additionally a centre for zinc smelting, particularly at Landore and Llansamlet. Brass foundries were also found near copper works and so were located near to Swansea in the south and Holywell in the north, as again were zinc works. Tin was plated in the Swansea area and around Llanelli. Expansion in the tinplate industry was particularly marked during the period after 1870, when output quadrupled to meet the needs of the developing canned food industry. By 1889, there were ninety-six tin works, with Swansea being again the chief harbour for export.

Up to now, development in the iron industry has been considered, together with that of some non-ferrous metals. All of these depended upon coal power and were located on the coalfields because of this, and it is the coal industry itself which will be examined next. The Welsh coal industry, which went back to mediaeval times, was, by the late eighteenth century, considerably stimulated by the growing needs of the iron or copper industries. The North Wales coalfield in Flintshire and Denbighshire also met the needs of local brick-works, but its development throughout the nineteenth century was on a more limited scale compared with that of South Wales. In South Wales, the softest, or bituminous coals were found in the south of the coalfield. The harder steam coals were found in the middle part of the field and this was the type used initially as fuel by the smelteries and by railway engines. The hardest coal, anthracite, was found in the north-west and this came to be used increasingly after the middle of the nineteenth century. Initially, extraction techniques were limited, so working was confined to areas where coal seams were near the surface, where coal could be mined from simple levels driven into the hillside, or from shallow pits such as the simple bell-pit, one of the early methods used, which was particularly favoured in Pembrokeshire. Once the steam engine had been adapted for pumping water and for hauling coal, it became possible to sink deeper mines. After the introduction of the safety lamp in the eighteenth century, mines were also somewhat less dangerous to work in, although many dreadful accidents still happened. Children often worked underground until the passing of the Mines Act in 1842 and long after that date women continued to be employed illegally.

Until the mid-nineteenth century, many of the coal mines in South Wales were being worked by the ironmasters in order to supply their own works, but after 1830 higher grade fuel from Abercannaid near Merthyr found increasing favour in London. It was supplied by one Lucy Thomas from her pit and sent via Cardiff, thus starting Cardiff's considerable coal export trade. After the removal of a heavy export tax in 1845 on coal, overseas demand for Welsh coal, particularly steam coal, became heavy. Large-scale coal exploitation was further stimulated by the construction of a rail network throughout the coalfield and so by the 1860s the Rhondda steam coals were readily available for export all over the world. This was, of course, the 'steam age', with locomotives, engines for heavy industry and even ships driven by steam power, so the demand for coal was apparently insatiable. Further docks were constructed at Newport, Cardiff, Barry, Port Talbot, Briton Ferry, Swansea and Llanelli, while exports rose, reaching their maximum in 1903 when south Wales produced one-third of all the world's coal exports. The Rhondda area became particularly associated in most peoples minds with coal mining. Samuel Thomas began his exploitation in the 1830s of the lower Rhondda and before the Marquis of Bute has a deep pit sunk in a previously inaccessible area of the Rhondda in the 1880s, this really initiated its phenomenal expansion in the second half of the century. Coal mining created virtually a single-industry region. All land uses were confined to the narrow, deeply entrenched river valleys, such that roads, railways, pitheads and mining spoil heaps were all confined to the valley floors, intermixed with housing, usually the characteristic terraces winding along the valley sides. The population of the Rhondda increased more than four-fold between 1871 and 1891.

Having examined economic activity concentrated on the coalfields, either dependent on coal as a fuel or the actual mining of the coal, there are two other industries which will now be mentioned, which were not connected with coal, but which also produced distinctive urban settlement. The first of these is the slate industry of North Wales which had been run by individuals or small groups in that area up to the 1780s and had important domestic markets in England and Ireland. However, the rapid expansion of the industry at the end of the eighteenth century was initiated by an enterprising member of the landed gentry, Richard Pennant, who owned the Penrhyn Estate in Caernarfonshire, which included Bethesda and its slate resources. In the 1870s he bought out the leases of many small undertakings and worked the quarries on a much more extensive scale. His example was followed at the Dinorwic Quarry in Llanberis and later at Nantlle, all in Caernarfonshire, and around Blaenau Ffestiniog and Corris in Merioneth. Within ten years, Caernarfonshire alone was producing 60% of Britain's slate. Other areas of production existed, as in Pembrokeshire, but development was less intense. New industrial communities developed, such as those at Llanberis, Bethesda and Ffestiniog and by 1881 there were some 14,000 quarry workers serving huge home and export markets.

Quarrymen were usually highly skilled, especially in splitting and dressing the slate and the work was often dangerous, both in hewing the rock and in blasting. Slate was a necessary commodity in the construction of many buildings, including workers' houses, in the nineteenth century. In 1882, Welsh slate composed 93% of the British output and, during the second half of the nineteenth century, Penrhyn and Dinorwic were the world's largest slate quarries. The quarries were linked by tramways or railways to the coast; Bethesda to Port Penrhyn at Bangor; Llanberis to Port Dinorwic, Nantlle with Caernarfon and Blaenau Ffestiniog with Portmadoc, thus also encouraging the growth and development of these port settlements. There was a boom in the slate industry from the middle of the nineteenth century until 1879, with the most prosperous years probably being the early 1870s, then followed by a depression. Industrial problems occurred at the major Penrhyn complex at the turn of the century, and the industry across Wales had declined drastically by the Great War.

The second industry away from the coalfields worthy of mention, and one of the oldest in Wales, is that of woollen manufacture, although much of the woollen industry was rural rather than urban. Until the end of the eighteenth century, the industry remained largely domestic, but with the introduction of new machinery, processes were mechanised and factories were established. For centuries, Welsh flannel and coarse cloth had been produced on a small scale for local use. The industry was particularly concentrated in the Severn Valley in Montgomeryshire, around Llanidloes, Newtown and Welshpool, and with Merioneth weavers around Dolgellau and Machynlleth.

Domestic output declined between 1840 and 1880 and, for a time, production was concentrated in Newtown and Llanidloes factories, using steam-driven machinery. However, this industry also went into decline because it could not compete with the greater mechanisation and scale of its competitors in Lancashire and Yorkshire, although woollen manufacture did survive well into this century in some more rural locations, such as the Teifi Valley.

The main industries in Wales which influenced urban development have been reviewed, namely coal mining, the iron and copper related industries, slate quarrying and woollen manufacture. By 1901, the pattern of urbanisation in Wales had been dramatically altered by the nineteenth-century extension of industrialisation. Of the ten largest towns in 1901, there were only two which had been in the 1801 list: Swansea and Merthyr Tydfil while Cardiff had become the largest city in Wales by 1881. The traditional regional centres of Carmarthen, the fourth largest town in 1801, and Caernarfon both declined after 1861. The rapid rise of the Rhondda Urban district is noteworthy, not a single town, but deemed an urban area by the census, rising considerably from 1871 onward. Most of the largest towns in 1801 had been small market centres and seaports but, by the beginning of the twentieth century, an array of industrial mining centres, seaports, resorts, transport centres as well as traditional market towns were part of the Welsh urban system. In spite of the mediaeval origin of many Welsh towns, urban Wales is largely the creation of development in the nineteenth century.

Merthyr Tydfil in the mid-nineteenth century

Having examined the main urban and industrial developments within Wales, Merthyr Tydfil, in the north-east of Glamorgan, has been selected to illustrate how a variety of sources may be brought together to investigate towns and their inhabitants in the nineteenth century. Merthyr is a town which should be of considerable interest to family historians, particularly those with, perhaps, mid and south Wales ancestors who may have worked in the town's iron industry. As mentioned earlier, for much of the nineteenth century, Merthyr was the largest Welsh town. In 1851, its population was over 46,000, twice the size of the second largest town, Swansea, and even greater than the combined population of both Swansea and Cardiff. It has been said that Merthyr Tydfil, in terms of numbers, was the first 'town' in Welsh history and for three generations the strongest concentration of Welsh people on earth.[13] Before the development of industry in the mid-eighteenth century, Merthyr was only a village, lying in the fairly wooded Taff valley, surrounded by scattered farms. By looking at contemporary prints (see Fig. 5-1), it is still possible to visualise the natural beauty which existed prior to rapid industrial growth which led to the changed landscape seen today.

A combination of an accessible supply of raw materials in the form of coal and limestone together with new production techniques, and particularly steam power, led to the growth of Merthyr's iron industry. It became the parent centre for the iron industry of South Wales, with the establishment over a twenty-five year period from the mid-eighteenth century of its four major satellite iron works at Dowlais, Cyfarthfa, Penydarren and Plymouth, and these were associated with some of the best-known names in the development of the iron industry. The Dowlais works were the first to be established in 1759 and became associated with the Guest family. The second ironworks were developed in 1763 by Anthony Bacon and later his nephew by marriage, Anthony Hill. These were the Plymouth works, built on land leased from the town of Plymouth. Bacon also initiated the Cyfarthfa works in 1785 but by 1794 these were in the outright control of the Crawshay family. The fourth ironworks was that at Penydarren, owned by the Humphrey family from Worcestershire. In the first decade of the nineteenth century, the Cyfarthfa works were described as:

> ... now by far the largest in this Kingdom; possibly indeed the largest in Europe and as far as we know, the largest in the world.[14]

Expansion of the ironworks at Merthyr and in other South Wales iron towns continued during the first half of the nineteenth century, particularly after the 1820s, with the demand for iron rails from the new railway companies, both in Britain and abroad. The Dowlais works supplied the rails for the Stockton and Darlington railway, the first passenger line in the world in 1821. The Penydarren works supplied the cables for Telford's Menai suspension bridge, completed in 1826. By 1845, the Dowlais works were certainly the largest in the world, with eighteen blast furnaces and employing over 7,000 people.

That is the industrial background to Merthyr, but what happened to the town itself during this period of unparalleled growth ? The remarkably rapid growth of this 'frontier' town of the Industrial Revolution had more than mere economic implications. Social factors were closely linked with the

Fig. 5-1: A view of Merthyr Tydfil in 1811

industrial development because of the enormous influx of workers into what was, in effect, a village. Some of these features were already apparent to a visitor to the area very early in the nineteenth century; especially with regard to rapid physical growth and its consequences:

> When the first furnaces and forges were erected there could not exist the slightest glimmering that this little obscure Welsh village would, in less than 40 years, grow up to such a magnitude, as to be far more populous than any other town in Wales. The first houses that were built were only very small and simple cottages for furnace-men, forge-men, miners, and such tradesmen as were necessary to construct the required buildings, with the common labourers who were employed to assist them. These cottages were most of them built in scattered confusion, without any order or plan. As the works increased, more cottages were wanted, and erected in the spaces between those that had previously built, till they became so connected with each other, as to from a certain description of irregular streets. These streets are now many in number, close and confined, having no proper outlets behind the houses. They are consequently very filthy for the most part, and doubtlessly very unhealthy. Such is the architectural character of Merthyr Tydfil, a place that never had a premeditated plan on which to be built, but grew up by accident.[15]

It is apparent from this and similar comments that the growth of Merthyr was unplanned and haphazard through much of its development and had implications in the field of public health, which came to a head during the mid-nineteenth century, and mention will again be made of this. So, the early nineteenth century town was dominated by its expanding ironworks and overwhelmed by the associated rapid population growth and the related problems of housing, sanitation and, from time to time, public order.

By the late 1840s, Merthyr Tydfil was characterised by two very different features. The first of these was that it was a town made up of several settlements which had only coalesced into one continuous urban area during the first half of the century. The second feature was the great limitation in the social class structure, a characterisation of a settlement which was completely the creation of industry. Rammell's Report to the General Board of Health made in 1850, observed that:

> The population consists entirely of: 1. Ironmasters (4 in number), their agents and workmen; and 2. Such professional men and tradesmen as are necessary for supplying the wants of the former. There are no men of middle station none of the ordinary class of 'residents' who are to be found … in every town … wherever a man made a fortune or even a sufficiency for the supply of his future days, he took leave of the town of Merthyr and settled in some other more agreeable or more healthy place.[16]

The 1851 enumerators schedules show that such higher status, or middle class, occupations were practised only by about 6% of household heads or 1½% of the total population in the 1851 census.[17] These 'men of middle station' although relatively small in number were of considerable significance in the growth of the organisation of public affairs in the town. The town in 1851 had no town hall, no local Acts for paving, lighting, cleaning streets or for any sanitary purposes and no workhouse. In effect, it was administered by the Parish Vestry, which had very limited powers, the Board of Guardians of the Merthyr Tydfil Union, formed in 1836 of eight adjoining parishes, and with the addition of a Turnpike Trust, responsible for occasionally cleaning the High Street. All were unsuited to the needs of a large urban community, particular in the supervision of public health. It was the iron-masters who were consistently against reform in local administration, since they saw that the paternal form of government, which gave them supreme power in parochial affairs, would not be maintained under a municipality. Hence, because of their influence, incorporation was aborted on a number of occasions and borough status was not granted until 1905. A government inspector of 1853 wrote:

> Merthyr presents one of the most strongly marked cases of the evil so frequently observed of allowing a village to grow into a town, without providing the means of civic organisation.[18]

The rate books in their own way, reveal the social bias within the town, since only one-seventh of the properties were actually rated.[19] This is a particularly good example of the kind of information which may be found in these documents. Owner and occupier of the property, its address and a description of its use.

Concern mounted during the second quarter of the nineteenth century about the high death rate, disease, overcrowding, lack of sanitation and clean water. In the first of the sanitary reports, 1845, it was stated that:

> This town is in a sad state of neglect ... The rarity of privies is one of the most marked characteristics of the town. The cinder heaps, as the refuse slags from the iron works are termed, and the river sides are frequented by persons of all ages and sexes, who manage the best way they can . There is no public supply of water ... the poorer classes are ill supplied. Pumps and wells are the chief sources but it may be doubted if it can be free from impurities derived from the house refuse, sinking into the ground in all directions.[20]

Another report, two years later found no improvements:

> In a sanitary point of view, the state of Merthyr is disgraceful to those who are responsible for it.[21]

Pressures for a solution to those problems culminated with the devastating cholera epidemic in the town during the summer of 1849, which claimed some 1,400 victims, producing the second highest death rate in Britain. A local Board of Health was elected in 1850, but no Medical Officer of Health was appointed until 1853, while in December of that year, a government Inspector, Dr. Holland, was still able to show that:

> The first circumstance that must strike every visitor at Merthyr is the extreme and universal dirtiness of the town. I have visited many dirty places [in] the worst towns ... but never did I see anything which could compare with Merthyr ... So universal is the presence of this filthiest of filth that it requires constant watchfulness to avoid treading in it.[22]

Just before the next major cholera outbreak in 1854, with 424 deaths, the first sanitary report was published, in which it was reported that Merthyr had the highest mortality level in the whole of Wales and ranked third only to Manchester and Liverpool. Infant mortality was particularly high and at mid century some 40% of children born in Merthyr would have died before reaching the age of five years, a similar level of mortality to that of Liverpool, the worst in Britain. Despite legislation, improvements in sanitary conditions were slow. Piped water did not reach Merthyr until 1860; a sewerage scheme was begun in 1864, but untreated effluent from this was discharged into the River Taff below Merthyr until 1872. Meanwhile, a further cholera epidemic in 1866 claimed 115 victims.

Another significant process which had affected the town was that of migration, both in terms of sheer numbers and in terms of intermixing. The growth of population during the first half of the nineteenth century has been called 'volcanic'.[23] For decades, South Wales ranked second only to the USA as an area of new settlement – as family historians with ancestral links in the area may have found out! The growing town and its iron industry were attractive, not only in terms of higher wages, but also in terms of what was considered to be a fuller life. The town grew to a certain extent in a series of regional quarters, as immigrants settled among friends in clusters of cottages. The population was, in the main distinctively Welsh in origin. It is not possible accurately to test the origins of the population until the 1851 census, since adequate birthplace information is not available before then. At the 1851 census, the published report shows that less than 9% of the parish was born outside Wales; in the town this rose to a little over 12%. The report shows that most of the immigration was relatively local from rural south and west Wales. About half of the non-Welsh migrants were English, especially from nearby Gloucestershire and Somerset; the remainder were Irish, who did not settle in large numbers until the 1840s, following the potato famine of 1845-6. Differences in origin meant to a certain extent differences in occupation. The iron-masters were English, as were a handful of their managers and a number of persons engaged in commercial activities in the town; the bulk of the iron workers and miners were Welsh and many of the labourers were Irish, as the census schedules show.

The main division, mentioned earlier, was the growth of the town out of the original village centre and its four satellite iron works (see Fig. 5-2).

Some of the characteristics of the different social areas of Merthyr at mid-century are now described. In between the commercial centre and the iron works were areas of mixed development and settlement. Surrounding all the main area of population was a rural-industrial fringe. The extraction of minerals and stone made the most impact on this landscape of this peripheral area, supplying the raw material for the furnaces. Coal miners are always termed 'colliers' in the census and earned about fifteen shillings per week while ironstone miners were returned as 'miners' and earned twelve shillings and sixpence a week.[24] The many small mining settlements were a distinctive part of this area. It was said that: '... the miners and colliers in and around Merthyr are gregarious in their dwellings',[25] a small row of cottages being more common than scattered single houses. Two characteristics of the inhabitants were large family size (high fertility in mining populations has been found in other areas) and birthplace:

> The miners and colliers are almost exclusively Welsh. As a class the miners are provident, temperate and regular in their work.[26]

Moving from the outskirts to the centre, the commercial centre of Merthyr extended from the old village centre around St Tydfil's church, northwards along the High Street. A newspaper report in 1800 stated:

> The shops are literally stuffed with goods. They are inconveniently small and low, but the most is made of the space – the windows and even the doorways displaying a profusion of wares – ironmongers, grocers, druggists, drapers and booksellers all thrive here. The market house may be termed 'a bazaar of shops'.[27]

Both census and trade directory information show that the main shopping area was in the central area of Merthyr, and with a smaller shopping centre at Dowlais, which also had a market hall. This central area also attracted by far the largest numbers of English migrants, especially those from the south-west counties; in the enumeration district around the market hall about one-fifth of the persons were English. The professionals, including clergy, doctors, lawyers, accountants and surveyors, were also found mainly in the central area and in small pockets of better quality housing in other areas.

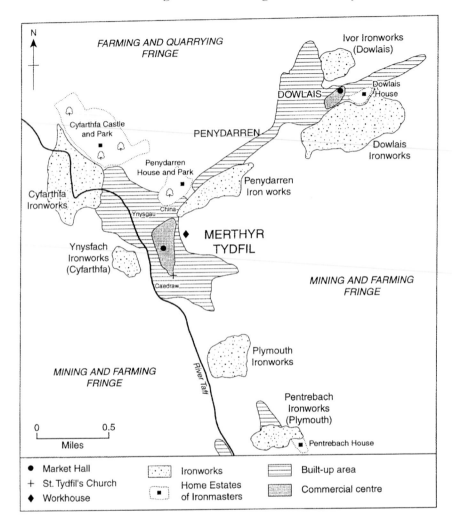

Fig. 5-2: Merthyr Tydfil in the Nineteenth Century

Continuing outwards from the centre, we come to what today would be termed the 'inner city areas', lying between the shopping area and the iron works 'villages', with nineteenth-century photographs giving the impression of small cottages and inns and beer houses (see Fig. 5-3). These areas provided the least attractive environment and received considerable attention in press and public health reports. The worst areas lay immediately north and south of the main retailing area, at Ynysgau-China and Caedraw respectively, while Dowlais had its own, though smaller, undesirable areas. These same localities registered large numbers of deaths in the cholera epidemics. The most notorious area was known under a variety of aliases, usually China or the Cellars. It was selected for special comment in the 1845 Parliamentary Report:

> The most wretched part of the town would appear to be that known as the Cellars ... and supposed to contain about 1500 persons. Though so named, they are not cellars, but a collection of small houses of two stories, situated in a depression between a line of road and a cinder heap ... abutting the river Taffe. The space between these houses is very limited; and an open, stinking, and nearly stagnant gutter, into which the house refuse is, as usual, flung, moves slowly before the doors. It is a labyrinth of miserable tenements and filth, filled with people, many of whom bear the worst characters.[28]

Fig. 5-3: Ynysgau, showing arch leading to Castle Street, *c.*1880

Reports vie in attempts to produce adequately sensational descriptions of the area. In 1847, the Commission on the State of Education in Wales succinctly described it as: '... a mere sink of thieves and prostitutes, such as unhappily constitutes an appendage to every large town.'[29]

The notoriety of the Cellars continued well in to the second part of the nineteenth century, with impressions from observers recording squalid housing and an absence of basic amenities, where the inhabitants lived on the fringes of society, in dire poverty, or as criminals, prostitutes, or vagrants. The census shows that these areas had a large unskilled labour force, often general labourers and also a large numbers of persons receiving parish relief. Fourteen deserted wives are given as having husbands gone to America. Lists produced by the Merthyr Poor Law Union give a better idea than the census of the extent of poor relief and at more frequent intervals, although no workhouse existed until 1853.[30] A further characteristic was the pressure of the Irish-born persons. The Irish were in general disliked by the Welsh because they were believed to cause a fall in wage rates and also lived in undesirable conditions, which encouraged diseases.[31] The Irish were fairly strongly segregated in the town, for example, China had a population which was nearly 30% Irish. In addition, the Irish tended to take in lots of lodgers and to subdivide their houses.

The final division includes the iron industry settlements. These varied considerably in character. Most companies provided some housing stock, at first as small terraces of traditional-type country cottages, but later as almost model housing. Dowlais was the largest of the iron-works settlements and the most independent. The town was set out regardless of the steep slope of the land; Dowlais House, the home of the Guests, the owners of the iron-works, was adjacent to both town and works, despite the outward moves of other iron-masters. An 1852 report stated that:

> His residence at Dowlais is a large, smoked, sooty-looking dwelling. Old Lady Lindsay, his mother-in-law, calls the house at Dowlais 'the cinder hole', but from it her son-in-law can command more influence than ever the Lindsay's could command in their castle![32]

Regarding the housing, one visitor found:

> ... they are mainly artisan habitations and as the doors were generally open a glance within showed the thrifty or the prodigal tastes of the owners. In some you saw neat substantial furniture. Pictures on the wall and a range of shining culinary utensils on the mantle-shelves, the cupboard full of crockery and glass in the corner. The dwellers of these cheerful habitations have not been in receipt of the highest wage, nor the smallest.[33]

The majority of the labour-force in the ironworks was Welsh in origin.[34] The iron-masters tended to employ English persons in positions of importance in the works – agents, clerks, the like, yet an examination of the salary list from the Dowlais works,[35] as well as being of interest for the pay, shows that fifteen out of the top thirty-five posts in the works did go to persons with Welsh surnames. Another very notable feature was the mobility of the Welsh rural immigrants. Once they had reached industrial South Wales, there was considerable movement from one iron-works to another in search of work because of fluctuations in employment, in the search for higher wages and because of industrial disputes. This 'floating' labour-force cannot be seen from the census schedules, but was established at 10,000 to 11,000 persons in 1849 in Merthyr.[36] Some indication of the 'floating' workers can be gauged by the large number of lodgers found in most of the iron manufacturing areas, unattached persons often joining relatives or friends from their home area. This added to the impression that lots of people from a certain area were living together.[37]

The iron industry employed many men in a whole spectrum of occupations, from managers, through skilled trades down to labourers. About 40% to 50% of the whole work-force was reckoned to be skilled. Rollers, producing iron rails, earned £2 to £4 a week; the majority of skilled workers, including puddlers and refiners, earned 20 to 25 shillings; labourers would have earned 10 shillings a week and women workers 6 to 7 shillings, although wage rates did fluctuate.[38]

The main image of the iron manufacturing areas is one of a respectable, rather than a rough, working-class population. It is rather ironic that Merthyr became a town in the complete sense at the very end of its main period of prosperity. Only one of the four iron-works, Dowlais, made a successful transfer to steel production. In the 1860s, the town acquired a town hall, increased parliamentary representation and sewerage and water systems. However, between 1851 and 1881, the population grew very little and at the 1881 census Cardiff had become the largest town in Wales.

During this discussion about Merthyr Tydfil various standard sources have been used. These include the census enumerators' schedules, newspapers, trade directories and maps and pictures. Other material has also been used, from the printed census, parliamentary papers, public health reports, rate books, poor law records and iron company papers. All of these add to our understanding of how people lived in the past and hence a deeper appreciation of family history in it fullest sense.

SELECT BIBLIOGRAPHY

General

These, and similar works, contain chapters of interest on social and
    industrial growth:
Evans, G., *A History of Modern Wales, 1815-1906* (Cardiff, 1989).
Moore, D. (ed.), *Wales in the Eighteenth Century* (Swansea, 1970).

Morgan, P. & Thomas, D., *Wales: The Shaping of a Nation* (Newton Abbot, 1984).

Williams, D., *A History of Modern Wales* (2nd ed., London, 1977).

Urban Growth

Carter, H., *The Towns of Wales* (2nd ed., Cardiff, 1966).

Griffiths, A., (ed.), *Boroughs of Medieval Wales* (Cardiff, 1978).

Soulsby, I., *The Towns of Medieval Wales* (Chichester, 1983).

Industrialisation

Dodd, A. H., *The Industrial Revolution in North Wales* (3rd ed., Cardiff, 1971; also reprinted Wrexham, 1990).

Hopkins, K. S., (ed.), *Rhondda: Past and Future* (Rhondda, 1975).

Jenkins, G., *The Welsh Woollen Industry* (Cardiff, 1969).

John, H., *The Industrial Development of South Wales, 1850-1950* (Cardiff, 1950).

Lewis, E.D., *The Rhondda Valley* (2nd ed., Cardiff, 1984).

Lindsay, J., *A History of the North Wales Slate Industry* (Newton Abbot, 1974).

Richards, A.J. *Slate Quarrying in Wales* (Llanrwst, 1995).

Williams, G. (General Editor), *Glamorgan County History* (Cardiff):
  Vol. V 'Industrial Glamorgan from 1700 to 1970' P. Morgan (ed.) (1980).
  Vol. VI 'Glamorgan Society, 1780-1980' A.H. John & G. Williams (eds.) (1988).

Merthyr Tydfil

Carter, H. & Wheatley, S., *Merthyr Tydfil in 1851: A Study of the Spatial Structure of a Welsh Industrial Town.* Board of Celtic Studies Social Sciences Monograph No. 7 (Cardiff, 1982).

Jones, I.G., 'Merthyr Tydfil: The Politics of Survival' in *Llafur* Vol. 2 No. 1 (1976); also reproduced in I.G. Jones, *Explorations and Explanations: essays in the social history of Victorian Wales* (Llandysul, 1987).

Merthyr Tydfil Historical Society, *Merthyr Historian* 8 Vols. (Merthyr Tydfil, 1976-1994).

Wilkins, C., *The History of Merthyr Tydfil* (2nd ed., Merthyr Tydfil, 1908).

NOTES TO CHAPTER 5

[1] The best account of urban development in Wales is Harold Carter's *The Towns of Wales* (2nd ed., Cardiff. 1966).

[2] W. Camden, *Britannia* ... Translated by P. Holland (London, 1610).

[3] G. Owen, *The Description of Pembrokshire.* Edited by H. Owen; Cymmrodorion Record Series No. 1 (London, 1892-1936).

[4] J. Speed, *The Theatre of the Empire of Great Britain Book 2* (London, 1610).

[5] T. Pennant, *Tours in Wales* (2nd ed., London, 1810).

[6] L. Owen, 'The population of Wales in the sixteenth and seventeenth centuries' *Trans. Cymmrodorion Soc.* (1959).

[7] Quoted in A.H. Dodd, *A History of Wrexham* (Wrexham, 1957).

[8] B.H. Malkin, *The Scenery, Antiquities and Biography of South Wales* (London, 1807).

[9] B.H. Malkin, op. cit.

[10] H. Skrine, *Two Successive Tours throughout the whole of Wales* (London, 1798).

[11] T. Pennant, op. cit.

[12] I.G. Jones, 'People and Protest: Wales 1815-1880' in T. Herbert & G.E. Jones (eds), *People and Protest: Wales 1815-1880* (Cardiff, 1988).

[13] G.A. Williams, 'The Merthyr of Dic Penderyn' in G. Williams (ed.) *Merthyr Politics: The Making of a Working Class Tradition* (Cardiff, 1966).

[14] B.H. Malkin, op. cit.

[15] B.H. Malkin, op. cit.

[16] T.W. Rammell, Report to the General Board of Health on a Preliminary Inquiry into ... the Sanitary Condition of the Inhabitants of the Town Of Merthyr Tydfil ... (London, 1850).

[17] 1851 Census Enumerators' Books for Merthyr Tydfil: PRO HO 107/2458-9.

[18] Dr P.H. Holland to General Board of Health PRO MH13/X/K513 (15 December, 1853).

[19] Merthyr Tydfil Rate Book for 1853 Merthyr Tydfil Borough Library.

[20] Second Report of the Commission of Inquiry into the State of Large Towns and Populous Districts: Appendix to Part I, Parliamentary Papers PP 602 (1845).

[21] Reports of the Commissioners of Inquiry into the State of Education in Wales: Appendix to Part I Parliamentary Papers PP 1847 XXVII (870).

[22] Dr P.H. Holland to General Board of Health, op. cit.

[23] G.A. Williams (1966), op. cit.

[24] T.W. Rammell, op. cit., and *The Morning Chronicle* (21 March 1850).

[25] *The Morning Chronicle* (27 March 1850).

[26] Ibid.

[27] The Morning Chronicle (18 April 1850).

[28] PP 1847 XXVII (870), op. cit.

[29] Op. cit.

[30] *Merthyr Tydfil Union List of Paupers,* Glamorgan Record Office U/M (1851).

[31] *The Morning Chronicle* (15 April 1850).

[32] *Bristol Times* (21 February 1852).

[33] E.F. Roberts, A visit to the iron works and environs of Merthyr Tydfil in 1852 (London, 1853).

[34] See A.H. John *The Industrial Development of the South Wales Coalfield* (Cardiff, 1950), but also confirmed by the Census Enumerators' Books.

[35] *Dowlais Iron Company Letters,* Glamorgan Record Office D/DG (1855-6 f.487).

[36] *The Westminster Review* (1849).

[37] Confirmed in the Census Enumerators' Books and see also PP 1847 XXVII (870) op. cit..

[38] Wage rates are quoted in several sources: T.W. Rammell, op. cit., *The Morning Chronicle* (21 March, 1850) and 'Dowlais and Penydarren Wage Rates' *Dowlais Iron Company Records,* Glamorgan Record Office D/DG Section C Box 5. Several lists of workmen appear in the Dowlais records of interest to family historians, for example, men in supervisory positions and persons consulting the company doctor.

6. PEOPLE IN MINING AND METALS: THE LLANELLI AREA, 1841–71

Malcolm Symons

The Llanelli area of Carmarthenshire was one of Britain's early coalfields, its bituminous coal having been exploited for a seaborne export trade since the sixteenth century.* In a similar manner to other parts of the South Wales Coalfield, metalliferous industry in the form of lead, iron and copper smelting had been introduced in the late eighteenth/early nineteenth centuries but, with the exception of copper, they had soon failed, leaving coal mining still unchallenged as the main employer of local labour in 1841. The introduction of tinplate manufacturing in 1846 produced rapid change and, by 1871, metalliferous industry had eclipsed coal mining as the area's staple trade. Tinplate, together with its allied iron and steel works, would dominate local employment into the second half of the following century.

This chapter, based on analysis of the manuscript census returns, examines population growth, population origins as indicated by place of birth, and male and female employment over the thirty years of important and lasting change between 1841 and 1871. Attention is drawn to the significant underestimation of workforces in coal mining and metalliferous industry resulting from use of the raw data of the 1841 manuscript census returns.

The Llanelli area

The Llanelli area of this study, covering some 21 square miles (approximately one-fortieth of the South Wales Coalfield), is shown in Fig. 6-1. Its boundaries, originally defined for research into coal mining history,[1] extend from Ordnance Survey National Grid line SN04 in the north to the shoreline of the Burry Estuary in the south. The major Moreb and Plas Isaf faults, which formed natural barriers to mining between the Llanelli

---

* This chapter is based on a talk given to the Second Stages Course, 'Occupations and the Records Relating to them', in September 1995.

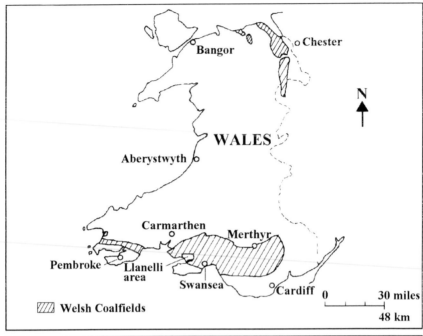

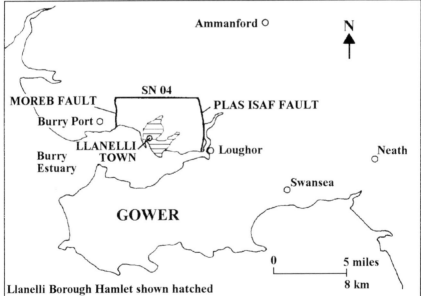

Fig. 6-1: The Welsh Coalfields and the Llanelli Area

coalfield and the neighbouring Burry Port and Loughor coalfields, are taken as the western and eastern boundaries respectively. During the period considered, most of the area consisted of agricultural land, industrial and urban growth being concentrated mainly in the three square miles of Llanelli Borough Hamlet.

A study area such as this is not ideal for the purposes of conventional demographic analysis as it intersects parish, hamlet and enumeration district boundaries – it includes part of four separate parishes with eight of the thirty-two enumeration districts intersected by the area boundaries. The Census Reports, those statistical publications compiled by the Census Office a year or two after the taking of the census providing details of areas defined by county, sub-district, parish and township boundaries, could not be utilised and resort had to be made to the manuscript census returns.[2] Research time was significantly increased but the specific and comprehensive data obtained more than justified the effort outlayed.

Population growth

The Llanelli area was the main focus of industrialisation for the county of Carmarthenshire, its population increasing from 11,101 (10.4% of Carmarthenshire's population) in 1841 to 22,107 (19.1%) in 1871.[3] More than 60% of this population was concentrated into Llanelli Borough Hamlet (about one-seventh of the area) which became increasingly industrialised and urbanised with each passing year.[4] The changes in population over the four census years are given in the Appendix (Table 1) to this chapter. An overall population increase of 99.1% occurred over the thirty-year period, decennial growth rates of 22.6, 26.2 and 28.7% between census years reflecting the growing workforce demand of a rapidly expanding centre of industry.

The male/female share of the population varied by less than 1% from equality in each census year suggesting an orderly social growth pattern unlike that experienced in parts of the neighbouring, rapidly industrialising county of Glamorganshire where males could exceed females by a significant margin.[5] Nevertheless, it was reported in 1854 that parts of Llanelli quite rivalled the notoriously overcrowded and unhealthy conditions of Merthyr Tydfil with beds occupied twice every twenty-four hours,[6] six confirming that the area did not escape the worst aspects of nineteenth-century industrialisation.

Population Origins

The area's population, little more than 3,000 in 1801,[7] increased to over 11,000 in 1841 and exceeded 22,000 by 1871, a growth far in excess of any form of natural increase. Where did all the people come from? For the purpose of this study it is assumed that the places of birth given in the 1841-71 manuscript census returns provide an answer to this question, although the synonymy of 'place of birth' and 'origins' must be treated with caution. To explain this, consider what is likely to have happened at Llanelli before 1841.

Up to *circa* 1790, the area's population would have possessed a long-established structure, consisting mainly of Welsh-speaking people domiciled locally for generations, with livelihoods based on the centuries-old local activities of coal mining, seafaring and agriculture.[8] The industrialisation of the late eighteenth/early nineteenth centuries, particularly the introduction of metal works, led to significant changes in this structure. An increased workforce was required and, whilst the unskilled labour could be recruited by internal migration from the surrounding Carmarthenshire countryside, the necessary core skills and crafts for the new processes had to be provided by more distant in-migration from already industrialised parts of England and Wales.[9] As the new skills become absorbed into general workplace practices, so the need for experienced, highly-paid workers from far afield diminished; and with little new industry introduced after the first decade of the century, a twenty- to thirty-year period of reduced long-distance in-migration ensued.[10] By 1841, when the first detailed census was taken, many of the original long-distance in-migrants of the early industrialisation period would have died, perhaps returned to their roots, their locally born children, by now adults, being indistinguishable from the progeny of long-established Carmarthenshire families, both being recorded as born in the county. As a consequence, only faint echoes of the extent of the early distant migrational flow survive in the 1841 returns, the true 'ethnic' origins of many being concealed by the listing of Carmarthenshire as their place of birth. The opening of the first tinplate works in 1846, followed by a further six similar establishments over the following twenty-five years, required a fresh influx of new skills and initiated a second phase of long-distance in-migration that would continue up to and beyond 1871.

Population origins are examined on the basis of whether or not a person was born in Carmarthenshire, the limited information on place of birth in the 1841 returns dictating this approach.[11] Because of indecipherable places of birth, omissions in the 'Where Born' columns, lack of information on those temporarily absent and missing pages, the numbers involved are slightly less than the population figures in Table 1.

The origins of the area's population, in terms of born, or not born, in Carmarthenshire for the four census years are given in the Appendix (Table 2). As more than 8 out of 10 of the population in each year was born in

Carmarthenshire, it would appear that the area's demand for labour was satisfied primarily by local people and by internal migration from the country's rural districts; the demand for core skills was evidently heavily outnumbered by that for semi-skilled and unskilled labour. The high percentage (87.3) born Carmarthenshire in 1841 could well be a result of the low rates of skilled in-migration required in the years of little new industry after 1810; the decrease to 82.7% by 1871 mainly reflecting the demand for new iron and tinplate manufacturing skills after 1846. Numerous new ventures – lead and silver smelting, iron shipbuilding, patent fuel manufacturing, general foundries, acid works plus all the services required for a rapidly expanding and increasingly affluent population – also contributed to this decrease, the opening of the South Wales Railway through Llanelli in 1852 linking the area to the national rail network and facilitating the ease with which long-distance in-migration could take place.

Llanelli Borough Hamlet, more heavily industrialised and urbanised than the rest of the area, would be expected to have a higher percentage of long-distance in-migrants. Appendix (Table 3) shows this to be the case, with 83.9% born Carmarthenshire in 1841, reducing to 79.5% by 1871. As the corresponding figures for the county of Carmarthenshire were 91.7% reducing to 86.3%[12] there is little doubt that Llanelli, with its complex of coal mines, factories, docks, transport networks and growing urbanisation, possessed a very different character to that of the rest of the county; the former a recognisable Victorian industrial township, the latter predominantly rural in aspect.

The origins of the population not born in Carmarthenshire are given in the Appendix (Table 4) in terms of born in other Welsh counties, England, Scotland, Ireland and Foreign parts; limitations of the 1841 returns preventing any distinction between other Welsh counties and England for that census year.[13] Between 1851 and 1871, approximately two out of three of the area's 'not born in Carmarthenshire' population had been born in other counties of Wales, 80% of them coming from the two adjacent counties of Glamorganshire and Pembrokeshire.[14] Approximately one in four had been born in England, a total of at least 914 being listed in 1871. A disproportionate percentage of those born in England appeared in the proprietorship, management, supervisory and professional ranks, which is not surprising as the bulk of capital investment into the area came from English sources both before and during the period considered.[15]

The preceding analysis, although simplistic and based on equating place of birth to origin, yields a convincing picture in conformance with the findings of other researches. With more than 80% of the population born in

Carmarthenshire and a further 9-10% having origins in the adjacent counties of Glamorganshire and Pembrokeshire, it would seem that the attraction of higher wages was tempered by reluctance on the part of both the industrially unskilled rural population and the skilled workers in other industrialised districts to migrate too far away from their home areas. Were it not for the industrialisation of the Llanelli area, Carmarthenshire would have lacked a centre of industry and its Welsh-speaking rural population would have had to leave the county to find work in industrialised Glamorganshire and Monmouthshire; in this respect Llanelli can be considered as the county's haven for the Welsh language during the mid-nineteenth century.

Employment trends

The doubling of the area's population between 1841 and 1871 was mainly due to the attraction of well-paid employment in a rapidly expanding industrial centre. Whilst most of the jobs were in predominantly male occupations, there was also a demand for female labour, particularly in the service sector. In order to assess the employment trends over the thirty years it is necessary to distinguish between male and female employment, consider the main occupations for each gender, and examine the extent and significance of occupational overlap between the genders. Interpretation of the raw data of the manuscript census returns has been used in estimating the male workforce, particularly in respect of child labour in 1841. Some interpretation has been resorted to in estimation of the female workforce in domestic labour and agriculture; but considerable reservations are held over the general accuracy of the female occupational returns.

The male and female workforces – the estimated male and female workforce numbers between 1841 and 1871 are given in the Appendix (Table 5).[16] The male workforce decreased from 65.1% to 61.9% of the male population over the period, the female workforce behaving in opposite manner and increasing from 12.7% to 19.6% of the female population. The decrease in male workforce percentage could be due to the Childrens' Employment and Education Acts of the 1840s, with boys both attending school for the first time and remaining at school to a more advanced age; the general increase in standard of living also playing its part by reducing the need for poorer families to put their sons to work at the earliest possible age. The increase in female workforce percentage probably reflects the demand for female labour in the expanding service industry sector of an increasingly affluent local society and, by the 1860s, the attraction of well-paid jobs in the new tinplate works: although more accurate recording of occupations by the enumerators in the later censuses should not be ignored as a contributory factor. The male workforce greatly exceeded the female workforce in each

year, the ratio of the workforces decreasing from 5.2 in 1841 to 3.0 in 1871, an imbalance numerically due to virtually all married women, and their teenage and older daughters, having no allocated occupations in the returns.
The main male occupations – there were four main fields of employment: coal mining, metalliferous industry, the port, and agriculture. The estimated numbers in each of these occupations[17] between 1841 and 1871 are given in the Appendix (Table 6). Coal mining and metalliferous industry were, by far, the largest employers, between them accounting for just over 36% of the male workforce in 1841, rising to almost 48% in 1871. Coal mining, the area's main occupation for centuries, peaked in terms of exports and almost certainly production between 1861 and 1871,[18] the plateauing of its workforce mirroring this trend. Metalliferous industry, consisting of only two copperworks and two foundries in 1841, grew massively over the following thirty years, an expanded copperworks, a lead and silver works, five foundries and ten iron or iron/tinplate works being in operation before 1871. As a consequence, metalliferous industry overtook coal mining as the main male occupation during the 1860s, the Llanelli area ceasing to be predominantly a coal mining community in employment terms in this decade. Llanelli's port, although an essential factor in the area's emergence as an important centre of industry, was not a large employer, accounting for less than 6% of the male workforce in all years. Agriculture, sufficiently important in 1841 to employ 12.6% of the male workforce, contracted to only 5.4% in 1871, the number of men and boys employed falling from a peak of 490 in 1851 to 361 in 1871. This fall can be attributed to acreage reduction, in some cases disappearance, of local farms absorbed by the industrial and urban spread and to the drift of farmers' sons from the land into better paid employment in the new works. Malthusian pressures of self-sufficiency had dissipated well before 1841 in any event, Llanelli's developed port having ensured supplies of grain and necessary foodstuffs for many years before the coming of the railway.
The main female occupations – consideration of the female workforce shows the main fields of employment as domestic labour, garment making, agriculture and, from 1861, metalliferous industry, almost entirely in the new tinplate works. The estimated numbers in each of these occupations[19] between 1841 and 1871 are given in the Appendix (Table 7). Domestic labour, accounting for at least 45% of the female workforce, was the largest single employment in all years, although the figures could be overestimated as a result of part-time working and the declared occupation of 'housekeeper' by many who would be regarded as non-employed housewives in later years.[20] Garment making increased from 11.8% of the

female workforce in 1841 to 18.6% in 1871 but the potential for casual, part-time or home working in this field of employment is self-evident. Nevertheless, a five-fold increase in the declared garment making workforce (from 82 to 411) over a period which saw only a two-fold increase in population is strongly indicative of an increasingly affluent society with rising living standards. The numbers in agriculture increased (from 138 to 167) but, as a percentage of the female workforce, decreased from 19.8 to 7.6% confirming the contraction of this previously important occupation.[21] Metalliferous industry, with no declared female employment in 1841, increased to 193 in 1871, of whom 190 were in the new tinworks.

There is no doubt that the extent of female employment listed in the manuscript census returns is not as accurate a reflection of the true picture as that obtained for male employment, omissions and lack of differentiation between part-time and full-time occupations introducing many uncertainties. **Overlap in the main male and female occupations** – assessment of the extent and significance of overlap in male and female employment brings into question the validity of combining two workforces with such dissimilar occupations. Overlap only really occurred in agriculture and, to a much lesser extent, in metalliferous industry after 1851; coal mining, domestic labour and garment making[22] being predominantly single gender occupations, the port totally a male employer. Agriculture, where there was real overlap, is examined in terms of the combined workforce to obtain an overall assessment of its contraction. Metalliferous industry and coal mining, where there was little overlap, are examined to determine the extent to which consideration of the combined workforce alters the statistics of the important watershed in the area's industrial character.

The estimated male plus female workforce numbers engaged in agriculture, metalliferous industry and coal mining between 1841 and 1871 are given in the Appendix (Table 8). Agriculture, whilst displaying only a marginal decrease in numbers (595 to 528), suffered a significant contraction in percentage terms, from 13.7 to 5.9% of the combined workforce; a result consistent with those obtained by separate consideration of the male and female workforces. Because of the genuine overlap in this particular occupation, the combined workforce proved to be a valid unit for the purposes of analysis. But use of the combined workforce yielded inconsistent results when applied to metalliferous industry and coal mining. The same general result of coal mining being displaced by metalliferous industry as the area's main employer during the 1860s was obtained, but the importance of the two occupations to the area's growth was devalued. They accounted for less than 31% of the combined workforce in 1841, rising to just over 38% in 1871, a significantly different result to that obtained from male workforce considerations alone (36% rising to almost 48%). There was little overlap in these occupations, female labour playing a very small role in industry during the period considered (as late as 1871 there were only 283 females in industrial occupations, just 3% of the combined workforce), and the validity of interpreting industrial developments and trends on the basis of the combined workforce must be questioned.

Workforce origins

The workforce would be expected to differ from the overall population in terms of origins as it would contain a higher percentage of long-distance in-migrants recruited for their skills. Appendix (Table 9), which gives the origins of the male and female workforce in terms of the percentage born in Carmarthenshire, confirms this to be the case.

The female workforce was consistent in origins over the entire period, lying in the very narrow range of 81.4%–82.8% born in Carmarthenshire. With most female occupations requiring little in the way of new skills there was no need to recruit from afar and, consequently, most of the workforce were locally born or were internal migrants from within the county. Nevertheless, in all years the female workforce contained a lower percentage of born in Carmarthenshire people than the overall population.

The male workforce displayed a different trend, decreasing steadily from 84.2% born Carmarthenshire in 1841 to 76.2% in 1871. This decrease was undoubtedly due to the long-distance in-migration needed to provide the necessary core skills in the new iron and tinplate works and also in other smaller new industries introduced to the area during the 1850s and 60s. A long-established industry like coal mining, on the other hand, not in need of an influx of new skills, did not exhibit any decrease, its male workforce remaining at more than 90% born in Carmarthenshire throughout the entire period (see Table 9). In all years the male workforce contained a significantly lower percentage born in Carmarthenshire than the overall population.

The born in Carmarthenshire workforce has been examined to determine the pattern of its regional origins within the county. For a first estimate, all members of the workforce born in parishes falling within a 10-mile radius of Llanelli's industrial centre (just south of the Town) were counted,[23] the intention being to repeat the analysis for increased radii (the most distant parts of Carmarthenshire lying some 35 miles from the Town). The results obtained, expressed as percentage of the male, female and combined workforces, are shown in the Appendix (Table 10) for 1851–71, only details of parish of birth not being given in the 1841 census. Irrespective of whether the male, female or combined workforce is considered, more than eight out of ten were born in the parishes falling within the 10-mile radius, a finding supporting the proposition that most internal migrants travelled the shortest possible distance to the nearest centre of industry to find employment.[24] As the parishes involved were entirely Welsh in culture and language, there is little doubt that the language of the workplace remained predominantly Welsh, even if that of the owners and managers was English. The overwhelming picture obtained from this first estimate obviated the need to repeat the analysis to include more outlying parishes.

Underestimation of the coal mining and metalliferous industry workforces in the 1841 manuscript census returns

There is general acceptance that the 'Profession, Trade, Employment or of Independent Means' column of the 1841 manuscript census returns contains serious deficiencies caused by omissions and incomplete descriptions of occupations but, paradoxically, this same inadequate column is invariably assumed capable of providing a reliable estimate of employment trends when used in conjunction with the 1851 and later returns, an assumption adopted in this present study. But how valid is this assumption? Evidence peculiar to the Llanelli area shows that use of the raw, uninterpreted data of the 1841 returns leads to significant underestimation of workforces in the main industries, bringing into question the accuracy of any calculated employment trend involving that census year.

This evidence contained in the Appendix to the Childrens' Employment Commission Report of 1842, provides detailed information of employment in coal mining and metalliferous industry at Llanelli between April and September 1841,[25] a period overlapping with the taking of the census in June of that year. For coal mining, a workforce of 1,222 (1,198 males, twenty-four females) was listed[26] but this included only the collieries of the large companies, the smaller concerns known to have been at work in the area in 1841 having no mention. A conservative estimate of ninety-five employees in these smaller mines[27] brings the coal mining workforce to at least 1,317. The 1841 manuscript census returns listed only 867 (863 males, four females) with identifiable coal mining occupations in the Llanelli area, an underestimation of 34.2% compared with the total based on the Childrens' Employment Commission evidence. A similar picture emerges for metalliferous industry with a workforce of 416 (412 males, four females) listed in the Appendix to the Commission's Report for the two copper smelting works in the town.[28] An estimate of eighty employees in the two foundries known to have been working in 1841[29] brings the metalliferous industry workforce to at least 496. The 1841 manuscript census returns contained only 300 (all males) with identifiable metalliferous industry occupations, an underestimation of 39.5% compared with the total based on the Commission's evidence.

Differences of this order of magnitude cast doubt on the conclusions of many demographic studies, particularly those based on the Census Reports whose statistics reflect the raw data of the manuscript census returns. It is therefore important that an assessment is made of the likely accuracy of the quoted Childrens' Employment Commission evidence and, if it is considered reliable, explanations sought for the underestimation of the coal mining and metalliferous industry workforces in the manuscript census returns.

The sub-commissioner appointed to collect evidence throughout South Wales for the Childrens' Employment Commission was Rhys William Jones, a Welsh-speaking colliery viewer and civil engineer residing at Loughor, near Llanelli. Most of his living was earned in the Llanelli area where he was engaged by colliery concerns, acted as mining and minerals agent for one of the area's large estates, and was involved in major harbour improvement schemes.[30] His local contacts would have allowed him access to information he would not readily obtain in other parts of South Wales, the disproportionate quantity of detailed evidence relating to Llanelli's coal and metal industries (some eighteen pages) in the Appendix confirming his close connections with the area. There was no reason whatsoever for the four large colliery companies who provided him with information to exaggerate the size of their workforce, if anything they were keen to play down the true extent of child labour in their mines; and Jones would have been well aware of the size of each concern anyway. Similarly, why would the two copper smelting companies wish to report a higher number of employees than they actually had? It could be suggested that many of the missing workers, in both coal mining and metalliferous industry, lived outside the Llanelli area, walking in to work each day and, thus, not showing up in the examined manuscript census returns. In the case of coal mining some of the 450 unaccounted-for workers may well have done this but, equally, just as many could have walked out of the area to work in the many collieries outside its boundaries and they would not have been included in the workforce numbers given in the Childrens' Employment Commission evidence. If one undeniable pattern emerges from the 1841 manuscript census returns it is that, at a time when twelve to fourteen-hour shifts were commonplace and public transport non-existent, people lived as close as possible to their place of work. With most of the area's collieries situated towards the docks and metal works, well away from its boundaries, it is probable that a large majority of the coal mining workforce lived within the Llanelli area. The possibility that the 196 unaccounted-for metalliferous industry workers lived outside the area is even more unlikely, the copperworks and foundries being situated in the southern part of the Borough Hamlet some three miles from the nearest boundaries. Taking everything into account, there appears to be no reason to doubt the reliability of the workforce numbers given in the Appendix to the Childrens' Employment Commission Report of 1842 other than to suspect that the total in coal mining would have been even higher if child labour had been fully declared.

There are two main reasons why the 1841 manuscript census returns underestimate the coal mining and metalliferous industry workforces. The first of these, already referred to, is unrecorded child labour. Proof of its widespread existence in Llanelli's coal mining industry was given by a local colliery agent in his evidence to the Childrens' Employment Commission:

> The youngest boys employed were from five to six years old; they kept the doors that directed the air-ways of the workings ... The door boys were mostly the sons, or near relatives, of the colliers; they were not very numerous, there were about 10 of them in the whole works, the oldest of whom were about 10 years of age; but they all came to the works from six to seven years old ... The next employment to which the boys are put is to 'cart' the coals cut by the cutters in the headings ... the boys so employed are called 'carters' and are the most numerous class of boys in the works. The youngest carters are about eight or nine and the oldest about 15 years old'.[31]

This was the child labour situation at just one colliery out of the many at work and yet the manuscript census returns for 1841 listed only 1 seven-years-old, 2 eight-years-old, 5 nine-years-old and 9 ten-years-old children with coal mining occupations in the entire Llanelli area. It is certain that most of the children working in the local collieries went unrecorded in the returns but the true extent of this omission is difficult to define. A nominal estimate was previously made when calculating the male coal mining workforce by including all colliers' sons aged nine upwards who had no allocated occupation and were not described as scholars (a total of 162) but, even if the limit was dropped to aged seven upwards (a total of 251), the coal mining workforce given by the returns would still fall short of the Childrens' Employment Commission total by some 200. The nature of the work in the metalliferous industries precluded the general employment of child labour[32] and it was not a contributory factor in the underestimation of the workforce.

The second reason for the underestimation of the two workforces is the incomplete description of occupations in the 1841 census. Skilled and unskilled workers such as smiths, carpenters, masons and labourers were invariably recorded in terms of their trade or craft only, with no reference to where they were employed. As collieries and metal works required all these categories of labour, many of these unallocated workers must have been engaged in the coal mining and metalliferous industries. One instance of this is to be found in the Childrens' Employment Commission evidence – the pitman and overman at the St. George's Pit near Llanelli, William Powell, in describing working conditions at the colliery, stated 'I have a son about 16 years old working in the smith's shop ...'. The manuscript census returns listed only one pitman by the name of William Powell, the occupation of his sixteen-year-old son being described simply as 'Smith';[33] he was not included in the coal mining workforce of 867 abstracted from the manuscript census returns. With a potential of 785 similarly unallocated but possibly relevant workers (114 smiths, 154 masons, 353 labourers, 108 carpenters, fifty-six engine men), the unrecorded child labour, the underestimated female labour and some other feasibly relevant occupations (accountants, agents, ostlers, wagoners *et al*), the pool to draw from easily surpasses 1,000, well in excess of the 646 (450 coal mining, 196 metalliferous industry) underestimation total.

Despite occupational descriptions becoming more detailed in subsequent census years, it is considered that the coal mining and metalliferous industry workforces given by the raw data of the returns remain under-estimations, albeit at a reducing scale, in 1851 and 1861, perhaps in 1871. The absence of detailed contemporaneous evidence of the quality available for 1841 prevents quantification of this opinion.

APPENDIX

Table 1: Population figures

Year	Population	Males		Females	
		Numbers	*%*	*Numbers*	*%*
1841	11,101	5,585	50.3	5,516	49.7
1851	13,613	6,760	49.7	6,853	50.3
1861	17,184	8,531	49.7	8,653	50.3
1871	22,107	10,850	49.1	11,257	50.9

Table 2: Born, or not born, in Carmarthenshire (CMN) – Llanelli Area

Year	Population with known place of birth	Born CMN		Not born CMN	
		Numbers	*%*	*Numbers*	*%*
1841	10,929	9,546	87.3	1,383	12.7
1851	13,528	11,339	83.8	2,189	16.2
1861	16,776	13,928	83.0	2,848	17.0
1871	21,939	18,144	82.7	3,795	17.3

Table 3: Born, or not born, in CMN – Llanelli Borough Hamlet

Year	Population with known place of birth	Born CMN		Not born CMN	
		Numbers	*%*	*Numbers*	*%*
1841	6,759	5,668	83.9	1,091	16.1
1851	8,551	6,977	81.6	1,574	18.4
1861	10,894	8,696	79.8	2,198	20.2
1871	14,682 *	11,679	79.5	3,003	20.5

* part of Westfa Hamlet is included in this figure

Table 4: Not born in CMN – places of birth

Year	Population with known place of birth	Numbers not born CMN				
		Wales (other)	*England*	*Scotland*	*Ireland*	*Foreign parts*
1841	1,383	1,296		15	64	8
1851	2,189	1,517	519	24	117	12
1861	2,848	1,875	782	42	124	25
1871	3,795	2,604	914	77	147	53

Table 5: Male and female workforce

Year	Male workforce (M)		Female workforce (F)		M/F ratio
	Numbers	*% of male population*	*Numbers*	*% of female population*	
1841	3,637	65.1	698	12.7	5.2:1
1851	4,271	63.2	1,213	17.7	3.5:1
1861	5,390	63.2	1,713	19.8	3.1:1
1871	6,720	61.9	2,208	19.6	3.0:1

Table 6: Main male occupations

Year	Male Workforce	Coal Mining	Metal Industry	The Port	Agri-culture	Other Occupations
1841	3,637	1,026	300	174	457	1,680
1851	4,271	1,095	616	239	490	1,831
1861	5,390	1,275	994	301	404	2,416
1871	6,720	1,270	1,947	372	361	2,770

Table 7: Main female occupations

Year	Female Workforce	Domestic Labour	Garment Making	Agri-culture	Metal Industry	Other Occupations
1841	698	343	82	138	0	135
1851	1,213	612	172	136	17	276
1861	1,713	820	322	132	74	365
1871	2,208	1,004	411	167	193	433

Table 8: Combined workforce in Agriculture, Metals and Coal

Year	Combined Workforce	Agriculture	Metal Industry	Coal Mining
1841	4,335	595	300	1,029
1851	5,484	626	633	1,098
1861	7,103	536	1,068	1,285
1871	8,928	528	2,140	1,285

Table 9: Percentage of workforce born in CMN

Year	Overall Population	Male Workforce	Female Workforce	Coal Mining
1841	87.3	84.2	81.7	93.7
1851	83.8	79.0	82.8	90.3
1861	83.0	78.6	81.4	94.2
1871	82.7	76.2	82.0	93.4

Table 10: Percentage of 'born CMN' workforce born in parishes within 10 miles radius of Llanelli Town, 1851-1871

Year	Male Workforce	Female Workforce	Combined Workforce
1851	83.1	83.1	83.1
1861	82.1	85.2	82.9
1871	80.9	86.7	82.5

BIBLIOGRAPHY AND FURTHER READING

Baber, C. & Williams, L.J. (eds), *Modern South Wales: Essays in Economic History* (Cardiff, 1986).

Children's Employment Commission (1842), First Report of the Commissioners, Mines; and Appendix to First Report, Mines, Part 2 (reprinted by the Irish University Press, 1968).

Church, R. (ed), *The History of the British Coal Industry, Vol. 3, Victorian Pre-eminence 1830-1913* (Oxford, 1986).

Edwards, J. (ed), *Tinopolis – Aspects of Llanelli's Tinplate Trade* (Llanelli, 1995).

Higgs, E., *Making Sense of the Census: The Manuscript Returns for England and Wales, 1801-1901* (HMSO, 1991).

Innes, J., *Old Llanelly* (Cardiff, 1902).

Lumas, S., *Making Use of the Census* (Public Record Office, 1992).

Minchinton, W.E., (ed), *Industrial South Wales, 1750-1914* (London, 1969).

Morris, J.H. & Williams, L.J., *The South Wales Coal Industry, 1841-75* (Cardiff, 1958).

Owen, D.H., (ed), *Settlement and Society in Wales* (Cardiff, 1989)

Rowlands, J. & S. (eds), *Welsh Family History: A Guide to Research* (2nd ed, FFHS, 1998).

Symons, M.V., *Coal Mining in the Llanelli area – 16th Century to 1829* (Llanelli, 1979).

Williams, J., *Digest of Welsh Historical Statistics, Vols 1 and 2* (Welsh Office, 1985).

NOTES TO CHAPTER 6

The anglicised spelling Llanelly was changed to the Welsh form Llanelli in 1965. Both spellings appear in these Notes.

[1] See M.V. Symons, *Coal Mining in the Llanelli area, 16th Century to 1829*, (Llanelli Borough Council, 1979), for details of the choice of boundaries.

[2] All manuscript census returns providing information on the parishes of Llangennech and Pembrey and the hamlets of Llanelly Borough, Berwick, Hengoed and Westfa within the parish of Llanelly were examined. These were: 1841, HO 107/1379; 1851, HO 107/2468, 2469; 1861, RG 9/4110-4115; 1871, RG 10/5464-5470.

[3] Carmarthenshire's population figures have been taken from Census of England and Wales 1871, Vol. 1, Counties, p. 506. They were: 1841: 106,326; 1851: 110,632; 1861: 111,796; 1871: 115,710.

[4] M.V. Symons, 'Coal Mining in the Llanelli area – Years of growth 1800-64', contained in *Modern South Wales, Essays in Economic History* (University of Wales Press, 1986), pp. 53-64.

[5] Brinley Thomas, 'The Industrial Revolution and the Welsh Language', in *Modern South Wales, Essays in Economic History,* (University of Wales Press, 1986), pp. 6-21.

[6] *Inspector of Mines Report for the South Western District* (1853), Herbert Mackworth, p. 186.

[7] It is difficult to assess the area's population in 1801. The approximate figure of 3,000 has been based on a statement that the population of Llanelli Town was about 2,000 at that time in J.L. Bowen, *History of Llanelly* (1886).

[8] Llanelli was described in 1803 as being inhabited 'principally by fishermen and colliers' and as late as 1821 as 'A miserable dirty place filled with miners and sailors' (J. Innes, *Old Llanelly,* 1902).

[9] For an appreciation of migration patterns during the nineteenth-century industrialisation of South Wales refer to : Muriel Bowen Evans, 'An aspect of Population History in Carmarthenshire', *The Carmarthenshire Antiquary,* Vol. XIX (1983), pp. 53-60; Brinley Thomas, op. cit.; Harold Carter, 'Urban and Industrial Settlement in the Modern Period, 1750-1814', contained in *Settlement and Society in Wales,* University of Wales Press (1989), pp. 269-296; W.T.R. Pryce, 'Migration: Concepts, Patterns and Processes', Chapter 19 in *Welsh Family History: A Guide to Research* (2nd ed., FFHS, 1998).

[10] This is inferred from the known pattern of industrial growth at Llanelli over this period.

[11] The 'Where Born' column in the 1841 returns required a Yes or No answer to the question of whether born in the same county, additional information being given if born in Scotland, Ireland or Foreign Parts.

[12] Census of Great Britain 1841 – Enumeration Abstract, p. 458 gives 97,547 out of a total population of 106,326 born in Carmarthenshire. Census for England and Wales – Population Abstracts Vol. 3, 1871, p. 609, gives 99,897 out of a total population of 115,710 born in the county.

[13] People born in Welsh counties other than Carmarthenshire and in England were not differentiated between in the 1841 returns, both groups being recorded only as not born in the county.

[14] The numbers born in Glamorganshire and Pembrokeshire were: 1851: 838 (G), 449 (P); 1861: 957 (G), 581 (P); 1871: 1,394 (G), 684 (P).

[15] See M.V. Symons, op. cit., (1979 and 1986).

[16] Assumptions have had to be made, particularly in respect of child labour, in estimating the male workforce. For 1841, all sons of colliers aged nine upwards without given occupations and not described as scholars have been assumed to be working with their fathers or near relatives, an assumption based on the evidence of the Children's Employment Commission Report of 1842. The same assumption has been adopted for all similarly undesignated sons aged ten years upwards of

labourers and those engaged in agriculture; remaining undesignated sons of other workers, or of widows, being included selectively on the basis of parent's occupational status, district of residence, size and age structure of family. The same criteria were adopted for 1851 and 1861 with the age limit for colliers' sons increased to ten years. For 1871, the age limit for all undesignated sons has been taken as twelve years upwards. In addition to child employment, allowances have been made in all years for mariners away at sea, visitors and for the likely workforce on missing pages. These assumptions increased the male workforce given by the raw data of the returns by 15.4% in 1841, 8.1% in 1851, 8.0% in 1861 and 5.2% in 1871.

Different assumptions have been made in estimation of the female workforce with no allowance for child labour. Women or girls described as 'Farmers' daughter' have been included selectively on the basis of age, size of farm and number of female servants working on the farm; women described as 'Housekeeper' but living with husband and children have not been included in the female workforce. It is not known if these assumptions increased or decreased the female workforce.

[17] The main fields of employment have been interpreted in the widest sense – coal mining including all underground and surface workers, agents and colliery proprietors; metalliferous industry similarly including all workers, managers, founders and owners; the port workforce involved everybody connected with the harbour – mariners, harbour masters, customs, shipping agents, ship builders, dock-workers, pilots, ballastmen, sailmakers, ships' chandlers; agriculture included all farmers, agricultural labourers, farm servants, farm bailiffs, shepherds.

[18] M.V. Symons, op. cit., 1986.

[19] Domestic labour has been taken to include all servants, housekeepers, housemaids, laundresses, charwomen, nurses, washerwomen, cooks and kitchen maids, apart from those living in at hotels, inns or public houses. Garment making includes all dressmakers, tailoresses, seamstresses, milliners, straw bonnet makers. Agriculture includes all farmers, selected farmers' daughters, farm servants, dairymaids, poultry maids. The metalliferous industry female workforce required little interpretation, the occupations being precisely stated, for example, scouring at tinworks, opening plates at tinworks.

[20] Compensating the overestimation possibility is the exclusion of female servants and housemaids residing at, and assumed to be working in, hotels, inns and public houses.

[21] As previously noted, it is difficult to decide if a 'Farmers daughter' was working on the farm, as distinct from residing there and performing household tasks. The increase in numbers from 138 to 167 could well be in error although the large decrease from 19.8 to 7.6% of the female workforce is convincing.

[22] Garment making is not as obviously a predominantly single gender occupation as coal mining and domestic labour because of the prevalence of male tailors. The

Llanelli area statistics for 1871 are: female garment makers (as defined in Note 19) 411; male garment makers (tailors, outfitters, hatters) 74.

[23] The parishes falling within a 10 miles radius of Llanelli Town were – Llanelly, Pembrey, Kidwelly, Llangennech, Llanedy, Llannon, Llandybïe, Llanarthney, Llanddarog, Llangendeirne, Llandyfeilog, St. Ishmael. The first six lay completely within the 10-mile radius; the final six lay partly within the 10-mile radius with the furthermost boundaries of Llandyfeilog and Llanarthney being up to 14 miles from Llanelli Town.

[24] W.T.R. Pryce, op. cit.

[25] Children's' Employment Commission, Appendix to First Report, Mines Part II (1842), evidence of Rhys William Jones, pp. 679, 688-90, 693-97, 702-07, 713-18.

[26] Ibid., p. 713.

[27] At least three substantial collieries (Bynea, Cwmddyche, Bryn) and one smaller pit (Dimpath) are known to have been at work in 1841 in addition to those listed in the Children's Employment Commission evidence. A nominal workforce of twenty-five at each larger colliery and twenty at the smaller pit give the additional figure of ninety-five.

[28] Ch. Emp. Comm., 1842, op. cit., p. 688.

[29] The owners of the two foundries at work in 1841 were John Waddle and Richard Nevill. The manuscript census returns for 1851 to 1871 list the number of men and boys they employed – Nevill, sixty in 1851, 154 in 1861; Waddle, forty in 1861, thirty-seven in 1871. The figure of eighty employed in the two foundries in 1841 is based on the assumption of forty in each foundry.

[30] Rhys William Jones was the third generation of his family to work as a colliery viewer, mining agent and civil engineer in the Llanelli area, his father Rhys and grandfather William having been active before him.

[31] Ch. Emp. Comm., 1842, op. cit., pp. 693-4.

[32] Ibid., pp. 688-9.

[33] The evidence of Ch. Emp. Comm., op. cit., p.717 and manuscript census returns 1841, H0 107/1379, Hamlet of Westfa, enumeration districts 10 (P), 13 (P) and 14, p. 29.

Fig. 7-1: The main locations of lead mining in Wales over the centuries

7. GREAT ENDEAVOUR FOR LITTLE REWARD: LEAD MINERS IN WALES

John Rowlands

The mining of lead in Britain has a history extending back at least 2,000 years.* Indeed, it was a feature of the Roman occupation of Britain that many of the temples and major public buildings in Rome are believed to have been roofed with British lead. The preference of the Romans for lead from British sources stems from its particular quality and the ease with which the ore could be won. As Pliny (AD 25-79) observed:

> ... [lead ore] was extracted with much greater difficulty in Spain and throughout Gaul, but in Britain it is found in the upper layers of the soil, and in such quantities that a law was passed without protest prohibiting the extraction of more than a fixed amount.

Within this context the history of lead mining in Wales also stretches back to Roman times when there was considerable activity in several areas. The chief areas of activity at this time (using modern day descriptions) were on the Flintshire/Denbighshire border, in the mountains between Llanidloes and Machynlleth, and also in the area inland from Aberystwyth (see Fig. 7-1).[1]

A particular attraction of this last area for the Romans would have been the significant quantities of silver which were often found in close association with galena, the major ore of lead. The existence of silver in commercial quantities in this area has had an influence over several centuries, not only for those directly involved in the mining of lead, but also on the general economy of this remote and often inhospitable part of Wales.

The middle decades of the nineteenth century, and the period 1850-60 in particular, were the high point for lead mining in Wales; that is, the high point for the number of miners employed and the amount of ore raised. However, the nineteenth century censuses show that, although between 11% and 16% of the male population of Wales were involved in mining or

---

* This chapter is based on a talk given to the Second Stages Course, 'Occupations and the records relating to them', in September 1995.

quarrying generally during the century, the proportion of lead miners was never more than about 1% and was often as low as 0.3%.

With such a small proportion of the population engaged in the mining of lead, it begs the question, 'Why should the topic be considered worthy of being included in a book of this sort?'

There are a number of factors which justify its inclusion here. First, lead mining is an activity which has been carried out in a reasonably significant way in each of the thirteen counties of Wales at one time or another. This may be compared to slate quarrying which has been largely confined to seven counties, and coal mining to only six. In England lead mining has been carried out in only twenty-three of the fifty-six counties.

	Percentage of male population					
	1841	1851	1861	1871	1881	1891
All Wales	0.54	1.03	0.88	0.73	0.69	0.31
Anglesey	Nil	Nil	Nil	Nil	Nil	Nil
Brecon	Nil	0.02	0.01	0.01	0.01	Nil
Caernarfon	0.03	0.31	0.28	0.13	0.39	0.23
Cardigan	**2.39**	**5.09**	**5.15**	**5.47**	**5.33**	**2.80**
Carmarthen	0.11	0.37	0.61	0.13	0.19	0.13
Denbigh	0.19	**1.98**	**2.30**	**1.31**	**1.90**	**1.08**
Flint	**5.05**	**5.40**	**3.79**	**1.99**	**2.49**	**1.85**
Glamorgan	0.01	0.02	0.01	0.01	0.01	0.01
Merioneth	0.27	0.40	0.13	0.01	0.20	0.04
Monmouth	Nil	Nil	Nil	Nil	Nil	Nil
Montgomery	0.24	**3.21**	**3.12**	**4.38**	**3.67**	**1.38**
Pembroke	0.06	Nil	0.01	Nil	0.01	Nil
Radnor	Nil	Nil	0.02	0.17	0.07	0.17

Source: Census, 1841-1891

Note: Where the county figures exceed the average for all Wales, they are shown in bold. If anything, all percentages are likely to be underestimates as there has been no re-allocation to lead mining from 'mining, other'.

Fig. 7-2: Men engaged in lead mining in Wales by county, 1841-1891

Second, there is the fact that national figures can often mask important local variations, and this is very much the case with lead mining. It can be seen in Fig 7-2 that the counties of Cardiganshire, Denbighshire, Flintshire and Montgomeryshire had significant percentages of their male populations (sometimes as high as 5.47%) engaged in lead mining. In the case of Cardiganshire, where lead mining is confined to the extreme north of the county, these county-wide figures obscure the fact that at times nearly 20% of the male population locally were employed in this way.

In addition, the influence of lead mining on several remote mountain areas of Wales was of great importance as it brought a measure of wealth to those areas in a way which would not otherwise have occurred. This in turn stimulated the whole of the local economy. Nowhere was this more in evidence than in the mountain estate of Hafod (Cardiganshire) during its ownership by Thomas Johnes in the late eighteenth and early nineteenth centuries.

Finally, and perhaps most important for family historians, lead mining was often a small-scale enterprise carried out by whole families (including the children). It could also draw in a wide range of incidental support – from carpenters, stone-masons, blacksmiths, suppliers of food and drink, providers of wagon transport for the ore, etc – in a way not paralleled in other industries. This can lead to skilled workers and even farmers being named in the records of a mine in a way one might not expect.

Lead mining in Britain

It is important to view lead mining in Wales within a British context, as it was to the major lead-mining areas of England that Wales had to look for the latest technology, for labour skilled in that technology, and in more recent times for adventure capital.

The main mining areas in England during Roman times were in Derbyshire and Yorkshire. To a much lesser extent – but close to Wales and hence of influence – lead mining was also carried out in Shropshire.

The main areas (in modern Wales) where there was activity during Roman times were:

- at Halkyn in Flintshire
- at Minera and near Abergele in Denbighshire
- near Capel Curig in Caernarfonshire
- at Llantrisant in Glamorgan
- in the mountains of Montgomeryshire between Llanidloes and Machynlleth
- and also over a wide area of north Cardiganshire

After the Romans

With the withdrawal of the Romans, lead mining went into severe decline in Wales and the metal appears to have been little used in the Dark Ages. It was not until the period of the building of castles, churches and the great religious houses from the eleventh and twelfth centuries onwards that anything approaching an industry became re-established.

During the middle ages lead appears to have been mined in most of the counties of Wales, albeit with no great intensity. The main areas – other than Flintshire, Denbighshire and Cardiganshire – which were active during this period were, on the Cardiganshire/Carmarthenshire/Breconshire border (to the north-east of Llandovery), in mid-Carmarthenshire and on the Wales/England border in the vicinity of Llanymynech.

In Wales the remoteness of many of these mining areas and the difficulties of transporting the ore (or the metal itself) to the potential markets held back any serious development until the sixteenth century, although lead for the great religious houses such as the Abbeys of Strata Florida (Cardiganshire) and Valle Crucis (Denbighshire) would have been supplied from local sources.

All this changed in the sixteenth century when, in 1568, Elizabeth I made the first serious attempts to exploit the mineral deposits of Wales. Her primary interest was not in lead, but in the silver and gold which could be found in close association with it. These precious metals were needed for coins to support the expanding economy as both had become increasingly difficult to obtain abroad because of the war with Spain. It was a measure of the Crown's interest in silver that it was decreed that anyone could mine for lead on their own land except where the value of the silver it contained was sufficient to cover the cost of refining the ore for lead.

Where the silver content was significant (as defined in this way), the mines were worked on behalf of the Crown by the Society of Mines Royal, much to the annoyance of local landowners. This annoyance stretched as far as obstructing the Queen's mining agents, which inevitably slowed up the already difficult process of winning the silver and lead from the inhospitable hills. Nevertheless, enough silver was mined in Cardiganshire for a Royal Mint to be established at Aberystwyth castle in 1637 and, for a period during the Civil War, coin from the Aberystwyth Mint contributed to the King's continuing ability to oppose Parliament.

However, during the seventeenth century the position of the monarch and the Society of Mines Royal was challenged and, in 1693, previous legislation which prevented landowners from profiting directly from silver-lead deposits on their land was repealed. Thereafter the mining of lead had a much larger part to play in the economy of Wales.

In the Flintshire/Denbighshire area the contribution to the economy related directly to the improvement in the national economy rather than to the silver content of the lead, which was low. Nevertheless, profits from lead mining stimulated a steady growth in such great estates as those owned by the Grosvenors of Halkyn, the Myddeltons of Chirk, and the Herberts of Powis Castle. On the other hand, in north Cardiganshire, where the silver content was much higher, dramatic improvements became possible in the estates of the Powells of Nanteos, the Prices of Gogerddan and in the Hafod estate which, by the end of the eighteenth century (under Thomas Johnes), had become a classic example of successful agricultural improvement in an upland area.

Of all the mines which contributed to the economy of Wales in this way, those near Halkyn, Minera and in north Cardiganshire survived into the early part of this century as commercial enterprises. The improvement in the economy of Wales which all this brought about touched upon the lives of a much greater proportion of the population than those directly involved in the industry itself.

Lead mining, lead miners and family history

There are seven main characteristics associated with the mining of lead which need to be borne in mind by all family historians who have ancestors who lived in lead-mining areas. They are:

1. It was largely carried out in the more remote rural areas.
2. It was subject to repeated boom and bust.
3. It was an industry with high mortality.
4. In some areas it involved whole families.
5. This resulted in significant in-migration (and out-migration) over time.
6. It introduced new forms of religious observance into some areas
7. It often involved the wider local community in a support role.
8. It introduced capital into under-developed areas and permitted agricultural improvements.

Rural areas: The mining of lead in Wales has always been carried out in sparsely populated areas. It was never carried out on a scale which could have brought about urbanisation, as was the case with the mining of coal or the making of iron or steel.

One particular disadvantage of this is that, in the more remote mines, the ore was being won far from its market, and the cost and difficulty of transporting it to those markets made the industry susceptible to national (or international) fluctuations in the price of lead. This had a profound effect the stability of the labour market in many areas (see 'boom and bust' below).

Another disadvantage is that church records (such as parish registers) for the isolated and sparsely-populated parishes which contained these mines, have not survived on any scale prior to 1813.[2] However, if they have survived, then individuals (especially in-migrants with distinctively different surnames) tend to stand out in those sparse populations.

Boom and bust: Lead mining in Wales has always been an industry swinging wildly between boom and bust. Because of this a stable mining tradition and skilled workforce never really developed, other than in Flintshire during the nineteenth century. In times of boom labour moved in from the more established lead-mining areas – usually in England; at times of bust that labour (or later generations which had descended from it) moved out. Often a decade, or even a generation, could separate the pinnacle of boom from the trough of bust, and it became a matter of chance whether or not the surnames of migrant miners became established in an area. Sometimes they did and, for example, English surnames such as Bonsall, Sheldon, Ball, Blackwell, Denman and Paynter (and many more) were to be found in the lead-mining areas of Cardiganshire in the early nineteenth century.

However, it should not be too readily assumed that because a surname or place-name looks unusual that it has come about as a result of 'foreign' influence. An example of this can be seen in the distinctly Italian-sounding Casara mine in north Carmarthenshire which derives its name from Cae Sara (Sara's field)!

High mortality: Lead mining was an industry with a high mortality rate because of the silica dust usually associated with it. A report on a strike at the Talargoch mine written in 1856 makes specific reference to this:

> The occupation of the miner at these works is considered an unhealthy one, partly on account of the smoke connected with the blasting, partly on account of the bad-ore dust flying about, and partly on account of the great depth of the mine, which in the lowest place is said to be 180 yards. When he is a little advanced in life, he very often suffers from shortness of breathing, and seldom does he reach the allotted period of human life, seventy years.[3]

As a result, re-marriage was common and families frequently had above-average numbers of 'step' relationships within them. This can often be a cause of tension within families and also a cause for confusion for family historians.

Family enterprise: In Wales there has always been the belief (also found in the north of England) that the family was not merely a social unit but was an economic unit as well. As a result, where a miner worked on his own account on someone else's land his whole family – including quite young children – often worked as a team with him. This was certainly the case in

Cardiganshire and some children started work as young as eight. It was also a cause for more general comment in the 'Blue Books' of 1847.[4]

The practice of using female labour was, however, less in evidence in Flintshire and Denbighshire where alternative opportunities, particularly for female labour, existed in the textile and paper industries.

In-migration: The influx of skilled labour into an area which usually accompanied a period of boom often had a profound and lasting influence on many remote and intensely Welsh areas in Wales. This influence manifested itself not only in the pool of surnames which existed in an area, but also in the use of the English language and the presence of religious congregations of a type not normally found in such areas. This, too, was often the subject of comment and, for example, in his report on the Talargoch strike, the incumbent goes on to say:

> The language spoken by the Talargoch miner in the common intercourse of life is Welsh, but many of them can buy & sell & carry on a simple conversation in English very well. The English language is much more commonly understood now in this district than it used to be before the Chester & Holyhead Line of Railway was opened. It is a curious fact that a good many of these miners bear English sirnames *(sic)*, thus showing their origin, but yet speak Welsh, and seem to differ in no respect from their neighbours the Joneses, the Hugheses, and the Williamses.[5]

Then again, the Episcopal Visitation for Minera Chapel (Denbighshire) in 1745 reports that:

> ... a number of miners have lately come to Minera from Ireland, Cornwall and other distant places. I was prevailed upon to oblige them with an English Sermon every other Sunday in the afternoon.[6]

A century later the 1881 Census shows that English surnames were still much in evidence in this same area. Indeed, one quarter of the miners at Minera in the late nineteenth century had surnames which have their origins outside Wales. These include names such as Oldfield, Mitchell, Bateman, Carrington, Collins, Kelly, Martin, Moss, etc.

Religion: Lead mining communities in Wales often display a denominational profile which is not shared by other communities in the area. This usually indicates that there has been an influx of miners from areas with a different religious tradition. For example, if your ancestors were Wesleyan Methodism in an area which was staunchly Calvinistic in tradition, it was not because John Wesley had been active and successful in that area. Almost certainly it was because there had been an influx of miners from other areas in which Wesley had been active and successful, as he made few direct inroads into predominantly Welsh-speaking areas.

Such was the case in the village of Tre'r Ddol in north Cardiganshire, where the Wesleyan congregation soon outgrew the original chapel built in 1845 (albeit there had been a Wesleyan presence in the area as early as 1806) and, despite it being extended in 1864, by 1877 a much larger chapel had to be built a few hundred yards away.

Earlier in the nineteenth century there were a large number of Italian miners in some north Cardiganshire mines. These men lived in barracks and two Catholic churches were built in this bastion of nonconformity to cater for their spiritual needs.

The generally high level of nonconformity in lead mining areas was another aspect commented upon in the report on the Talargoch Strike. In this it is stated that:

> The greater number of the Talargoch miners are in the habit of attending occasionally some Dissenting place of worship or other on Sundays, but only a minority of them attend the different parish churches in their respective neighbourhoods.[7]

However, it should not be assumed that all lead miners were nonconformists. Allegiance to the Established Church by miners over a long period can be seen in a petition to the Bishop, dated 26 June, 1745 which was attached to the Episcopal Visitation for Minera Chapel for that year.[8] In that petition – whose primary purpose was to secure an English sermon once or twice a month – it was clearly stated that the Chapel '…had been erected by miners in earlier times' and that the present miners '…Have a great desire to Lead a Christian Life in Keeping the Holy Sabath (*sic*)'.

Wider community involvement: It has been mentioned earlier that lead mining as an activity drew in people from the community at large to provide essential support services. As a result, carpenters would be employed for lining the shafts and the tunnels; smiths would be engaged in a wide variety of forge work; while masons were employed to erect buildings, line adits, etc. Farmers would be called on to provide horses for transporting the ore, and this could extend to providing fodder for those horses. Meanwhile, not to be outdone, the farmers' wives would provide bread, butter, eggs, meat, etc, for the miners.

This involvement of the wider community features prominently in accounts of the Llangunnog mine (Montgomeryshire).[9] Those accounts – which have well over 100 pages of detailed entries covering the period 1729-36 – record (for a small part of 1731) payments which include:

Frank Burton & partners	for full bargains	£41 3s 4d
John Davies	for leather pipe	£7 14s 0d
Richard Bunting and son	smelters	£11 5s 0d
Jenkin Thos.	for 8 bedsteads	£2 16s 0d
Eliz: Rogers	grass for wagon horses	£10 10s 0d
Mary Herd & Jane Bidden	for making sheets	£0 5s 10d
Hum: Humphrys	for 285yds of Linnen cloth	£11 0s 7d

Entries such as this represent about one-fifth of those which might be found on a typical page in these accounts. It is not often within Wales that one finds the activities of quite ordinary people (as individuals) being recorded in such detail for the early part of the eighteenth century.

Farming connections: It is traditional in Wales for farming and mining (of all sorts) to be closely connected. Indeed, it was sometimes difficult to distinguish whether a man was a miner doing a bit of farming to supplement his income, or if it was the other way round. As a result, it would be quite common for two months to be lost to lead mining each year because of the competing demands of sowing crops, peat cutting (for winter fuel) and the harvest. All this was tolerated by the mine owners because it enabled men to supplement their income, which in turn enabled them to keep wages down.

For many miners, however, a sudden surge in income resulting from a particularly profitable bargain would offer the prospect of being able to escape the demands and dangers of mining. Many (but by no means all) grasped this opportunity as can be seen in the report on the Talargoch Strike, which records that:

> Some of them have saved money; some have built houses for themselves as well as for letting to others; and some having been successful as miners, have changed their original occupation for that of farming; but too many of them alas! do not think of a rainy day, and of making hay during shun-shine (*sic*).[10]

And sometimes the sun really did shine. Indeed, the Talargoch Strike came about because the mine owners sought to change the terms of existing bargains after one group of miners had found large quantities of lead in a very unfavourable location and had been earning up to £120 per month.

Records relating to lead miners

Information about individual lead miners may be found in a wide variety of records. These can range from the obvious, such as parish registers, monumental inscriptions and the census, to the far-from-obvious, such as estate letters and accounts, episcopal visitations and chapel year-books or chapel histories, etc. However, these may be best considered under five main heads, namely:

Records of Church and Chapel
Monumental Inscriptions
Census Records
Estate Records, and
Newspapers and other Miscellaneous Reports.

Records of Church and Chapel: One obvious place to find evidence of individual lead miners is in parish registers. Between 1754 and 1837, any record of marriage should be found in parish registers (provided they have survived). They may also be found there outside this period even though one, or even both, of the parties involved might be nonconformist.

The same cannot necessarily be said of baptismal and burial records in areas with a high level of nonconformity. However, baptism in the Established Church held potential advantages (in the event of a need for poor relief), and burial in the churchyard was in most cases not an issue of denominational significance. Because of this, church records should not be discounted even when searching for evidence of those with known nonconformist allegiances. It must also be remembered that in Wales the Calvinistic Methodists did not formally break away from the Established Church until as late as 1811. Prior to that date a dual allegiance – to both Methodism and the Church – existed in many parts (see Chapter 4).

When reading these records – and marriage records in particular – care must be taken to avoid confusion between minors and miners through the correct reading of the actual word (see Chapter 8, page 127) and assessing it in its proper context. This needs to extend to a healthy caution about the accuracy of published transcripts.

Where chapel records exist for baptism, burial or marriage (in the event of a chapel being licensed after 1837), they can furnish comparable information.[11, 12]

Year-books and histories can also be of particular importance. The former can record the arrival of individuals within the community, while the latter can give a useful insight into the fluctuations in the numerical strength of a particular congregation consequent upon boom and bust.

At another level we have seen earlier that Episcopal Visitations can give quite detailed assessments of the personal and spiritual well-being of the parish as well as of its congregation.

Monumental Inscriptions: Inscriptions on gravestones can often give information not readily available from other sources. They are after all personal statements within a family, and those providing that information would have been privy to details not easily found elsewhere.

For example, a gravestone at Eglwys Newydd (Cardiganshire) commemorates the death of John Eddy in 1860 as well as the deaths of several of his children, the last of whom died at Wadsley, Yorkshire, in 1886. Now, the surname Eddy is not one which originated in Wales and it would be reasonable to suppose that it was present in this lead mining area of north Cardiganshire as a result of in-migration from England. It would also be tempting (in the absence of any other evidence) to assume that there may have been a connection with the Wadsley area of Yorkshire. However, also in that same churchyard is a gravestone which records the following:

> In memory of Elizabeth, wife of Benjamin Eddy, parish of St Austell Cornwall who died May 20th 1852 age 43 years.
> Also of the above-named Benjamin Eddy who died November 8th 1853 aged 43 years.

It would be hard to imagine that two people living in this remote area and holding the surname Eddy could have come other than from the same place; in this case St Austell in Cornwall.

In addition, of course, the names on other gravestones at Eglwys Newydd tell their own story of an indigenous workforce supplemented by significant in-migration, and names such as Prout, Collins, Messer, Dunn, Davey, Glanville, Davidson, Terrill, Buzza and Ball may be readily found. Two of these, Davey and Buzza, are almost certainly also of Cornish origin.

The Census: The value of the nineteenth century censuses when pursuing the family history of an individual or family is well known and doesn't need to be repeated here. However, information about the occupations being generally pursued by the population of an area can give a insight into the nature of the community in which an ancestor had lived and the degree to which lead mining might have influenced that community. The 1881 Census for Talybont (a village on the edge of the lead-mining area of north Cardiganshire) is a good example of this.

Occupation	No.	%
Mining (agents, miners, ore dressers, mine labourers)	52	34.4
Woollens (Manufacturers, carders, weavers, spinners)	21	13.8
Trade (smiths, carpenters, painters, moulders, masons)	19	12.5
Agriculture (farmers, millers, gardeners, ag. labs, shepherds)	16	10.5
Retail (grocers, chemists, coal merchants)	14	9.2
Religion/Education (ministers, schoolmasters, pupil teachers)	10	6.6
Crafts (shoemakers, saddlers tailors)	9	5.9
Officials, (rate collectors, receiving officers, clerk of works)	3	2.0
Miscellaneous (servants, gen. labs, carriers, independent, etc)	8	5.3

Fig. 7-3: Male adult employment in Talybont (Cardiganshire), 1881

It can be seen from Fig. 7-3 that male employment in lead mining at 34.4% was two-and-a-half times greater than the manufacturing of woollens, the next most common occupation. It should be noted, however, that this list relates solely to those living in the village of Talybont and excludes the majority of those within the parish of Llangynfelyn who were engaged in agriculture.

Estate Records: Organised mining on any scale would have been carried out either by major landowners on their own land, or by mining companies under a contractual agreement with the landowner. In the case of the former the work may have been done partly by bargain and partly by waged labour. It is not surprising, therefore, that details of who was paid what should appear in the records of an estate.

A good example of this can be found in the records of the Chirk Castle Estate relating to the Llangunnog Mine (Montgomeryshire) for the period 1729-36.[13] The account book shows that, between Midsummer and Christmas in 1735, the total payments by bargain were £667 2s 4d, and for wages £353 19s 6½d.[14] Needless to say, the specific bargain struck with a group of miners (in which each individual might well be named) would also have been recorded.[15]

Newspapers, etc: A dangerous industry like lead mining is bound to feature in newspapers from time to time as disasters occur. However, strikes and disputes of all sorts are also a valuable source for newspaper copy.

In addition, many disputes, especially those between landowners, can often end up in court and may, therefore, be recorded in a further way.

With imagination a wide range of incidental material can be flushed out from local sources, including the journals of local or family history societies, as well as the more specialist journals dealing primarily with the technical aspects of mining as well as general (and particular) impacts on local society.

In conclusion

Anyone with ancestors who are firmly-rooted in the lead-mining areas of Wales could well have a wealth of incidental information available to them which relates to those ancestors, even if they were not directly involved with lead mining themselves. As much of family history research in Wales involves a desperate search for incidental information to fill gaps caused by the lack of survival of more standard sources, those with ancestors in the lead-mining communities of Wales are blessed – potentially at least – with a decided bonus.

BIBLIOGRAPHY

The majority of books and booklets relating to lead mining which have been published deal with the technicalities of mining rather than the contribution made by the ordinary individuals. The only exception to this is where a particularly prominent owner, agent or engineer was involved. Nevertheless, many of these can be well worth reading (or at least dipping into) for the insight they give into the harshness of the terrain where much of the lead mining activity took place in Wales, as well as the resulting hardships experienced by our ancestors.

Bick, David, *The Old Metal Mines of Mid Wales* (Parts 1 to 6; 1974-1991). Originally published as separate booklets they are now available in a single volume (Pound House, 1993).

Bick, David, *Frongoch Lead and Zinc Mine*, British Mining Monograph No. 30. (British Mine Research Society, 1996).

Carr, Tina and Schöne, Annemarie, *Pigs and Ingots: The Lead/Silver Mines of Cardiganshire,* (Y Lolfa, 1993).

Hughes, Simon (ed), *History of the Cardiganshire Mines*, Absolom Francis (1884). Mining Facsimiles Reprint No. 14, 1987.

Lewis, W. J., *Lead Mining in Wales* (UW Press, 1967)

NOTES TO CHAPTER 7

[1] It is interesting to note that, in 1998, a hoard of Roman coins from the period AD 260-293 was found in the village of Penrhyncoch, a short distance inland from Aberystwyth. See *The Cambrian News*, Thursday 17 December 1998.

[2] See *Welsh Family History: A Guide to Research* (2nd ed, 1998), Fig. 4-1.

[3] NLW: SA/MISC/364 (St Asaph Miscellaneous Manuscripts), p. 3. This 24-page booklet of handwritten text entitled 'The Talargoch Strike' was written by the incumbent to his Bishop and describes a wide range of aspects associated with the mining of lead and its impact on the local community. I am uncertain who precisely the incumbent was, as the Talargoch mine was partly in the parish of Dyserth and partly in the parish of Meliden.

[4] Reports of the Commissioners of Inquiry into the State of Education in Wales, 1847. Three parts.

[5] NLW: SA/MISC/364, p. 4.

[6] NLW: Church in Wales Records, SA/QA/3, No. 53, answer to Question IX.

[7] NLW: SA/MISC/364, p. 3.

[8] NLW: Church in Wales Records, SA/QA/3, No. 53.

[9] NLW: Chirk Castle MS 12435F.

[10] NLW: SA/MISC/364, p. 2.

[11] Ifans, Dafydd (Ed.), *Cofrestri Anghydffurfiol Cymru/Nonconformist Registers of Wales* (NLW, Aberystwyth, 1994).

[12] Rawlins, Bert J., *The Parish Churches and Nonconformist Chapels of Wales: Their Records and Where to Find Them Vol. 1, Cardigan, Carmarthen and Pembroke* (Celtic Heritage Research, Salt Lake City, 1987).

[13] Chirk Castle MS 12435F, Account Book of the Llangunnog Mine.

[14] The principle of mining 'by bargain' was first introduced in Cardiganshire by the Company of Mine Adventurers. It was a form of piecework whereby the right to work a seam was granted by auction to the lowest bidder; the bid sum being the price per ton to be paid to the miner by the mining company. It had the safeguard that the price could be varied (either way) if found to be wholly unreasonable.

[15] An example of this is to be found in Powis MS 21939, Frongoch Mine Bargain Book, 1792-98.

8. READING OLD DOCUMENTS: STRATEGIES FOR SUCCESS

Susan J. Davies

Anybody who has already persevered with family or local history back to the early nineteenth century and beyond will have encountered documents which are difficult to read, sometimes because of poor condition but often because of unfamiliar writing.* Some may be put off by the difficulties; others try hard to develop skill but feel despair.

This chapter is based on long teaching experience in a university context and regular sessions for family history groups, with resulting awareness of the best routes to success. While there is no need to impose an academic approach on everybody, it has advantages in learning to read old documents, and the key points can be grasped by all. This skill is part of **palaeography,** the study of old handwriting, and it is a rare skill in our modern society, even among professional historians. It always brings a personal sense of achievement, a feeling of real contact with the past – and many requests from others for assistance! Time devoted to learning is time well spent.

The message of this chapter is twofold. First, to emphasise that there is a wealth of written information of local relevance which has accumulated in bulk from the sixteenth century onwards when, for example, parish registers began: this is a rich resource for the family historian who has the reading skills to exploit it. Second, to make clear that everyone can succeed in reading old documents. Although special skill is certainly necessary, acquiring it is not beyond anybody, regardless of age or experience, since time, interest and maturity will compensate for lack of any recent educational opportunity. The essential equipment is appropriate guidance on methods of approach and careful practice. Personal confidence will then grow, together with ability to solve the 'difficult bits'!

---

* This chapter is based on talks given to the Second Stages Courses held in 1993, 1994 and 1995.

Appropriate guidance takes three forms, constituting the three essential lines of approach to reading old documents:

1. Preparatory study/reading in order to understand the purpose and function of the particular documents in question.
2. Background information which will provide a context for appreciating the way in which documents were written at different times.
3. Technical advice on identifying and reading particular styles of handwriting.

Preparatory study/reading can be tackled individually, with the aid of appropriate reference books. This is a very important preparatory stage which alerts the searcher to the kind of information and vocabulary which he or she should expect to encounter in the original documents.

Background information is difficult to acquire without help: it is not conveniently conveyed by reference books and is rather specialised, yet it is crucial to retrieving information from documentary evidence.

Technical advice is particularly difficult to grasp without initial instruction and advice.

These requirements may seem formidable; they are the tools of the professional historian. Yet the dogged determination which comes from a personal mission to make clear the role of the family in one's own, and the collective, past will usually provide the 'amateur' with motivation and strength to tackle all necessary source material, however difficult, with excellent results.

The rest of this chapter will concentrate on guidance for the second and third of these points, for which introductory support, combined with careful practice, is necessary to successful progress in reading old documents.

Background matters

Rapid growth of a paper and parchment 'mountain' was a feature of Tudor times. Primarily a **manuscript** (hand-written) mountain, with very little representing the then new technology of printing, it comprises documents of diverse kinds, whether 'official', as part of the business of government, the Church, local administration or commerce, or 'personal', in the form of correspondence, accounts, family/estate papers, etc. The mountain continued to grow thereafter, adding a wealth of written evidence for the family historian at both national and local level, now largely preserved in archive repositories and made accessible through their catalogues and indexes. The term **documents** will be used here in a broad sense, to mean all kinds of manuscript material which contain information.

Learning to read all these documents requires knowledge of the various writing styles which were used and their characteristic letter shapes, together with some broader understanding of handwriting development. During past centuries, handwriting has generally been conservative and slow to change, one style remaining in use for several hundred years before giving way to another. Most people aimed to copy the particular style of the time, and especially that which they were first taught. The opportunity to learn was not as widespread as it is today, but improved from the sixteenth century with additional schools and the work of peripatetic writing masters who taught all who wished to learn (and could pay). Writing was still, however, more of a male opportunity, and confined to the upper classes, the government secretariat, the clergy, and the scholarly and mercantile ranks of society, and this was to remain true until the later nineteenth century. This situation, though limiting in a social context, provides a good opportunity to appreciate what kind of writing was taught and helps to explain why certain styles predominated, namely, those fostered by government and taught in schools and by the writing masters.

A constant guiding principle, implicitly acknowledged and continued to the middle of the present century, favoured standardised writing style and letter formation, according to the particular script in use, in the joint interests of clarity, efficiency, widespread understanding and legal validity. Any abbreviations used were equally controlled within an accepted, widely understood system which dates back to medieval times; it had been established for use with Latin but was subsequently borrowed, as appropriate, for writing English and other vernacular languages, surviving to the eighteenth century. While this may seem confusing to the newcomer to palaeography, the degree of consistency and conformity to rules which occurs in the writing of old documents is actually encouraging. Discover the standard styles and necessary rules and successful reading will follow!

Other, more subtle, factors are also significant in influencing old handwriting, such as the age of the writer or the place of writing. For example, an elderly person might use a writing style learnt in youth which appears archaic for the given date, while provincial areas (like Wales), far from the seat of government in London, reflected changes of writing style more slowly, perhaps with a differential of a century or more.

Not only the writing style but also the word patterns of formal documents are traditionally conservative and long-lasting. Many date back to the medieval Latin forms, which were both concise and precise, and some are echoed in English to the present day. Just as wills commonly began with several lines similar to:

In the name of God Amen ... on the (date) in the year ... I ...of the parish of ... in the county of ... and diocese of ... sick in body but of whole and perfect remembrance ... do make this my last will and testament in manner and form following ...

so too does the current language of legal conveyance of property in Britain still reflect medieval phraseology and terminology, first set down in Latin. Deeds and court records contain a particularly high proportion of long-lasting common form. Few people realise that Latin continued in use in Britain for some official records (especially the most formal court records) until the 1730s, when its use was finally abolished by Act of Parliament. This explains the continued survival of associated word-patterns in their English equivalents; this is not an attempt to reproduce antique quaintness or to create obscurity! It is, instead, a continuation of long historical development and legal precedent which constitutes a further useful aid to successful reading, certainly in the case of formal documents such as deeds and wills, also court and church records, the majority being written in English from the sixteenth century.

Established precedent and common form was also observed in the pleasantries of private correspondence and the courtesies of modes of address. For this reason, familiarity with classic English literature in the works of Jane Austen, Charles Dickens and others can be very helpful in tackling ancestral correspondence and the more spontaneous writings which the family historian may wish to study.

Other language matters relevant to reading old documents are more general and pervasive, but sometimes clouded by current experience. For example, apparent rapid change in the form and use of English in present times, together with opposing views on the merits of teaching a formal writing style, can obscure the fact that written English before the middle of this century remained rather formal and well-structured in careful sentences, following rules of grammar and syntax. Here again, classical literature will help to prepare the mind for what to expect when reading manuscript documents, especially correspondence, from bygone times. The pleasure of 'transporting' oneself back to the language and social circumstances of bygone times is thus justifiable in research terms!

A final point in the language context relates to spelling, more particularly to a common lack of standardised spelling in English before the eighteenth century, and even then a tendency to fluctuate, so that names, for example, may be spelled in several different ways within one document. Spelling may also reflect regional origin. In Wales, English spelling in general may be more phonetically based, while particular details, such as a double **ss** where a single **s** is expected, may provide evidence of spoken accent. Yet it would be dangerous to suggest that factors affecting spelling in Wales could be reflected so simply: here we have to consider exclusion of the Welsh language following the Acts of Union, and a tendency for the gentry to be educated outside Wales, etc; also some determined efforts to anglicise place names, combined with basic ignorance of such names by many whose duty it was to set them down in writing. Both personal and place-names in Wales present their special problems, together with anglicised attempts at Welsh names for objects. In all cases, accurate reading of each word, letter by letter, is particularly important, before any further interpretative efforts are made. Such difficulties abound in private correspondence, requiring both palaeographical care and detective work, whatever the century of origin. Even Welsh phonetic spelling varies through the centuries, whether or not under English influence, e.g. use of **v** where modern Welsh would use **f**.

All these issues of language, grammar and syntax serve to strengthen the importance of careful, accurate reading of what is actually set down in writing. It is recommended that individual letters and forms of spelling should always be identified and noted as they occur in the original document, without attempts at 'modernisation'.

Today's handwriting scene is very different. From the mid-twentieth century, personal styles of writing have become generally accepted, and our younger 'scribes' appear to have little concept of any need for consistency and legibility in letter formation! For those who foresee the consequences, the potential reading problems for our descendants are serious. At the same time, current developments in word-processing and electronic communication will result in our bequest of information to posterity being very different from that of earlier generations, containing, for example, few draft copies to indicate evolving thought, and few written records of any kind for many transactions.

Little has yet been noted about particular styles of writing, except the importance of studying them and taking an informed interest in their development. The history of one style will illustrate the value of this approach in anticipating what to expect in documents. The Copperplate style of handwriting, familiar to our immediate ancestors early in the present century as the common cursive style, was widely written from the eighteenth, but has a long history and a strong influence on the present. Unless very careless, this is clear, legible and pleasing, with a familiar right-hand slope and loops on ascending and descending letters. It developed from Italic script (still familiar today from its use in print, *like this*) which came from Italy as long ago as the fifteenth century, and was called after its country of origin as it spread widely in western Europe. The version which is commonly known to us as Copperplate (because it was engraved on copperplate for printing copybooks designed to teach writing) developed in

England in the seventeenth century, and was successfully exported back to continental Europe through commercial and trading activity, this time identified as the English Round Hand. British imperial expansion ensured its use in distant parts of Empire, where the style has a long and continuing history of use.

Such historical information not only explains the nomenclature but also the spread of use and persistence of one particular style of writing. It also provides a context for learning to read that particular style. Exceptions to common developments are also significant in this instance: in Germany, for example, Italic was known as the Latin Script and restricted to writing Latin. This largely explains why development of handwriting and printing style in Germany was different from that of the rest of Western Europe and why interesting consequential features are seen in handwriting in the USA, where links with immigration from different parts of Europe can be highly significant among the various influences on handwriting development. Thus, the historical context is always an important consideration, and an aid to understanding. Much study of handwriting in the USA has been linked with **calligraphy**, which considers handwriting as an art form. A palaeographical approach differs in that it aims to evaluate context, origins and relationships as well as to study the script itself.

Clearly, the Copperplate/Round Hand style of writing was very long-lasting, thus illustrating the conservatism of handwriting. It has additional familiarity because its ancestor, Italic, is also the ancestor of our modern printing type, used widely in Western Europe and providing the basic letter forms not only for printed books but also for teaching children to read and write. If this were the only style used in old documents there would be few problems, allowing for some careless versions, but there were others, and also mixtures of two at times of changing fashion in handwriting; these, unfortunately, are less 'user friendly'!

What styles of handwriting were used and how are they identified?
These vary in appearance, and sometimes in the context of use. Reading is always easier if one can first identify which style is being used. Identification is made by using a combination of overall appearance and letter-shapes. Some letter-shapes are very unfamiliar to the modern eye, so it is necessary to learn to recognise their characteristic forms, just like learning to read for the first time.

As for general approach, some prefer to start with the more recent and familiar styles, working backwards in time to the less familiar. This raises a significant difficulty in that, without knowledge of earlier practice, one cannot recognise archaic survivals from an earlier style. Experience suggests another approach, namely, to start with the handwriting scene in the sixteenth century – a time when written material and its survival is noticeably increased – and work forwards, considering the chronological development of handwriting to the nineteenth century, thus accommodating any features which occur later than might be expected.

Three styles of writing were used in Britain during the sixteenth century. One was the surviving medieval style, widely used by government and the Church from the twelfth century, chiefly for writing Latin. It is often called Court Hand, and is related to the heavy Gothic script used for books. It cannot be considered here because it requires a knowledge of Latin and a full grasp of the medieval abbreviation system, although nobody should regard it as too difficult to learn – it just needs time (or another chapter to itself). For the present, it is sufficient to say that it continued in use in the more formal records of central government and the law courts (e.g. the Plea Rolls of the Court of Great Sessions in Wales), and it is most likely to be met in these circumstances, also, perhaps, in a broader legal context, and certainly in some kinds of deeds, such as Fines/Final Concords. It disappears with the abolition of Latin in the 1730s, after seven centuries in use.

The second style, called Secretary Hand, was in widespread use in the sixteenth century, having gained popularity in the fifteenth (it came from Europe in the 1370s). It was the most popular everyday and business style, and was also used for the bulk of routine administrative and governmental business, literary writing and correspondence. It is, therefore, of particular importance in the context of reading documents of value to family history in the sixteenth century and later. It is not easy to read because letter-shapes are unusual to the modern eye, and the writing often suffered from the detrimental effects of being written quickly.

Secretary Hand was very well written in the sixteenth century, especially in Elizabethan times, and many beautiful examples survive. It remained fairly pure until the later part of the century, when it first shows the influence of the third style of handwriting, namely, Italic, which has already been mentioned. Italic was known in Britain earlier, and was favoured by Tudor royalty and the nobility, but it is not generally noticeable in surviving documents before the late 1500s, when the gentry began to use it, primarily for their signatures. It began to exert influence on Secretary Hand, as seen in the imposition of a right-hand slope which does not suit the Secretary style and distorts the letters. Gradual substitution of some of the (simpler) Italic letter shapes, including capitals, also occurs. This represents the beginning of a subtle sequence of change from one dominant style of handwriting to another, as follows: pure Secretary Hand > Secretary with Italic influence > cursive Italic with Secretary influence > cursive Italic.

The phase of mixture of Secretary Hand with Italic varies in place and time, but generally continues from the last quarter of the sixteenth century through the first quarter of the seventeenth, culminating in the victory of Italic in its cursive, almost-Copperplate form by the 1650s. However, while this timing may be substantially true in England, Wales reflects a different pattern. Here, Secretary Hand persists much later in a pure or mixed Secretary/Italic form, and will be encountered in the late 1600s, with substantial reminders surviving into the eighteenth century. The final phase is observed in cursive handwriting which regularly slopes to the right and which appears to be primarily Italic-based, but which still contains identifiable Secretary letter-shapes; if this mixture is recognised, reading difficulties are minimised.

The victory of Italic, as the cursive Copperplate/Round Hand style, reduces the problems of reading old documents thereafter, because letter-shapes are more familiar. Of course, the influence of speed and carelessness, which results in letters being incompletely formed, is still problematic, and demands the same methodical, careful approach which is needed by Secretary Hand, but for different reasons. Thereafter, right through to the early 1900s, there is no further major change of writing style, but an increase in very cursive and more careless execution as the volume of less formal writing grew. Anybody who has struggled with nineteenth century manuscript sources will appreciate this point.

How to start reading:

A. General guidelines on method of approach

1. Be systematic and careful. This means following the guidelines below and going slowly, reading letter by letter. Making mistakes is part of the process and should be viewed as progress, not failure! As skill develops, mistakes will be more quickly recognised and not repeated.

2. Do not rely on guesswork. If you must guess, and have a good clue to support your guess, you should then prove that your idea is correct by reading the actual letter-shapes. You may, of course, discover that your guess was wrong.

3. Always start by taking a calculated look at a document, considering its nature and date of origin – you may find this information in the finding aid which you have used to locate the document. Next, try to identify the style of writing used. Only then should reading begin, by first allowing the eye to become accustomed to the general appearance of the writing, then picking out some recognisable features such as names and dates,

and finally starting at the beginning, reading each word slowly, letter by letter. A reference list of letter-shapes and stylistic features which belong to the particular style of writing is often helpful, especially for capital letters.

Note: A natural wish to discover the content quickly means that this slow method is unpopular at first, but it produces the best cumulative results which will encourage improvement with each document read. It will also enable the persistent searcher to progress successfully to increasingly difficult material. Some published reading aids do not distinguish between the principal styles of old writing and present a range of letter-shapes, belonging to different styles, on a 'pick and choose' basis. This does not inspire confidence or develop skill.

4. Remember that the scribe was using standard letter-shapes, and that personalised and peculiar letter shapes are not common in documents before our own times.

5. Expect to meet examples of abbreviations. Remember that the system followed rules and is not haphazard (see below).

6. Comparison is always important when reading difficult writing. If you fail to read a word or letter, look for another which is similar and see if that is easier, then go back to the first example. Similarly, use comparison to help with any idiosyncrasies.

Note: it is usually possible to pick out small words like **the** and **and**. These will establish the shapes of certain letters and combinations; use them to help with other words. It is a fact that the answer to most reading difficulties may be found within the document itself or in others which are related.

7. If you cannot read a word, copy it carefully in your notes so that you can look at it again. If you can read the letters but cannot solve a vague abbreviation mark, copy the letters and put an apostrophe at the end of the word to indicate abbreviation. This is good editorial practice!

8. Do not be surprised by curious spelling, as already explained. If in doubt, try reading aloud phonetically: some words are more easily recognised by sound.

9. If you are dealing with a particular type of document, there are almost certainly some similar examples in print which will provide a reading and study aid, e.g. court records and wills/probate records.

10. If anybody is looking at seventeenth or eighteenth century court records, which seem illegible and are in Latin, it is worth checking those in the series which survive from the period of the Commonwealth (the 1650s). For a few years, the use of Latin and archaic writing was abolished, and the records were written in English. Of course, they may not be particularly easy to read by modern standards and the scribes, who were used to writing legal phraseology in Latin, floundered with the

equivalent English version, resorting to a language style which was almost an exact parallel of Latin word order. With the restoration of the monarchy in 1660, Latin and the medieval writing style returned.

B. Abbreviations and contractions used in writing English in the sixteenth and seventeenth centuries, and sometimes persisting to the eighteenth

Abbreviation marks devised for precise use with Latin in medieval times were carried over into English, where appropriate, and sometimes used less precisely,

> e.g.   ℘ = per, par, por (℘ish = parish)
> ℘ = pro (℘fit = profit)

– the common **bar** mark (‾) was widely used, most often for an omitted **m** or **n** (com̅on = common). When written quickly it is often curved, and it may be attached to the final letter of the word.

– a mark rather like a large 'apostrophe' (ꝰ) represents **er** or **re** (pꝰsent = present), sometimes **ri**. A similar mark at the end of a word, especially a name, is often a general abbreviation mark.

– a 'looped' sign at the end of words (ꝫ) represents **es** in English plural endings.

Otherwise, common practice was to use some initial letters, followed by one or more letters in a 'superior', or raised position, perhaps with additional abbreviation marks:

e.g. M^r	= Master	tenem^t	= tenement
M^ris	= Mistris	testam^t	= testament
S^r	= Sir (also ꝼ or β)	a ℘℘tinꝫ	= appertinances
Mad^m	= Madam	℘liam^t	= parliament
K^t	= Knight	pꝰsentm^tꝫ	= presentments
M^tie	= Majestie		
A^oD^ni	= Anno Domini		
w^ch	= which		
y^r, y^or	= your		
o^r	= our		
w^th, w^t	= with		

Note: Sometimes, superior letters were used when no contraction had taken place,

> e.g. afte^r   = after

Also, when the superior letter is an **r**, it is often in the **secondary** form, like a small **2** , and may be difficult to recognise, looking like a 'squiggle', or even a small number **3**.

Generally speaking, the incidence of abbreviation used in writing English was much less than in Latin. The same is true of other vernacular languages.

Use of the 'thorn': The **thorn** is a very old letter-shape, runic in origin. By the sixteenth century it looks like a **y**, but its descender does not curve. It was used in medieval times for the **th** sound in English, because the Latin alphabet had no way of representing that sound. The thorn continued in regular use until the seventeenth century, and even the eighteenth in some cases. Beware of the following, and other similar examples involving the thorn (represented here by **y**):

y^e = the
y^t = that
y^{er} = ther ($y^{er}w^{th}$ = therwith)
y^{em} = them

The following matters often present reading problems because of abbreviation:

1. Months: Names of months are often abbreviated by using superior letters:

e.g. $Sept^{ber}$
Oct^{ber}
Nov^{ber}
Dec^{ber}

Beware of these later versions, 7^{ber}, 8^{ber}, 9^{ber}, X^{ber}, representing **Sept**ember, **Oct**ober, **Nov**ember and **Dec**ember.

2. Titles and proper names: These are heavily abbreviated, often using superior letters. Abbreviated titles sometimes end with a mark similar to a modern colon (**:**). Abbreviated proper names often use the common **bar** mark:

e.g. Lo: = Lord, Lord's, Lordship etc.
LL: = plural of above
Lop: = Lordship (plural Lopps !)
Ho: = honour, honour's, honourable etc.
La: = Lady, Ladyship etc.
Thō = Thomas
Wā = Walter
Iā = James
W^m or
Wm̄ = William
Jn̊ = John

3. Money: Abbreviations of financial denominations, especially **£ s. d.** (pounds, shillings and pence) often cause difficulty, since these represent the Latin words **libra** (pound), **solidus** (shilling) and **denarius** (penny), also **obolus** (halfpenny) and **quarta** (farthing). Continuing use of abbreviated forms of the following Latin words in accounts can also be confusing until recognised: **dimidia** (half), **per annum** (yearly), **summa** (total) and **summa totalis** (often reduced to **sum' tot'** = total), **In primis** (first – in a list) and **Item** (likewise, also).

li   = pounds (𝓉𝒾,𝓉𝒿) the modern form is £
s   = shillings (ς , ∫)
d   = pence (∂-,∂)
ob   = a halfpenny (ob)
q̄u   = a farthing (q̄u)
dīa, dī   = a half (dīa, dī)
N.B.   lib   = a pound in weight (lib)

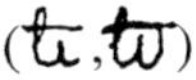

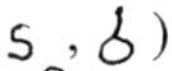

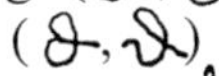

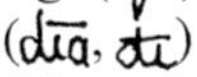

Forms of numbers: Roman numerals are still widely used in the sixteenth century, with some unfamiliar forms:

e.g. iij   = 3   (the final **i** of two or three is written as **j**)
        �   = 5
        ꝑ   = 10

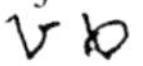

Beware of a double **xx** used in a superior position for counting in scores (20s):

e.g. iij^{xx} = 60

Miscellanea: Small, rather unimportant words frequently cause reading problems, e.g. the abbreviated forms **etc.** and **viz. Etc.** is abbreviated using these same letters, but in the letter-shapes of the contemporary style of writing, representing the Latin **et cetera** (and others). **Viz.** is an abbreviated form of **videlicet** (namely), which also transferred from Latin use to English, but the **z** is not a letter: it is an old abbreviation mark, rather like a **3** extending below the line (vi₃), which was used for **et** and has become misrepresented by the letter **z** in modern print.

Personal and place names in Wales: These seem unfamiliar in abbreviated form and, if written fully, in spelling, because of uncertainty over the written forms of older Welsh names and of those which contain combinations of consonants and special sounds. Two examples of written personal names from the sixteenth century are 'Ritheraghe' (Rhydderch) and 'Gwen Over' (Gwenhwyfar). Standard abbreviation marks are usually used for contracted personal names, but may be absent, e.g. the **bar** in **dd**(David or Dafydd), **Ein** (Einion), **Gm** (Gwilym), **llm** or **llen** (Llewelyn) and **lls** (apparently used for Llewelyn and Lewis), also **Ieu** (Ieuan/Ievan), where the capital letter is often followed by several unclear letters with a superior **a** and a **bar**. The **er** and **es** abbreviations are also used, as in **M$^{)}$edydd** (Meredydd) and **R$($**(Res/Rees).

Place names may also show specific abbreviation marks e.g. **Carm$^{)}$then** (Carmarthen) and **Caern$^{)}$von** (Caernarvon), which use the **er** mark more loosely for **ar**. More often, the final portion of the name is represented by one or more letters in raised position, as in **Lanf^{l}** (Llanfihangel) or **Lland^{ll}** (Llandysul); the not infrequent use of double **ll** – where a single **l** only is needed, as in Llandysul – can be rather confusing.

Special abbreviations used in Wales: In general, there is no difference in the use of abbreviations in writing in Wales but, for the **ch** sound in Welsh, it became common to use a very old letter which looks rather like $_3$, and was used in medieval English for a guttural **gh** sound (and called a yogh/yok). It is used in words like **co$_3$/go$_3$** (coch/goch) as a name element, also in abbreviations of **verch** (daughter), which may appear as **ver$_3$** , **v$^{)}_3$** , or **v$_3$**.

C. Letter-shapes and alphabets

Successful reading of old handwriting depends heavily on being able to recognise letter-shapes which may be very different from those in use today, and on appreciating which letter-shapes occur in which style of handwriting. Recognition is made more difficult by the fact that some may closely resemble modern letters, e.g. a popular Secretary **e** (see below) is circular in form, looking rather like an **o** with a small loop in the middle. Correct reading is crucial to proper interpretation, as in the description **miner** (occupational), as opposed to **minor** (under-age)!

Secretary Hand letter-shapes, both lower case and capitals, pose by far the greatest problems, especially the unfamiliar 'straight' **c**, the careless **h**, and the 'twin-stemmed' **r** which has loops at the lower corners (see the alphabet below, with modern letters on the left). Italic-based writing is much more familiar, apart from some flourished capitals and the persistence of long **s**, especially in the middle of words and in double **ss**, where the first may be long and the second short. Identifying Secretary letter-shapes is just as important in reading a mixed Secretary/Italic style as it is in purer Secretary Hand, because of the need to recognise them in unexpected places.

As mentioned earlier, a style of writing is identified by a combination of overall appearance and letter-shapes. Mixtures are identified in the same way. To illustrate this, the following versions of one place name, Llantilio Pertholey, Abergavenny, are given below in three styles, all of which may

may be encountered in the seventeenth century: (a) medieval 'Court Hand', (b) Secretary Hand and (c) Italic/Copperplate.

a)   *Llantilio Pertholey Abergavenny*

b)   *Llantilio Pertholey Abergavenny*

c)   *Llantillio pertholey Bergavenny*

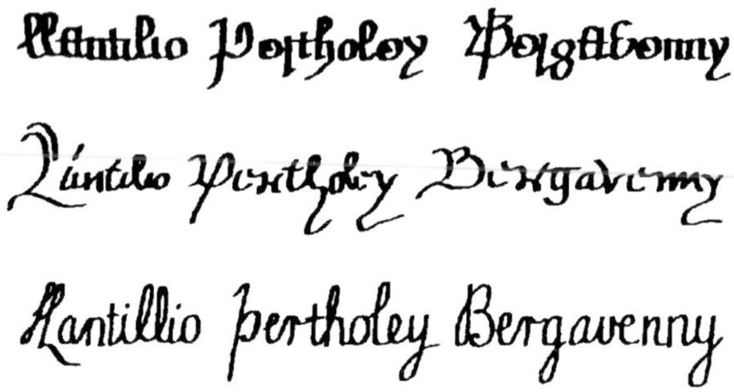

Fig. 8-1: Llantilio Pertholey, Abergavenny

Note the very different forms of **a**, **g**, and **r**, which are often used as one of the factors in distinguishing between styles (a) and (b). The first two are contemporary examples, dating from c1600, while (c) dates from *c*.1700.

APPENDIX A
Secretary Hand: some capital letter forms

A		**N**	
B		**O**	
C		**P**	
D		**Q**	
E		**R**	
F		**S**	
G		**T**	
H		**U**	
I		**V**	
J		**W**	
K		**X**	
L		**Y**	
M		**Z**	

APPENDIX B

Secretary Hand: lower case letters, 15th – 17th centuries

In the case of **a, c, d, e, h, p** *and* **r,** *the third and any fourth*
examples represent the common forms of these letters from
the mid-16th century

a	a tt lu
b	b bb = lb or $\mathscr{B}$
c	τ Υ $\acute{\tau}$
d	δ ∂ ∂ or $\sim\!\!\mathscr{J}$ at the beginning of words
e	Θ c^a $\acute{c}$ (or a Greek $\in$)
f	$\wp$ f
g	g $\mathcal{Y}$ g
h	b $\mathcal{h}$ $\int$ $\int$ beware th- $^{t\!\wp}\{$ or $\{$
i and j	not often dotted. These two letters are interchangeable, depending on their position in the word (usually **j** at the beginning and **i** in the middle).
k	$\mathcal{R}$
l	ℓ ll = $\mathscr{X}$
m	$\mathcal{M}$ or $\mathcal{N}$ which is partly angular and partly rounded
n	$\mathcal{N}$ rather angular, can be mistaken for **u**
o	beware the double **oo** which looks like ∞
p	$\wp$ $\wp$ $\mathcal{P}$ $\mathcal{P}$

APPENDIX B (CONTINUED)
Secretary Hand: lower case letters, 15th – 17th centuries

q   *q ꝗ ɋ*

r   *v u ʋ ʃ* or the secondary form, 2 or Z

s   *ſ ſ* at the beginning or middle of words, but ʓ or ƀ at the end (ʓ is early)

t   *ł t*

u and v   These two letters are used interchangeably, usually **v** at the beginning of words (*ᴜ ʋ*) and **u** in the middle (*ɯ*).

w   *ᴡ* or *ᴡɔ* which is partly angular and partly rounded

x   *ᴇ* beware of confusion with **p**

y   *ʏ ʏ* Note that the thorn has a straighter descender *Y*

z   *ʒ ʒ*

Note:

1.   ligatures with long s, e.g. *ſł* = **st**, *ſʃ* = **sc**, *ſʃ* = **sh**, *ſƀ* = **se**

2.   beware of diagonal crossing of double letters with looped ascenders, e.g. *ᴕ* = **ll**

3.   use alphabet for capital letters, remembering that **I** and **J** are the same, also **U** and **V**.

SELECT BIBLIOGRAPHY

Principal authorities on palaeography in England and Wales:

Denholm-Young, N., *Handwriting in England and Wales* (Cardiff, 1954).

Hector, L.C., *The Handwriting of English Documents* (2nd ed., London, 1966; and recent reprint).

Johnson, C. & Jenkinson, C.H., *English Court Hand 1066-1500,* 2 parts (Oxford, 1915).

Jenkinson, C.H., *The Later Court Hands in England, 15thC to 17thC,* 2 parts (Cambridge, 1927).

Parkes, M.B., *English Cursive Book Hands 1250-1500,* (Oxford, 1969; and later revision).

Petti, A.G., *English Literary Hands from Chaucer to Dryden* (London, 1977). Very good introduction on the development of handwriting in Britain.

Reference works *re* Latin, archaic English, abbreviations, dates, etc

Cheney, C.R., *Handbook of Dates for Students of English History* (Royal Hist. Soc., 1945 and later).

Fryde, E.B., Greenway, D.E. et al., *Handbook of British Chronology* (3rd ed., Royal Hist. Soc., 1986).

Gooder, E.A., *Latin for Local History* (2nd ed., Longmans, 1978).

Martin, C.T., *The Record Interpreter* (1892 and later, esp. Phillimore, 1982, with additional introduction).

Milward, R., *Glossary of Household, Farming and Trade Terms from Probate Inventories*, Derbyshire Record Society Occasional Paper no. 1, (3rd ed., 1986).

Morris, J., *Latin Glossary for Family and Local Historians* (FFHS, 1989).

Stuart, Denis, *Latin for Local and Family Historians* (Phillimore, 1995).

Webb, C., *Dates and Calendars for the Genealogist* (Society of Genealogists, 1989).

Also, the large *Oxford English Dictionary* is particularly helpful for archaic English words.

Useful reading aids, most containing transcribed facsimiles (those marked * are inexpensive)

Borthwick Wallets: a series of facsimiles of manuscripts (13th-17th centuries) with transcriptions and notes, published by the Borthwick Institute of Historical Research, University of York.*

Dawson, G.E. and Kennedy-Skipton, L., *Elizabethan Handwriting 1500-1650* (London, 1968).

Ison, Alf, *A Secretary Hand ABC Book* (Reading, 1982; reprinted 1996).*

Grieve, H.E.P., *Examples of English Handwriting 1150-1750*, Essex Record Office Publications, No. 21, 1954.*

Emmison, F.G., *How to Read Local Archives 1550-1700:* Historical Association-Pamphlet (first published 1967).*

Morgan, Gerald, 'Welsh names in Welsh wills', in *The Local Historian,* Vol. 25, No. 3 (August, 1955).

Munby, L., *Reading Tudor and Stuart Handwriting* (Phillimore, 1988).*

Newton, K.C., *Medieval Local Records: a reading aid:* Historical Association Pamphlet (first published 1971).*

Preston, J. F. & Yeandle, L., *English Handwriting 1400-1650* (New York, 1992).

Stuart, Denis, *Manorial Records* (Phillimore, 1992).

Wolpe, B. (ed.), *A Newe Booke of Copies 1574* (London, 1962). This is a writing master's manual, which is a very useful learning aid.

Background information on manuscript source material, collections & accumulations

Alcock, N., *Old Title Deeds* (Phillimore, 1986).

Bevan, A. (ed.), *Tracing Your Ancestors in the Public Record Office* (5th ed., PRO, 1999).

Emmison, F.G. & Grey, I., *County Records.* Hist. Assoc. (London, 1961).

Franklin, P., *Some Medieval Records for Local Historians* (FFHS, 1994).

Hey, D., *The Oxford Guide to Family History* (Oxford, 1993).

Iredale, D., *Enjoying Archives* (1973, and Phillimore, 1985).

Kitching, C.J., *Archives, the very Essence of our Heritage* (Phillimore, 1996).

Morton, A. & Donaldson, G., *British National Archives and the Local Historian.* Historical Association (1980).

Munby, L.M., *Short Guides to Records, First Series 1-24*, repr. and ed. K.M. Thompson. Historical Association (1994, 2nd series forthcoming).

Olney, R., *Manuscript Sources for British History: their nature, location and use.* IHR Guides no. 3 (1995).

Prescott, A., *English Historical Documents* (British Library, 1988).

Riden, P., *Record Sources for Local History* (Batsford, 1987).

Tate, W.E., *The Parish Chest* (3rd ed., Cambridge, 1969, repr. Phillimore, 1983).

West, John, *Village Records* (London, 1962, and Phillimore, 1982).

West, John, *Town Records* (Phillimore, 1983).

9. USING PETER BARTRUM'S *WELSH GENEALOGIES*

Michael Powell Siddons

The attachment of the Welsh to their pedigrees and the importance of pedigree in mediaeval Welsh law are well established.[*] Pedigrees were at first transmitted orally, and were only later committed to writing. Knowledge of pedigrees was part of the duties of the bards, and these sang the praises of their patrons' ancestors in verse, and collected the pedigrees of the leading families. Two bards, Gruffudd Hiraethog and Lewys Dwnn, were appointed deputy heralds for Wales by the English Kings of Arms in the sixteenth century, and visited all parts of Wales recording the pedigrees of the gentry. The traditional pedigrees were not constructed from record evidence, and indeed such evidence is not available for most of the older Welsh pedigrees, and where it does exist is patchy. In those cases where record evidence allows us to test the traditional pedigrees, they show a surprising degree of accuracy.[1]

Dr Peter Bartrum has compiled two monumental series of volumes of Welsh genealogies, the first presenting the pedigrees from the earliest accepted lines from about 300 A.D. down to about 1415,[2] and the second covering another 100 years, that is from the generation born around 1415 until that born about 1515.[3] For the sake of convenience these two series are commonly known as *WG 1* and *WG 2*, and the work as a whole as *WG*. The first series (*WG 1*), occupies approximately 950 pages of pedigrees and 940 pages of indexes, and the second (*WG 2*), covering only a further 100 years, is nearly twice as large, with 1775 pages of pedigrees and 1840 pages of indexes. They form the most complete and reliable collection of the traditional Welsh pedigrees which has ever been made, and it is difficult for anyone who studies any aspect of mediaeval Wales, whether history, literature or even the study of personal names, to avoid using them.

---

[*] This chapter is based on a talk given to the Second Stages Course, 'People, Places and Pedigrees', held in September 1996.

Earlier attempts have been made to compile comprehensive collections of pedigrees covering the whole of Wales. The earliest of these were the collections of Peter Ellis (d.1637) and Jacob Chaloner (d.1631), who were followed by Robert Vaughan of Hengwrt (1592?-1667), Griffith Hughes (*fl*.1634-65), deputy herald for North Wales, Owen Salesbury of Rûg and John Salesbury of Erbistock (compiled *c*.1630-77), David Edwardes (d.1690), deputy herald for South Wales, William Lewes (d.1722) and Hugh Thomas (1673-1720), another deputy herald. The last of these great compilations was the Golden Grove Book (*c*.1765), now in the Carmarthenshire Record Office at Carmarthen, which incorporated most of the work of David Edwardes and William Lewes, including large sections of David Edwardes's work without even changing the cross-references. Although these collections set out to cover all Wales, they were all more complete either for the families of north or for those of south Wales. The families were grouped together under the names of the patriarchs, or ancestor figures, from whom they claimed descent. Non-Welsh families which had migrated into Wales and settled there were grouped under the heading of *advenae*, or incomers. The compilers of all these collections made a strenuous effort to follow up the lesser branches of the families involved, and many obscure lines were included. The compilers all wrote in English except Robert Vaughan, who wrote in Welsh. The latter, Griffith Hughes and Peter Ellis wrote their pedigrees in semi-tabular form with marginal links to indicate descent. The others all wrote in drop-line pedigree form. They tried hard to give cross-references for marriages, except for Griffith Hughes who entered them only in a few cases.

In Bartrum's two large works the pedigrees are arranged in alphabetical order of the patriarchs from whom the families descended, with immigrant or *advenae* families, together with some border families which intermarried with Welsh families, placed under their surnames. In *WG 2* the genealogies are brought down to the generation born in the early 1500s, and many of the persons included lived until nearly 1600. This second series includes in addition many immigrant and border families not included in *WG 1*, and Welsh families which attained prominence later than the period of *WG 1*. Some pedigrees which do not form a group descending from a common ancestor are arranged under territorial groupings such as Blaen Iâl or Dinhengroen in *WG 1*, and Brycheiniog, Morgannwg or Tegeingl in *WG 2*.

Aim

It is important to bear in mind what was Dr Bartrum's aim when he set out to make his compilation of pedigrees. This is stated clearly on page 2 of the introduction to *WG 1*: 'The purpose of the present work is to reduce the [traditional] pedigrees into order as far as possible and to make the results available in convenient form.' Later on the same page he says: 'It is hoped that the tables will provide a reliable skeleton as a basis for further research.' He did not set out deliberately to include record evidence, but accepted it if it came his way. A general search of record evidence was, he said, beyond the scope of his study, 'and must be left to specialists in their various fields'.

It is likely therefore that persons concentrating their research on a particular family or a limited district will find additional elements in the pedigrees.

Method

1. To try to find for each generation sources as nearly as possible contemporary.
2. To find where mistakes had occurred owing to miscopying and misidentification.
3. To establish the most reliable texts.

If we consider how before the days of printing the pedigrees were copied from one manuscript to another, with mistakes and misreadings in one copy being themselves copied, with further mistakes and misreadings at each copying, it is easy to see how the texts became corrupt. Some of these miscopyings were due to misreadings of names. When the same name occurred twice in a pedigree, a careless copier might omit the words between them. In many families the generations alternated between two names, e.g. Rhys ap Dafydd ap Rhys ap Dafydd ap Rhys ap Dafydd and so on, and it was easy through carelessness to omit one Rhys ap Dafydd, or insert an extra one.

What Dr Bartrum did was to seek out all the earliest texts, and for the later generations the most nearly contemporary texts, since they would normally be the least corrupt. He edited the oldest texts in a series of studies in which he established the most reliable texts,[4] and made full copies of nearly all the major manuscripts written up to about 1580. This allowed him to compare the pedigrees as given in the different manuscripts, and to see where the text had become corrupted.

Since the sources are not all agreed as to the descent of certain lines, Dr Bartrum has in some cases found it necessary to indicate this uncertainty by giving more than one possible descent. Examples of this are to be found in *WG 1* on pp. **Bleddyn ap Maenyrch** 12 and 28, and in *WG 2* on pp. **Bredwarden** (B,C) and **Gwynfardd** 4(A).[5]

Bartrum has numbered the generations, allowing three male generations for 100 years, which has usually been found to be approximately satisfactory, the numbers indicating as far as possible the approximate date of birth.[6] By this means he was able to point out some gross discrepancies between the generation numbers of husband and wife. Because women married younger, many wives have a generation number higher than that of their husbands, but if, for example, a wife of generation 10 is found married to a husband of generation 12, this indicates the need for careful re-examination. There are, of course, cases where generations are longer or shorter, and there are authenticated examples, even in the early seventeenth century, of a father being born only sixteen or seventeen years before his son. It is therefore sometimes necessary to alter a generation number up or down. Discrepancies between generation numbers of husbands and wives are shown in the tables by putting the spouse's generation number in a square box, and discrepancies in numbering successive generations in a family by putting the younger generation's number in a circle. Examples of both these are seen in Fig. 9-1 (p. **Adam ab Ifor** 2).

The generation numbers are sometimes taken to be Dr Bartrum's firm opinion as to the date of each individual, whereas they are simply his guide to the successive generations of the members of a lineage, and especially in relation to the generation numbers of their spouses. Dates, where known from independent sources, should be used to confirm or correct generation numbers.

The first fifty-four pages of *WG 1* form a separate section containing the earliest pedigrees, with many ancient kings, heroes and saints, and uses an earlier generation numbering system. Since most of the traditional pedigrees are traced back to patriarchs or ancestor figures, the descendants of each patriarch are grouped together, and the pedigrees arranged in alphabetical order of patriarchs. In some cases an intermediate ancestor has been the chosen ancestor figure, Hywel Fain, for example, is himself usually considered to be descended from Elystan Glodrydd. Dr Bartrum informs me that this was in most cases because he had some doubt whether the traditional descent of the intermediate ancestor from the patriarch was really founded. Other cases in point are Trahaearn Goch of Llŷn and Cynfelyn ap Dolffin. The pages bear at the top right the name of the patriarch and a number, e.g. **Adam ab Ifor** 1 (see Fig. 9-2). This indicates that that page is page 1 of the section containing the descendants of Adam ab Ifor. Since there was not room for all these descendants on one page, the reader is referred to pages 2 and 3 for the others. The pages are also numbered consecutively throughout the volumes at the top of the page, but Dr Bartrum tells me that this was only done in order to make sure that the pages were bound in the correct order. When he wishes to refer to a page he gives the patriarch's name and number at the top of the page, e.g. **Adam ab Ifor** 2, and not vol.1, p.2. This method of numbering has the advantage of indicating at once with which 'tribe' one is dealing.

Since Dr Bartrum foresaw when compiling *WG 1* that in the future he or another might wish to continue the pedigrees, he placed a letter, A, B, C, etc, under the name of the last person in a line of descent which continued beyond the period covered by *WG 1*. This allowed him in *WG 2* to continue that line by using these letters, e.g. in *WG 1* on **Adam ab Ifor** 2 a letter A is placed under 12 Gwilym ap Hopkin ap Philip of Trefildu, and the letters B, C and D under others on that page with descendants, so that their descendants are to be found in *WG 2* on pages marked **Adam ab Ifor** 2. Those from A in *WG 1* are given on **Adam ab Ifor** 2(A), and since there was not room for the others on this page, they are to be found on the next page, **Adam ab Ifor** 2(B, C, D).[7] Since it was not always possible to put all the descendants of a particular line, e.g. from A on *WG 1*, **Cydifor ap Dinawal** 6, on to one page, it was sometimes necessary to have in *WG 2* several pages to accommodate them. In this case we thus have pages **Cydifor ap Dinawal** 6(A1), 6(A2) and 6(A3), where for certain lines the reader is referred from 6(A1) to 6(A2) and 6(A3). This numbering may appear rather complicated, but since the division between the series *WG 1* and *WG 2* is horizontal, i.e. by chronological period rather than by pedigree, it enables the reader to know at once where he should look when following a family from *WG 1* to *WG 2*. In this example a pedigree on p. **Cydifor ap Dinawal** 6 in *WG 1* is continued in *WG 2* on pages whose heading begins **Cydifor ap Dinawal** 6.

Dr Bartrum did not foresee a further continuation after *WG 2*, but gave references, under the last generation named, to sources where the reader could find continuations of many of the pedigrees.

The pedigrees are presented in drop-line form, with the marriages indicated where possible, and also the reference to the pedigree of the spouse, where known. Where the order of marriages is known, this is indicated by (1) =, (2) =, etc. Where the order is unknown, the marriages are marked (a) =, (b) =, etc. In the case of multiple marriages of the father, where the mother of a child is known this is indicated by the same figure or letter above his or her name. The descendants of the daughters are to be found under their husbands' pedigrees. Illegitimate unions are shown by double wavy lines ≈ and illegitimate descents by single wavy lines ~. Where no reference to a tribe is given for a spouse, it means that his or her family is unknown, or does not appear in *WG*. In order to save space the references to the pedigrees of spouses are abbreviated, and Bartrum has given a list of the abbreviations of the names of the patriarchs, families or area groupings which he has used.[8] The names of places where the family is recorded as having lived are indicated below each line. Where families had more than one residence, sometimes at a distance one from another, more than one place-name is given. Since nearly all of the period covered by *WG 1* and *WG 2* falls before the Acts of Union of England and Wales (1536-43), the mediaeval territorial units have been used.[9]

Indexes

Since very few Welsh families had surnames during the period covered by this work, the indexes of personal names are in patronymic form, except where there is an established surname. Many Welshmen had epithets or cognomens added to their name, such as Fychan, which led to the surname Vaughan, Llwyd, which gave Lloyd, and so on, and it is sometimes difficult to tell when an epithet has become a surname. The name is indexed under three generations, that is the subject, his father and grandfather, and the index is in alphabetical order of the first name and then the second and third names. Epithets and surnames are ignored in the order, so that John ap Roger ap Gwilym comes before John Llwyd ap Roger ap John. Some Welsh names have strictly Welsh and also anglicised spellings, e.g. Rhys and Rees, Hywel and Howell. In different sources the same person may have his name spelt in more than one way. Since indexing varying spellings of the same name would lead to confusion it has been necessary to standardise the spelling, and names have all been standardised in *WG* on the Welsh forms as found in the earlier manuscripts.

The generation number is given, e.g. 12 Dafydd ap Gwilym ap Jenkin, since this gives some indication of the date at which the subject lived. The index refers to the patriarch and page number where the subject's pedigree is given, e.g. **Adam ab Ifor** 2(C), and also gives references to the earliest sources in which the person concerned is cited. This is particularly valuable, since it allows the reader to see how nearly contemporary is the source concerned. The abbreviations used for the manuscripts and other sources to which reference is made are listed in the introduction of *WG 1*, pp.10-18 and additional sources in *WG 2*, p. iv. A reference beginning with the word 'see', for example 'see **Godwin** 7(B)', means that the name referred to, while occurring on the page indicated, is not that of a member of the family whose pedigree is given there, but is that of a spouse, or an ancestor of a spouse. It can also indicate a family whose pedigree is not given elsewhere in the collection, but which intermarried with the family whose pedigree is recorded on that page, e.g. the descendants of Jenkin ab Ila are indexed under 'see **Llywelyn Eurdorchog** 7(B)'. The indexes of personal names for

WG 1 cover all Wales, and are divided into men and women of different periods; in *WG 2*, which only covers about 100 years, they are divided by region of residence rather than by period. On each page of the pedigree tables is placed a letter indicating in which regional index the personal names occurring on that page are to be found. The areas covered by each index and the key to these letters is to be found in the introduction to *WG 2*, p. ii. There are also indexes of surnames and of place-names.

In the absence of surnames in Wales in earlier days, the importance of place-names cannot be over-emphasised. There may be many men called John ap Dafydd ap Hywel at a given time in a given district, or even in a given parish, but John ap Dafydd ap Hywel of Gilfach-wen is a much more identifiable person.

Additions and Corrections

In the nature of things such collections of pedigrees can never be final, since new sources are found, new identifications made, record evidence made available, and research on particular families or areas published. A series of 'Additions and Corrections' has therefore been published. These lists have now reached five for *WG 1*, and one for *WG 2*, and the total number of pages of additions and corrections has now reached 261 for *WG 1*, and 226 for *WG 2*, but Dr Bartrum has already collected material for further lists for both *WG 1* and *WG 2*.[10] In these additions and corrections the circles and squares used for discrepancy of generation numbers were omitted owing to the difficulty of using them with the word-processor.

A worrying fact is that few copies of *WG 1* and *WG 2* have been brought up to date by entering these additions and corrections, so that if reference is made to information contained in them a reader might look for it in vain in the copy to which he has access. In the manuscript room at the National Library of Wales all these supplements of additions and corrections have been placed in a box which is kept with the published series of *WG 1* and *WG 2*. It may be that in other libraries they have not been acquired, or else are not kept with the original volumes. In view of the many additions and corrections which have been published it is greatly to be hoped that a new edition of both works could be published, perhaps on CD-ROM, which would incorporate the new material while respecting the pagination of the original, so that published references would still be valid, although this would be a major undertaking. A microfiche edition was made of *WG 1* which incorporates the first list of additions and corrections.

The next step

The present writer has for a number of years been preparing a further collection of pedigrees (WG 3), continuing those which already appear in the previous series for a further century or so, thus bringing them down as far as persons born in the early part of the seventeenth century, and also, as was the case in *WG 2*, adding further families not covered in the earlier series. Although the pedigree tables of WG 3 are now fairly advanced in rough draft form, much work remains to be done before they can be made available, and final paging is not yet established, nor indexes compiled.

It is hoped that a reading of Dr Bartrum's introduction and of this chapter will help the reader new to the work to understand its nature and aim, and make it easier to become familiar with its use.

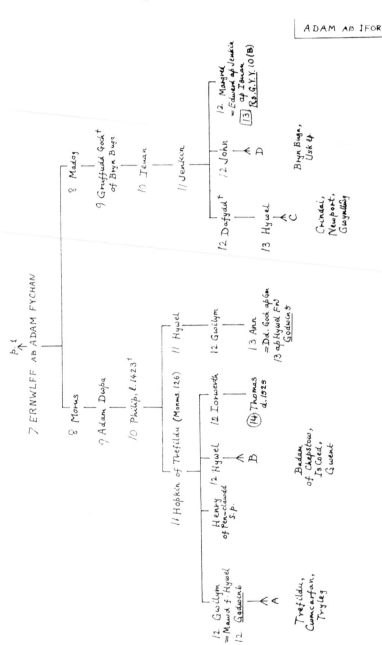

Fig. 9-1: *Welsh Genealogies (AD 300–1400)* – Adam ab Ifor 2

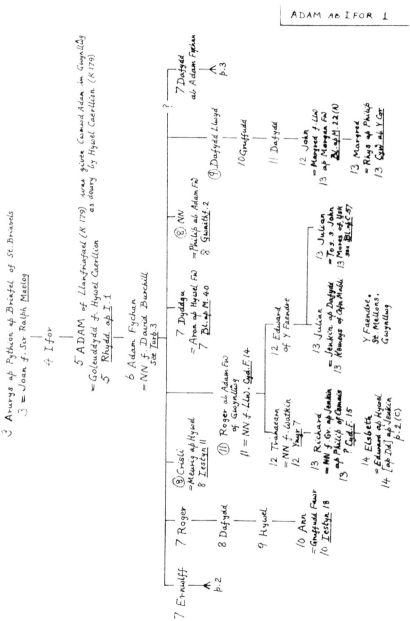

Fig. 9-2: Welsh Genealogies (AD 300–1400) – Adam ab Ifor 1

1

ADAM AB IFOR 2(A)

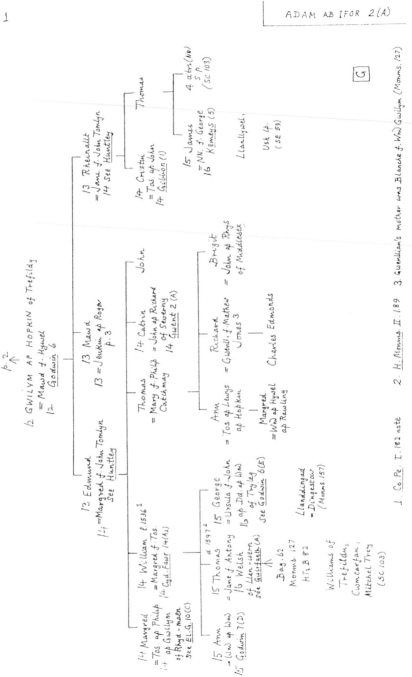

Fig. 9-3: *Welsh Genealogies (AD 1400-1500)* – Adam ab Ifor 2(A)

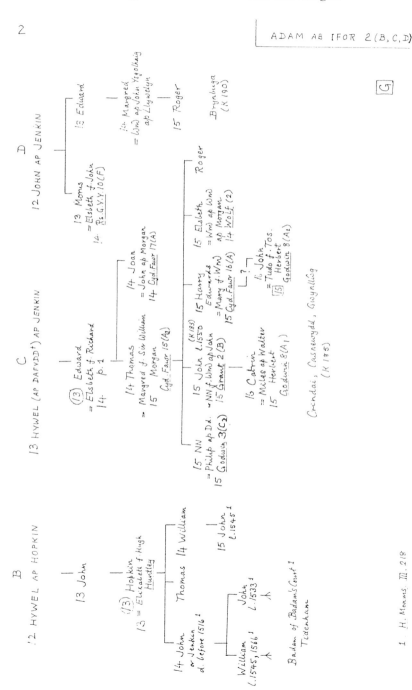

Fig. 9-4: *Welsh Genealogies (AD 1400-1500)* – Adam ab Ifor 2(B, C, D)

NOTES TO CHAPTER 9

[1] The background to this chapter is discussed by the present writer in 'Printed and Manuscript Pedigrees', in *Welsh Family History: A Guide to Research*, ed. John & Sheila Rowlands (2nd ed., 1998), 211-29; see especially 224-6.

[2] P.C. Bartrum, *Welsh Genealogies A.D. 300-1400* (8 vols, Cardiff, 1974, microfiche edition 1980).

[3] P.C. Bartrum, *Welsh Genealogies A.D. 1400-1500* (18 vols, Aberystwyth, 1983).

[4] *Early Welsh Genealogical Tracts* (Cardiff, 1966); 'Pedigrees of the Welsh Tribal Patriarchs', *NLWJ*, XIII (1963), 93-146, XV (1967), 157-66.

[5] The page numbering is explained later in this chapter.

[6] The dates indicated are listed on p. 6 of the introduction to *WG 1*.

[7] These pages are reproduced in Figs 9-2 to 9-4.

[8] On pages 20-4 of the introduction to *WG 1*. Abbreviations used for Christian names are listed on p.19.

[9] Melville Richards, *Welsh Administrative and Territorial Units* (Cardiff, 1969), will be found useful.

[10] List V for *WG 1* and List I for *WG 2* were published by the National Library of Wales in 1996.

10. SOURCES FOR SURNAME STUDIES

Sheila Rowlands

This is a brief, necessarily selective, and largely chronological survey of sources available, both manuscript and in print, for those researching the history of individual Welsh surnames.[*] Although it is well known that the majority of the surnames held by Welsh people are of patronymic origin and that relatively few such names are in use by a high proportion of the population, it is also true that there are many unusual patronymic names in use, as well as many long-settled surnames in (chiefly) the anglicised areas. There is no reason why those researching Welsh families should not share the universal fascination with surnames, though – as with all genealogical research – we must accept that the history of a name does not always throw light on the history of an individual family. For the latter, nothing can replace working systematically backwards, proving links all the way. With the less common Welsh names, however, there is always the possibility that an individual's research can throw light on surname studies generally.

This survey stops short of the nineteenth century. Anyone wishing to find the distribution of surnames in Wales in the later part of that century has an excellent tool in the transcribed and indexed 1881 census, widely available. The 1851 census has also received much attention from family history societies. There is a very full consideration elsewhere of all the surnames in use in Wales from 1813 to 1837, a key period for the settling of surnames and for using distribution-patterns to trace possible geographical origins,[1] and I do not propose to go over that ground but to concentrate on material available for earlier centuries. In doing so we shall be able to observe the developing history of Welsh personal names.

The Sources
The sources used for a study of surnames in Wales are not intrinsically different from those for anywhere else. One must begin with what is in print,

---

[*] This chapter is based on a talk given to the Second Stages Course, 'People, Places and Pedigrees', in September 1996.

whether it be books and articles on the subject or published transcripts of documents.

The *Bibliography of the History of Wales* is an excellent source for all that is in print, including useful lists of names, but is neglected by many family historians, keener to explore original documents. It is available on microfiche, so is relatively inexpensive, and should be found in larger libraries. The paperback guide to using the *Bibliography* requires initial study, but once one has found one's way round the system, the fiches themselves cover books and articles, such as those in local history journals, divided into chronological periods and subject-headings.[2]

For the period since the *Bibliography*, the *Welsh History Review* (twice-yearly) summarises new material in historical journals. It does not include articles in family history society journals but abstracts of many of these feature in the digest section of *Family History News and Digest*.

Family historians often neglect to check every newly discovered surname in the basic genealogical guides, found in good reference libraries, yet many names of Welsh origin are in these records of three-generation pedigrees.[3]

Thirteenth and Fourteenth Century Sources

If we turn to earlier centuries to seek evidence for the existence of names in an area, we are probably dependent on sources which have been transcribed and published – fortunately many have been, and the Bibliography to this chapter lists a range of these for several areas of Wales, together with the all-important category of works which provide details of their history and background.

Let us turn first to a late thirteenth-century document, the 1292-3 lay subsidy for Merioneth,[4] in which we are able to see the Welsh patronymic naming-system in full flow. (Women appear in such tax lists, but as their names rarely gave rise to future surnames, dwelling on examples from these categories is a luxury where space is short.) For the most part, names follow this pattern: Meurig ap Iorwerth, Eynon ap Cadwgan, Adaf ap Ednyfed.[5] A man was known, and placed in society, by his descent, so that long patronymic strings could be recited in, say, title deeds; for example: Owen ap Gwilym Duy ap Ievan ap Philip Scolayg.[6] However, official lists frequently confined themselves to two elements only, usually the name of son and father. Surnames as such did not exist except for incomers.

The 'profile' of forenames[7] is very Welsh: Blethin, Cynwrig, Ednyfed, Gronw, Gurgenau, Heilin, Ithel, Madog, Meilir, Rhirid, Tudur. These names gave rise in due course to fixed surnames, though by the time this occurred they had been overwhelmed numerically by the influx of Anglo-Norman forenames.

There are far fewer names of saints or of biblical characters than will be observed later, the major exception being David, already quite frequent. John, in the form of *Iohannes*, is found infrequently, Ieuan – a Welsh interpretation of *Iohannes* – rather more often. Pious forenames do appear, however: Wasdewi, Wasmihangel and Waspatrick, all eventually leading to rare (and now probably extinct) surnames, reflected devotion to the saints David, Michael and Patrick.

Another type of name in this list is forename plus adjective: Gronow Voyl, Ieuan Vachan, Iockyn Hen, Lewelin Duy, Madoc Gam, Meilir Goch, Philip Loyt.[8] Here the important name is the forename, with the second element intended to distinguish between people of the same name. At this time and place the epithet is not likely to be fixed or hereditary but, sooner or later, such words did become fixed, forming the second largest group of Welsh surnames.[9] As with comparable English surnames, less flattering epithets, such as *crach* ('scabby'), did not tend to survive, but some compound Welsh descriptive names in this list, such as *pengrych*,[10] came down at least to early modern times in other areas.

In this list we find early evidence of the use of Gwyn (usually as Wyn), 'white, fair', as a forename, though this usage became less common later, to be revived in the modern era.

Occupational names, though forming a significant element of English surnames, are not numerous in the list, but examples are to be found: David Saer (carpenter), David Crouthur (one who played the *crwth,* a musical instrument). Of the few names of this type listed, a good proportion are in Latin – *cantore, carpentario, fabro* (and *aurifabro*), *sutore* – and it is not clear whether such terms, or their Welsh equivalents, would have been used in common speech. Probably not, but among these are Adaf Medico, Eynon Medico and Ieuan Medico, and *meddyg* 'doctor', is found later in Wales as the surname Meddick. English influence on names of administrators is clear in the name of Candalo (Cynddelw) Cachepol.[11]

The final main category of name is forename plus location, another numerous class in England but rare in Wales. Tudor Glyne was from Glynllifon;[12] Iockyn Dolgen's home was in Dolgain, Trawsfynydd; Ieuan Pen[…]thkur is described in a note as being possibly of Pennaethgwr, Win Mautho as presumably from Mawddwy; David Trefas (but it is his wife who is listed) was of Trefaes.[13] They, and a very small number more with similar names, do not seem to have passed their bynames on in such a way as to contribute to the later pool of surnames and there are no examples of topographical names, the equivalent of Green, Hill, etc, in England.

I have dwelt on these names, and types of names, from an early period in an area which – though subject to English taxation – was fairly untouched by English social practice, in order to highlight the relative significance of the main categories of name. Most are patronymic, a further important category are descriptive, but few people thought it necessary to identify a person by either his work or his geographical origin – and this was to be the pattern throughout the long centuries when surnames were slowly adopted in Wales.

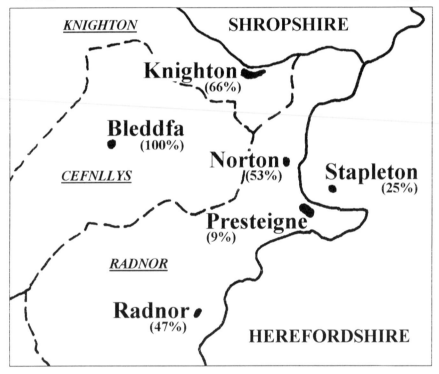

Fig. 10-1: Places on the Wales-England border with varying degrees of Welshness reflected in names

A Border Area

We shall move briefly, for contrast, to the same period in a distinctive area on the English border, Radnorshire, where the late thirteenth-century tax assessments are also readily available in published form.[14] Although the list contains many *ap* names, there is quite a high proportion of adjectival, occupational and locative names. Many of the latter categories are in Latin and once more it can be difficult to know how a person was really referred to. M.A. Faraday surmises, interestingly, that 'de Cimeterio' may equal Gravenor, a surname found in these parts in later times. Another later name, Bond or Bound, seems to be represented by Thomas le Bonde. Here also is an early appearance of a characteristic local name, Badland. It was borne by Nicolas de Badilond in 1293, and he may have owned or come from the small farmstead of that name near New Radnor.[15] M.A. Faraday's analysis of the names indicates the diminishing degree of Welshness (that is, fewer patronymic and Welsh adjectival names and more occupational and locative ones) as the border approached: he concludes that in 1293 Bleddfa was 100% Welsh, Knighton 66%, Norton 53%, Radnor 47%, Stapleton 25% and Presteigne 9% (see Fig. 10-1).

Thirteenth Century Administrators
Documents relating to the Lay Subsidy of 1292 exist for other part of Wales, including a schedule of taxors and jurors.[16] The men listed here are 'the more lawful and wealthier men' of the Marcher lordships, yet a great number of their names are purely Welsh and 'genealogical': that is, they are chiefly two-element patronymic names. The twelve jurors of Whitecastle (in the area which was to become Monmouthshire) are Robert ap Phelip, Seisild ap Adam, David ap Yeuan, David ap Cnaytho, Meirich ap Yeuan, Wilym ap Adam, Yuan ap Wasteylou,[17] David ap Seysil, Madoc ap Meirich, William Sely, Kenewriec ap Griffin, Maddoc ap Kneytho. Among these names can be seen traditional Welsh forenames: Cneitho, Cynwrig, Madoc, Meurig, Seisillt, Selyf, as well as the incoming Anglo-Norman names: Philip, Robert, William, etc, which were to take on greater importance in the time ahead.

    Although it is not appropriate to give extensive examples from this list, the striking thing is how many men entrusted with the supervision of the tax were clearly of Welsh origin. Nevertheless, in many areas, incomers are easily detected by their names, bearing the stamp of the English pattern. At Kidwelly,[18] for instance, among the patronymic names, are elements which are recognisable as surnames: Thomas Blaunchard, Martyn de Coldecote, John Coleman, Jordan Eliot, Adam Payn.

    In any given area in Wales such names were unlikely to survive, for their bearers might leave for other areas of occupation or, if they stayed and intermarried as so many did, might adopt the native naming-pattern. However, there is sufficient continuity in some places to state categorically that some of these names survived and became part of the pool of surnames. Recorded in Haverfordwest are men whose surnames were passed on, if not always to the present day, at least to early modern times: Geoffrey Brown,

John Robelyn, John Reynbaud, William de Buleton, Walter Alard. The same is true of Pembroke and Tenby men: William le Weyte, Philip Demeyt, William Reymond, William Wiseman.[19]

Although among the Welsh population patronymic names outnumber all others, a good few descriptive names are to be found: Llewelyn Bongam, Madoc Cam, Rhys Cethin, Griffith Hagar, Philip Hir, Ieuan Tew.[20] Those who found themselves addressed or recorded thus had a more distinctive name than the forename of their father was likely to be and it seems probable that such names became fixed earlier in border areas.

Thus we can observe that, by the late thirteenth century, in the marcher or border areas of Wales, there were already many indicators of the long-term influence of English administration and social practice.

Deeds and Documents

A generation later, much of the great area of the diocese of St David's was surveyed[21] and we have further evidence of the largely patronymic pattern in Welsh areas, with 'English' surnames for incomers in areas on the coast of southern Wales.

We must accept that, from the point when we have found a name in one of these lists, we should seek further examples in other documents for the area, in the hope of proving continuity. Searching large collections of deeds and documents, whether in local or national repositories, can never be as easy as searching published lists. However, schedules exist which commonly indicate the personal names to be found in the documents themselves, and many county record offices have indexes of such names.[22] The possibilities in such collections may span the period from mediaeval to modern times.

Fifteenth Century Personal Names

When we consider the distribution of modern Welsh surnames, we have reason to be grateful for the work carried out by P.C. Bartrum on the forenames in use in Wales in the fifteenth century.[23] The popularity of some names can be demonstrated as regional by this time and this may help to explain some aspects of regionality in settled surnames.

The most striking aspect of Dr Bartrum's tables is that Welsh forenames were fading whilst the 'new' Anglo-Norman names were growing in popularity: Edward formed 2% of names throughout Wales, Hugh 2%, Jenkin 2%, Robert 3%, Richard 3%, William 5%, Thomas 8%, with John (usually confined to religious before the Normans came) forming 12% and its variant Ieuan 8%. David, used before the Normans but boosted by their devotion to the patron saint's cause, is a special category but came close behind John at 11%. It is worth repeating that these names led to the common Welsh surnames Edwards, Hughes, Jenkins, Roberts, Richards, Williams, Thomas, Jones, Evans and Davies.

We cannot here study the regionality in the fifteenth century of all these forenames but a few may be taken as examples: Robert was a name of the north-west part of Wales, present but small in numbers in the south; Jenkin, 1% or less in all other areas, formed 4% in two large regions of south-west and south-east Wales; Thomas, though used in all regions and never falling below 3% anywhere, rises to 12% in Brycheiniog and Gwent in the south-east.

Of the 'traditional' Welsh forenames the most used were: Gruffudd 6%, Hywel 5%, Llywelyn 6%, Morgan 3%, Owain 2%, Rhys 5%. Modern derivatives are Griffiths, Howells, Llewelyn, Morgan, Owen and Rees, all substantial surnames in modern Wales.[24] Names such as Bleddyn, Caradog, Ednyfed, Einon, Gwion, Llywarch, Trahaearn, Tudor, etc, were used in the fifteenth century but normally in smallish traces in specific regions; surnames formed from such names as these are inevitably less common.

The point to be made is that modern Welsh surnames, by virtue of their patronymic nature, came from the pool of forenames in use as surnames were settling. The fifteenth century is too early to form firm conclusions yet, already by that time, some names had come to dominate the scene.

Sixteenth Century Border Surnames

Lists of names become more numerous by the sixteenth century and are increasingly useful in the study of surnames.[25] Montgomeryshire is particularly rich in such lists. In the case of the 1574 Muster,[26] one must note the strong preponderance of patronymic names even as late as this (well after Tudor ordinances to abandon the practice) in an area with many English influences. Some forenames of men and their fathers (with *ap*) are distinctive and gave rise to surnames typical of the area: Austin, Gervaise, Jeffrey, Lucas, Oliver, Piers, Reynold. Among names of this sort of purely Welsh origin are Cadwaladr, Einion, Gutyn, Lello, Meredith, Rhydderch, and Tudor; while Games, Lloyd and Vaughan are representatives of adjectival names, which are relatively few. What we do notice a large quantity of are names of mediaeval English origin: occupational – Benbow, Fletcher, Mason, Taylor, Turnor, Weaver; locative – Astley, Broughton, Habberley, Madeley, Mytton, Sambrook, Swancott.[27] These are not necessarily isolated examples, but often represent a handful of adult men, who must have been in the county some time. Murray Chapman has provided evidence for the positive settlement of Englishmen and their families in Montgomeryshire in this century, thus throwing light on the history of many such surnames.[28]

Seventeenth Century Lists

Perhaps the most significant aid to researching surnames in Wales in the seventeenth century is provided by the good number of Hearth Tax assessments and returns which have survived, especially as several are accessible in print.[29] The 1670 Hearth Tax for Glamorgan[30] allows one to observe differences in characteristics between upland and lowland parishes. Take, for example, upland Llangiwg (Llanguicke), with many three-element patronymic names such as Morgan William John, Richard ap John Richard, John Thomas Walter, as well as two-element ones which often retain *ap*: David ap David, Richard ap John and Leyson Richard.[31] The native naming-pattern clearly survived here at this date. Llangiwg and nearby parishes contain a sizeable number of people called Hopkin, whether as forename or father's name/surname, another example of the local popularity of a forename leading to a widespread but localised surname in the following century.

If we turn to another part of Glamorgan, the prosperous and more anglicised Vale, a quite different pattern emerges: for the most part, people have two names and *ap* rarely appears. In St George's parish, recognisable surnames are found in greater numbers – examples are Bassett, Gibbon and Wrench. Mault Lougher bears that unusual thing, a locative place-name.[32] In nearby St Brides super Ely there is an even rarer survival of the occupational Goyder.[33]

Although a few Pembrokeshire parishes are defective in the printed 1670 Hearth Tax,[34] the large number of names which have survived give an excellent picture of the surnames of the county in the later seventeenth century, and this is enhanced by the inclusion of the names of paupers (i.e. those exempt from tax). It would be extravagant to claim for it status as a quasi-census but it remains the earliest near-complete list of householders. Thus we can draw tentative conclusions about the antiquity, or otherwise, and continuity of 'local' names. Of names mentioned under 'Thirteenth Century Administrators' above, Boulton, Brown, Demet, Reymond, Reynbott, Roblin and White remain evident and such examples could be repeated many times. Most settled surnames like these tend to survive in the anglicised south of the county. When we look at the Welsh-speaking hundreds we find many late survivals of the patronymic system: Llanwnda parish has John Thomas Kethin, William ap William, and many people with common and typical Welsh names like Evan Griffith, Thomas Harry and Rice Lewis. Yet, in southern parishes we have long-settled names such as

Husband, Prout, Codd, Tasker, Tucker and Nash alongside less-common Welsh patronymic names, Gwyther, Knethell and Cadogan, rarely found by this time in the north. Regardless of this, a very high proportion of surnames in the southern hundreds are also traditionally Welsh: Williams, Thomas, John, Howells, etc, reflecting the mixed nature of the population.[35]

The good survival and relative completeness of hearth tax lists should not deter us from looking at other possibilities in the same century, many of which are covered in the very useful Gibson Guides.[36] Though other tax lists, muster rolls, etc, are inevitably less comprehensive in their coverage of the adult population, characteristic names are quite frequently found in them, often supporting conclusions derived from fuller lists. One large area of Wales, the diocese of St Asaph, is covered by *notitiae*, dating from the 1680s, listing heads of households by name (as well as giving other family details). This late seventeenth century quasi-census is an invaluable source for surnames.[37]

Eighteenth Century Lists

We move finally to a century which is notorious in Wales for lack of continuity in documents, making linear research difficult in many areas. Nevertheless, for the purposes of studying surnames, much exists, though this is perhaps where it needs to be emphasised that the International Genealogical Index (IGI) is of little or no value for those studying Welsh surnames in quantity, partly because of enormous gaps in the source-material and partly because there is inadequate provision for dealing with the complexities of patronymic names.

By this century, probate indexes provide extensive evidence for surnames, at least for that proportion of the population which had something to dispose of. Increasingly, Welsh probate indexes at the National Library of Wales have been computerised and the resulting printouts on open shelves reveal much information in convenient form.[38] A study of Llandaff Probate Index in the eighteenth century reinforces earlier indications of the late survival of names of patronymic origin in many parishes in Glamorgan and in western Monmouthshire. Names in this list for this century include: Arnold ab Arnold, David ab Evan, Thomas ap Hopkin, Rice ap Jenkin, Howel ab John, and there are numerous examples of *ab/ap* before such potential patronymic surnames as Griffith, Harry, James, Llewelyn, Meredith, Morgan, Robert, Watkin, etc.

Land Tax assessments provide long lists of names which, though often difficult to search because of their arrangement by hundred, provide valuable evidence of where names were, especially after 1780.[39] Records of the land tax, used to establish voting rights, continued to be well kept until

1832, so that the later information on surnames is replicated in the 1813-1837 marriage registers which have been studied.[40]

After this we are moving towards the great nineteenth-century sources, including civil registration and the census, where most researchers are equal.

BIBLIOGRAPHY

Periodicals

Family History News and Digest, the official journal of the Federation of Family History Societies (FFHS), published twice-yearly in April and September. FFHS, The Benson Room, Birmingham & Midland Institute, Birmingham B3 3BS.

The Welsh History Review/Cylchgrawn Hanes Cymru published twice-yearly by the University of Wales Press, 6 Gwennyth Street, Cathays, Cardiff CF2 4YD.

Standard Genealogical Sources

Barrow, G.B., *The Genealogists' Guide: An index to printed British pedigrees and family histories, 1950-1975* (1977).

Marshall, G.W., *The Genealogists' Guide*, 4th ed. (Baltimore 1967).

Whitmore, J.B., *A Genealogical Guide: An index to British pedigrees*, (1953).

Bibliographies, Background and Location

Jones, P.H., *A Bibliography of the History of Wales*, microfiche (1989). E.g. 1EH46, miscellaneous lists of names; 1EH62, individual families.

County-based histories and periodicals, etc. See Bibliography in J. & S. Rowlands (ed.) *Welsh Family History: A Guide to Research (WFH)*, (2nd edition, 1998).

Franklin, P., *Some Medieval Records for Family Historians* (FFHS, 1994). Background to records in print.

Gibson, J., *The Hearth Tax and other later Stuart Tax Lists and the Association Oath Rolls* (FFHS, 2nd ed., 1996). Gibson Guides are the best indication of what survives in each county, plus location; each has a guide to background.

— *Quarter Sessions Records for Family Historians* (FFHS, 4th ed., 1995).

Gibson J. & Dell, A., *Tudor and Stuart Muster Rolls* (FFHS, 1991).

— *The Protestation Returns 1641-42 and other contemporary listings* (FFHS, 1995).

Gibson J. & Medlycott, M., *Local Census Listings 1522-1930* (FFHS, 3rd ed., 1997).

Gibson J., Medlycott, M. & Mills, D., *Land and Window Tax Assessments* (FFHS, 2nd ed., 1998).

Rogers, C.D., *The Surname Detective* (Manchester University Press, 1995). Although it covers England only, it provides inspiration for possibilities in Wales.

West, J., *Village Records* (Phillimore, 1982) and *Town Records* (Phillimore, 1983) have useful bibliographies and lists of published records, including some Welsh references.

Select Primary and Secondary Sources

The following list is of sources referred to in the talk on which this chapter is based, not all of which could be accommodated here.

Bartrum, P.C., 'Personal Names in Wales in the Fifteenth Century', *National Library of Wales Journal* (1965-6).

Benwell, R.M. & G.A., 'Interpreting the Census Returns for Rural Anglesey and Llŷn', *Transactions of the Anglesey Antiquarian Society* (1973).

Charles, B.G., *Calendar of the Records of the Borough of Haverfordwest 1539-1660* (1967).

Davies, J.H., 'Cardiganshire Freeholders in 1760', *West Wales Historical Records* iii (1913).

Faraday, M.A., 'The Assessment for the Fifteenth of 1293 on Radnor and other Marcher Lordships', *Radnorshire Society Transactions* (1973).

Green, F., 'Pembrokeshire Hearths in 1670', *West Wales Historical Records,* ix-xi (1923-5).

Griffiths, J., 'Documents relating to the early history of Conway', *Trans. of the Caernarvonshire Historical Society,* 8, (1947), pp. 5-9.

Henson, N., *Bangor Probate Records, Vol. 1: Pre-1700* (NLW, 1980).

Jones, D.H., 'The Freeholders of Neath Hundred 1634', *Trans. of Neath Antiquarian Society,* 6 (1936-6). (Abstracted from T. Maber, below.)

Jones, F., (ed.), 'The Subsidy of 1292', *Bulletin of the Board of Celtic Studies,* XIII (1948-50). Schedule of jurors and assessors appointed for South Wales and the marches, 1291.

Jones, N.C., *Archdeaconry of Brecon Probate Records, Vol. 1: Pre-1660* (NLW, 1989).

Maber, T., *The Names of all the Freeholders in Every Parish in the Ten Hundreds of the County of Glamorgan in the Year that Watkin Lougher was High Sheriff 1634* (Neath, 1949).

Matthews, A.W. (ed.), 'Carmarthenshire Taxation 1560-1. Eastern District', *Trans. Carmarthenshire Antiquarian Society,* 7, 1911-12. (Transcript of Lay Subsidy Roll, PRO 220/108.)

— 'Carmarthenshire Accounts of Poll Tax for 1689-90', *Trans. Carmarthenshire Antiquarian Society,* 6, 1910-11. Transcript of Carmarthenshire Subsidy Roll.

Morgan, R. (ed.), 'A Powys Lay Subsidy Roll', *Montgomeryshire Collections*, 71 (1983).

'Muster of Montgomeryshire Men, Horses, etc, made in 1574', *Montgomeryshire Collections*, 22, (1888).

Nicholas, T., *Annals and Antiquities of the Counties and County Families of Wales* (1872, repr. Baltimore, 1991).

NLW: *Guide to the Department of Manuscripts and Records* (Aberystwyth, 1994).

NLW: Probate Indexes, arranged by diocese.

NLW/SA/Misc/1300-1490. Parochial Notitiae, Diocese of St Asaph, *Montgomeryshire Collections*, 55-74 (1957-86). See Gibson & Medlycott (1997) for fuller details of parish/date.

Owen, D. Huw, 'The Englishry of Denbigh: An English Colony in Medieval Wales', *Trans. of the Hon. Society of Cymmrodorion (THSC)*, (1975).

Owen, H., 'Pembrokeshire Lay Subsidies 1543', *West Wales Historical Records* iv, 169-174 (1914).

Owen, H. (ed.), *A Calendar of the Public Records Relating to Pembrokeshire*, 3 vols. (1918).

Parkinson, E. (ed.), *The Glamorgan Hearth Tax Assessment of 1670* (South Wales Record Society, 1994).

Pierce, T. Jones & Griffiths, J., 'Documents relating to the early history of the Borough of Caernarvon', *BBCS*, ix, 236-46 (1937-8).

'Powis 21901 – NLW', *Montgomeryshire Collections*, 72 (1984). Assessment for a loan.

Taylor, A.J., 'The Earliest Burgesses of Flint and Rhuddlan', *Flintshire Historical Society Trans.*, 27-29 (1975-80).

Williams, D.E., 'A Short Enquiry into the Surnames in Glamorgan from the Thirteenth to the Eighteenth Centuries', *THSC*, (1962).

Williams-Jones, K. (ed.), *The Merioneth Lay Subsidy Roll* (UW Press, 1976).

Willis-Bund, J.W. (ed.), *The Black Book of St David's*, Cymmrodorion Record Series, 5, (1902).

NOTES TO CHAPTER 10

[1] John and Sheila Rowlands, *The Surnames of Wales* (Federation of Family History Societies, 1996). This has an extensive bibliography on the subject. See also Chapter 11 in the present work.

[2] See the Bibliography to this chapter for details of the printed sources in this section.

[3] Marshall (1967), Whitmore (1953), Barrow (1977).

[4] PRO E 179/242/53, published in Williams-Jones (1976); the introduction to the latter explains the background to the tax.

[5] *Ap* means 'son of'. It is the lenited form of *map*, *mab*, 'son', cognate with the Gaelic *mac*. *Ap* is supposed to become *ab* before a vowel, but there is often inconsistency in lists of names.

[6] F. Jones 'An approach to Welsh Genealogy', *Transactions of the Honourable Society of Cymmrodorion 1948* (London, 1949), pp. 346-7, gives several similar examples for the fourteenth and fifteenth centuries.

[7] It is best to use the neutral term 'forename', since many traditional Welsh names were of Celtic origin and should not strictly be called Christian names.

[8] Voyl = *foel* 'bald', Vachan = *fychan* 'smaller', *hen* 'old', duy = *du* 'dark' (as in hair or complexion), *gam* 'lame', *goch* 'red', Loyt (Lloyd) = *llwyd* 'grey'.

[9] Extensive lists of adjectival names are given in Morgan and Morgan (1985) and Rowlands and Rowlands (1996).

[10] 'Pengrek' is annotated as if it refers to Pencraig, a place-name, but is *pengrych* 'curly-headed'.

[11] Catchpole = bailiff and became an English surname.

[12] Prys Morgan, 'The Place-name as Surname in Wales', *NLWJ*, XXIX, 1 (1995).

[13] See Williams-Jones (1976).

[14] M.A. Faraday (1973).

[15] Michael Faraday, 'Badland, the Story of a Radnorshire Surname', *Cronicl*, 9, 1984 (Journal of Powys Family History Society).

[16] PRO E 179/242/48, published in Francis Jones (1948-50).

[17] Yuan (a variant of Ieuan) was son of Gwasteilo, a devotional name meaning 'servant of [St] Teilo'.

[18] In modern Carmarthenshire.

[19] In modern Pembrokeshire.

[20] *Bongam*, 'bandy-legged'; *cam* 'crooked', became Games; *cethin* 'swarthy', etc; *hagar* 'ugly', became Haggar; *hir* 'tall', became Hier; *tew* 'fat'.

[21] Willis-Bund (1902). Although doubts have been cast on the fourteenth-century date, surname evidence supports this.

[22] See NLW *Guide to the Department of Manuscripts and Records*, for available schedules at NLW; also individual county record office publications.

[23] Bartrum (1965-6). Although the names in the study are taken from families in mediaeval pedigrees, a large number of small freeholders claimed descent from such families in later centuries; in any case, forenames in use in better-off families have always influenced the general population.

[24] For comparison, the figures for Wales 1813-37 are: Griffiths 2.58%, Howells 0.62%, Llewelyn 0.37%, Morgan 2.63%, Owen 2.08% and Rees 1.83%.

[25] For example, Gibson & Dell (1991, 1995) list many such rolls for Welsh counties at the PRO, NLW and British Library.

[26] 'Muster of Montgomeryshire Men, Horses, etc, made in 1574', *Montgomeryshire Collections*, 22 (1888) [State Papers Domestic, Eliz 1574].

[27] From a place in neighbouring Shropshire.

[28] Murray Ll. Chapman, 'The Records of the Courts of Great Sessions for Wales', Chapter 17 in *WFH*; and Chapter 12 in the present work. Having the advantage of seeing the latter before publication, I have been able to minimise my own coverage of this period.

[29] Gibson (1996) provides details of manuscript and printed copies, where they have survived, county by county.

[30] Parkinson (1994).

[31] Leyson is an example of a Welsh forename (Lleision) which gave rise to a characteristic Glamorgan surname.

[32] Lougher: locative surname from Llwchwr/Loughor, village and river (latter forming boundary between Carmarthenshire and Glamorgan).

[33] Goyder: occupational from *coedwr* 'woodman', does not seem to have flourished outside Glamorgan and became very rare by the early nineteenth century.

[34] *West Wales Historical Records*, ix-xi.

[35] See *WFH*, p. 70.

[36] Gibson & Dell (1991, 1995).

[37] Gibson & Medlycott (1997).

[38] N. Henson (1980) and N.C. Jones (1989) are published indexes for an earlier period which repay study, though space has not permitted them to be covered here.

[39] Gibson, Medlycott & Mills (1998).

[40] Discussed in Rowlands and Rowlands (1996).

11. THE HOMES OF SURNAMES IN WALES

John Rowlands

No matter where a person's family history interests lie – be it in Wales, in England, or elsewhere – they cannot avoid an involvement with surnames.* They are, after all, the oral and written markers whereby people are identified, both in real life and in the multitude of documents which family historians use in their researches.

However, the perception of surnames in Wales is that virtually the whole of the population of the Principality is called Jones, Davies, Williams, Thomas or Evans in a blanket sort of way. Anyone holding that belief – usually as a result of hearing, or reading, one of the many joking references to Wales being 'the land of the Joneses' – might be excused for reaching the conclusion that the pursuit of Welsh ancestry must, as a result, be an impossible task. In fact it is a wholly wrong conclusion. Unfortunately, however, the thinking which lies behind it has been given a measure of official support as when, in 1856, the then Registrar General, George Graham, observed that:

> The name John Jones is a perpetual incognito in Wales, and being proclaimed at the cross of a market town would indicate no one in particular.[1]

As a result of a comprehensive survey of the occurrence and incidence of surnames across Wales during the period 1813-37, it is possible to consider whether this statement does indeed hold true not only for the surname Jones, but also for all the other surnames which are particularly common in Wales.[2] From this we find that there is, in fact, a considerable variation across Wales in the incidence of even the most common of surnames.

In the case of the surname Jones we find (see Fig. 11-2) that, whereas more than 30% of the population have held that surname in the area around Bala in Merionethshire (Penllyn Hundred), barely 1% have done so in the area around St David's in Pembrokeshire (Dewisland Hundred). As a result,

---

* This chapter is based on a talk to the Second Stages Course, 'People, Places and Pedigrees', in September 1996.

the effect of the name John Jones being proclaimed at the market cross of those two places would be dramatically different. This single example clearly illustrates that there is a far greater variation in the incidence by location of individual surnames within Wales than is commonly supposed. As a result, those who turn away from their Welsh lines because of a perceived problem with surnames are doing so quite unnecessarily and are, therefore, missing out on a part of their background which need not be a closed book.

Surnames in Wales and England: Some Comparisons

I have referred above to 'common surnames in Wales'; but what is meant by 'common', and how does the incidence of these surnames in Wales compare with surnames such as Smith or Brown in England? Fortunately, by combining the information contained in the Report of the Registrar General published in 1856 (in which he gives details of the incidence of the fifty most common surnames in England and Wales combined) and that derived from the survey referred to above, it is possible to derive separate listings for each country, and hence to draw some broad comparisons.

A list of the ten most common names in each country is given in Fig. 11-1 and clearly shows that 'common' in a Welsh context covers a dramatically greater proportion of the population than is the case for England.

	WALES		ENGLAND	
	Surname	%	Surname	%
1.	Jones	13.84	Smith	1.37
2.	Williams	8.91	Taylor	0.68
3.	Davies	7.09	Brown	0.57
4.	Thomas	5.70	Jones	0.43
5.	Evans	5.46	Johnson	0.38
6.	Roberts	3.69	Robinson	0.36
7.	Hughes	2.98	Wilson	0.36
8.	Lewis	2.97	Wright	0.34
9.	Morgan	2.63	Wood	0.33
10.	Griffiths	2.58	Hall	0.33
	Total	**55.85**	**Total**	**5.15**

Fig. 11-1: Comparison of the 10 most common names in Wales and England

However, these figures for all-Wales, high as they are, mask an even more dramatic picture which can exist at the local level. For example, in our survey we found that the ten most common names in the Uwchgwyrfai area

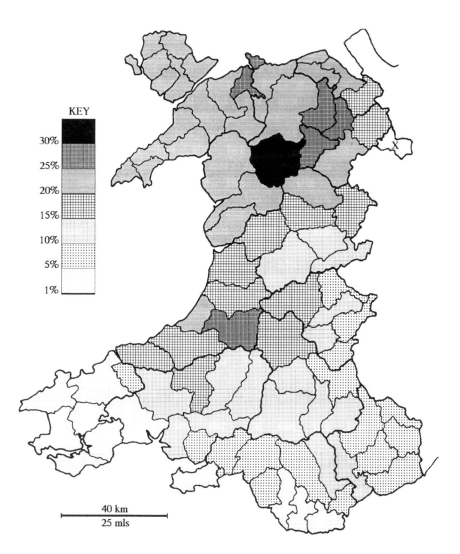

KEY

30%
25%
20%
15%
10%
5%
1%

40 km
25 mls

Fig. 11-2: Distribution and incidence of the surname Jones

of Caernarfonshire covered more than 90% of the population. Those names (in the early part of the nineteenth century) were:

Jones (22.87%), Williams (18.40%), Roberts (13.28%), Hughes (7.78%), Griffiths (7.39%), Thomas (5.37%), Owen (4.86%), Evans (4.17%), Pritchard (3.65%) and Parry (2.92%).

It can be seen that, not only are the percentages for each of these names very high, but also three of them – Owen, Pritchard and Parry – do not appear in the all-Wales list. This, together with the information about the surname Jones given in Fig. 11-2, gives a firm indication that different areas of Wales have different levels and mixes of surname, and this is the theme which forms the basis for this chapter.

Types of Surnames: Further Comparisons

Another area in which comparisons may be made relates to the different types of name which exist in England and Wales.

It is generally accepted that surnames may be subdivided into four main groups; namely those derived from personal names, locational names (place-names and topographical features), occupations and from descriptions (physical descriptions and nicknames). It can be seen in Fig. 11-1 that all the surnames included in the list for Wales are derived from personal names alone, while the list for England contains surnames from each of the four groups: personal names (Jones, Johnson, Robinson, Wilson), locational names (Hall, Wood), occupations (Smith, Taylor, Wright) as well as a descriptive name (Brown).

These lists are, however, very short. If we extend them to cover the thirty-five most common names in each country we find that Wales still remains firmly wedded solely to surnames derived from personal names, and the proportion of the population covered by these names rises to 80.64%. That extended list (of thirty-five) for Wales is (in descending order of incidence):

Jones, Williams, Davies, Thomas, Evans, Roberts, Hughes, Lewis, Morgan, Griffiths, Owen, Edwards, Rees, James, Jenkins, Price, Morris, Richards, Lloyd, Phillips, Parry, David, Harris, John, Powell, Pritchard, Howells, Watkins, Rowlands, Bowen, Humphreys, Ellis, Pugh, Llewelyn, and Hopkins.

In comparison there is an increase in the number of surnames in each of these groups in the extended list for England and the proportion covered rises to 11.71%. However, the list for England does not include any surname (at this level of incidence) which have been derived from place-names – such as Chester, Shrewsbury, Bristow, etc.

The extended list for England (by group and descending order within each group) is:

Personal names: Jones, Johnson, Robinson, Wilson, Thompson, Williams, Jackson, Harrison, Davis, Martin, Harris, Allen, Watson, Edwards and Roberts. (Total: 4.28% of population)

Locational names: Wood, Hall, Green, Hill, Moore, Shaw and Lee. (1.86%)

Occupations: Smith, Taylor, Clark(e), Wright, Walker, Turner, Cooper, Ward, Baker, Parker. (4.46%)

Descriptive names: Brown, White. King (1.11%)

Why such differences?

It is not the intention to discuss in detail here the processes whereby two such radically different surname patterns should have developed in close geographical proximity to one another, as it has been more than adequately discussed elsewhere.[3] However, it is worth refreshing our memories on the main influences which have brought this about as it not only helps to explain the differences between the two countries but also the variations within Wales.

In England surnames were taken progressively between the twelfth and fifteenth centuries in response to the needs of growing towns and increasing bureaucracy. Generally it came about earlier in southern England than in the north, and it did so in societies which found no difficulty in taking names from a wide range of common sources. Today the survival of more than 30,000 surnames in England bears testimony to just how varied those sources could be.

In Wales surnames only started to be taken on any scale in the sixteenth century, a full hundred years after they had become the norm in England. Prior to the sixteenth century the traditional naming system in Wales involved a person having a given name and attaching to it the given name of (normally) the father and, if necessary, the given names of as many earlier generations as would uniquely identify the bearer within their particular community. With the Acts of Union (1536-43), the people of Wales became fully subject to English law and administration for the first time. They also became subject to pressures to conform to English practices regarding surnames.

However, things did not change overnight, nor did they change in an even way across Wales. Instead surnames were adopted earlier by the gentry than the ordinary people, earlier in those areas subject to greatest English influence, and earlier in the richer lowlands than the poorer, more isolated upland areas. The process of transition took place over an extended period and it was not until the mid-nineteenth century that the patronymic system could be said to have been fully replaced.

Now, any system which had given names at its core – as was the case with the patronymic system – inevitably used given names as the basis for its settled surnames. As the pool of given names in use was small (compared to the many which could be derived from locations, occupations or descriptions), the resultant pool of surnames in Wales was, inevitably, equally small. When we take into account variations in the popularity of individual given names by place, over time, and within the different levels of Welsh society, it is easy to see that the surnames which stemmed from them did not exist across Wales in a even sort of way as is commonly supposed.

Further Influences
In addition, however, other powerful influences were also at play and these helped to bring further variety to the surname scene in Wales. Chief amongst those influences were;

- the existence of the word *ap* (meaning 'son of') in the traditional patronymic system and its subsequent incorporation (for a period) into settled surnames
- the dropping of the use of *ap* and its consequent absence from those surnames which became settled after this had happened (again for a period)
- a final period which saw the addition of a final possessive 's' to many surnames which had previously been without them, as well as for those surnames which were being newly taken
- the preference for using Old Testament given names within the older nonconformist denominations (most notably the Baptists and the Independents)
- the survival of certain adjectival and old Welsh names in some clearly defined areas, and
- the steady migration of people into Wales from areas with different surname structures and traditions such as England, Scotland and Ireland. This steady migration was to become a flood by the mid-nineteenth century.

Surnames incorporating *Ap*: The use of the word *ap* was originally an integral part of the patronymic naming system and, hence, gave rise to a person being known as Thomas *ap* Howell (Thomas the son of Howell). In those areas in which the change to settled surnames took place while this was still in use – generally to about the middle of the seventeenth century – the *ap* element often became incorporated into the new surname; thus

Thomas *ap* Howell would become Thomas Powell and Thomas *ab* Owen would become Thomas Bowen (reflecting that *ap* normally becomes *ab* before a vowel).

Most of the surnames which fall into this category (and in our survey we found thirteen of them) are to be found in those areas which had been subject to greatest and earliest English influence.[4] As one would expect (see Fig. 11-3), there is a concentration of these surnames on the English border and along the coastal belt of South Wales extending into Pembrokeshire. Interestingly, a small number have a strong localised presence in the heartland of Wales, as is the case with Pugh in Merionethshire, Pritchard in both Anglesey and Caernarfonshire, and Parry across much of North Wales.

The dropping of *Ap*: In time the use of *ap* (or *ab*) was dropped despite the continued use of the patronymic system. When eventually settled surnames were taken in areas in which this had already happened, we find that our Thomas *ap* Howell and Thomas *ab* Owen (above) have become just plain Thomas Howell and Thomas Owen. This could well have been a feature of surname development in those areas during the seventeenth and early eighteenth centuries.

Of particular interest, however, is the effect this had on those holding the patronymic names David or John. In those areas in which surnames became fixed relatively soon after the dropping of the *ap* prefix this resulted in the survival as surnames of David and not Davies, John and not Jones as would be the case later on. Thus we have a high incidence of both David and John as surnames in south Glamorgan (often well in excess of 5%), in south Carmarthenshire (sometimes exceeding 5%), and in the northern part of Pembrokeshire (often approaching 5%).

In all these areas the surnames Davies and Jones have, as one might expect, a relatively low incidence. The fact that the surname John has an incidence of 4.60% in the St David's area of Pembrokeshire goes a long way to explain the relative absence (referred to earlier) of the surname Jones in that area.

Adoption of the possessive 's': In time, however, a further change took place and many surnames derived from a given name such as Howell and Jenkin either took the form Howells or Jenkins immediately or acquired the final possessive 's' after a short period. Perhaps this reflects a continuing tendency to associate a man with his father long after the patronymic system had been abandoned.

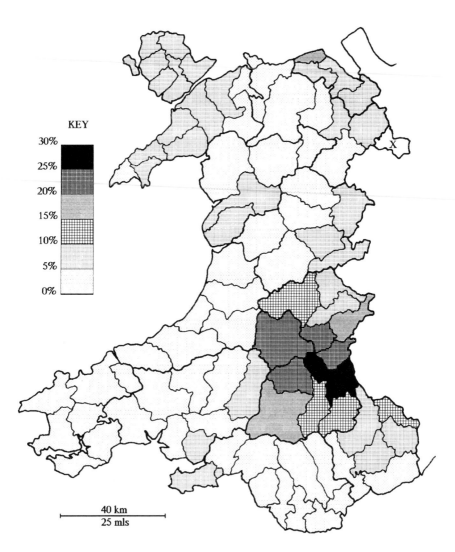

Fig. 11-3: Incidence by location of surnames incorporating *Ap*

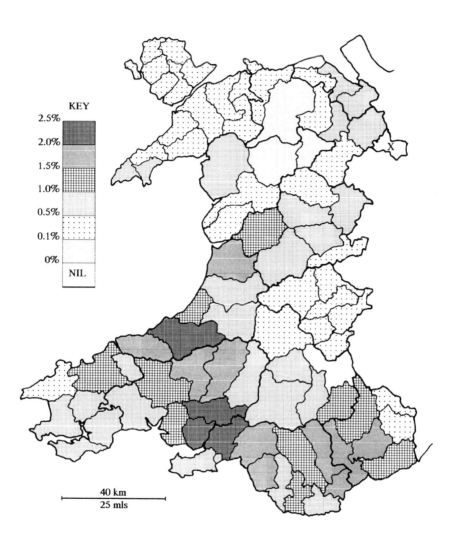

Fig. 11-4: The incidence by location of Old Testament surnames

In the case of the writer's own surname of Rowlands, this became fixed as the surname Rowland in central Cardiganshire in the mid eighteenth century and did not acquire the final possessive 's' until about a century later. My great-great-grandfather (1772-1819) was always known as William Rowland, his son (1816-1887) was sometimes John Rowland and sometimes John Rowlands, while his son (1861-1939) was always David Morgan Rowlands.

The whole process of transition typified by the change from *ap* Howell to Howell to Howells, has resulted in some areas having Howells but not Powell, Evans but not Bevan, etc. In other areas where settled surnames were taken at the beginning of the transition process, the converse would be true. All of this results in basically the same surname having identifiably different 'homes' through taking different forms.

Names from the Old Testament: Another major influence on surname patterns stemmed from a preference for using Old Testament given names within the 'Old Dissenting' denominations (the Baptists and the Independents), rather than the names of English kings and Christian saints which were favoured by Anglicans and Methodists. Where those Old Testament names were in the pool of given names when the transition to settled surnames was taking place, they became fixed (as surnames) within that society. This accounts for the high proportion of surnames of seemingly Jewish origin – such as Aaron, Enoch, Gabriel, Habakkuk, Isaac, Mordecai, Salathiel, Samuel, etc – in many parts of South Wales.

As the proportions of the population holding allegiance to the different nonconformist denominations varies significantly across Wales, it comes as no surprise to find that this type of surname (of which we found fifty-five separate examples in our survey) has an identifiable regional emphasis.[5]

The distribution and incidence across Wales of surnames derived from Old Testament given names is shown in Fig. 11-4. The main areas of concentration of this type of surname (1%-2.5% of the population) are the same areas in which the Old Dissenters have traditionally been strongest.

It should be noted, however, that the surname Daniel has been excluded from consideration, largely because it is impossible to determine what proportion is derived from the Old Testament name compared to that derived from the ancient Welsh given name of Deiniol. In any case, however, it was extensively used as a given name throughout Wales for a considerable length of time and its incidence as a surname (0.66% in Carmarthenshire) is such that its inclusion would have masked the essentially local presence of the main body of less common Old Testament surnames.

Resulting differences across Wales

Perhaps the best way of seeing the effect of all these different factors is to consider the purely theoretical case of four separate people each holding exactly the same name (Hywel ap John) at the beginning of the seventeenth century but living in different areas of Wales and, hence, in areas in which settled surnames would have been taken at different times. If we assume that the given names of their descendants were exactly the same in each succeeding generation, we find (see Fig. 11-5) we end up at the beginning of the nineteenth century with four people, each with the given name John, but each holding a completely different surname, namely: John Powell, John David, John Isaac and John Jones

	EARLY[6]	INTERMEDIATE[7]	LATE (A)[8]	LATE (B)[9]
1600	Hywel ap John	Hywel ap John	Hywel ap John	Hywel ap John
	John ap Hywel	John ap Hywel	John ap Hywel	John ap Hywel
	David POWELL	David ap John	David ap John	David ap John
	Thomas POWELL	Thomas David	Thomas David	Thomas David
1700	William POWELL	William DAVID	William Thomas	William Thomas
	Isaac POWELL	Isaac DAVID	Isaac William	Isaac William
	John POWELL	John DAVID	John Isaac	John Isaac
	Thomas POWELL	Thomas DAVID	Thomas ISAAC	Thomas John
1800	John POWELL	John DAVID	John ISAAC	John JONES

Fig. 11-5: Theoretical case showing the effects of surnames settling at different times in different places

Descriptive (or adjectival) surnames: Despite their limited presence in the pool of surnames in Wales, these surnames display a distinctive pattern which finds their occurrence largely confined to the 'Marcher' areas on the English border and the coastal regions of south Wales. In all we found twenty-one surnames in this category.[10]

Surnames of ancient Welsh origin: Rather surprisingly the number of surnames in this category is very small, albeit if one includes common surnames such as Owen (Owain), Rees (Rhys), etc, the proportion of the population which they cover is quite high. However, as the more common surnames in this category are more than adequately covered elsewhere, discussion here is confined to the distribution patterns shown by the rarer surnames which, while they do not cover great numbers of people, nevertheless are a clear (and important) link with an ancient past.[11]

In our survey we found over fifty surnames in this category. Some have become anglicised over time but many retain their ancient form. A list of the rarer names which we found – with the ancient form in brackets – is as follows:

Blethyn, Caddick (Cadog), Cadogan (Cadwgan), Cadwallader, Connah, Craddock (Caradog), Cunnick, Cynvin, Dedwith, Devereux, Eynon/Einon, Gronow (Goronwy), Guyon, Gwalchmai, Gwion, Gwyther, Hiley (Heilin), Ithell, Kendrick (Cynwrig), Leyshon (Leision), Llewelyn, Llywarch, Maddocks (Madog), Meredith, Meyler, Meyrick (Meurig), Poiskin (ap Hoesgyn) Povah (ap Hwfa), Pridy (ap Meredith), Prothero (ap Rhydderch), Rees (Rhys), Rhydderch, Tudor, Wogan (Gwgan), Yorath (Iorwerth).

In addition, there were many other surnames with *ap* derivations such as Price and Preece from ap Rhys.

The incidence of the variants Gwynne and Wynn

The notion that surnames in Wales have their 'homes' is given further support when we consider the incidence of the two variants Gwynne and Wynn, which are descriptive names derived from the Welsh word *gwyn* meaning white, or fair of complexion.

If we draw a line east-west across the narrowest part of Wales – effectively along the boundary between Montgomeryshire and Radnorshire and then across Cardiganshire to just south of Aberystwyth – we find that 93% of those named Wynn are found to the north of this line, and 94% of those named Gwynne are found to the south of it.[12]

So far the examples I have used have been aimed at establishing that even though the surname scene in Wales is markedly less varied than in England, nevertheless there have been influences at play which have created a subtle form of variety which offers considerable hope for family historians.

Some indication of that variety is to be seen in the thirty-fold difference between the incidence of the surname Jones in the Bala and St David's areas (see Fig. 11-2). If similar variations are a characteristic of less common names than Jones, then there is every likelihood that some names would be absent from certain areas. Information of this nature (which on the face of it might seem to be rather negative) has its positive side in that it enables one to identify where *not* to look for people with that surname.

Using the results of our survey we can explore this possibility further by looking in more detail at the thirty-five most common names for Wales which are listed on page 164. As a result, we found that only five – Thomas, Lewis, Griffiths, Edwards and Morris – are found throughout Wales and do not display any marked concentration in any one area. On the other hand, the remainder – excluding Jones which has been considered earlier (see Fig. 12-2) – often show a distinct identity with quite specific areas of Wales. The main place (or places) in which the remaining twenty-nine surnames occur in greatest concentration is as follows (the percentage given immediately after the name is the average incidence across the whole of Wales):

Williams (8.91%): Found throughout Wales with particular concentrations (16%-23%) in Caernarfonshire and Anglesey.

Davies (7.09%): Found throughout Wales with significant concentration centred on south Cardiganshire (up to 22%).

Evans (5.46%): Similar distribution to Davies. Strongest in south Cardiganshire (18%).

Roberts (3.69%): Largely confined to North Wales (up to 18%); limited incidence in Montgomeryshire.

Hughes (2.98%): Found throughout Wales. Main areas of incidence (up to 14%) as for Roberts.

Morgan (2.63%): Chiefly found in South and Mid Wales. Some concentration along a line from Newport (Monmouthshire) to Aberaeron (Cardiganshire).

Owen (2.08%): Chiefly in North Wales (up to 10%) and south-west Wales.

Rees (1.83%): Largely confined to South and Mid Wales. Maximum incidence (up to 7%) in the area just north of Swansea (Glamorgan).

James (1.51%): Chiefly found south of Montgomeryshire. The main concentration is in north Pembrokeshire (over 6%).

Jenkins (1.48%): Almost identical incidence to that for James with main concentrations (over 5%) in mid Cardiganshire and in the Vale of Glamorgan.

Price (1.35%): Found consistently on the Wales-England border but extending well into Wales. Heavy concentration (up to 12%) in Breconshire and Radnorshire.

Richards (1.26%): Found everywhere except where Pritchard is present (*q.v.* below). No particular concentration.

Lloyd (1.19%): Low incidence in North-west and south-east Wales. Found generally elsewhere (up to 4%).

Phillips (1.18%): Largely confined to South Wales with main concentration (over 5%) in Pembrokeshire.

Parry (1.08%): Found right across North Wales (up to 7%) and in south-east Wales (up to 3%) but low incidence elsewhere.

David (0.99%): Almost wholly confined to Glamorgan, Carmarthenshire and Pembrokeshire. Maximum incidence nearly 8% (Glamorgan).

Harris (0.87%): Chiefly found in South Wales, but with little incidence in Glamorgan. Never found in any significant concentration.

John (0.86%): Virtually the same pattern of incidence as for David. Maximum incidence 6% in Glamorgan.

Powell (0.73%): Similar distribution to Price. Maximum incidence (over 8%) in Breconshire.

Pritchard (0.68%): Largely confined to Anglesey and Caernarfonshire (up to 4%) and also Breconshire (over 8%) and Monmouthshire (over 2%).

Howells (0.62%): Found throughout Mid and South Wales but very low frequency in Breconshire where Powell is dominant.

Watkins (0.57%): Virtually identical to Price and Powell but with lower incidence (up to 4%).

Rowlands (0.56%): Mainly found in Mid Wales and Anglesey. Maximum incidence 4% in south Merionethshire.

Bowen (0.45%): Found at generally low incidence in Mid and South Wales and on the Wales-England border. Maximum incidence of over 2% in south Carmarthenshire.

Humphreys (0.45%): Principally a name of North Wales. Maximum incidence just over 3% in Denbighshire.

Ellis (0.44%): A mirror image of Humphreys. Maximum incidence of over 3% in north Montgomeryshire.

Pugh (0.39%): Same pattern as for Price, but also with high incidence (over 5%) in south Merionethshire.

Llewellyn (0.37%): Confined to South Wales – chiefly Pembrokeshire (2%) and Glamorgan (nearly 3%).

Hopkins (0.32%): Largely confined to Glamorgan (over 3%) and parts of Monmouthshire.

While these thirty-five most common names cover a large proportion of the population, more than 5,000 other names were found to occur in Wales in the early part of the nineteenth century. These range from those having only a single occurrence (and there were many) to names such as Bevan, Rogers and George which only just failed to get into this main list.

In conclusion

It can be seen from the above that there is a significant variation by location in the incidence of even the most common of surnames in Wales. In the case of less common surnames the variation can be sufficiently great to point to one, or a small number, of likely places of origin; all of which can be of great value where families have migrated to other areas.

Further ways in which all this can be put to use for family history research are described elsewhere.[13] However, it is hoped that, in time, details of the incidence by location of all 5,358 which we found in our survey will be on deposit at the National Library of Wales, the Society of Genealogists and the National Genealogical Society at Arlington, Virginia (and possibly elsewhere), so that others may be able to pursue their own particular surname interests.

NOTES TO CHAPTER 11

[1] Sixteenth Annual Report of the Registrar General, Abstracts for 1853, published in 1856.

[2] Rowlands, John and Sheila *The Surnames of Wales for Family Historians and Others* (FFHS Birmingham and GPC Baltimore, both 1996). [Hereafter referred to as Rowlands and Rowlands, *Surnames.*]

[3] See Chapter 3 'The Adoption of Surnames' in Rowlands and Rowlands, *Surnames.*

[4] See also Chapter 6 'Further Uses of the Survey' Rowlands and Rowlands, *Surnames.*

[5] See Rowlands and Rowlands, *Surnames*, Chapter 6 and in particular Figs. 6-1 and 6-2.

[6] Preliminary work suggests that the areas in which surnames were taken 'early' (pre-1640) take in those offering easy access from England, including the South Wales coastal belt. This includes the greater part of Flintshire, Montgomeryshire and Monmouthshire; a smaller proportion of Radnorshire and Breconshire together with the Vale of Glamorgan, the Gower Peninsula and south Pembrokeshire (south of the linguistic divide known locally as the Landsker).

[7] The 'intermediate' period (say 1640-1720) takes in a significant proportion of Denbighshire, the North Wales coastal strip as far west as Caernarfon (together with the adjacent part of Anglesey), the remainder of Montgomeryshire and Radnorshire. In South Wales there were some inroads into the higher land adjacent to the Vale of Glamorgan and also adjacent to south Pembrokeshire together with a narrow strip of south Carmarthenshire.

[8] By far and away the largest area of Wales (but one of low population) took surnames 'late' (say 1720-1800). This includes the larger part of Caernarfonshire and Anglesey (in the north) and Breconshire and Carmarthenshire (in the south), as well as the whole of Merionethshire and Cardiganshire. This area is commonly referred to as the heartland of Wales.

In this example the influence of nonconformity has led to an Old Testament given name being used one generation prior to settled surnames being taken and, hence, its entry into the pool of surnames in the next generation in that area.

[9] As for note 8 but with the surname becoming settled two generations after the Old Testament given name was used and, hence, it not becoming part of the pool of surnames in this area.

[10] See Rowlands and Rowlands, *Surnames,* Fig. 6-4 and Appendix B.

[11] Morgan, T.J. and Prys, *Welsh Surnames* (UW Press, Cardiff 1985).

[12] See also Rowlands and Rowlands, *Surnames*, Fig. 4-18.

[13] See Rowlands and Rowlands, *Surnames,* Chapters 6 and 7, and also Appendix C.

12. AN ENGLISH SETTLEMENT IN WESTERN MONTGOMERYSHIRE DURING THE TUDOR PERIOD

Murray Ll. Chapman

Montgomeryshire was one of the newly created shires resulting from the Acts of Union.* Its area had, hitherto, comprised some thirty-two separate lordships, each with its own separate jurisdiction, laws and customs. The Acts of Union, 1536-1543, swept away all the old laws and customs and provided a uniform system for the administration of justice in Wales as in England through the establishment of the Courts of Great Sessions. These courts administered justice according to the laws of England. The Acts of Union therefore afforded the same protection to Welshmen as well as Englishmen. This was particularly important to any in-migrants from England who chose to establish themselves in any of the newly shired counties. New administrative areas (hundreds) were also established by the Acts within the counties.

There are indications that, following the passing of the Acts of Union, there was a significant in-migration of English families to Montgomeryshire and, in particular, to the lordship of Arwystli in western Montgomeryshire during the period 1572-1580. At that time Robert Dudley, Earl of Leicester, held the lordship of Arwystli, with other lordships, from the Crown.

There are a variety of reasons as to why people should move, be they economic, religious, social or political. Professional people such as clerics and lawyers move from place to place to take up new appointments so as to further their careers. Traders, craftsmen and servants move to places where there is a demand for their services. The letting of land to farmers can also result in the movement of families from one area to another.

In some instances the movement is enforced, as was the case in the Vale of Clwyd following the Edwardian conquest of Wales.[1] In other instances

---

* This chapter is based on a talk given at the course, 'Genealogy on the Wales-England Border', held at Gregynog in September 1997.

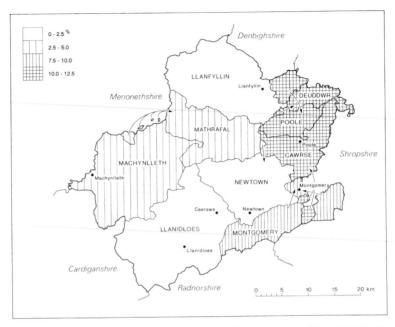

Fig. 12-1(a): English style names in Montgomeryshire, 1543-45

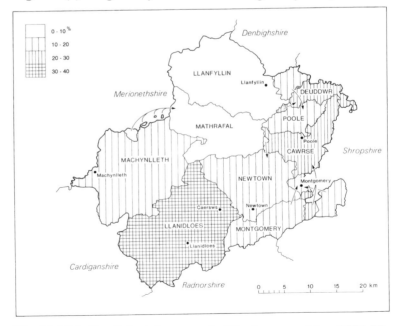

Fig. 12-1(b): English style names in Montgomeryshire, 1574-77

there was a deliberate policy to repopulate areas through a carefully managed process by the Crown, as occurred in Munster, Ireland, following the forfeiture of the Earl of Desmond's estates as a result of rebellion.[2] The evidence for the in-migration of English families to western Montgomeryshire during the period 1572-1580, presented below, is shown to be a result of incentives provided by the Earl of Leicester with the help of the Crown.

Occurrence of English-style personal names

Determination of the occurrence of English-style surnames within Montgomeryshire has been made from the Lay Subsidy rolls and also from the records of the Courts of Great Sessions. The Muster Roll of 1574 provides further data.

Lay Subsidy Rolls: For Montgomeryshire, the Lay Subsidy rolls for the years 1543 and 1545[3] survive and provide a comprehensive schedule of all those who were assessed in each township. Of the 2,695 persons assessed, only about 130 persons had English-style surnames, i.e. less than 5% of the total. The distribution of English-style surnames recorded in the 1543 and 1545 Lay Subsidy rolls indicate regional variations, ranging from about 10% in Eastern Montgomeryshire to practically zero in the west (see Fig. 12-1a). The higher percentage of occurrence in the east can be expected due to it abutting the border with England. Of those who used English-style surnames only, about half were English in-migrants, i.e. only about 2.5% of the total population of Montgomeryshire.

Later Lay Subsidy rolls indicate changes in the incidence of English-style surnames but, unlike the Lay Subsidy rolls which survive for the reign of Henry VIII, the records are generally based on parishes and with a smaller number of persons assessed for tax. Fig. 12-2 summarises all the data abstracted from the rolls and this clearly shows an increase in the occurrence of English-style surnames although the increase is variable for each hundred.

Great Sessions – Criminal Proceedings: Data obtained from the criminal proceedings of the Montgomeryshire Court of Great Sessions (for which records survive from 1541 to 1830) indicate that, for the period 1541-1580, just over one in five persons used English-style surnames, some 840 names out of a total of nearly 4,000. By the Commonwealth period, 1650-1660, the ratio of English-style surnames to Welsh patronymics had increased to just over four out of every five of the population. This is not an indication of a major influx of English in-migrants between these two periods, but rather the increasing use of English-style surnames.

Hund. / Manors:

- **Machynlleth:** Cyfeiliog
- **Llanidloes:** Arwystli, Carno
- **Mathrafal:** Caereinion (Iscoed and Uwchcoed)
- **Llanfyllin:** Llanfyllin, Llanwddyn, Mochnant, Mechain Uwchcoed, Nantymeichiad, Plas Dinas, Brithdir
- **Newtown:** Cedewain, Llanllugan
- **Montgomery:** Montgomery, Kerry, Hopton, Bishop's Teirtref, Halcetor
- **Poole:** Broniarth, Mechain Iscoed, Ystrad Marchell, Tirymynech
- **Deuddwr:** Deuddwr, Bausley
- **Cawrse:** Teirtref, Leighton, Llannerch Hudol, Over Gorddwr, Nether Gorddwr, King's Teirtref, Rhos-goch

Year	Machynlleth	Llanidloes	Mathrafal	Llanfyllin	Newtown	Montgomery	Poole	Deuddwr	Cawrse
1543	—	—	—	3.5	—	—			—
1545	2.8	0.9	3.5	2.2	5.0[2]	8.6	5.8	13.2	12.1
1546	—	0.6	—	—	—	—	12.5	11.6	—
1547	5.5	2.7	—	—	16.7	—	—	—	10.7
1556	0.0	5.3	8.7	6.9	19.3	15.0	22.0	17.6	20.5
1562	0.0	10.0	21.0	8.9	20.7	8.9	illegible	31.6	17.5
1571[1]	0.0	31.8	14.0	4.5	18.9	10.2	13.2	—	23.6
1571[1]	2.6	26.2	8.3	7.0	22.6	6.1	10.0	23.0	21.4
1573	0.0	26.0	8.5	11.5	19.7	16.7	13.7	34.4	25.4
1574	13.8	39.8	4.5	9.8	19.3	23.0	19.6	17.4	20.1
1577	3.2	39.4	11.5	6.4	?	13.3	15.0	32.4	22.4
1588	illegible	22.5	11.1	3.3	21.4	13.4	15.4	22.7	21.0
% diff.[2]	0.0	21.6	7.7	1.1	16.4[3]	4.8	5.7	9.8	8.9

[1] There are two sets of muster rolls available for 1571

[2] This % difference relates to the years 1543/5 and 1588

[3] The actual figure for 1545 for the Newtown Hundred is uncertain. For the purposes of this table it was estimated to be 5%.

Fig. 12-2: **The percentages of English families (based on surnames) in each hundred assessed for tax in the lay subsidy rolls and 1574 muster roll for Montgomeryshire**

As with the Lay Subsidy rolls, it is difficult to determine how many of those adopting English-style surnames were actually English people. The problem is further compounded by some families adopting both English-style and Welsh patronymics in parallel, e.g. Ieuan Fletcher of Guilsfield who occurs in 1563 was also known as Ieuan ap David;[4] Rees Crockett of Newtown who also occurs in 1563 was also known as Rees ap Morris;[5] Richard Breeze of Newtown, labourer, occurs in the Gaol File for 18 July 1575, but he was also known as Richard ap Hugh.[6] The name Derwas (which is a Welsh name) first occurs in 1562 when John Derwas, of Llandrinio, complained of a riotous assembly by a group of people who chased away a red cow from out of his pasture. He was also known as John ap Owen.[7]

Some of the surnames are based on the trade or craft of a person such as Barker, Baker, Butcher, for which it is not possible to distinguish the families' places of origin. Other surnames are from the places of origin, e.g. John Knutsford of Llanbryn-mair whose name first occurs in the Gaol Files in 1570[8] and clearly suggest that he was an English man who moved into the area from Cheshire. William Medlicot of Gwern-y-go, who occurs in 1541,[9] only moved a short distance from the township of Medlicot in western Shropshire.

In some instances the Gaol Files provide evidence from where a family moved from England to Montgomeryshire. As an example, the family of Sheene are first mentioned in the records in 1567.[10,11] Joan Sheene, the wife of David Thomas alias David Velyneth of Mochdre was charged with the burning of the house of Gwen verch Rees of Mochdre on 25 July 1575. Thomas Sheene of the parish of Newtown and John Sheene of Aston, co. Hereford, and Robert Sheene, his son, were similarly charged for the same offence. What is clear from this case is that there is a family connection between the Sheenes of Aston co. Hereford and those living in Montgomeryshire, and it is likely that the Sheenes of Montgomeryshire originated from Herefordshire.

Taking account of the above it is estimated for the period 1541-1580, that of the 840 families who used English-style surnames, 401 were English in-migrants, i.e. about 50% of those in Montgomeryshire who adopted English-style surnames during this period were English in-migrants. The English in-migrants therefore represented about 10% of the population of Montgomeryshire.

The Acts of Union
The Acts of Union 1536-1543 created Montgomeryshire from lordships or manors which had, hitherto, been distinct and separate administrative areas.

The Acts removed the sovereignty of the lords of such lordships or manors and created a new system for the administration of justice.

In the case of Montgomeryshire a significant number of the lordships were held by the Crown prior to the Act and had been acquired as a deliberate policy to annex Wales to England.[12] This did not mean that the Crown lordships were subject to the rule of Westminster. They were governed according to the law and custom of the particular lordship. The Acts of Union not only unified these areas but provided a uniform system of justice.

The lordships of Cedewain, Kerry, Montgomery and Halcetor came into the hands of the Crown by descent from the Mortimer family. On the other hand the lordships of Arwystli and Cyfeiliog were purchased by the Crown from Sir John Dudley, Kt., in about 1531. A survey of the lordships of Arwystli and Cyfeiliog was carried out prior to their purchase.[13] One extract from the survey records that:

> The people for the most part desire to have the laws of England ministered amongst them by the English ministers that the eldest son should inherit the whole land according to the law of England.

Another passage in the survey records:

> Also, if justice were kept there according to the law of England by Justices as is in North Wales and yearly the sheriff [appointed, there] would be great profits yearly come to the king's highness by reason of the same and the country better inhabited and land better let on and woods better sold which is now little worth there.

Here, then, is a suggestion that greater revenue would accrue to the Crown by the country being better inhabited provided that the law of England was administered there. In many respects, this survey sets out the very reasons for the Acts of Union and clearly indicates the deliberate policy of the Tudors in this regard.

Prior to the 1536 Act of Union, the condition and state of the inhabitants in each of the lordships was variable. For the lordship of Cedewain, a charter exists from Richard Plantagenet, Duke of York, dated 31 August 1444, at Montgomery Castle, which granted amongst other matters the release of all natives of Cedewain lordship from every yolk of bondage and servile condition.[14]

As late as 1536, Sir John Dudley, Kt., lord of Deuddwr lordship, by his grant dated 4 February at Dudley Castle, Warwickshire, released from service and servile conditions of villeinage certain inhabitants of his manor of Deuddwr.[15] By the Acts of Union, all these mediaeval forms of bondage were swept away and the lateness of Sir John Dudley's grant must be viewed as his last opportunity to reap some financial benefit from his grant, which would otherwise have been denied him by the Act of Union.

Why should there be in-migration?

The new administrative and legal system introduced by the Acts of Union would have brought certain professional persons into the county but this would only be a relatively small number. The fundamental reason for in-migration into Montgomeryshire is as set out in the prophetic statement contained in the 1531 survey of the lordships of Arwystli and Cyfeiliog,[16] viz: '... if justice were kept there according to the law of England ... the country (would be) better inhabited and land better let on'. The introduction of English law was achieved by the 1542-43 statute 'An Act for Certain Ordinances in the King's Dominion and Principality of Wales'. In Montgomeryshire, the new legal system was already in place before this time, with the first Court of Great Sessions held at Montgomery before Sir Nicholas Hare, Kt., Chief Justice, on 12 September 1541.

What do the records reveal?

The Appendix to this chapter lists English-style surnames obtained from the Great Sessions Gaol Files which are considered to be of English families which moved into Montgomeryshire during the period 1540-1580. It notes the year that the names first occur in the records. The list cannot be regarded as absolute but is sufficient to indicate if there are any discernible concentrations of English families in one place when compared with another and is indicative only of the period when there was any in-migration. The list, however, does not indicate movement of English families from one area of the county to another. From the details given in this Appendix, an analysis has been made noting the location of English in-migrants in each of the lordships of Montgomeryshire for the periods 1540-1563 and 1564-1580 (see Fig. 12-3).

The selection of lordships to carry out this analysis rather than, say, parishes or hundreds is simply because a lordship was not only an administrative area but a territorial division subject to ownership. For the period under consideration, a significant number of the lordships in Montgomeryshire formed the barony of Powis which was owned by the Grey family. As noted above, the Crown also held a significant number which they had gradually acquired over a great many years.

Fig. 12-3 clearly indicates that the incidence of English families in the Crown lordships is nearly twice that in the barony of Powis and nearly three times that in all the miscellaneous lordships. More significant, though, is the large number of English family names which occur in the lordship of Arwystli for the period 1564-1580 which, at sixty-nine, is over three times

LORDSHIP	1540-1563	1564-1580	TOTALS
Crown Lordships			
Arwystli	10	69	79
Cedewain	28	17	45
Cyfeiliog	7	7	14
Halcetor	3	4	7
Hopton	0	2	2
Kerry	16	10	26
Montgomery	5	2	7
	69	**111**	**180**
Powis Lordships			
Broniarth	1	1	2
Caereinion (Iscoed & Uwchcoed)	15	20	35
Carno	1	1	2
Llanfyllin	7	7	14
Llannerch Hudol	4	2	6
Llanwddyn	0	0	0
Mechain (Iscoed & Uwchcoed)	4	5	9
Mochnant	0	4	4
Nantymeichiad	1	0	1
Plas Dinas	4	3	7
Teirtref	10	8	18
Tirymynech	3	2	5
Ystrad Marchell	1	3	4
	51	**56**	**107**
Miscellaneous Lordships			
Bausley	1	0	1
Bishop's Teirtref	4	2	6
King's Teirtref	4	2	6
Leighton	6	1	7
Nether Gorddwr	3	2	5
Over Gorddwr	2	4	6
Rhos-goch	0	1	1
Deuddwr	22	10	32
	42	**22**	**64**
Unknown	23	31	54
GRAND TOTALS	**185**	**220**	**405**

Note: The minor manors of Llanllugan and Brithdir in Mochnant are not shown separatey but are included in Cedewain and Mochnant respectively.

Fig. 12-3: English In-migrants to Montgomeryshire, 1540-1580
(Source: Montgomeryshire Gaol Files)

that for any other lordship for the same period. More detailed (year by year) analysis of the Great Session Gaol Files shows that there is a noticeable increase in the years 1572-1580 for the lordship of Arwystli (forty-five families) which does not occur in any other lordship.

A comparison of the data obtained from the criminal proceedings of the Great Sessions with the data obtained from the Lay Subsidy Rolls (summarised in Fig. 12-2) confirms the same trends with a significant increase in the occurrence of English-style names in Arwystli for the period 1570-1580. The 1574 Muster Roll of Montgomeryshire men (also summarised in Fig. 12-2) provides further confirmation of the relatively large number of families with English surnames in Arwystli[17] (see also Fig. 12-1b, which illustrates the occurrence of English surnames in 1577).

What were the circumstances for in-migration to Arwystli?

Arwystli was a Crown lordship which was farmed out successively to various courtiers. By patent dated 19 April 1572, the lands in the lordships of Arwystli and Cyfeiliog and the towns of Machynlleth, Llanidloes and Caersws were granted to Robert Dudley, Earl of Leicester.[18] He also held the lordship of Denbigh and the manors of Chirk and Chirkland by grant from the Crown dated 9 June 1563.

On 9 July 1576, the Queen granted to Leicester the right to alienate all lands comprised in grants to him and his heirs *inter alia* to hold by service of the fortieth part of a knight's fee the lands granted to him by the patent dated 19 April 1572 and 9 June 1563 for a period of four years 'from the present date he may on every such alienation reserve and create such tenures as he pleases whether by rent and fealty, by fealty alone or other service of him and his heirs as of any manor of his or otherwise notwithstanding the statute of Westminster of Quia Emptores or any other law'.[19] Leicester used this right, which is recited in a deed dated 20 June 1578, when he granted his lands in the manor of Arwystli Iscoed to John Hubband, Kt., Edward Herbert, William Baynhan and John Nutall, esqs., at an annual rental of £55 3s. 9d.[20] The recital records that the tenants of the Earl's manor of Arwystli Iscoed had petitioned him and had provided him with a certain composition for which an agreement was then made between the Earl and his tenants by virtue of the licence granted by the Queen. The names of all of Leicester's tenants in each of the townships are recorded in the deed. The following English names occur: Nicholas Bennett, Lawrence Beck, Roger Gardener, Richard Cox, Henry Ingram, David Halcetor, and Robert Mason. Although Leicester yielded up the lordships of Arwystli and Cyfeiliog to the Crown on 9 January 1581 he continued to administer his freehold estates there.[21] For this purpose, Leicester appointed John Hubband, Kt., of Leominster,

Herefordshire, as his commissioner authorised for the survey, letting and setting of all his lands and tenements within the lordships of Arwystli and Cyfeiliog.[22] By his last will and testament, Leicester's lands passed to University College, Oxford.

It is clear that a significant in-migration of English families into Arwystli occurred during the time that Leicester held the lordship (19 April 1572 to 9 January 1581). Direct proof of the in-migration of English families to Arwystli is provided in the case of John Thornhill of the parish of Llangurig which was heard in the Montgomeryshire Court of Great Sessions held at Newtown commencing Monday 30 June 1578.

John Thornhill's case

Thornhill, who was about forty years old, complained in 1578 to the Council in the Marches of Wales that he was a poor Englishman, born in Derbyshire, with a wife and small children.[23] He said that in about 1576 he left Derbyshire and came to Montgomeryshire to live 'for that he was not able to come by any habitation in the said county of Derby for relief and maintenance of himself and his poor family'. He complained that he had been wrongfully accused of sheep-stealing by two local Welsh men. David Lloyd Jenkin, the local Justice of the Peace, examined witnesses and, in his letter forwarding their depositions to the Chief Justice, recorded that the 'matter was then vehemently suspicious and yet is to be the deed of the said Thornhill or some of his family'. David Lloyd Jenkin then went on to defend the integrity of the two Welsh men, stating that one of them, Thomas David, was then the lord's bailiff 'and such as hath done good service in the country as it is not unknown to all the worships of this shire'.[24]

Thornhill called the following witnesses:[25]

- John Bamford of the parish of Trefeglwys, aged 60 years. Bamford said that he had lived in the same town where the plaintiff, Thornhill, was born, which was called Bamford, co. Derby.
- Henry and Margaret Gregory of the parish of Llangurig, aged about 60 years who said in like manner as John Bamford.
- Robert Hatfield of the parish of Llangurig, aged 20 years. He said that he was born in the town of Bamford.
- Nicholas Bennett of the parish of Llandinam, aged 54 years. He said that he had known John Thornhill for thirty years.

Other witnesses who were called on Thornhill's behalf and who had known him from the time he had come to Montgomeryshire were: Thomas Bowring of Llandinam, aged 40, John Cottrell of Llandinam, aged 50, Ralph Cottrell of Llandinam, aged 40, William Downes of Llanidloes, aged 60, George

Wosencroft of Llanidloes, aged 60, John Wilson of Llandinam, aged 44, John Wilson of Llanidloes, aged 40, George Ashton of Llanidloes, aged 55, Ralph Marple of Llangurig, aged 60 and Thomas Cowper of Llandinam, aged 43. One of the witnesses, Nicholas Bennett, is recorded as holding property from the Earl of Leicester in the townships of Hengynwydd and Dethenydd in the parish of Llandinam.[26]

Here, then, is direct proof of English in-migration to Arwystli and more importantly, the date of in-migration is during the time that Robert Dudley, Earl of Leicester held the lordship. Thornhill came to the parish of Llangurig at the time that Leicester was granted the right to alienate land in the lordship in what ever form he chose.

The names of Bamford, Hatfield and Thornhill are of three communities in the Peak District of Derbyshire in close proximity to each other. What Thornhill's case illustrates is:

1. A group of people from the same community in Derbyshire moved together into Montgomeryshire.
2. The names of the places from whence they moved were adopted as their surnames.

What was the attitude of locals to the newcomers?

Thornhill's case also well illustrates the resentment which was felt by the indigenous local population to the English newcomers. The malicious charge of sheep-stealing, if it had succeeded, could have resulted in the hanging of Thornhill. This would have instilled fear into the other English in-migrants who would then have been liable to further intimidation by the local population.

Thornhill, as part of his defence to the trumped-up charge obtained a letter from his previous landlord in Derbyshire.[27] The letter, dated 1 June 1578 at Sheffield, from George Talbot, Earl of Shrewsbury to Sir John Throckmorton, Chief Justice of the Montgomeryshire Court of Great Sessions, was a key piece of evidence and is reproduced in its entirety below:

> After my hearty commendations/ Where I am given to understand that one John Thornhill is at this present by sinister practises of some lewd persons wrongfully troubled and charged with felony before you and others of her majesty's Council there, and thereby like to be put in great peril of his life, I have thought good (because the said Thornhill has been born and brought up hereby upon my lands and ever before his departure hence of good fame and conversation, as the whole country will respect no less) to request you to have good consideration of the same his cause which as I am credibly informed proceeds altogether upon the malicious and wicked practise of his adversaries And so I heartily bid you farewell.

The letter from the Earl of Shrewsbury is remarkable in a number of ways. Firstly, it must have involved a great deal of effort and influence to obtain it and, secondly, it contains a veiled direction to the Chief Justice 'to have good consideration of the matter'. Thornhill was acquitted and continued to live in Llangurig.

But how was the letter from the Earl of Shrewsbury obtained? Thornhill, a tenant farmer,[28] would not have the necessary influence and, perhaps, wherewithal to obtain such an important letter. He was not even able to write.[29] The influence of the Earl of Leicester is likely to be behind its procurement, for failure to have Thornhill acquitted from the trumped-up charge would discourage English families from moving into Arwystli and elsewhere. Leicester certainly took an interest in the affairs of Montgomeryshire, as evidenced in 1580 by his influence in the procurement of Griffith Lloyd as 'an impartial sheriff' for Montgomeryshire.[30]

Thornhill next appears in the Great Sessions in 1597 to prosecute a felony against Evan Lewis of Llangurig who stole his brown cow, valued at 40 shillings.[31] Lewis confessed to the felony. The examinations of Thornhill and Lewis were taken before the Council in the Marches of Wales and not the local Justice of the Peace. This is understandable due to Thornhill not trusting the local JP in view of the problems he had encountered in 1576 over the trumped-up charge of sheep stealing.

Another Englishman who complained about unfair treatment from the indigenous local people was Thomas Law of Dolfor, in the lordship of Kerry. He submitted a petition to the Chief Justice of the Montgomeryshire Court of Great Sessions held at Montgomery commencing Monday 5 April 1568.[32] In his petition, Law complained that at nine o'clock on 5 March 1568, Lewis ap Ieuan of Cynhinfa, had stolen two 'burthones' of his hay, valued at one shilling. Law prosecuted a bill of indictment against Lewis ap Ieuan and was assisted by two of his neighbours who had responded to the outcry he had raised at the time of the felony. The jury had not found his bill to be true and Law alleged that this was because Lewis ap Ieuan was 'a gentil and well frended and alied' in the country. Law further claimed that because he was an Englishman and a stranger, the jury refused to find his bill to be true 'to the great emboldisshinge of like offendors' and to his and 'others pore men great fear and discomforte to inabite in the said sheere'.

Was there a deliberate policy to repopulate Arwystli?

All the evidence presented above indicates a noticeable in-migration of English families to the lordship of Arwystli. It indicates that shortly after the Act of Union, there were virtually no English families in that lordship but from mid-1560 the number of English families which moved to Arwystli increased, and significantly so between 1572-1580.

Could this in-migration of English families to western Montgomeryshire be considered to be an English plantation? A comparison can be made with the settlement of English and Welsh families in county Kerry, Ireland[33] (being a part of the Munster Plantation), following the forfeiture of the Earl of Desmond's estates through rebellion in 1583.[34]

The Munster Plantation was carried out in a very orderly manner and was a deliberate policy by the government to repopulate the province of Munster with English and Welsh families. The estate of the Earl of Desmond was divided into seigniories of 12,000 acres, decreasing to proportions of 8,000, 6,000 and 4,000 acres. For a full seigniory the Undertaker (the name given to the holder of the seigniory) had to settle ninety-one families, including his own. Additionally, the nature of the tenancies was ordained.

Details of the seigniories granted and the number of households[35] that were actually established in co. Kerry from English and Welsh families show strong parallels with the situation in Montgomeryshire. For example, in Kerry there was (on average) one household for every 470 acres compared to one household for every 560 acres in Montgomeryshire (see Fig 12-4). The acreage of Montgomeryshire (510,111)[36] is about half that of county Kerry (1,030,193).[37] Data are only available to compare the population of these two counties for the year 1733, being about 34,000 for Montgomeryshire[38] and 71,730 for co. Kerry.[39] The density of population is virtually the same for each county (approximately one person per 16 acres).

On a county-wide basis, the in-migration of English families to Arwystli during the period 1572-1580 (forty-five families, which represents one English family per 11,330 acres) is very comparable to the plantation of English and Welsh families in county Kerry (ninety-one families, which represents one family per 11,320 acres).

Although the extent of the in-migration of English and Welsh families to Munster was much greater than that of English families to Arwystli, comparisons between the two indicate that their intensity was virtually the same. For those who settled in the Irish seigniories the acreage occupied is known but the same is not true for those who settled in the lordship of Arwystli. The Earl of Leicester, as lord of Arwystli, probably had possession of a significant proportion of Arwystli's 109,586 acres,[40] but how much is not known. It is also not known how many English in-migrants occupied land granted by the Earl of Leicester.

Nevertheless, it is possible to estimate the acreage of the land occupied by the English in-migrants in Arwystli from data contained in the Lay Subsidy Roll for 1577. This shows a most significant number of families with English-style names (nearly 40%) in the hundred of Llanidloes which comprises the same extent as Arwystli.[41] Of the twenty-six persons with English-style names in this tax assessment it is considered that fifteen were English in-migrants who came to Arwystli since 1572.[42] They therefore represent about 23% of the total assessed for tax. To have been assessed the in-migrants must have occupied land and so it would not be unreasonable to assume that it would have been in the same proportion as their number, i.e. 23% of 109,586 acres (25,205 acres) (see Fig. 12-4).

County	In-migrants in the county			Land occupied by in-migrants	
	Number of in-migrants	*acreage of county*	*in-migrants/ acre of county*	*acreage of land[43] occupied*	*in-migrants per acre*
MGY	45	510,111	11,330	25,205	560[44]
KER	91	1,030,193	11,320	42,818	470

Fig. 12-4: Comparison of in-migration to Montgomeryshire (MGY) with county Kerry (KER), Ireland, in the later sixteenth century

The comparison clearly points to the fact that the intensity of in-migration was very similar in Arwystli as it was in co. Kerry and, for that matter, in Munster.

There is no direct evidence which suggests that there was a policy to populate the lordship of Arwystli with English families but the facts show that a large proportion of those that did come to Arwystli did so from north Derbyshire. The Earl of Leicester's right, granted by the Crown, to alienate land in whatever form he chose can be considered as the inducement to encourage people into Arwystli, but this seems to have been granted by the Crown as a special favour to further reward Leicester rather than as a deliberate plantation policy. The explanation for so many families moving from north Derbyshire may well have been due to very close liaison between the Earls of Leicester and Shrewsbury; the former seeking new tenants and the latter putting them out.

Postscript
Today, there persist in Arwystli some of the surnames: Wilson, Ingram, Bamford, Bennett and Ashton.

APPENDIX: SURNAMES OF ENGLISH IN-MIGRANTS IN MONTGOMERY-SHIRE LORDSHIPS ABSTRACTED FROM THE GAOL FILES, 1540-1580
NOTE: For the list which follows, (1) Place-names in parentheses give the parishes of residence, (2) Surnames in italics belong to women, (3) There is an alphabetical sequence of surnames, with given names, in *Montgomeryshire Collections*, Vol 87.

ARWYSTLI: Aderley (Llanwnnog) 1565; Ashley (Llandinam) 1574; Ashton (Llanidloes) 1568; Bamford (Trefeglwys) 1578; Barret (Llanwnnog) 1570; Bayley (Llanidloes) 1545; Bent (Llandinam) 1572; Bere (Llanwnnog) 1568; Bidell (Llandinam) 1574; Blesse (Llanwnnog) 1574; Bostock (Llandinam) 1573; Botley (Trefeglwys) 1576; Bound (Llandinam) 1574; Bowring (Llandinam) 1578; Brate (Trefeglwys) 1545; Brenton (Trefeglwys) 1566; Bridgewater (Llandinam) 1573; Brightman (Llangurig) 1578; Bromall (Llanwnnog) 1567; Bronsmaker (Trefeglwys) 1576; Brown (Trefeglwys) 1567; Brynton (Llanidloes) 1577; Bullock (Penystrywaid) 1552; Castry (Trefeglwys) 1576; Cleaton (Llanidloes) 1573; Cleyton (Llandinam) 1574; Colley (Llandinam) 1565; *Corbett* (Trefeglwys) 1567; Corfield (Llandinam) 1565; Cotterell (Llandinam) 1578; Cowley (Llanwnnog) 1570; Cox (Llandinam) 1573; Downes (Llanidloes) 1578; Drewry (Llandinam) 1565; Edge (Llandinam) 1576; Foden (Llandinam) 1573; *Furd* (Trefeglwys) 1576; Gamage (Llanidloes) 1567; Gardener (Llanwnnog) 1559; Geers (Llanwnnog) 1563; Gregory (Llangurig) 1578; Haines (Llandinam) 1571; Hall (Llandinam) 1572; Hallam (Llangurig) 1580; Hatfield (Llangurig) 1578; Hoghe (Llandinam) 1545; Homes (Llandinam) 1564; Ingram (Llandinam) 1564; Jorden (Llandinam) 1574; Kay (Llanidloes) 1544; Loton (Trefeglwys) 1576; Lovesey (Llandinam) 1574; Lowe (Llandinam) 1572; Lyne (Trefeglwys) 1580; Madley (Llandinam) 1574; Marple (Llangurig) 1578; Meden (Llanidloes) 1573; Oakley (Llanwnnog) 1569; Orchard (Trefeglwys) 1570; Paddy (Llanwnnog) 1572; Parr (Llanidloes) 1573; Parrance (Llanwnnog) 1569; Peat (Llanwnnog) 1563; Proudlove (Llanidloes) 1580; Rabon (Llanwnnog) 1572; Smith (Llanwnnog) 1573; Sonamore, John (Llanidloes) 1568; Steadman, Thomas (Trefeglwys) 1566; Stranmore (Llanidloes) 1567; Thornhill (Llangurig) 1578; Tore (Llanidloes) 1572; Tyry (Llanwnnog) 1568; Wainwright (Llandinam) 1574; Watson (Trefeglwys) 1568; Wheldon (Llangurig) 1572; Whitall (Llanidloes) 1542; Wilson (Penystrywaid) 1563; Wosencraft (Llanidloes) 1578; Wright (Llangurig) 1579.

BAUSLEY: Calcott (Alberbury) 1556.

BISHOP'S TEIRTREF: Colborne (Lydham) 1562; Fermor (Churchstoke) 1562; Horton (Churchstoke) 1571; Middle (Mainstone) 1574; Penchard (Mainstone) 1558; Pinches (Churchstoke) 1551.

BRONIARTH: Humpetch (Guilsfield) 1579; Mullener (Guilsfield) 1561.

CAEREINION: Bailiff (Llanfair) 1571; Barber 1541; Bell (Llangadfan) 1569; Bennet (Llanfair) 1560; Bentall (Llangynyw) 1553; Berkley (Llangadfan) 1569; Birch (Llanfair) 1563; Blower (Llanfair) 1557; Bowdler (Llangadfan) 1574; Bridges (Llanerfyl) 1545; Carlys (Llanfair) 1553; Chester (Llangadfan) 1569; Chidlow (Llanerfyl) 1563; Farley 1561; Fox (Garthbeibio) 1561; Harding (Castell Caereinion) 1572; Hawkyn (Llangadfan) 1569; Littlehales (Llangynyw) 1571; Lydles (Llangynyw) 1579; Maunsells (Llanfair) 1578; Middleton (Llanfair) 1565; Onslow 1543; Powner 1567; Ralph (Llangadfan) 1569; Ridgeway (Llanfair) 1560; Rudge (Llanfair) 1577; *Sandford* (Llanfair) 1573; Setterdown (Llangadfan) 1569; Skelhorne (Llangadfan) 1572; Sydlow (Llangadfan) 1569; Ward,

(Llanfair) 1555; Whiler (Llangadfan) 1569; Whittingham (Llanfair) 1571; Yope 1553; Yres (Llanfair) 1544.

CARNO: Cryrior (Carno) 1550; Parton (Carno) 1569.

CEDEWAIN: Aloe (Aberhafesb) 1580; Alwell (Tregynon) 1540; Anolene (Tregynon) 1551; Arneway (Tregynon) 1558; Astley (Tregynon) 1553; Bebb (Llanllwchaearn) 1554; Blackman (Tregynon) 1574; Blackwey (Llamyrewig) 1574; Bocke (Aberhafesb) 1570; Breeze (Newtown) 1575; Brey (Berriw) 1545; Bright (Llanllwchaearn) 1560; Butler (Newtown) 1567; Clerk (Tregynon) 1550; *Collett* (Newtown) 1576; Cook (Manafon) 1554; Dode (Llandysul) 1553; Everall (Berriw) 1575; Feldwall (Newtown) 1544; Feysey (Llanwyddelan) 1555; Goldigar (Newtown) 1561; *Gowdegay* (Llamyrewig) 1545; Habley (Newtown) 1575; Hamlet (Manafon) 1579; Hardeman (Aberhafesb) 1558; Harman (Newtown) 1552; Harvey (Newtown) 1545; Ireland (Berriw) 1575; Lawrence (Llamyrewig) 1553; Markes (Llandysul) 1553; Marton (Newtown) 1560; Paramore (Llanllwchaearn) 1554; Parks (Llanllwchaearn) 1554; Phipps (Betws Cedewain) 1575; Piper (Newtown) 1565; Plesyngton (Aberhafesb) 1561; Purcell (Llandysul) 1572; Radling (Llandysul) 1551; Sheene (Newtown) 1568; Thelwall (Newtown) 1545; Tryror (Tregynon) 1571; Turner (Newtown) 1553; Weaver (Tregynon) 1541; Wilkes (Newtown) 1550; Wooding (Tregynon) 1569.

CYFEILIOG: Barker (Machynlleth) 1541; Cadman (Llanbryn-mair) 1580; Cotton (Machynlleth) 1578; Crompton (Llanbryn-mair) 1561; Crowther (Llanbryn-mair) 1572; Forbes (Machynlleth) 1543; Ghwoslowe (Machynlleth) 1580; Hamond (Llanbryn-mair) 1571; Kelly (Machynlleth) 1557; Knutsford (Llanbryn-mair) 1563; Kylam (Machynlleth) 1550; Shapptor (Machynlleth) 1567; Wynyatt (Llanbryn-mair) 1560; Yealet (Machynlleth) 1580.

DEUDDWR: Arrowsmith (Llandrinio) 1573; Atkinson (Llansanffraid) 1562; Banaster (Llandysilio) 1540; Buckworth (Llandrinio) 1574; Burgess (Llandrinio) 1551; Carde (Meifod) 1544; Clouse (Llandrinio) 1560; Crump 1551; Duckett (Meifod) 1557; Dutton (Meifod) 1562; Gratewood 1542; Grum (Llandrinio) 1568; Haughton (Meifod) 1574; Haward (Llandrinio) 1562; Hignett (Meifod) 1562; *Hobby* (Llandrinio) 1572; Holland (Meifod) 1545; King (Llansanffraid) 1567; Leyland (Llandrinio) 1559; Loskyn (Llandysilio) 1563; Lucas 1551; Maesbrook (Meifod) 1557; Mase 1551; Mytton (Meifod) 1566; Rider (Meifod) 1567; Robson (Llandrinio) 1570; Sandbroke (Meifod) 1559; Symkis (Llandysilio) 1572; Waring 1562; Whigsaw (Llandysilio) 1544; Whittington (Llandrinio) 1542; Wythenbury 1562.

HALCETOR: Aldwell (Churchstoke) 1557; *Baker* (Hussington) 1561; Heighway (Snead) 1564; Mountford (Churchstoke) 1576; Poyner (Churchstoke) 1580; Symonds (Snead) 1564; Woodward (Churchstoke) 1545.

HOPTON: Titley (Churchstoke) 1569; Wheler (Churchstoke) 1579.

KERRY: Ames (Kerry) 1554; Bates (Kerry) 1562; Berret (Kerry) 1540; Bromley (Kerry) 1569; Bromlow (Kerry) 1554; Bugorcome (Kerry) 1542; Crokett (Kerry) 1550; Dolley (Kerry) 1550; Dudleston (Kerry) 1565; Dudlick (Kerry) 1574; Filie (Kerry) 1573; Habberly (Kerry) 1561; Holies (Kerry) 1559; Knott (Kerry) 1557; Law (Kerry) 1568; *Leighton* (Kerry) 1574; Medlicott (Kerry) 1541; Nedeham (Mochdre) 1556; Owley (Kerry) 1565; Paige (Kerry) 1554; Penny (Kerry) 1566; Prince (Kerry) 1569; Sale (Kerry) 1563; Tailor (Kerry) 1563; Tyler (Kerry) 1542; Wellings (Kerry) 1578.

KING'S TEIRTREF: Allen (Forden) 1575; Fewtrell (Forden) 1574; Hinton (Forden) 1559; Jackson (Forden) 1544; *Saxsues* (Forden) 1563; Symond (Forden) 1544.

LEIGHTON: Aldrich (Trelystan) 1561; Awport (Trelystan) 1554; Betchcott (Trelystan) 1578; Digri (Trelystan) 1562; Gest (Trelystan) 1561; Lee (Trelystan) 1561; Milward (Trelystan) 1549.

LLANFYLLIN: Actyn (Llanfyllin) 1566; Borage (Llanfyllin) 1566; Burcoid (Llanfyllin) 1570; Burton (Llanfyllin) 1570; Corser (Llanfyllin) 1561; Davyson (Llanfyllin) 1563; Garner (Llanfyllin) 1550; Golborne (Llanfyllin) 1563; Huxley (Llanfyllin) 1561; Latham (Llanfyllin) 1563; Ove (Llanfyllin) 1556; Pinckam (Llanfyllin) 1579; Poole (Llanfyllin) 1571; Stirrope (Llanfyllin) 1579.

LLANNERCH HUDOL: Cawbot (Castell Caereinion) 1572; Cowper (Castell Caereinion) 1558; Cowres (Poole) 1562; Goldsmith (Berriw) 1540; Heyford (Poole) 1563; Spencer (Castell Caereinion) 1550; Wilde (Castell Caereinion) 1569.

MECHAIN: Done (Llanfihangel-yng-Ngwynfa) 1560; Hallmark (Meifod) 1567; Hockleton (Llanfechain) 1572; Jervis (Llanfechain) 1576; Long (Llanfechain) 1561; Perrock (Meifod) 1551; Savage (Meifod) 1551; Sydley (Llanfechain) 1576; Wilcox (Meifod) 1579.

MOCHNANT: Holden (Llanrhaeadr) 1568; Malton (Llanrhaeadr) 1574; Naggington (Llanrhaeadr) 1571; Rotley (Llanrhaeadr) 1569.

MONTGOMERY: Billings (Montgomery) 1560; Blocke (Montgomery) 1560; Broughton (Montgomery) 1566; Dudstone (Montgomery) 1554; Foster (Montgomery) 1571; *Wood* (Montgomery) 1557; Yonge (Montgomery) 1562.

NANTYMEICHIAD: Fytcher (Meifod) 1544.

NETHER GORDDWR: Elkes (Alberbury) 1553; *Kerby* (Alberbury) 1576; Porter (Alberbury) 1556; Pothan (Alberbury) 1542; Wang (Alberbury) 1576.

OVER GORDDWR: Bromlow (Trelystan) 1570; Clempston (Forden) 1564; Heath (Alberbury) 1570; Lingen (Trelystan) 1553; Ridge (Trelystan) 1571; Warters (Trelystan) 1542.

PLAS DINAS: Ballior (Llansanffraid) 1550; Cliff (Meifod) 1561; Howgreve (Meifod) 1563; Ratcliff (Llansanffraid) 1576; Roderop (Meifod) 1563; Swan (Llansanffraid) 1575; Whitfield (Llansanffraid) 1575.

RHOS-GOCH: Whatley (Trelystan) 1577.

TEIRTREF: Alcock (Buttington) 1561; Astowe (Buttington) 1556; Bailey (Buttington) 1556; Brasier (Buttington) 1579; Bratt (Buttington) 1545; Brome (Buttington) 1561; Colfax (Poole) 1568; *Deacon* (Buttington) 1577; Egerton (Buttington) 1577; Fletcher (Buttington) 1562; Focks (Buttington) 1577; Hands (Buttington) 1580; Juckes (Buttington) 1556; Minton (Buttington) 1561; Nicolls (Poole) 1566; Smith (Buttington) 1579; Swanick (Buttington) 1561; Tolpyn (Buttington) 1550.

TIRYMYNECH: Buckley (Guilsfield) 1577; Gilbert (Guilsfield) 1545; Rughley (Guilsfield) 1560; Salisbury (Guilsfield) 1561; *Stanley* (Guilsfield) 1570.

YSTRAD MARCHELL: Annysley (Guilsfield) 1580; Nash (Meifod) 1567; *Pallen* (Guilsfield) 1578; Striven (Guilsfield) 1545.

NOTES TO CHAPTER 12

[1] D.H. Owen (1975), 'The Englishry of Denbigh: an English colony in medieval Wales', *Transactions of the Honourable Society of the Cymmrodorion*.

[2] *The Munster Plantation: English Migration to Southern Ireland 1583-1641*, Michael MacCarthy-Morrogh, Oxford. 1986.

[3] PRO: Lay Subsidy Roll for 35 Henry 8; E 179/222/337 (for Llanfyllin hundred), E 179/222/359 (for Poole hundred), E 179/222/357 (for Deuddwr hundred), Lay Subsidy Rolls for 37 Henry 8; E 179/222/342 (for Newtown hundred), E 179/222/344 (for Cawrse and Mathrafal hundred), E 179/222/383 (for Montgomery hundred), E 179/222/348 (for Llanidloes and Machynlleth hundreds), E 179/222/353 (for Poole, Llanfyllin and Deuddwr hundreds). For the evaluation of the number of persons assessed the data contained in roll E 179/222/353 has been ignored as it is included in the other rolls. A transcript of all the lay subsidy rolls for Montgomeryshire is contained in the Leonard Owen manuscripts held at the National Library of Wales: MS 18163 D. pages 1-164 and 169-244.

[4] National Library of Wales: Montgomeryshire Court of Great Sessions Gaol Files: WALES 4/125-2 m.62.

[5] NLW: WALES 4/125-1 m.40.

[6] NLW: Montgomeryshire Court of Great Sessions Plea Roll: WALES 24/48 m.8.

[7] NLW: WALES 4/124-5 m.62.

[8] NLW: WALES 4/124-5 m.13.

[9] NLW: Montgomeryshire Court of Great Sessions Plea Roll: WALES 24/2 m.8.

[10] NLW: WALES 4/126-2 m.8.

[11] PRO: Lay Subsidy Roll E 179/222/375 dated 1571 records a Thomas Sheene in the parish of Newtown.

[12] Act of Parliament: 27 Henry 8, c.26 'An Act for Laws and Justice to be ministered in Wales in like form as it is in this Realm. Clause 3, in particular notes that 'many of the said lordships Marchers be now in the hands and possession of our sovereign lord the King and the smallest number of them in the possession of other Lords'.

[13] PRO: SC 12/17/99.

[14] NLW: Powis Castle Deeds and Documents: A copy of the charter is contained in a large vellum covered book, pages 49-51, which records a survey of the lordship of Cedewain in 1609.

[15] Cardiff Central Library: Register of Deuddwr Deeds: MS 5.2 m.5 dorso.

[16] PRO: SC 12/17/99.

[17] *Montgomeryshire Collections*. Volume 22, pp. 119-138. Muster of Montgomeryshire Men in 1574. A complete schedule of names is included for each hundred for those who were mustered to serve as horsemen, pikesmen, arquebusiers (soldiers with hand guns), archers and bill men.

[18] NLW: Powis Castle Deeds and Documents: 11427.

[19] PRO: C66/1137/m.33; NLW: Powis Castle Archive 11426.

[20] NLW: Powis Castle Deeds and Documents: 12773. The deed contains the names of 214 tenants of the Earl of Leicester in certain townships in the manor of Arwystli Iscoed. 176 are Welsh patronymic and of the thirty-eight which are English-style surnames, only eight are clearly English families. This is a relatively low number when compared with the numbers given in the Lay Subsidy Rolls for 1571, 1573, 1577 and 1588 which record a much higher percentage of English-style names, and also less than the numbers which can be derived from Table 2 and stated in Table 4.

[21] PRO: C 66/1200/mm. 33-41.

[22] NLW: Powis Castle Deeds and Documents: 12611.

[23] NLW: WALES 4/129-1 mm. 24-25A.

[24] NLW: WALES 4/129-3 m.65.

[25] NLW: WALES 4/129-1 mm. 59-64.

[26] NLW: Powis Castle Deeds and Documents: 12773.

[27] NLW: WALES 4/129-1 m.66.

[28] John Thornhill is recorded in the Lay Subsidy roll dated 1588 [PRO: E 179/222/377] being assessed in goods (*in bonis*) and not in land (*in terris*), indicating that he was a tenant farmer.

[29] NLW: WALES 4/129-1 m.73. The examination of John Thornhill taken at Llanidloes on 22 December 1577 before Morgan Gwynne and David Lloyd Jenkin, esqs., JPs. Thornhill was only able to subscribe this document with his mark.

[30] Calendar of State Papers 1547-1580, Volume CXLIV. Letter from William Herlle to the Earl of Leicester dated 17 November 1580 in which Sir Edward Herbert thanks Leicester for procuring an impartial sheriff in Montgomeryshire for which office Griffith Lloyd is much to be preferred.

[31] NLW: WALES 4/138-2 m.171.

[32] NLW: WALES 4/126-1 m.5.

[33] The selection of co. Kerry, Ireland, has been made because its population density in 1733 was the same as that for Montgomeryshire. The date of 1733 has been selected simply because it is the earliest one for which comparable data are available.

[34] *The Munster Plantation: English Migration to Southern Ireland 1583-1641*, Michael MacCarthy-Morrogh, Oxford. 1986. The Earl of Desmond's forfeited estates amounted to 294,072 acres (Table 1, pp. 291-2) and extended through cos. Kerry, Limerick, Cork and Waterford with a small area in Tipperary.

[35] Ibid.: Table 2, p. 23. The total number of households which settled on all of the forfeited estates in 1584 was 512, of which 91 households settled in co. Kerry.

[36] *Digest of Welsh Historical Statistics, Volume 1*. John Williams. Welsh Office. 1985. p. 40.

[37] *The Ancient and Present State of the County of Kerry*. Charles Smith. Dublin. 1979; being a reprint of the original edition published in Dublin, 1756, p. 43.

[38] *The Crisis of Community, Montgomeryshire, 1680-1815.* Melvin Humphreys. Cardiff, 1996. p.75. The population for the year 1733 has been taken as the average for the years 1731 (34,601) and 1736 (33,415).

[39] *The Ancient and Present State of the County of Kerry*, p. 43. For the year 1733, 14,346 families are recorded in co. Kerry. For the year 1754, the number of households is 10,228 with a population of 51,140 people. This would suggest a population in 1733 of 71,730.

[40] The acreage has been derived from the first edition of the Six-Inch Ordnance Survey Maps, viz: Carno (11,004 acres), Llandinam (18,565 acres), Llangurig (33,362 acres), Llanidloes (16,312 acres), Llanwnnog (10,910 acres), Penystrywaid (1,248 acres) and Trefeglwys (18,547 acres).

[41] Carno has been included as part of Arwystli for the purposes of this assessment.

[42] PRO: E 179/265/4/ Those considered to be English in-migrants are: (Llangurig) Thomas Wright, William Warden, George Doggin; (Llanidloes) George Ashton*, Ralph Bennett, Thomas Hurle, John Wilson*; (Trefeglwys) Nicholas Bennett*, Christopher Cleaton, John Dothell, Thomas Buxton, Alan Jordan; (Llanwnnog) Richard Swancott, Richard Wilson*, William Dewson. Those marked with an asterisk were witnesses at the trial of John Thornhill. Note also Thomas Buxton whose name suggests that he, too, came from North Derbyshire.

[43] The acreage of land also includes wastes and commons.

[44] This is virtually the same intensity as that for the total in-migration to Munster where 512 families occupied 294,072 acres (1 in 574).

13. ORDINARY PEOPLE IN THE RECORDS OF THE GREAT ESTATES

Graham C.G. Thomas

Good book-keeping is a requisite of any successful business.[*] This is a maxim as equally true for the running of any estate, large or small, in past centuries as it is for the management of any small business or multi-conglomerate today. For the landowner, there has always been the need to establish his legal right and title to his estate and, although the act of transferring property was by livery of seisin, namely, the symbolic cutting of a turf and handing it to the new owner, it has been advisable that all transactions, whether they be the acquisition of property, the settlement of it or the disposal of it, should be recorded in writing. He has also needed to be aware of and record the extent of his estate, the nature of its cultivation, its division amongst his tenants, and its annual value; that is, the incomings from rents and dues paid by his tenants, admission fees paid by new tenants for their leases, sales of crops, cattle, timber, minerals, etc, balanced by outgoings in the form of money expended on labourers' and servants' wages, provisions, and general maintenance. On such a gentleman's estate, these activities would generate a substantial amount of documents which, deposited in a recognised repository and adequately scheduled, can provide the genealogist with a wealth of information.

Land Tenure and Title Deeds

Before discussing the kinds of documents likely to be encountered among the muniments of a typical country estate, something should be said about the nature of land tenure.[1] The basic administrative unit in England and Wales was the manor, in which different kinds of land tenure usually operated. There were the freeholders who held their property indefinitely, paying a minimal chief rent to the lord of the manor. Freehold tenure might be either in fee simple, by which the property could pass on the death of the

---

[*] This chapter is based on a talk given to the Second Stages Course, 'People, Places and Pedigrees', in September 1996.

owner to whomsoever he chose by his last will and testament or any other legal instrument to be his rightful heir, male or female, and it could be sold freely; or in fee tail, by which the property could pass only to a specified class of heirs, depending on the terms of the original grant, and it could not be sold. There were the leaseholders who held their land by lease for a specified term of years, such as twenty-one years, paying an annual rent to the owner who retained the freehold. A lessee could assign his lease to another party who would then pay the rent to the owner or he could sub-let the property for a period less than the original lease. Often leasehold tenure was for lives. However, there was a difference between leases for lives and leases for lives or ninety-nine years. In the former, the property was let for an indeterminate period of time dependent upon the duration of the lives of certain named individuals, usually three in number. When one of the lessees died, the lease was surrendered and a new one drawn up replacing the deceased lessee with the name of another. By such a method, the lessees acquired a virtual freehold estate and continuity of family occupation was assured. In the latter, no such freehold estate was created as a definite date was specified for the termination of the lease. Finally, there were the customary tenants or copyholders who held their property according to the custom of a particular manor. Any changes involving the ownership of the property would have had to be presented at the following meeting of the manorial court and recorded in the court rolls and a copy of the proceedings then given to the owner. They would have to do various services such as suit of court.

Most landowners in England and Wales came from the ranks of the yeoman or freeholding class. Many built up large estates by buying out less successful freeholders or by making advantageous marriages. The advisability of keeping a written record of any change in the ownership or status of land meant that each property transaction was accompanied by title-deeds and other documents relating to it. Over the centuries various types of title-deeds[2] were used to record the conveyance of freehold property in fee simple, including, for example, deeds of enfeoffment or deeds of gift, leases and releases, bargains and sales, and bargains and sales with feoffment. In the case of property held in tail, two kinds of fictitious suit were devised to bar or break the entail and to convey it, the one being the final concord or fine and the other the common recovery. Documents relating to these actions likely to be encountered among estate archives are one or two of the three copies which were made of the fine (the third called the foot was retained among the court's records), and an exemplification of the recovery.

A title-deed names the parties involved in the transaction, the property conveyed and often the tenants, together with the witnesses to the deed and to the livery of seisin. Sometimes, they contain recitals of previous transactions relating to the property with the names of previous owners. It was also usual for the person acquiring the property to acquire all previous surviving deeds relating to it. Often a bundle of deeds would contain an abstract of title summarising in chronological order the deeds and other papers in the bundle. From such documents the genealogist can establish the succession of owners of the property over a period of time. Leasing of property on a gentleman's estate was done, as explained above, by a lease for a fixed number of years. Two copies were made, the one given to the lessees and its counterpart kept amongst the estate muniments. A record of rents normally collected biannually at Lady Day and Michaelmas from the tenants was entered in a rental or rent-roll. These usually name each tenant and the property, give the amount of rent due, the amount collected and the amount unpaid. Often, they record the name of any tenant who has died since the previous collection, and the name of the new tenant, sometimes explaining the family relationship. The presence in an estate archive of a series of rentals for an extended period of years can be used effectively to trace the succession of tenants of a property and their family connections.

Most land proprietors were not lords of the manor in which they owned land but held their property of the lord, paying him an annual chief rent. Therefore, manorial documents such as court rolls, extents, custumals are only found, unless they have strayed, among the muniments of an estate whose owner was also lord of the manor, but where they are present they can provide information not only about the tenants living in the manor but also the freeholders.[3] Often, the lord would keep a record of the chief rents due to him in a chief rental and from a series of such rentals the names of successive owners of properties within the manor can be ascertained.

Powis Castle Estate Muniments

The substantial Powis Castle estate muniments, deposited in the National Library of Wales by successive earls of Powis between 1933 and 1990, have been chosen to demonstrate how the records of a large estate can provide valuable information for the genealogist and anyone researching the families of a particular locality. What singles the Powis Castle estate out from most other estates in Wales is the fact that its nucleus is a barony with a chief lord at the top of the hierarchical pyramid, under whom came the freeholders who paid him chief rents and the leaseholders who paid him rents. Some of the freeholders such as the Vaughans of Llwydiarth held substantial estates comprising tenements leased to tenants who in turn could, depending on the nature of their leases, either farm their holdings or sub-let them. For administrative purposes, the barony was divided into the manors of Caereinion Uwchcoed and Iscoed, Deuddwr, Llanerchudol, Mochnant, Mechain Uwchcoed and Iscoed, Teirtref, Ystrad Marchell, and the boroughs of Llanfyllin and Pool. Additional manors were acquired either by purchase or marriage. Each manor was usually composed of a number of townships grouped together. During the Middle Ages, each township usually consisted of the *tir cyfrif* ('the accountable land') and the *cytir* ('the waste'). The accountable land was divided into messuages usually farmed by freeholders, and the waste was used for free pasturage and grazing. By the time of the Restoration of the Monarchy in 1660, when documents relating to the barony become more substantial, most of the accountable land within the barony was in the hands of freeholders. The number of leaseholders paying rent directly to the lord appears to have been small. There seems to have been some leasing of parcels of the demesne land and the waste by Magdalene Herbert and her son Sir Percy Herbert at the end of the sixteenth century and the first quarter of the seventeenth century.

Manorial Documents
The Powis Castle archives contain a fine series of manorial court-rolls. These list the names of the inhabitants of each manor who did suit to the manorial court; often there are comments by the side of the names of individuals explaining their absence from court, such as 'sick', 'essoined', or 'dead'. The heirs of both freeholders and customary tenants would have to pay a heriot on the death of each principal owner or tenant and the admittance of a new holder of the land would need to be registered on the court roll. Encroachments on the lord's waste would also have to be recorded and a fine or amerciament levied.

To illustrate these proceedings, I have chosen the records of the Court Leet and Court Baron of the manor of Tirymynech for the years 1557-1618, and the roll of the Court Leet and Court Baron of the manor of Mechain Iscoed, held, 18-19 October 1785, at the dwelling house of Thomas Edwards, Innholder.[4] In the first, apart from the usual lists of tenants doing suit of court, there are notices of the death of tenants and the admittance of new tenants including the following:

> 22 November 1576, Hugh ap John has died and John ap Hugh Lloid now
>> admitted
> 29 April 1578, Humphrey ap John Goch has died, and Thomas ap
>> Humphrey his son now admitted
> 30 April 1601, Henry ap John Bedo has died, Jasper ap Harry his son
>> now admitted

30 September 1607, Jane verch David, widow, late wife of Gruffudd ap Robert has died, and Richard Gruffudd her son now admitted 24 April 1617, Robert Lloyd, gent., has died, Humphrey Lloyd, gent., his brother, now admitted.

In the roll for 28 September 1618, we learn that David ap Ieuan Howell and Lowry his wife ran a tavern in Trefnant without a licence. In the second document, there is a list of the jury arranged according to the townships in which they live, the jury's ratification and confirmation of presentments and amerciaments. For example:

> We do present William Williams of Bryncynfelin for continuing an enclosure on the waste in this township of Bryncynfelin containing in length five yards and in breadth one yard by the same more or less, he having removed his Hedge and taken the same into his garden – amerced 1d.

The roll also records that John Dickin late of Pool has died since the previous court seized of a real estate in the manor and that according to the custom of the manor there is due to the earl of Powis the sum of 6s 8d in lieu of a heriot. This is followed by the signatures or marks of the jurymen, and a list of the inhabitants of the township of Bryncynfelin who ought to do suit and service at the Court Leet, which in turn is followed by the presentments of the petty constables of the townships within the manor, first listing the names of the inhabitants of the townships. The presentations usually involve encroachments on the waste.

Manorial surveys are also valuable for providing the names of inhabitants. Among the Powis Castle archives is a bound volume[5] which contains copies of the surveys made by Robert Fludd between May and July 1609 of the manors of Montgomery, Kerry, Cydewain including the borough of Newtown, and Halcetor. Each survey lists the names of the inhabitants, distinguishing between freeholders, leaseholders and copyholders, the property they hold (in the case of leaseholders, sometimes details of their leases) and the rent or chief rent payable from each, for example, the freeholders of Wig township in the lordship of Kerry:

> Margaret verch Richard for one tenement & certain land per annum *xd.*
> James David ap Ieuan for one tenement & certain land per annum *xjd.*
> John James for one messuage & certain land per annum *xvd.*
> David ap Edward for a messuage voc' *Giggvran* per annum *vd.*
> Mathewe Moris, gent., for one messuage & certain land per annum *vd.*

Powis Castle document 9689 is a series of interrogatories or questions administered, 31 March 1697, in a cause in the Court of Exchequer, London, between William, earl of Rochefort (complainant) and John Noell, esq. (defendant) concerning the manor and lordship of Ystrad Marchell [= Tirymynech] in mortgage to the defendant, with depositions of witnesses. This document records answers given by the tenants living within the manor to the questions put to them, and also includes the age of each witness, for example, Thomas Field of Tirymynech, yeoman, aged 60 years, Judith Pugh of Tirymynech, widow, aged 60 years, Joseph Nicholls of Burgedin, yeoman, aged 42 years, and Robert Griffythes of Tirymynech, tanner, aged 34 years.

Estate Rentals

The Powis Castle muniments contain an excellent series of estate rentals, extending from 1745 to 1941, which provide information regarding the leasehold tenants. The most convenient way of using the rentals is to search them at regular intervals of five years and note the changes in tenure. If any had taken place within any five-year period then the rentals for the intervening years may be examined in order to pinpoint the year the change took place. To illustrate this method, I have taken the entries for the township of Cnewyll in the parish of Llanerfyl within the manor of Caereinion Uwchcoed for the period 1790 to 1815.[6] In 1790 there were four tenants in the township:

1. David Humphreys paying £3 for *Coed y Bank* tenement.
2. Evan Watkin paying £4 7s 8d for *Ffrydd y Drum* and another *ffrith*.
3. Morris Evans paying £4 4s 0d for *Pen y Foel* tenement.
4. Griffith Evans paying 6d for *Cae Bach* and 7s for unnamed lands.

By 1796 (the volume for 1795 is missing), Evan Watkin had been replaced by John Jones; by 1800 David Humphreys had died and his widow Margaret Humphreys was tenant. An examination of the rentals for the intervening years shows that John Jones first appears in the 1796 rental, the property having been left vacant for some years following Evan Watkin, and that David Humphreys' widow first appears as tenant in the rental for 1797. From 1800 onwards each successive rental is augmented by rents charged for more and more enclosures of the waste within the township – in 1800 by rent for a house and enclosure on *Cnewyll Common* leased to Oliver Ingram; in 1805 by rent for a cottage and garden called *Plocksin* on *Moel Bentyrch* leased to Richard Ingram; in 1810 by rent for two enclosures on *Moel Bentyrch* leased to Robert Davies and a house and garden and two enclosures on *Y Drum Common* leased to Evan Watkins. By 1815, Evan Watkins had died and Elizabeth Watkins his widow was tenant.

Leases

The presence of leases, especially those for lives amongst estate archives, provides additional information regarding the tenants and their families, for example, a lease, dated 6 October 1760, to Ann Davies, widow, of property in Guilsfield for ninety-nine years dependent on the lives of Alice Wawen, widow, her daughter, and Hannah Wawen and Alice Proudley, her grand-daughters; and a lease, dated 25 March 1862, to Thomas Edwards of Cyffin, Llangadfan, labourer, of property in Llangadfan, for ninety-nine years dependent on the lives of his daughters Ann Edwards, aged twenty-two years, and Elizabeth Edwards, aged twenty years. It is endorsed with a note, dated 13 April 1908, referring to Thomas Jones son of Ann (she had died 7 April 1908) and Elizabeth the other daughter who had married some thirty years previously and had gone to America.[7]

Chief Rents

A characteristic of chief rents paid by freeholders, which can be used to great advantage in tracing the history of a property and its owners is that, unlike rents collected from leasehold properties, they remain constant, and if a property should become divided, then the chief rent payable on it would also be divided accordingly. This means that the succession of freeholders of a property, even if it is unnamed, can be traced easily in a series of chief rentals. In a chief rental of the manor of Llanerchudol for the year 1559, not in the Powis Castle archives,[8] there were four freeholders in the township of Gaer, in the parish of Castell Caereinion, who paid a combined annual chief rent of 31s 9d: David Lloyd, 9s 7d; Ieuan Gwyn Madog, 6s 2d; Hugh ap Richard, 5s 8d; Robert ap Ieuan ap Gyttyn, 10s 4d. The total chief rent of 31s 9d had not changed almost a hundred years later according to the earliest surviving chief rental for Llanerchudol in the Powis Castle archives, the one for 1655.[9] However, the number of properties listed had increased to seven, indicating that two of the original messuages had been divided in the intervening years. The original property paying 9s 7d was now divided into three messuages:

1. Mr John Whittingham: for a tenement with several parcels thereunto adjoining containing 30 acres lying at the side of a common called *ye Golva*, 2s 2d.
2. Jane Whittingham, widow: for a tenement called *Llan y Gaer* with other several parcels thereunto adjoining containing 50 acres lying by the aforesaid common called *Mynythe y Gaer* in the occupation of Thomas Swingle, 5s 0d.
3. Mr John Whittingham: for a tenement with several other parcels containing 40 acres lying at the side of the common called *ye Golva* in the occupation of Humphrey Richard, 2s 5d.

and the original messuage paying 6s 2d was now divided into two messuages:

4. Mr John Whittingham: for a tenement with other parcels containing 50 acres lying at the side of the road that leadeth from *Poole* to *Pont y Swccod* in the occupation of David ap Hughe, 3s 0d.

5. Richard Griffiths: for a tenement with several other parcels thereunto adjoining containing 30 acres lying at the side of the said common called *ye Golva* called *Kae Iago*, 3s 2d.

The other two tenements remained undivided:

6. Richard ap Hughe: for a tenement called *Lletty yr Wen* with several other parts thereunto adjoining containing 40 acres lying at the side of a common called *Mynydd y Gaer*, 5s 8d.

7. John Calcott: for a tenement called *Lletty y Lliwydd* with several other parcels thereunto adjoining containing 4 acres lying at the side of the aforesaid common called *Mynydd y Gaer* in the occupation of Humphrey Hughe and Richard ap Hughe, 10s 4d.

The same arrangement holds in the chief rentals for 1676[10] and 1680-1,[11] except that by 1680-1, Daniel Whittingham had succeeded both John Whittingham and Jane Whittingham. The freeholders of the properties can be traced in subsequent chief rentals until 1724. There is then a large gap in the series until 1777.[12] By then, further regrouping of the properties had taken place. Property 6 had become two tenements, both owned by 'Madam' Waring, paying 4s 4d and 1s 4d; property 4 had become combined with property 1 to form *Ty 'n y Pwll Farm* paying 5s 2d.

Marriage Settlements

An important document often encountered among estate muniments is the marriage settlement, whereby the father of one of the parties married or about to be married conveys property to trustees, usually to provide a dower for the bride. Much genealogical information can be obtained from such documents. For example, in 1560 a prenuptial settlement[13] was drawn up by Robert Middleton of Middleton and Richard Purcell of Onslow, Shropshire, gentlemen, regarding the forthcoming marriage of their respective children, Hugh Middleton and Alice Purcell, whereby Robert Middleton covenants that he will at a future date convey property to trustees to provide a dower for Alice the bride, one of the properties however to descend to her only after the death of Alice Middleton, widow of Peter Middleton, deceased, late brother of Robert Middleton. Attached to this document is a deed, dated 3 May 1606, between (1) Roland Middleton of Priest Weston and (2) John Middleton of Churchstoke, described as Roland's cousin, and Edward Thomas of Bishop's Castle, described as brother of Roland's wife Jane. This Roland Middleton was the eldest son of the union between Hugh Middleton and Alice Purcell and the document was executed by Roland in order to fulfil the covenants in his parents' marriage settlement. The uses recited are to Alice Middleton (now the widow of Hugh Middleton) for life, then to Jane Middleton the wife of Roland and their heirs, and in default of such heirs then to the other sons of Hugh and Alice, namely, Alexander, John, Peter, William, Lodowick, and Charles. Thus quite a detailed pedigree can be compiled from the two documents.

Title deeds can provide much more information than just the names of the parties. The property involved is usually named along with the names of any tenants. Deeds relating to sizeable estates usually name each tenement and tenant. In the marriage settlement mentioned above, the property described includes a water-mill in the tenure of William Sambroke, a messuage in Kinton in the tenure of Humffrey Mathewes, a messuage in Sydnall in the tenure of Ieuan Whatley, three messuages in Little Weston in the tenures of Thomas Oley, John Bordley and Ieuan ap Hugh, and a capital messuage in Priest Weston in the tenure of Thomas Speake.

Evans Family, Llangadfan

In 1832, Edward Herbert, Viscount Clive, purchased on behalf of his father, the earl of Powis, from Maurice Evan Evans of Holborn in the city of London, carpet warehouseman, and Margaret his wife, property called *Blowty Farm* in the township of Blowty, a messuage called *Tycoch* formerly called *Pen Mopart Farm* otherwise *Tyddyn y Mopart*, and parcels of land which had been allotted to Maurice Evans out of the waste lands called *Yr Allt Cae Dwr* in the township of Moelfeliarth, and *Gowriad* otherwise *Gwrid* in the township of Cyffin, all in the parish of Llangadfan, Montgomeryshire. With the purchase came a bundle of deeds relating to the property,[14] the earliest dated 20 September 1544. In it Res ab Ieuan Bedo and John ab Ieuan Bedo his brother, sons and co-heirs of Ieuan ap Bedo of Llangadfan, quitclaim to Mathew ap Ieuan ap Bedo their brother all their interest in four tofts called *Tythen y Tyr Beell, Tythen lle Yskybor Vawr, Llety yn y Llan, Lletty Vorth Goch* lying within the parish and fields of Garthbeibio in the lordship of Caereinion Uwchcoed, and a parcel of land lying in a place called *Mobpart* and parcels of meadow called *Rrankyve Newydd* in the township of Llamysten in the parish of Llangadfan.

The next document was drawn up in 1613, by which John Ieuan of Garthbeibio, yeoman, leases to his father Ieuan ap Mathew ap Ieuan for sixty years a moiety of a messuage in Llangadfan and Garthbeibio. This Ieuan ap Mathew would have been the son of Mathew ap Ieuan ap Bedo of the 1544 document. By 1648, John Ieuan's own son William John had married Jane the eldest daughter of David Morgan of Bryngwaethan, gentleman, and on 20 September 1648 a covenant was drawn up in pursuance of the marriage to levy a fine of a messuage in which John Ieuan (John Evans) lived called *Tyddyn y Bryn Tayl* in Blowty, Llangadfan. There are a number of deeds drawn up in the 1660s involving Evan ap John ap Evan of Garthbeibio, yeoman, in connection with the messuage called *Y Ty yn Moparth*, including one, dated 9 July 1667, in which he conveys the property to a trustee to the uses of himself and Jane his wife. Between 1676 and 1742 there is a series of marriage settlements:

> 23 September 1676: Morris Evans son of Evan John Evan and Elizabeth, daughter and heir of William John Evan.
>
> 4-5 May 1713: Evan Morris only son and heir of Morris Evans and Elizabeth, daughter of Robert Thomas David of Llangadfan, yeoman.
>
> 9-10 December 1742: Morris Evans of Blowty and Mary Owens, daughter of Ann Thomas now wife of Joseph Thomas of Llysin, gentleman, by John Owens her former husband.

From 1743 onwards, the family was forced to mortgage its lands: Morris Evans (by now the surname Evans was fixed) in 1743, 1749, and 1761; John Evans of Llangadfan, son and heir of Morris Evans, deceased, in 1775; and Maurice Evans, late of Pool, but now of Oxford St, Middlesex, mercer, eldest son and heir of John Evans, late of Llangadfan, gentleman, in 1811. Finally in 1832, Maurice Evans's son, Maurice Evan Evans of Holborn in the city of London, carpet warehouseman, and Margaret his wife sold the property to the Powis Castle Estate. Thus from this bundle of documents, a pedigree of the Evans family of Garthbeibio and Llangadfan, Montgomeryshire, can be traced back from 1832 to 1544, to the children of Ieuan ap Bedo (see Fig. 13-1).

Estate Workers and Labourers

Information concerning estate workers and labourers can be obtained from ledgers recording payment of wages. The kinds of information given vary from ledger to ledger and from estate to estate. A register[15] of workmen on the Walcot estate, part of the Powis Castle estate, commencing 1898, is particularly detailed, giving not only the names of the employees and their weekly wages but also their ages when they started working on the estate and whether they belonged to a club. Additions in red ink even record whether they had died or left their employment. For example, among the men working in the gardens there were John Edward, who started work in May 1901, aged 14 years, earning 6s a week, a member of the Foresters, and Meyrick Thomas, who started work in November 1898, aged 17 years, earning 14s a week, a member of the Oddfellows, and who left his employment in April 1903. An interesting, contemporary, social comment is

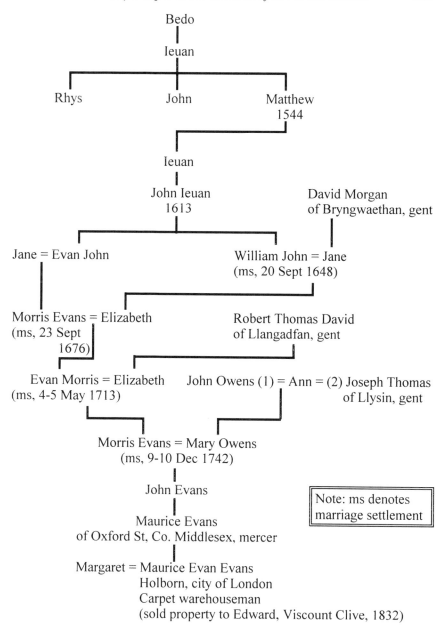

Fig. 13-1: Blowty Farm, Garthbeibio

seen in the main reason given for workmen leaving their employment between 1914 and 1918, namely, to join the army. For example, Harry Jones, who had started work in January 1911, aged 23 years, earning 18s a week, and Charles Baker, who had started in February 1910, aged 22, earning 16s a week, both left in August 1914 to go to war.

Family Papers

Other important classes of records which need to be touched on before concluding are family papers and the records generated by the management of the household as opposed to the estate. Family correspondence can provide information about the circles in which members of the family moved, their friends, the way they lived and the social events they attended. If a member of the family held some official position in society, the muniments may include documents which he acquired while fulfilling his duties. For example, if he held some legal position such as magistrate, his papers may include quarter session records or calendars of prisoners. If he was a Member of Parliament, his papers may well include poll-books listing the names of electors.

Household Accounts

Household accounts such as housekeepers' or butlers' ledgers, tradesmen's bills and vouchers can provide information regarding 'downstairs' life in the big house, including the names of servants and workmen engaged in its maintenance.

A volume[16] of sundry expenses for the year 1774 amongst the Powis Castle archives records payments under several headings.

Under 'House Bills', Elizabeth Davies was paid £1 2s for 22 days assisting in Powis Castle kitchen; Ann Griffiths 12s for 24 days assisting in kitchen; Mary Humphreys 8s for 16 days assisting in the cook's scullery; Abigail Proudley 11s for assisting at Powis Castle as under-chambermaid.

Under 'Stable Bills', payments in August and October were made to Isaac Jones for two bushels of oats, £1 4s; Richard Jones for two bags of oats which Molly Greatrex had to feed fowls, £1 4s; William Ellis for assisting in the stables and going on errands, 8s 6d.

Under 'Horse Hire, Messengers and other Incidentals', payments were made to William Thomas for carrying a letter from Powis Castle to Newtown, 1s; John Edwards an Old Bailiff of Pool and Llanfyllin Hundreds for giving an account of freeholders, 14s; and Mr Wright for fifteen advertisements in different evening papers, £3 8s 3d.

Among the payments 'paid on account of Montgomery's Election' are those to Richard Barnes, carrier, £3 13s; Ralph Thomas, postmaster, £4 4s; William Nave for bonfire liquor, £8 12s; and to 'a strange musician' 5s.

Among the accounts of tradesmen's bills recorded in an account book, dated October 1776,[17] for work done upon sundry farms on Heathley, Rockley, and Lymore estates, we find, for example, Charles Pugh's bill for thatching, 16s; John Davies's bill for mason work, 2s 8d; Mr Evans for twenty-one thrave of thatch straw for his own repairs, £1 11s 6d; and Edward Turner's bill for gate hinges, 10s 4d.

These records help to set particular individuals in particular circumstances at particular times, and could well reward the searcher for that elusive ancestor.

NOTES TO CHAPTER 13

[1] See A.W.B. Simpson, *A history of the land law* (Second edition, Oxford, 1986).

[2] For guides to title deeds, see N.W. Alcock, *Old title deeds: a guide for local and family historians* (Chichester: Phillimore & Co. Ltd, 1986); A.A. Dibben, *Title deeds 13th-19th centuries* (London: The Historical Association, 1971).

[3] For guides to manorial records, see Mary Ellis, *Using manorial records* (PRO, Readers' Guide No 6, 1994); P.D.A. Harvey, *Manorial records* (British Records Association Archives and the User No 5, 1984); Denis Stuart, *Manorial records: an introduction to their transcription and translation* (Chichester: Phillimore and Co. Ltd, 1992).

[4] NLW, Powis Castle Estate Archives, 1933 deposit, manorial records, Tirymynech, a bound volume and unbound files, 1557-88, 1600-18; and Mechain Iscoed, 1785.

[5] Ibid., 1982-3 deposit, uncatalogued.

[6] Ibid., 1982-3 deposit, RL12-39, general rentals, 1790-1815.

[7] Ibid., 1982-3 deposit, uncatalogued.

[8] NLW, Bodewryd MS 103, p. 168.

[9] NLW, Powis Castle Archives, 1990 deposit, chief rental of the manor of Llanerchudol, 1655.

[10] Ibid., 1982-3 deposit, RO1, chief rental, 1676.

[11] Ibid., 1982-3 deposit, 'Old Hughes's Book'.

[12] Ibid., 1982-3 deposit, RO25, chief rental, 1777.

[13] Ibid., 1982-3 deposit, box 14, uncatalogued.

[14] Ibid., 1982-3 deposit, D27/48/1-29.

[15] Ibid., 1982-3 deposit, uncatalogued.

[16] Ibid., 1982-3 deposit, uncatalogued.

[17] Ibid., 1982-3 deposit, uncatalogued.

14. AN INTRODUCTION TO MAPS OF WALES FOR FAMILY HISTORIANS

Sandra Wheatley

All family historians find it necessary sooner or later to use maps.* At first, perhaps, a road atlas from the family car is adequate to locate ancestral villages or towns, but eventually more detailed or specialised maps are required. It is always desirable, where possible, to look at maps contemporary with the period in which your ancestors lived, since such maps will show the area as it was in their lifetime. Most areas have altered rapidly in the last two hundred years, particularly with changing agricultural practices, urban expansion and developing canal, road and rail networks. The use of maps, and also of pictures and actual visits to areas of ancestral interest, all go hand in hand and add considerably to broadening family history by the visualisation of the locality and circumstances in which our ancestors lived:

> Family history without maps is like painting with your eyes shut. Even if you know personally the areas from which your ancestors came they will certainly be different now from what they were 50 years ago let alone one or two hundred.[1]

Before even beginning to look for maps, however, it might actually be necessary to find out *where* a place is. There are two modern gazetteers which should be available in public libraries. These are the *Bartholomew Gazetteer of Britain* and the *Ordnance Survey Landranger Gazetteer*, which gives a grid reference for all names found in the current Landranger series of maps.[2]

Following these, there are two modern standard Welsh works, which may help in different ways: *A Gazetteer of Welsh Place Names*, by Elwyn Davies, which gives the correct Welsh version and spelling of common place-names, and *Welsh Administrative and Territorial Units*, by Melville Richards, which explains how administrative areas, such as counties,

---

* This chapter is based on talks given to Family History in Wales Courses from 1986 to 1998.

hundreds, commotes, were divided historically and includes lists of these and some maps.

One major cause of confusion is the fact that in the past, the spelling of place-names could vary considerably. This is especially true in Wales, where place-names on maps and in official records such as the census were often recorded phonetically by non-Welsh speakers who would use, perhaps, *v* instead of *f*, *l* instead of *ll*, and could make various other changes, but only experience will prevail here. An additional pitfall is that Welsh and English versions of the same place may exist in parallel, such as *Llanbedr-pont-Steffan* and *Lampeter*. If the meanings of place-names are sought, then specialised books exist for this, including general ones and even a limited number of publications for specific counties.[3] For the mid-nineteenth century, a very useful gazetteer exists, which was published by Samuel Lewis in various editions from the 1830s to the 1850s. His *Topographical Dictionary of Wales* was issued in two volumes; other volumes were also produced for England, Scotland and Ireland. These should be found in main reference libraries and record offices. A great wealth of contemporary information is included, covering local landowners, industries and agriculture, church and chapels, schools and charities, in addition to standard topographic detail.

Of course, family historians will always need information on parishes and parish boundaries, and one item with which most family historians will already be familiar, and have found indispensable, is *The Phillimore Atlas & Index of Parish Registers*. This is usually readily available in main libraries, but individual maps may be purchased.[4] The atlas divides Wales into four sheets: North Wales, Central Wales, South Wales and Monmouthshire. The maps are particularly useful in identifying groups of adjoining ancient parishes, when a wider range of parish registers needs to be searched, and also for locating boundaries of probate jurisdictions, which are colour-coded in this publication. Pre-1832 parochial boundaries are shown, with the date of the first entry in each parish register. The index section of the atlas is also of value, since it gives an overview of the public availability (at date of publication) of parish registers, transcripts, nonconformist registers and parishes in the International Genealogical Index.

For many people the word 'map' probably means either a pink-covered Ordnance Survey Landranger Map, a local A-Z town street map or the well-thumbed family road atlas, yet the scope for family historians is much broader and more useful than this. So, the remainder of this chapter is divided into three sections, to illustrate the main groups of maps likely to be encountered. These are:

1. Earlier published maps, available from the late sixteenth century onward, and usually issued at a county level;
2. Manuscript maps, which include tithe maps, enclosure maps and estate maps and which are associated mainly with the second half of the eighteenth century into the mid-nineteenth century; and
3. Ordnance Survey maps and plans which for Wales, in general, cover the period from the second quarter of the nineteenth century up to the present day.

The books by Hindle and by Smith are both recommended as useful reference works for most aspects of historical maps, while the shorter booklet by Hodgkiss will also provide a briefer introduction to the subject. With regard to map availability, generally speaking, county record offices, main county and city public libraries, together with the National Library of Wales, all have excellent collections of maps associated with their respective areas, and these would be the first place to look.[5] Note that some libraries may produce useful leaflets on historic maps. Copies of maps may often be supplied for very modest sums by use of photocopying machines, or rather more expensively by photographic methods. Some record offices produce facsimile copies of a selection of their maps of special interest. Further notes on availability will be made during each section.

Earlier Published Maps

A number of earlier maps were published on a county by county basis and these can take us from the sixteenth century into the nineteenth century. Although increasingly rare, original printed copies are still available for sale, from these early editions. Most people find these older maps fascinating, with their artistic appearance and sometimes unusual cartographic embellishments but, although often thought of as only colourful accessories for the study wall, they are, in their own right, useful and informative historic documents.

For more than two centuries before the Ordnance Survey began, private map makers were producing county maps and atlases, and these were relatively common from the 1570s onwards. The first printed map series of the Welsh counties were surveyed by a Yorkshire man, Christopher Saxton, and were published in 1579 as his *Atlas of England and Wales*, in both hand-coloured and plain versions. Saxton issued the sheets for Wales in seven sheets, by grouping some counties together; only Glamorgan, Monmouthshire and Pembrokeshire were produced as separate sheets. All had fine engraving and decoration and attention was paid to the coastline, rivers, lakes and settlements, although a detailed survey of the mountainous areas was not, apparently, undertaken and some pictorial hills seem to have been added haphazardly. It has been suggested that the hills which Saxton climbed to do his surveys were drawn more prominently on his maps, while more significant hills were often omitted! Complete accuracy is not, therefore, necessarily a strong point with these early maps. Compared with all of the information given on the First Edition Ordnance Survey maps, not many features are shown. Towns, villages, parks and hills are shown in semi-pictorial form, while road information is completely missing. In addition, the scale is obviously too small for much local detail; nevertheless, these maps are of interest to see if one's ancestral villages were included.

In 1611, John Speed, another well-known surveyor, produced *The Theatre of the Empire of Great Britaine*, a grandiose title for his atlas of sixty-seven maps, which included those for the thirteen Welsh counties. In one corner (or sometimes more), he indicated a 'bird's eye view' town plan, a form which was popular in Tudor and Stuart times – see Fig. 14-1.

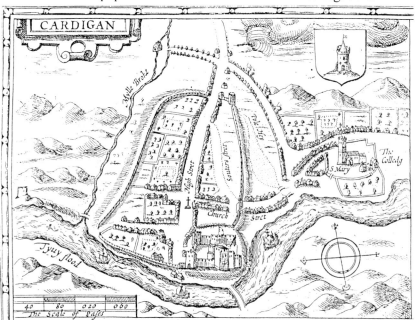

Fig. 14-1: Detail from Speed's map of Cardiganshire

Speed also showed the boundaries of the administrative areas called 'hundreds' into which counties were divided, and a descriptive text about the county was provided on the reverse of each sheet. A different type of map, but mentioned here for convenience, and produced later in the seventeenth century was published by John Ogilby in his *Britannia* of 1675.

Ogilby was a road surveyor and this work was a road atlas; maps were drawn in 'strip' form, showing all the main routes, including thirteen for Wales. Settlements on or just off these route-ways were illustrated semi-pictorially, together with adjacent landscape features. The maps are of interest for contemporary place-names and road networks and also for showing what are now abandoned villages and also lost historic monuments. *Britannia* has been reprinted on a number of occasions and will probably be found in most large libraries; revised versions were also published into the following century.[6]

Further county maps were produced during the seventeenth, eighteenth, and into the early nineteenth centuries, frequently newer editions of previous surveys, but sometimes showing new detail. The surveys by Robert Morden at the end of the seventeenth century were the first series to show the main road network for Welsh counties, while John Cary's maps are noteworthy for Welsh counties for the mid-eighteenth century. One of the last series of county maps to be issued was published as an atlas to accompany Samuel Lewis's *Topographical Dictionary*, in various editions from 1832 to 1849. These included all the Welsh counties and later versions gave Poor Law Union boundaries. Finally, for a number of counties, there were predecessors, although privately produced, to the early Ordnance Survey maps.[7] The 1795 North Wales sheets by Revd John Evans and the 1803 Joseph Singer sheet of Cardiganshire both received Royal Society of Arts gold medals for the quality of engraving, while the Glamorgan and the Monmouthshire sheets have been re-issued.[8]

This section has only touched on the vast publishing field of county maps, and mentions a mere handful of the surveyors. You can read more if you look at the books by Hindle, Smith, Booth and West in the Bibliography; at the end of this, you will see that bibliographies of maps for some of the individual Welsh counties exist, if further examples are desired. Reproductions of some maps, more especially those by Saxton and by Speed, are readily available for very modest sums, and can be added to your family history files as further illustrative material.[9]

Manuscript Maps

The term 'manuscript map' means one which was hand-drawn, rather than printed, which means that in general there will only be one copy in existence. There are three groups of maps, and also some miscellaneous ones included for convenience, which are discussed under this heading. For most parishes within Wales, there are tithe maps and apportionments and these will date from around the 1840s. For some areas also, there are enclosure award maps and documents, probably covering the period from the mid-eighteenth to the mid-nineteenth century. Finally, some areas may be covered by estate maps, which in Wales would probably date from the eighteenth century or early nineteenth century. So, all three categories of map will potentially take us across a period before the more detailed Ordnance Survey maps of the 1860s and will usually themselves show more detail than the earlier county-type of map, considered in the previous section. In addition, all three categories of map may have accompanying documents which could contain lists of named occupiers of land, and hence add directly to family history.

Tithe Maps: The tithe surveys are an extremely valuable source of information, extending over nearly 80% of English and Welsh parishes, and dating from 1838 to 1854. A small amount of background detail may be helpful here. Tithes traditionally represented one-tenth of annual produce of the soil. They date from the early middle ages, and were compulsory, being extracted by the church for support from the laity. When Henry VIII seized much of the Church's property in the 1530s, following his break from Rome, many tithes were sold off to private buyers, so that from this time onward parishioners might find themselves paying tithes to some great landowner residing outside the area. The tithes from the enormous ancient parish of Llanbadarn Fawr, Cardiganshire, for example, had been appropriated by the Chichester family from Devon, who were not only English landowners but also Roman Catholics. This payment in tithes to virtual strangers added to their unpopularity, particularly in Wales. Resistance and discontent came to a head during the late eighteenth and early nineteenth centuries, when agricultural improvements and investments continually involved farmers in increased tithe payments, while over this same period there was growth in numbers of dissenters, who disapproved of their money going to support the established church. In 1836, the Tithe Commutation Act legislated for the districts where the obsolete system of tithes in kind still remained. A system was introduced to eliminate tithe payments gradually over the next century, and a government department, the Tithe Commission, was established. The agreement made with each parish was recorded and the resulting documents have become a valuable historical source. In Wales, there were 1,129 Tithe Districts, each often covering the area of a parish, This exercise was conducted in all except twenty-five of these districts, where either the tithes were already commuted, or instead they were monastic lands. That brief summary, then, should illustrate the reason why the tithe documents were drawn up.

Only three copies were made of the tithe map and its accompanying schedule, or apportionment, for each parish or district. The original and definitive set of documents was retained by the Tithe Commission in London and these have now been deposited in the Public Record Office. A second copy went to the relevant diocesan office and for Wales these are now at the National Library of Wales (NLW), as the repository of all Church in Wales records. The third copy was held by the parish incumbent and may not have survived; if the parish copy did survive then it is likely to be lodged at the county record office or possibly even again at the NLW. The NLW has made micro-print copies of many of the tithe maps, and photocopies can be made of these at very modest cost. The original maps are frequently large, rolled items and may be fragile, and so are not produced unless absolutely necessary.

We will now consider the information to be found on the map and in the schedule or apportionment. It must be stressed that the map always needs to be used together with the schedule. The maps, at a first glance, seem very bare; the general impression is of a lot of fields with no names or labels, except for the field or parcel numbers, although fields, dwellings, roads, common land, wastes and rivers can be seen. However, the whole key to these maps lies in the hand-written apportionment or schedule and the map field numbers link the two together. By looking at the column headings in the apportionment, we can immediately appreciate why these documents are of interest for family historians, since 'occupiers' of land are listed. Also given are the landowners, sometimes field names and an indication of land use, and then acreages and tithe values (see Fig. 14-2).

Variation does occur in the quality of the maps. The accuracy of the survey may not have been perfect, since only twenty-seven out of over 1,000 maps in Wales were awarded First Class Certificates for land measurement. So, if field shapes are compared on equivalent tithe maps and large-scale Ordnance Survey plans, then discrepancies may occur. Some apportionments do not record land use, although this will not be of concern unless a study of an ancestral farm is being undertaken. Tithe maps are best used in rural areas or in urban fringes, since they do not usually lend themselves to use in towns, where individual occupiers will usually be listed in a block group as 'sundry occupiers'. Outside of towns, some quite small dwellings are listed separately with named occupiers, although grouping may again occur.

The tithe documents can be slightly frustrating for family historians to use, since the arrangement in the apportionment is alphabetic, but by landowner, so that if a particular parcel number or an individual occupier is being traced, then a longer search will be involved. However, the one enormous bonus of having prominence given to landowners means that

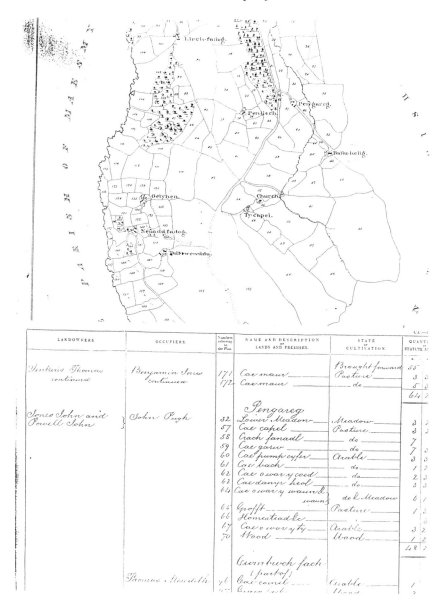

LANDOWNERS	OCCUPIERS.	Numbers referring to the Plan.	NAME AND DESCRIPTION OF LANDS AND PREMISES.	STATE OF CULTIVATION.	QUANTI STATUTE M	
				Brought forward	55	
Jenkins Thomas continued	Benjamin Jones continued	171	Cae maur	Pasture	3	3
		172	Cae maur	do	5	3
					64	2
			Pengareg			
Jones John and Powell John	John Pugh	32	Lower Meadow	Meadow	3	3
		57	Cae capel	Pasture	3	2
		58	Cach fanadl	do	7	
		59	Cae garw	do	7	3
		60	Cae pump cyfer	Arable	3	3
		61	Cae bach	do	1	3
		62	Cae o war y coed	do	2	3
		63	Cae danyr heol	do	3	3
		64	Cae o war y waund swaun	do & Meadow	6	1
		65	Grofft	Pasture	1	3
		66	Homestead &c			
		67	Cae o war y ty	Arable	3	2
		70	Wood	Wood	1	2
					48	2
			Cwmbwch fach (part of)			
	Thomas Meredith	71	Cae cornil	Arable	1	
			Graen bach	Wood	2	

Fig. 14-2: Part of the Tithe Map and the associated schedule for Llangynnog, Breconshire

these provide a key for access into estate records and hence perhaps into a further source for family history. Of course, property could and did change hands, but knowledge of the landowner of a particular area in the middle of the nineteenth century is a very good starting place for entry into estate records and a potentially very fruitful field for further researches. This may be particularly beneficial in those areas of Wales where parish records have not survived as well as one might have hoped.

The value historically of these tithe documents is enormous. They are not only useful for attempting to broaden the knowledge of our own ancestors, whether tenant or landowner, in the middle of the nineteenth century, but also for looking at land use at that period and for examining the estates of the landed gentry and the rural landscape in general. One particular use to which tithe information may be put is its combination with census data, to carry out what has been termed 'house repopulation', which consists of matching properties from the tithe apportionment with the nearest census listing in time, either that of 1841 or 1851.[10] Even when the two document dates are close, complete matching of tithe occupiers with census household heads is not possible, because of in- and out-migration and death. However, this technique may be helpful when attempting to establish in which property an ancestor lived, where there is some confusion.

Enclosure Maps: The late eighteenth century and much of the nineteenth century in Britain covered a period of considerable agricultural change, one aspect of which was Parliamentary Enclosure. This was generally undertaken in order to make farming more productive and efficient, with the aim of extending the area of land under cultivation and hence use land more profitably. In Wales, where enclosure was not generally as prevalent as in England, this was often done by enclosing common land, moors, marshes and other relatively marginal land. 'Wastes' were especially prevalent in areas of higher land; in central Wales, for example, these accounted for at least 40% of this area in 1800. In Wales as a whole, there were only thirteen parliamentary enclosures before 1790, while over 50% of enclosure took place after 1840.[11] For any parish where Parliamentary Enclosure took place, there should be a specific set of documents generated, which were a copy of the actual award, an award map and the specific Local Act, unless the procedure was carried out under a General Enclosure Act. The award document would usually list allottees, to whom specific plots were granted, and these plots would be referenced by numbers on the accompanying map; thus, as with the tithe map, the enclosure map must be seen with its associated documents in order to be of use for tracing specific names to areas on the ground. Geographic coverage is not as wide within Wales as for the tithe surveys, since only 227 enclosure awards were made in the principality. Enclosure documents are to be found either in county record offices or in the Public Record Office, and all are listed in the book by Chapman.[12]

Estate Maps: From the late sixteenth century up to the nineteenth century, records of the landed gentry may include a series of maps of the family estates, although early maps, from before the eighteenth century, are fairly uncommon. These maps, for the estates belonging to a family, may survive as individual documents or might be bound into volumes for a whole estate. Numbers of surviving estate maps suggest that the survey of these estates had become a fashionable practice for the gentry and other landowners from the late eighteenth century and into the early nineteenth century. The surveys, of course, also had very practical applications where sale of land was involved or boundary disputes arose. Activity of land surveyors, that is, the men who were responsible for producing these maps in Wales, was scarce before 1750 and grew then to a peak around 1830 and fell dramatically when Ordnance Survey maps became available after mid-century. So, although the earliest estate mapping in Wales dates from late Elizabethan times, until the second part of the eighteenth century estate surveys remained the reserve of only the great landowners.[13] At about this time, during the agricultural revolution, there was an increasing awareness of the value of detailed estate plans to use in the estate management for improved farming techniques and hence more landowners began to commission estate surveys. Between a third and two-thirds of the total area of Welsh counties were occupied by large estates, which were almost certainly mapped, although smaller estates may have been less likely to undergo a survey.

These maps can be very attractive documents, with careful hand water-colouring and sometimes quaint pictorial representation of various features, both adding to the usually high standard of decoration. It should be noted that their accuracy and quality vary enormously; all were hand-drawn, were usually at a large-scale and were produced individually. They remain valuable documents not only of the farming economy, but of the whole rural landscape, giving a detailed topographical picture, since surveyors often showed minor features, such as pits and quarries, forges, furnaces, mills, collieries and other industrial structures, in addition to the expected individual field boundaries, farms, barns, cottages, roads, lanes and bridges. Of particular interest to family historians is the fact that some estate plans are accompanied by written surveys, not only detailing names of fields and holdings with acreages of different plots, but possibly also giving named tenants. The maps would also have been used with estate rentals. Do note, however, that not all land in the past belonged to estate owners who could afford to employ a surveyor. Further, by their very nature, estate plans were designed only to show the lands of a single landowner, so that in general only that landowner's property is outlined, although adjoining landowners may be indicated. Thus, this category of map was produced to represent the holdings of an estate at a particular point in time and each would be unique and hand-drawn.

With regard to the availability of estate plans and associated documents, NLW has an impressive collection, while some estate maps are in other repositories, such as the National Museum of Wales in Cardiff, the county record offices and in city or county libraries. Many landed estates still exist today and have retained their estate documents for continued use, rather than deposit them for public availability. Alternatively, the documents reside with land agents, solicitors or surveyors. Occasionally, even, these documents find their way into auction rooms or to antiquarian map dealers and are sold privately to collectors. In general, if you wish to have copies made of any of these estate maps, they would have to be made photographically, at the discretion of the archivist, since the maps will probably be too large, too fragile and too valuable to place on a photocopier.

Miscellaneous: Following on from estate maps, Sale or Auction Estate Particulars may also be of interest to family historians. Although not in any sense manuscript maps, the survival rate of these useful documents, by their ephemeral nature, is low, so that it is suitable to include them in this section. Many large estates disintegrated from the 1860s onward and the selling-off process involved the detailing of estate particulars, including small summary maps and printed descriptions, sometimes giving partial land-use with acreages and lists of tenants. These would have been distributed to prospective buyers. Some have found their way into solicitors' archives, others into private hands, but whatever the source, as with estate plans, the main repositories would have an index to those which have been deposited for public access. Note that similar maps may also be found in amongst leases within estate records.

One further group under manuscript map are the Valuation Maps from the Finance Act of 1910-11, otherwise known as Lloyd George's Domesday. These used the Ordnance Survey 25-inch series of maps as a base, onto which were drawn by hand the boundaries of individual properties for taxation purposes. As with the tithe maps, the numbers written onto the maps refer to the record books, which list both property owners and property occupiers. NLW has some of these working maps, but others are deposited at the county record offices, which also have the Valuation Record Books, while the Public Record Office has retained the field record books and record plans. This may be a useful source for anyone 'stuck' at the beginning of the twentieth century, wanting to follow the history of a family holding or to know where an ancestor lived.[14]

So, all of the manuscript maps sources discussed can be of direct use to family historians by virtue of their accompanying lists which name persons occupying, or even owning, land at a certain time. Tithe and estate maps are of further unique value in preserving field and farm names, which might otherwise be lost.

Ordnance Survey Maps

Most people are familiar with the modern Ordnance Survey folded map series, especially the Landranger series at 1:50,000 scale. These are found in many book shops and stationers and replaced the old pre-metric 1 inch to the mile map series. Also currently available are the Pathfinder Series, now being superseded by the Explorer maps (both at 1:25,000 scale and relatively inexpensive). This scale has only been published since 1945 but is quite useful at the local level, because it shows both modern field boundaries and community boundaries which, in rural parts of Wales, may still be the same as parish boundaries. However, more useful for family historians are the larger-scale Ordnance Survey maps at 6 inches and at 25 inches to the mile, especially in the older editions dating from the second part of the nineteenth century and the first decade of the twentieth century. Place-names, houses or industries which have now disappeared will probably be recorded on these earlier plans.

The Ordnance Survey is our national mapping organisation and was set up originally in the late eighteenth century for military purposes, in order to produce accurate 1 inch to the mile maps for south-eastern England during the Napoleonic Wars. The first ever Ordnance Survey map was for Kent, and was published in 1801. Index sheets are available, showing dates of publication for the First Series of these maps and showing how the series expanded out northwards and westwards, until by 1844 much of southern Britain was surveyed, including Wales.[15] The Welsh sheets were published over the period 1818 (south Pembrokeshire) to 1842 (north-east Flintshire). Later versions of these First Series sheets are available as fairly cheap reproductions, which are fair value for money and are excellent for looking at the Victorian countryside and future suburban areas.[16] Those familiar with these maps will know that a great wealth of contemporary names are given, often down to individual farms, the contemporary road network is easily appreciated, and railways may also be shown in the facsimile editions.

Relief is illustrated by hachuring, which tends to make the hills look quite dramatic, but can make these maps difficult to read by not improving the legibility of labelling. These sheets are generally far more reliable in terms of survey accuracy than anything produced before, and are of considerable value when used to amplify contemporary documents, such as the census enumerators' schedules. Superior reproductions of the First Edition 1-inch series have also been published, to a higher standard of printing, and should be available in larger libraries and record offices.[17] The original series was revised on a number of occasions and both First and Second Editions provide a useful picture of the landscape during a period of considerable change, but particularly in developing industrial areas, both urban and rural.

During the 1860s, mapping on more modern lines began with the survey of a more detailed series of maps at a 6 inches to one-mile scale. These had a very high standard of engraving and give considerable landscape detail, including field boundaries in rural areas and have many other features shown and labelled (see Fig. 14-3).

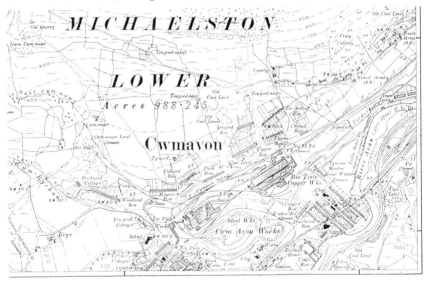

Fig. 14-3: Cwmavon, Glamorgan – detail from OS Map, 6 inches to 1 mile, (x 0.80), 2nd ed., 1900

For the nineteenth century and until after the Second World War, the 6-inch series (1:10,560 scale) and its even more detailed counterpart at 25 inches to one mile (1:2,500 scale) were surveyed and published in county blocks, and hence are known as the 'County Series'. The 25 inch to the-mile plans were based on the same survey information as the 6-inch maps, but were only published for lower levels, less than 1,000 feet high. The hand-coloured editions are particularly attractive. All buildings are individually shown and street names are given, so that these are useful for finding individual properties, ancestral houses, inns, chapels and so on. Both First Editions (1860 to 1888 in Wales, depending on county) and Second Editions (1896 to 1906 in Wales) show industrial and port features, and housing, which may no longer exist. In rural areas every field is shown, with an acreage and parcel number, together with woodland, scrub and quarries and farms and cottages which were inhabited by our ancestors, but which may now be ruined or even have gone without trace. Both the 6-inch and the 25-inch maps are detailed and informative, so that addresses given in other documents such as the census, or trade directories may often be pin-pointed on one of these maps, and in relation to schools, churches and areas of industrial activity.

Around the middle of the nineteenth century, the Ordnance Survey began a special series of town plans which are very detailed, being on a very large scale of around 10 feet to one mile (1:500 or 1:528). For anyone interested in Victorian towns, these are essential. Every property boundary and every building is shown individually (see Fig. 14-4). Far more labelling exists than on the 25-inch series, with all public houses, courts and alleys, banks and churches named. On some sheets, even the interiors of public buildings are shown, such as hospitals, workhouses, railway stations and prisons. These plans usually date from the 1870s and 1880s; occasionally, they were revived in the first decade of the twentieth century. The hand-coloured versions are especially attractive.

With regard to obtaining copies of these older Ordnance Survey maps, all maps over fifty years old are out of copyright, so there is usually no problem in obtaining photocopies, since the 6-inch and 25-inch to the mile maps were produced on strong paper (although do note that photocopying is always at the discretion of the archivist or librarian). NLW has good coverage for much of Wales and county record offices should have sheets covering their own area. Alan Godfrey is republishing 25-inch maps for selected urban areas, although only a limited number for Wales have been issued so far; copies of these are often on sale at local outlets.[18] Some county record offices have also produced some urban facsimile plans.[19]

Only the main types of maps have been introduced in this brief outline and others do exist which may be of interest, including further town plans (in addition to those generated by the Ordnance Survey, e.g. the John Wood surveys of some towns in Wales *circa* 1830), transport maps (in addition to the strip road maps of Ogilby), marine charts and military maps.

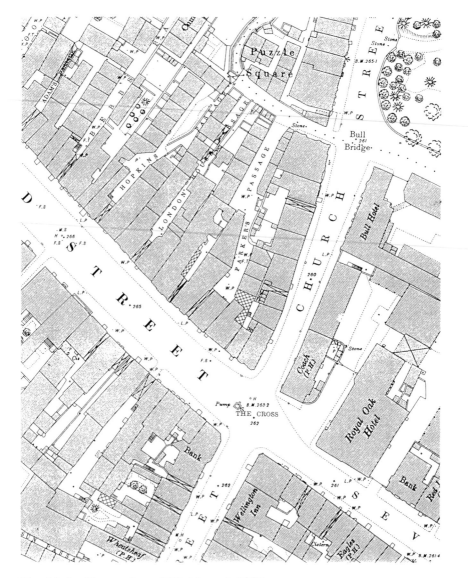

Fig. 14-4: Town plan of Welshpool, 1885
           Detail from 1:500 scale plan (reduced)

More information will be found from works on the reference list and all should provide fruitful ideas for broadening, as well as illustrating, family history researches.

SELECT BIBLIOGRAPHY

1. General

Davies, Elwyn (ed.), *A Gazetteer of Welsh Place Names* (Cardiff, 1967; paperback, 1996).

Hindle, Paul, *Maps for Historians* (2nd ed., Chichester, 1998); first published as *Maps for Local History* (London, 1988) and may still be found in some libraries.

Hodgkiss, A.G., *Discovering Antique Maps.* Shire Discovering Series No. 98 (Princes Risborough, 1977).

Humphery-Smith, Cecil (ed.) *The Phillimore Atlas and Index of Parish Registers* (2nd ed., Chichester, 1995). Note: individual maps are available from The Institute of Heraldic and Genealogical Studies, Northgate, Canterbury, Kent.

Jones, Bedwyr Lewis, 'Place Names', Chapter 8 in John & Sheila Rowlands (ed.), *Welsh Family History: A Guide to Research* (2nd ed., 1998).

Lewis, Samuel, *A Topographical Dictionary of Wales* (2 volumes, London, 1st ed., 1833; also various later editions, to 1850).

Lias, Anthony, *A Guide to Welsh Place Names.* Welsh Heritage Series No. 3. (Llanrwst, 1994).

Mann, Oliver (comp.), *Bartholomew Gazetteer of Britain* (Edinburgh, 2nd ed., 1986).

National Library of Wales, *Guide to the Department of Pictures and Maps* (Aberystwyth, 1997). Bilingual outline summary to the holdings.

The Ordnance Survey Gazetteer of Great Britain (London, 2nd ed., 1989).

Place Names on Maps of Scotland & Wales Ordnance Survey, Southampton (1973).

Richards, Melville, *Welsh Administrative and Territorial Units* (Cardiff, 1969).

Smith, David, *Maps and Plans for the Local Historian and Collector* London (1988).

2. Ordnance Survey

Harvey, J.B. & Phillips, C. W., *The Historian's Guide to Ordnance Survey Maps* (London, 1984). A very good summary, now out of print, but available at some libraries.

Oliver, R., *Ordnance Survey Maps – a concise guide for historians* (London, 1993). A comprehensive guide, but rather too technical for the beginner.

The Old Series Ordnance Survey Maps of England & Wales – A Reproduction ... *Volume VI: Wales* (Harry Margary, Lympney Castle, Kent, 1992).

3. Other Maps

Booth, John, *Antique Maps of Wales* (2nd ed., Westbury, Wilts, 1978).

Chapman, J., *A Guide to Parliamentary Enclosures in Wales* (Cardiff, 1992).

Davies, Robert, *Estate Maps of Wales 1600–1836* (Aberystwyth, 1982). A National Library of Wales Exhibition Catalogue, with a very useful commentary – now out of print.

Foot, William, *Maps for Family History.* Public Record Office Readers' Guide No. 9 (London, 1994). Gives details of three groups of maps held in the PRO: Tithe Surveys, the Valuation Office Survey & the National Farm Survey.

Harvey, J.B., *Maps for the Local Historian* (London, 1964). Covers town, estate, enclosure, tithe and county maps and has extensive further references; a very good summary, now out of print, but available at some libraries.

Wallace, H. (ed.), *Historians' Guide to Early British Maps* Royal Hist. Soc. Guide No. 18 (London, 1994). Useful reference section and bibliography, followed by guide to repositories holding pre-1900 British maps.

West, John, *Village Records* (3rd ed., Chichester, 1997). Has useful sections on county maps, tithes, enclosures, plus an extensive bibliography.

Welsh County Bibliographies, etc, covering mainly pre-1900 maps
(Most of these are published in county history society journals)

Brecon: *Brycheiniog* Vol. XVI (1972)

Cardiganshire: *Ceredigion* Vol. 2 (1955)

Carmarthenshire: *Carmarthenshire Antiquary* Vol. 13 (1977) – estate maps only

Denbighshire & Flintshire *Guide to the Parish Records of Clwyd* (Hawarden, 1984). Includes checklist of enclosure awards, tithe maps and some other manuscript maps

Glamorgan *Morgannwg* Vol. XIX (1975) – eighteenth-century printed maps only, and

Hilary M. Thomas, *A Catalogue of Glamorgan Estate Maps* (Cardiff, 1992) – an illustrated guide produced by Glamorgan Archives;

Merioneth *Journal of the Merioneth Historical & Record Society* Vol. 1 (1951);

Monmouth D.P.M. Michael *The Mapping of Monmouthshire* (Bristol, 1985);

Montgomeryshire *Montgomeryshire Collections* Vol. 75 (1987);

Pembrokeshire, Cardiganshire & Carmarthenshire *The Carmarthenshire Antiquary* Vol. 6 (1970) – concerning printed maps

Radnor *Trans. Radnor Soc.* Vol. 47 (1977) ; also published as a National Library of Wales booklet (Aberystwyth, 1977) – now out of print.

NOTES TO CHAPTER 14

[1] Michael Gandy *An Introduction to Planning Research: Short Cuts in Family History* (FFHS, 1993).

[2] All books mentioned in the text are listed in the Bibliography of this chapter.

[3] Chapter 8 by Bedwyr Lewis Jones in *Welsh Family History* (see Bibliography) is a very useful overview; some simple books on Welsh place-names are included in the Bibliography.

[4] See Bibliography for address; the same publisher also produces maps for the pre- and post-1852 General Registration Districts in England and Wales.

[5] Glamorgan, Flintshire and Denbighshire Record Offices have produced several facsimile maps.

[6] Ogilby – see Bibliography; reprinted London (1939) and Amsterdam (1970); also note J. Owen & E. Bowen *Britannia Depicta or Ogilby Improv'd* (London, 1720 and later).

[7] Summary of the large-scale, generally pre-Ordnance Survey, county maps for Wales:

North Wales: Anglesey, Caernarvonshire, Denbighshire, Flintshire, Merionethshire and Montgomeryshire	1795	Rev. John Evans	¾" to 1 Mile
Cardiganshire	1803	Joseph Singer	1" to 1 Mile
Denbighshire & Flintshire	1720	William Williams	1" to 1 Mile
Glamorgan	1799	George Yates	1" to 1 Mile
Glamorgan, Brecon & Radnor	1828	Christopher Greenwood	¾" to 1 Mile
Monmouthshire	1785	Robert Snell	1" to 1 Mile
	1830	Christopher Greenwood	1" to 1 Mile
Pembrokeshire	1827	I. C. Campbell	1" to 1 Mile

[8] The Glamorgan sheets were reprinted for the South Wales Record Society and Glamorgan Archive Service (1984); the Monmouthshire sheets were also reprinted by the South Wales Record Society (1985).

[9] Saxton and Speed maps are readily available in cheap reproduction form from many booksellers, county record offices, the National Museum of Wales, Cardiff, and from the British Museum, London. 'Parchment' Speed is available from The

Olde Map Co., Sennen Cove, Penzance, Cornwall TR19 7DF. Reprinted collections also exist.

[10] D.R. Mills, 'The technique of house repopulation' in *Local Historian* Vol. 13, pp. 86-97 (1978).

[11] John Chapman's *Guide* in Bibliography.

[12] See Chapman, *op. cit.*: see his bibliography for articles of local interest.

[13] See work by Robert Davies in Bibliography for very useful information on estate maps in general and holdings of these in NLW in particular.

[14] These maps are described in the PRO publication with a slightly misleading title: *Maps for Family History* – which describes only three kinds of map; see Bibliography.

[15] See Smith or Hindle for further detail.

[16] David & Charles, Newton Abbott, Devon, have published versions of the 1st edition 1 inch to the mile Ordnance Survey maps. These maps are often on sale in local bookshops.

[17] Harry Margary, Lympney Castle, Kent. This should be available at larger libraries.

[18] Alan Godfrey maps may be ordered through booksellers, or by post from: Alan Godfrey Maps, 12 The Off Quay Building, Foundry Lane, Newcastle NE6 1LH.

[19] Glamorgan Record Office has been particularly productive in this area.

15. THE NATIONAL MONUMENTS RECORD OF WALES

Hilary Malaws

This chapter explains the role and importance of the National Monuments Record of Wales (NMRW) to the family historian.* The NMRW holds the national collection of photographs and surveys, together with related maps and written records, of the built heritage of Wales from the earliest times until the present day. This mass of information about archaeological and historical sites and buildings is a public resource maintained by the Royal Commission on the Ancient and Historical Monuments of Wales (RCAHMW) and is becoming better known among family historians undertaking research on buildings and their related social history.

The Royal Commission's title may not immediately suggest fruitful ground for the family historian but the wording of its first Royal Warrant (dated 1908) provides a strong clue:

> ... to make an inventory of the ancient and historical monuments and constructions connected with or illustrative of the contemporary culture, civilisation and conditions of life of the people of Wales and Monmouthshire from the earliest times ...

This requirement has allowed RCAHMW to undertake major studies of the traditional architecture of farmhouses and cottages, the impact of the industrial revolution and the spread of nonconformist chapels, in addition to castles, churches, great houses and archaeological sites such as hill-forts and cairns. The synthesised results of such studies are generally published but the mass of related records produced as part of the projects are made available to the public through the NMRW.

Since 1908 the Royal Warrant has been updated to reflect the developing role of the RCAHMW in the understanding of the built heritage of Wales,

---

* This chapter is based on a talk given to the 'Second Stages in Researching Welsh Ancestry' Course in September 1991.

but the basic purpose of creating a record or 'inventory' as described above is as central to its work today as it was at the beginning of the century. The greatest change has been in the depth of recording as knowledge of the disciplines involved has grown and in the techniques used to make the record. From a family historian's point of view perhaps the most significant developments have been the increasing interest in social history as it affects the development of buildings and the extension of interest to more recent structures of the nineteenth and twentieth centuries.

The NMRW was formally established in 1963 and brought together for public use the records created and gathered by RCAHMW with the Welsh records held by the former National Buildings Record (NBR), an archive created during World War II at the height of the blitz on London. Founded in 1941, the NBR was a testimony to the dedication of a small group of far-sighted people, who, appalled by the scale of destruction of some of Britain's finest architecture, were determined to make photographic and drawn records before further important buildings were destroyed. They began by identifying and collating existing photographic and drawing collections, and undertaking a rapid photographic survey of important buildings ahead of bombing raids. Other organisations, notably the Courtauld Institute, whose Conway Library formed the nucleus of the new collection, and the Central Council for the Care of Churches, made considerable contributions by making their own records available.

The cessation of hostilities failed to stem the tide of destruction begun by enemy warfare; in fact the rate of reconstruction and development of war-damaged towns and cities, the rapid closure of old industries, and the increasing inability of many country house owners to maintain their ancestral homes, made the work of photographing and recording buildings even more urgent.

The vast scale of the work to be undertaken led to close co-operation between the NBR and the three Royal Commissions on Ancient and Historical Monuments (for England, Scotland and Wales) who were finding themselves increasingly involved in recording buildings threatened with destruction. The organisations' joint commitment to threatened structures led naturally to the assimilation of the NBR within the individual Royal Commissions in 1963 and the title of the NBR was broadened to reflect the wide range of archaeological and historical records already held by them. The transfer of the Welsh records to NMRW enhanced the Royal Commission's own collections immeasurably, with particularly good photographic cover of houses large and small, many of which had subsequently been destroyed or heavily altered.

The NMRW is a 'place of deposit' for public records as designated by the Public Records Act and holds selected public records created by other relevant government departments in addition to those of RCAHMW itself. These include listed buildings and scheduled ancient monuments records from Cadw: Welsh Historic Monuments and plans of public buildings, such as post offices and law courts, created by the Property Services Agency. From the earliest days of the NBR the importance of collecting information about records held elsewhere was recognised and this work has continued ever since. In addition, private individuals and other organisations have also been encouraged to deposit records or to loan them for copying, thus enabling the NMRW to develop as a national information centre for the built heritage where the staff are usually able to direct researchers to relevant collections in other repositories if the information is not available in the NMRW itself.

The continuing work of the Royal Commission (which celebrated its ninetieth anniversary in 1998) ensures a regular flow of new surveys, photographs and reports to the NMRW. This is a symbiotic process whereby existing archives may be analysed and interpreted to support a field project and this analysis, together with new field surveys, will then be added to the collections. The Royal Commission places considerable emphasis on recording buildings 'threatened' by conversion, re-development or demolition; particularly those which are listed as being of architectural or historical interest. (The actual 'listing' is the responsibility of Cadw: Welsh Historic Monuments.) Ironically, demolition often provides the key to unravelling the building's history – revealing hidden construction details which enable the Royal Commission's staff to interpret phases of construction and use of the building. This work means that records of a wide range of buildings, from clay cottages and terraced houses to large country estates and Victorian factories, are constantly being added to the collections.

Parallel to such general recording, thematic surveys are carried out of *types* of structure under threat, such as farm buildings, collieries and chapels. As part of these thematic surveys considerable information is amassed about records held elsewhere and this is also incorporated in the NMRW. The result is an amalgam of information, both historic and contemporary, relating to the architectural development and social history of individual buildings or types of structures. An important facet of this diverse information is that the staff of RCAHMW, who are specialists in various aspects of the built heritage, interpret the material and assess its value using their expertise and up-to-date knowledge, and add this to the existing records, to the ultimate advantage of users of the NMRW.

Current projects on which staff are engaged illustrate the wide-ranging concerns of the RCAHMW. These include an intensive study of the timber-building tradition in Radnorshire, basic recording of all Nonconformist chapels in Wales, creation of a database of historic gardens and the Welsh Uplands initiative, which seeks to identify the diversity and distribution of human activity in the hill regions and thus promote greater understanding of the uplands environment and its role in the history of Wales.

Aerial photography is used for most of RCAHMW's projects. It provides a powerful tool for recording many aspects of the historic landscape and built heritage of Wales, from the earliest times until the very recent past. The aerial viewpoint can give a fresh and often dramatic perspective of sites, buildings and landscapes which can be difficult to appreciate or interpret at ground level. Several thousand oblique air photos are taken each year illustrating a range of subjects from prehistoric settlements and Roman remains, to historic gardens, farm buildings, wartime structures and industrial landscapes, and these are all made available in the NMRW.

The Royal Commission works closely with other organisations, voluntary groups and individuals and examples of co-operative ventures include the chapels project, which is being taken forward with Capel (the Chapels Heritage Society), and the Defence of Britain project, co-ordinated by the Council for British Archaeology, which relies mainly on volunteers to record the remains of second world war structures across Britain. Wales was at the forefront of developments in the industrial revolution and the evidence of former industries can be found throughout the country. The rapid industrial change that growing technological knowledge brought about continues still and RCAHMW has set up a specialist panel (the Welsh Industrial Archaeology Panel) to provide advice and act as a discussion forum to determine priorities for recording in this vast subject area. In addition to recording the remains of structures directly involved with past industries, the Royal Commission is concerned with recording the industrial processes carried out and has recently completed a survey of the coal preparation process at a since-demolished South Wales colliery. It is also concerned with the related social 'infrastructure': housing, religious buildings, and public facilities such as schools and hospitals.

RCAHMW is in the process of computerising information from the NMRW and, through the Extended National Database index (ENDEX), plans to bring together the records of many related organisations which will act ultimately as an index to the information held by other bodies concerned with the archaeology and architectural heritage of Wales, as well as to those held in the NMRW. It is also working with other archive repositories in

Wales to establish a Welsh Archives Network enabling remote searching of the archive holdings. The task of creating a detailed computerised index linking sites to NMRW records (both paper and computer-based) will take many years to complete but ENDEX already holds core information on many thousands of sites and buildings.

The development of the database will, amongst other things, make searching for names of people associated with the structures much easier, and it is anticipated that users will eventually be able to access the NMRW from remote locations and view a selection of archive items and information on a local computer. Selected project information and database records will also be made available on the Internet via the RCAHMW's web pages (the web site already carries details of current projects and information on the NMRW). However, using the NMRW does not mean simply gaining access to dry facts; it also allows users to draw upon the expertise and knowledge of the Royal Commission's specialist staff.

Collections in the National Monuments Record of Wales
A description of some of the main collections in the NMRW is given below but as these are being added to on a daily basis it is always worthwhile contacting staff to discuss research queries and establish what records may be of assistance. Offers of items loaned for copying or to be gifted to the collections are received gratefully and, if for some reason the NMRW is unable to accept the offer, advice on other appropriate repositories will be given.

The main record file series: This series, previously known as the parish files (from early inventory days when information was collated on a parish basis), form the core of the collection and are the starting point for most area-based searches. The collection includes over 1,100 boxes and is presently arranged in five main class groups – earthworks, defensive, ecclesiastical, domestic and industrial – ordered by Ordnance Survey quarter-sheet with sites located by eight-figure grid-reference. The records include photographs, drawings, reports, house sale particulars, correspondence, etc, all accompanied by a headed strip listing core information about the site. Many of the records include some information about people connected with the structures such as architects, engineers, industrialists or domestic families, but naturally the principal information concerns the structure itself.

Photographs are a particularly important part of this collection and comprise about one million negatives and their associated prints, among them historically important and fragile examples of early photographic techniques. The vast majority of the collection is in black and white format although some colour prints, slides and transparencies are held, particularly where colour is important to understanding the building concerned. Included are both specially commissioned photographs and the work of the RCAHMW photographers, in addition to collections acquired from both private and official sources. The historic collections include some of the earliest known photographs of particular structures and represent the work of many of the most important landscape and architectural photographers of the time. Broadly covering the period from 1860 to the present day, the photographs show both exterior and detailed interior views of buildings, as well as street-scapes and general views depicting buildings in their settings.

Fig. 15-1: Tŷ-maen, St Brides Major, Glamorgan, in 1986

Often there is considerable social history displayed in the photographs, from portrayals of village life and special events to the furnishings and decoration of individual living rooms. The types of buildings represented are extremely varied; as might be expected the larger country houses are well-represented but there are also many examples of humbler establishments (see Fig. 15-1), including mud-walled cottages and terraced houses. There are also photographic surveys of associated buildings and features such as out-houses and gardens, as well as churches, schools, public buildings, farm buildings, mills, smithies and other types of industrial buildings. Some historic processes, such as iron-founding and printing, are well represented.

The drawings collection: This collection comprises over 50,000 drawings of many types. Measured drawings, surveys, cut-aways and reconstructions prepared by the Royal Commission in the course of its work are well represented, as are copies of local authority building control plans. The cut-away and reconstruction drawings are useful for showing how buildings were originally used and how machinery (such as fulling stocks) once fitted – see Fig. 15-2. There are also special collections such as architects' drawings.

Fig. 15-2: Tŷ-maen, St Brides Major, Glamorgan. Cut-away reconstruction of the house in the early seventeenth century

The air-photographs collection: The collection includes around 200,000 photographs (taken from both vertical and oblique positions), some taken for specific archaeological purposes by the RCAHMW and others by the Royal Air Force and Ordnance Survey for mapping and other reasons. The photographs were taken over the period from the 1940s to the present and are a valuable record of buildings since destroyed, of former garden designs and of archaeological features hidden on the ground but visible from the air under certain conditions and known as crop or parch marks. The historic vertical air-photographs are in black and white format but the RCAHMW photography includes colour transparencies as well. The collections are particularly useful for showing changes in local landscapes over the last fifty years or so, and when used in association with the large-scale map collection demonstrate clear patterns of land use spanning the last century.

The map collection: About 30,000 large-scale Ordnance Survey maps are held, covering the whole of Wales in several editions and at various scales. Perhaps the most important series in the collection is a set of original surveyors' maps of the 25-inch to the mile second series. Although unfortunately incomplete, this set shows earlier survey detail in pale blue, with the survey to be published overlying in black. It is thus possible to identify features from an earlier period, but in most cases post first-edition, that were no longer visible by the date of the second series survey around the turn of the century. It is a particularly valuable source for studying the development of industrial features and the alteration and extension of building plans and garden design. A few of the maps were never subsequently published at this scale, and therefore form a unique record.

The library collections: The library collection has been developed to provide printed sources to complement the unpublished information available in the archive. About 12,000 books and periodicals are available as a reference collection and include a wide range of comparative material for archaeology, architecture and related subject areas in Wales, Britain and elsewhere. There is a large collection of national and local journals, society newsletters and annual reports and a particular strength is the growing collection of out-of-print contemporary engineering manuals. A set of scheduled monument and listed building lists issued by Cadw and its predecessors, together with accompanying maps, are held for the whole of Wales and are periodically updated.

The maritime archaeology collection: This is an embryonic collection of information relating to historic wrecks which complements the wrecks database now being compiled. At present it includes a few photographs together with completed recording forms specially designed by the Royal Commission. Copies of the designation documents are also held for officially protected sites.

Special collections: In addition to the main collections there are numerous special ones donated or loaned by other organisations or individuals. Some examples are given here to illustrate the diversity of these collections and their possible interest to family historians:

The Ordnance Survey collection: A set of archaeological record cards for about 25,000 sites (including some domestic houses) containing brief descriptions and references and including sketches, photographs and antiquity models compiled to assist the Ordnance Survey's mapping work. An annotated set of maps and various notes, reports and off-prints accompany the cards.

The R.E. Kay collection: A large set of notebooks compiled by the late Richard Kay (of Hereford) from 1946 to the early 1990s. These consist of meticulous records made from field observation of a broad range of archaeological monuments and buildings throughout Wales and elsewhere.

The Arthur Chater collection: An extensive collection of black and white photographs of archaeological sites and monuments of all periods and historic landscapes in the former county of Cardiganshire, taken between 1950 and 1990. An important sub-set of photographs covers gravestone inscriptions.

The Rokeby collection of railway photographs: The Welsh section of a Britain-wide collection of photographic albums compiled by the late Reverend Rokeby and consisting of black and white photographs of most railway stations and halts in Wales.

Arrangements for public access

Access to the NMRW is free of charge and can be obtained either by visiting the public search room in Aberystwyth or by post, fax, telephone or e-mail (see details below). A charge is made for supplying copies of items in the archives and a charge may also be made if value-added services, such as complex searches, are requested. Although advance notice of visits is not essential, it is very helpful and may avoid a wasted journey or a delay while material is retrieved from store. Requests for information on several sites or general areas are best met by making arrangements to visit, but staff will endeavour to supply detailed responses to anyone unable to visit in person. For practical reasons it may be necessary to limit such requests to information on two or three sites, so it is worth prioritising areas or sites of interest in order to get the most benefit from the service. It will help to supply as much locational information as possible and, in particular, the national grid reference if this is known. Where information is not available within the NMRW, staff will aim to direct researchers to relevant sources elsewhere.

Group visits are welcomed by arrangement and can be combined with tours and/or talks by the staff as appropriate, and of course staff may also be available to give illustrated talks to interested groups at their own meeting places; please contact the address below for further information. Free leaflets describing the NMRW and the work of the RCAHMW can also be obtained on request.

Contact information
National Monuments Record of Wales, RCAHMW, Crown Building, Plas Crug, Aberystwyth, Ceredigion SY23 1NJ.
Tel: 01970 621200. Fax: 01970 627701.
e-mail: nmr.wales@rcahmw.org.uk. Web site: www.rcahmw.org.uk

Search Room and Library opening hours
Monday – Friday: 9.30 – 16.00

Selected list of RCAHMW and other publications
Houses of the Welsh Countryside by Peter Smith, HMSO, 1988 (Second enlarged edition, first published 1975).

[Glamorgan: The Greater Houses] An Inventory of the Ancient Monuments in Glamorgan Volume IV: Domestic Architecture from the Reformation to the Industrial Revolution Part I: The Greater Houses (HMSO, 1981).

[Glamorgan: Farmhouses and Cottages] An Inventory of the Ancient Monuments in Glamorgan Volume IV, Part II: Farmhouses and Cottages (HMSO, 1988*).

Llantwit Major and Cowbridge: A Study of the Historic Domestic Architecture [Extract from the above Inventory] (RCAHMW, 1989).

Crewe, P. & Musson, C., *Snowdonia from the Air: Patterns in the Landscape* (Snowdonia National Park, 1996).

Hague, Douglas, *Lighthouses of Wales: Their Architecture and Archaeology* (RCAHMW, 1994).

Hughes, Stephen, *The Archaeology of the Montgomeryshire Canal: A Guide and Study in Waterways Archaeology* (4th ed., RCAHMW, 1988).

— *The Archaeology of an Early Railway System: The Brecon Forest Tramroads* (RCAHMW, 1990).

Hughes, S., Malaws, B., Parry, M. & Wakelin, P., *Collieries of Wales: Engineering and Architecture* (RCAHMW, 1994).

Musson, Chris, *Wales from the Air: Patterns of Past and Present* (RCAHMW, 1994).

Suggett, Richard, *John Nash – Architect/John Nash – Pensaer* (National Library of Wales/RCAHMW, 1995).

16. WRITING AN ESTATE AND FAMILY HISTORY: THE VAUGHANS OF TRAWSGOED

Gerald Morgan

My ambition, in publishing *A Welsh House and its Family: the Vaughans of Trawsgoed*, was to attempt more than simply an account of family members generation by generation.* It was to relate the family to the growth of its estate in Cardiganshire, to indicate the relationship of that estate to the local landscape and economy, and to demonstrate the place of the family in county and national social and political life. Such an ambition strains one's resources of both knowledge and time. Skills in the whole range of palaeography, genealogy and heraldry, architecture, garden history, art, the tracing of sources, and in interviewing, as well as a grasp of local and national social, political, agricultural and economic history are not granted to many, and certainly not all to me. I had lived in the shadow of Trawsgoed, so to speak, for sixteen years before time was granted me by a change of work. For twenty years I lived in what had been Trawsgoed properties: in the farmhouse at Tan-yr-allt (Abermagwr), built in the eighteenth century from local bricks, and in Wenallt House, where I wrote the first draft of the book. This was at the time the Llanafan vicarage, given by the seventh Earl of Lisburne to the Church in Wales, but is now a private house. At worship in Llanafan church one would be surrounded by Lisburne family memorials and gifts; it was virtually an estate chapel. I came to know the local landscape well, and gained acquaintance with a generation of people whose parents had worked on the Trawsgoed estate or been its tenants, and I had a nodding acquaintance with members of the Earl of Lisburne's family before I started serious work.

Such a background was invaluable when time became professionally available to research and write seriously, and through holding adult education classes it was possible to learn more. There was time to arrange to

---

* This chapter followed from a talk given to the Second Stages Course, 'People, Places and Pedigrees', in September 1996. See also the Foreword to this book.

meet members of the Vaughan family, who were always helpful, especially with the temporary deposit of valuable family albums and documents in the National Library of Wales. Essentially a historian in this field should research backwards: the documents of the past are in safe keeping, and with rare exceptions will remain available, but the living are not with us for ever; they should be consulted while they enjoy their full faculties. So too with the landscape: it lives and changes, landmarks disappear, boundaries are obliterated, houses restored or demolished. Yesterday's photograph is today's witness, especially if it is labelled.

The historian of a landed family is faced with a very different task from that of people working on their own non-landowning families. Few of us leave much permanent imprint on the landscape – at the most, we may build a house and create a garden where none existed. But the impact of a family like the Vaughans was enormous, and stretched over centuries, with the result that the landscape itself is a source, albeit often a baffling one. The mansion house is an obvious starting-place, and the historian must begin by asking why is the house situated where it is. In the case of Trawsgoed, the reasons are evident. The site is on well-drained land, but has a good water supply from a stream which seemingly never dries. The land is level and open – a rare thing in Ceredigion. The presence of surrounding woodland is deceptive; most of it was planted in the eighteenth century or later, partly for privacy, partly for shelter, partly for ornament, partly to encourage game. However, nothing about a site should be taken for granted. The present B4341 road passing so conveniently nearby (but not too close) was a turnpike creation of the 1780s; prior to that, the road pattern of the area was almost completely different, as is shown in estate maps.

For the house itself, the files kept at the Royal Commission on the Ancient and Historical Monuments of Wales (at Aberystwyth) are vital, although not every mansion in Ceredigion has yet received the treatment from the inspectors that Trawsgoed has enjoyed. Indeed many historic houses have been destroyed, in which case one may begin by consulting Thomas Lloyd's *Lost Houses of Wales*. Assuming its survival, the historian must gain access and examine the building. By the time I saw it first in 1973, Trawsgoed mansion had been much altered since its sale to the government in 1947, but its basic structure seemed unchanged, and it had benefited from a high standard of maintenance. The house has two parts, an older core of vaguely classical appearance, with a huge and ugly wing added in 1891. Dating the earlier part of the structure is not simple. A print of 1684 shows a completely different Trawsgoed, apparently a large gabled structure of the earlier Stuart period, quite possibly built by Sir John Vaughan (1603-

74), the most important (and wealthy) member of the family. The rebuilding is referred to in the correspondence of Wilmot Vaughan, first Earl of Lisburne (d.1800), during the 1770s, and although there is no detail it was obviously extensive. However, the library is not only Victorian in decoration, it may have been an actual infill between two wings of the early or immediately pre-Victorian period, while the front portico was probably added at about the same time.

Inside, only the magnificent Victorian library remained much as it had been when photographed in 1888. This reference shows the importance of photographs; the family has a fine collection of albums from 1888 onwards, to which I was kindly given access. These also throw much light on the history of the gardens which surround the house. Garden history is a recent specialism and a difficult one, since people can usually alter their gardens with less effort than their homes. Maps, plans and other documents add enormously to our knowledge, but nothing is so important as knowing the present garden, without which the documentary sources may easily be misinterpreted. The present Trawsgoed garden is largely Edwardian, imposed on previous gardens of which some documentary evidence survives, as well as a splendid grove of oaks close to the house.

The impact of a great landowning family on the landscape is extensive. Owners and/or their agents and stewards had considerable influence in every kind of planning. They might decide to replace a poor building with a better; they might insist on the planting of hedgerows, a process which can be confirmed by examining leases in the estate archives. Estate maps of the late eighteenth century show that there were still striplands of a mediaeval pattern surviving in the landscape, often belonging to someone other than the owner of the surrounding land. Much effort was expended in exchanging such strips, and indeed whole farms, the intention being to consolidate the estate. Of course all that cost money for legal fees. Thus a map of 1771 of the Trawsgoed demesne land (the land surrounding the mansion) shows a strip in the middle of the great Palu meadow; the strip belonged to the Hafod Uchdryd estate, which had access and the right to grow hay there, but nothing else. The same map also shows the fencing of a small deer park which can be traced in its completeness in an earlier map; no trace of the park remains. What does remain is a small group of oak trees which marked the original drive to the main entrance from what was the main Llanfihangel-y-Creuddyn to Llanafan Bridge road, all of which can be traced on the maps.

One effect of estate ownership on the landscape is not easily visible, but nevertheless important, that of the interchange of lands between neighbouring tenancies, and the amalgamation of tenancies. This was the result of at least two processes. The first was the acquisition of additional holdings, still often traceable in field-names. Thus the 1781 map of Wenallt (Llanafan) shows the upper half of the large farm as 'Tyddyn-y-bedw', so indicating that an originally separate farm had been swallowed up.[1] Another process was the amalgamation of units for economy of scale; thus Tan-yr-allt (Abermagwr) was for at least a century united with Penpompren, though they are now distinct; during the 1920s Tan-yr-allt's fields were all (bar one) rented out to other holdings, but they were reunited when the farm was sold after the second World War.

The hunger of the great landowners for further acquisitions ('much wants more') is well-evidenced in the landscape by the enclosure of common land. Contrary to folk-belief, common land does not belong to the public. It is land in Crown or private ownership over which certain other people (commoners) have rights, such as pasture, firewood-collection and the digging of peat. Indeed, desperate and landless members of the public frequently squatted on land which they perceived as tenantless. Their dwellings still survive on Welsh roadsides, as well as on sites such as Rhos-y-gell (north of Pont-rhyd-y-groes) and the mountain slopes above Ysbyty Ystwyth. A whole village, Cnwch Coch, has its origins in squatting on common land whose ownership was shared between Trawsgoed, Cwmnewidion and Nanteos. The Vaughans protested against the squatters, but themselves benefited from enclosures elsewhere which ended access to what had once been commons. The monopoly over the shooting of game which was enjoyed for centuries by landowners is also evidenced in the landscape, particularly in the plantations around Trawsgoed, and in the family's interest in the land of Cors Caron (Tregaron Bog). This interest, perceived as vital to family status and individual pleasure, is also evident from the game books which were kept by landed families, and which in the case of Trawsgoed are still in family ownership.

There is further evidence of family history in the other buildings which great landowners contributed to the landscape. As well as the mansion itself, its many outbuildings, and as well as the farm-houses, there are often many other buildings whose existence is owed to such patrons. In the case of Trawsgoed, there is the dower-house of Birch Grove, intended as a residence for adult heirs in waiting and for dowagers; Llanafan village school, whose full title is still The Earl of Lisburne School; there is the village hall (Neuadd Lisburne), and although the site of the parish church is ancient, the present building was paid for by the fourth Earl of Lisburne (d.1873). The relationship of many great families to the nonconformist denominations was often difficult, but they were often willing to provide land on lease at a peppercorn rent.

Finally, as far as the landscape is concerned, there is the industrial involvement of landowners, particularly in mining and quarrying. In the case of Trawsgoed, the family owned several of the major leadmines of north Cardiganshire, and their impact on the landscape was considerable. One has only to contemplate the site of Fron-goch (Trisant), with its attractive reservoir and hideous pollution, to realise how important this was. Over generations, rivers and water-sources were poisoned, fish, otters and birds disappeared, but royalties from the lead and zinc were a major contribution to the family's income, though not very well documented in the surviving sources.

During the process by which historians familiarise themselves with house and landscape they will meet their second major source, those men and women who were tenants or who are the children of tenants, estate workers or their children, or simply those who by long familiarity have some insight into the estate and family history. The evidence of living witnesses about the distant past is not at all dependable, but stories they tell may shed light even on much earlier times. For example, several local tradition-bearers told me a story of how the Vaughans had supposedly acquired land at Maenarthur (Pont-rhyd-y-groes). The story is actually a folk-tale which sheds light, not on actual events, but on popular beliefs, in this case, that the landed classes were so rapacious as to be capable of lying and cheating to achieve their ends. Of course, oral evidence can be difficult to handle; local gossip may or may not be true, and might well give serious offence if published, whether true or not.

A third non-documentary source may be the family's collection of portraits and heirlooms. These have always formed a small but vital part of the identity of gentry and aristocratic families. With the disappearance of families through a lack of heirs, or with the sale of the mansion and estate, they may have been sold, stolen, scattered or lost, surviving at best in the chilly isolation of a museum or art gallery – most often consigned to the basement or other store. In the case of Trawsgoed the family has retained a collection of heirlooms going back to the eighteenth century, and has kept the nucleus of a fine collection of portraits both of family members and other individuals. The historian must be wary; some families, strapped for cash, sold their best paintings and had copies made to replace them on the walls. Many of the Nanteos portraits have returned to the mansion, but without identification. Neither is the case with the Trawsgoed collection. Among the finest works are a magnificent portrait of the first Sir John

Vaughan (d. 1674), and one of the second Earl of Rochester, rake and poet, whose daughter Malet married John Vaughan, ennobled as the first Viscount Lisburne in 1695. On that occasion, or shortly afterwards, the viscount was presented with a state portrait of William III. These portraits were a vital part of a gentry or aristocratic family's identity, a reminder of the length of its conscious past, of its status in society.

Inevitably and naturally, however, the estate historian will gravitate to the materials available in printed and manuscript sources. There are obvious places to start, first of all with books and journals, of which the county history, if there is one, must be the first. In the case of Trawsgoed there is more in the 'Notes on County Families' in the 1907 edition of Meyrick's county history than in the original edition, along with useful details of the county's parliamentary elections and the Vaughan participation.[2] Then there are useful volumes such as Burke's *Peerage*, Debrett's *Peerage and Baronetage*, and particularly *The Complete Peerage*, edited by H.A. Doubleday and Lord Howard de Walden (London, 1932). Even the latter is not infallible; their claim that Dorothy Hill, adulterous wife of the second viscount Lisburne, had been previously married to a Mr Waller is not credible. For the growth of estates in south-west Wales, the works by Howell Lloyd and D.W. Howell listed in the bibliography at the end of this chapter are essential background reading.

In the case of a member of the family who played a part in history, so to speak, there may be entries in the *Dictionary of Welsh Biography down to 1940* and the *Dictionary of National Biography*. Obituaries of many leading gentlemen were published in the *Gentleman's Magazine* for much of the eighteenth and early nineteenth century; they are sometimes vague on detail, but always a pleasure to read. Often a prominent family member may have published a book; Sir John Vaughan's law reports were collected and published by his son Edward after his death in 1674. The wonderful project on the history of Parliament, in course of publication, already includes invaluable information about Members of Parliament and references for further research, especially Hughes's history of Cardiganshire's parliamentary representation (see Bibliography). The second Sir John Vaughan was a lieutenant-general in the British Army who fought in the American War of Independence; his interesting career has not yet been fully investigated, but should prove of particular interest. He played an important part in helping his elder brother, Wilmot Vaughan the first Earl of Lisburne, to keep the estate solvent.

There will almost certainly be references to any estate and its family in local history journals; the historian in west Wales is fortunate in that the volumes of *Ceredigion* have been indexed to 1990. Local newspapers are a necessary but frustrating resource; it was only by a fluke that I discovered from the *Welsh Gazette* of the 1920s that a respectable Aberystwyth citizen had been instrumental in saving from the wrath of the law Wil Cefn Coch, the poacher who killed Lord Lisburne's gamekeeper in 1868, by enabling him to escape to the United States.

Half-way between the printed material and the manuscript is the academic thesis, existing in the uneasy limbo of typescript, only available in the National Library of Wales or equivalent institution. Where these exist they are invaluable, because their authors have spent years doing spadework that there is no need to repeat, and which is available for use without any payment other than acknowledgement. Two such theses exist on Trawsgoed, one by (now Emeritus Professor) J. Gwynn Williams on Sir John Vaughan of Trawsgoed (MA, 1952), the other on the growth and economic development of the Crosswood estate by J.M. Howell (MA, 1956). It was a source of great regret to me that I was unable to trace Mr Howell, who I understood emigrated to New Zealand.

Then we come to documentary sources. Here again the process of investigating an estate-owning family is different from that used by most family historians. Their first sources are usually parish records and the census, in order to build up a genealogy. In the case of aristocratic and gentry families, however, the genealogy is already established, and is often traceable in published sources. That is not to say that it is necessarily complete or accurate; for example, illegitimate children begotten by male members of the family (or more rarely, born of female members of the family) are not usually included, and even when their existence can be traced, they usually vanish without leaving further trace of their existence. All these points can be illustrated from the history of the Vaughans. Thus John Vaughan (d.1741), the second viscount Lisburne, is recorded as having one legitimate daughter, Malet. But his wife Dorothy, who left him in 1729, gave birth to a son, Edward Vaughan, in 1733, whose claim to the Trawsgoed inheritance might well have succeeded had he not been persuaded to abandon his claim in 1754, thus admitting his illegitimacy. John Vaughan himself left money in his will to his illegitimate son, of whom there is no further trace. Moreover, his unmarried sister Letitia seems to have behaved as loosely as her brother; a lawyer scrawled on one of the documents in Edward Vaughan's lawsuit that she was the mother of twins. Edward Vaughan's lawsuit generated a wonderful pile of revealing documents; despite his loss of the Trawsgoed estate, he retained the Lisburne coat of arms for himself and his descendants and, thanks to the man who was almost certainly his real father, David Lloyd of Brynog (Felin-fach), he became squire of Green-grove. This was a remarkable achievement in terms of contemporary mores.

Nevertheless, although they may be incomplete, gentry genealogies can be invaluable sources for the historian. The seventh Earl of Lisburne (1892-1965) commissioned a family genealogy from the College of Arms, a beautiful volume handwritten and illuminated on parchment. The Earl himself added frequent notes in green ink and, although they spoiled the appearance of the book, they are a precious resource, giving exact dates and places of birth, marriage and death for a number of family members from the late seventeenth century onwards, citing a lost 'Green Book' as his source. Welsh genealogies have always been notorious for their length, and that of the Vaughans is no exception; Adda ap Llywelyn Fychan, who married the heiress of Trawsgoed early in the fourteenth century, claimed descent through his father from Collwyn ap Tangno, a shadowy twelfth-century North Wales patriarch, and through his mother from the tenth-century king Hywel Dda. Constructive genealogy, as we may call it, was not unknown in any historical period, but through his recent ancestors Adda ap Llywelyn (like his wife Tudo) claimed free status and the right to own land. A host of Welsh gentry families can be traced in the splendid collection of genealogies made by Alcwyn Evans (NLW MS 12359), a photocopy of which is on the open shelves of the Gwenogvryn Evans room in the National Library of Wales. The major source for early genealogies is P.C. Bartrum's massive collection; not easy of access but magisterial in its depth, this too is on open shelves in the Gwenogvryn Evans room and in other major libraries in the United Kingdom and overseas.

Genealogies, challenging though they may be to compile or adjust, are not history, only a source, and the further back they go, the more phantasmal are the names. However, Professor Ralph Griffiths has constructed a splendid resource in his list of Cardiganshire and Carmarthenshire office-holders in the late mediaeval period (see Bibliography). He has plundered the recesses of the Public Record Office to construct lists of office-holders under the Crown during the period between the conquest of Wales and its union with England in 1536/43. Such office-holders (stewards, reeves, beadles) were drawn from the class of small landowners, and members of the Vaughan family appear among them, with dates usefully attached. Thus we know that Adda ap Llywelyn Fychan was beadle or administrator of Creuddyn, escheator of South Wales (Carmarthenshire and Cardiganshire), deputy steward of Cardiganshire, and attorney to the constable of Cardigan

Castle. He survived the Black Death of 1349-50 and service in France, perhaps dying about 1360.

The combined impact of the Acts of Union, the dissolution of the monasteries (1536-39) and the confiscation of a great deal of other Church land had an enormous impact on the Welsh economy. Careers in the burgeoning legal system became possible, and legal fictions made the purchase of land much easier than it had previously been. The office of Justice of the Peace, though unpaid, brought status and influence. The foremost men in every county strove to become Members of Parliament, sheriff (an annual appointment) and Lord Lieutenant. Fortunately the Trawsgoed archive opens at this very time, with the 1548 marriage settlement of Morris ap Richard Fychan and his wife Elliw, an heiress of Llanilar, who brought nine farms to her husband, thus probably doubling the size of the Trawsgoed estate. A substantial archive was an inevitable concomitant of an estate ; only thus could its owner prove title to his lands and manage his resources. Examination of the succession of documents will reveal a pattern of acquisition by purchase, by inheritance, by marriage and by mortgage. That is to say that the loan of money to a struggling freeholder, if not repaid, led to the land's acquisition by the lender. Some estates were built up by the purchase not of freehold but of leases. Thus the Hafod Uchdryd estate was created in Cwmystwyth by the Herberts through the purchase of leases from the farmers who had originally obtained them from the abbots of Strata Florida. When the freehold of Cwmystwyth came into the hands of John Vaughan in 1632, he sold the relevant leases to Morgan Herbert. Among other documents in the Trawsgoed archive are exchanges of lands with Hafod Uchdryd on the pattern described above.

Leases of land to tenants are important for the evidence they contain of changing practice. They may prescribe the laying of quickthorn hedges, the liming of land and the maintenance of a dungheap. Timber is not to be cut without permission. The Trawsgoed leases contain numerous references to mediaeval rents of hens, eggs, geese and days of labour. The days of labour – carrying corn, carrying turf, reaping and harrowing – had largely faded out by 1700, but the renders of hens and eggs continued into the nineteenth century. That this was not a documentary formality is shown by the survival of an Aberystwyth printer's record noting the printing of posters for the collection of these renders. During the seventeenth and eighteenth centuries many leases were for twenty-one years or for three lives, for a down payment and a fixed rent. With slow but steady inflation it is likely that landlords felt themselves disadvantaged by such an arrangement, and by the early nineteenth century leases were for one year at a time. These documents can be examined alongside rentals, which usually name the tenant, the farm and the rent paid (or in arrears). J.M. Howell made much use of these rentals in his research. Unfortunately they were rarely kept in standard form from year to year, and farms suddenly disappear, only to reappear in a later year. Whole sections of the estate may be missing. Thus I found it impossible to establish how much truth there is in the frequent assertion that some families held the same tenancies for numerous generations. Even more conspicuous by their absence are any agent's notebooks of day-to-day expenditure such as are found in the Gogerddan archive. These survive from the late eighteenth century, giving a vivid picture of the huge range of activities involved in the daily running of a great estate.

Particularly interesting for the estate historian are the surveys which were commissioned by owners from time to time. These are even more valuable when accompanied by maps. In the case of Trawsgoed the maps made in 1756 have all disappeared, save only the demesne map itself, but a partial survey of 1771 survives, with several exquisite maps including the demesne, and the maps of 1781 nearly all survive, in three splendid volumes in the National Library of Wales. They are the work of Thomas Lewis, a well-known surveyor of whose work a good deal survives. Unfortunately he quarrelled with the first Earl and his agents, one of whom dismissed his work as being valueless. However, that seems to be a gross exaggeration.

As well as maps of the estate, a rich archive will contain other plans and visual material. The Trawsgoed archive includes a good deal of detail about lead-mining: plans show workings and boundaries, designs for buildings and other mining details. There are garden plans, plans for conservatories, dairy houses and a golf-course, not to mention plans showing where a railway line will run. The National Library maintains a collection of estate sales catalogues, giving the dates, places and times of sales, listing the properties to be sold with some detail, and often containing maps. Naturally the collection has gaps, and some catalogues survive only in part. The best are those on which someone, perhaps the agent, noted the prices bid for each lot, as in the case of the sale of most of the Abertrinant estate in 1830. I have referred elsewhere in this chapter to the value of photograph albums; the National Library's collection of photographs, prints and original landscape drawings and paintings can offer valuable background to the study of an estate's history.

Unfortunately, many archives (especially of smaller estates) have disappeared in large part or entirely. However, the National Library of Wales not only acquired the Trawsgoed archive but, to the happiness of the Trawsgoed historian, printed a detailed calendar by Francis Green in 1927;

there is a typescript supplement of additional deeds and documents on the open shelves at the Library. Green's work is astonishingly accurate; in years of poring over it and the archive, I have only discovered one avoidable error. However, calendars can be misleading. Two documents each given a single-sentence description may turn out to be of totally different length and value to the researcher; only consultation of both will reveal that one is worthless and the other important. Moreover, it may be only serendipity that leads to the discovery that there are other relevant archives. For example, it was only by chance that I discovered that the National Library also held a collection called Lisburne/Northumberland, unscheduled. Consultation at the National Library of the computer printout of the National Register of Archives revealed that the Shropshire Record Office held several interesting letters from John Vaughan (d.1721), the first Viscount Lisburne.

Some archives are of course more exciting to the researcher than others. The Nanteos and Gogerddan archives both contain far more correspondence than does the Trawsgoed archive, a good deal of which consists of deeds of purchase and tenancy leases. However, letters can be traced in other sources, often through references in articles in local history journals and in the card indexes in the Gwenogvryn Evans room; thus I discovered some of the correspondence of Wilmot Vaughan the first Earl of Lisburne in NLW MS 14215. Another useful source is the indexes to the many publications of the Historic Manuscripts Commission; it was through these I first discovered that the Lisburne title had previously been bestowed on one Adam Murray by James II, but after Murray's death the title was revived ('of the second creation' in the jargon) by William III for the benefit of John Vaughan. Nevertheless, despite the fascination of personal letters and references in diaries, it is deeds of land that form the backbone of original research on estate history, for thus can one find at what periods the estate grew fastest, at what periods it may have stood still, and when retrenchment or dispersal became necessary.

Reference has already been made in passing to documentary sources outside the family's own archive. Naturally the archives of neighbouring families and of families which intermarried with the subject of one's research need to be checked. Wills and other probate records can yield valuable details of the wealth of individuals, as well as genealogical details, for the seventeenth and eighteenth century family members. Unfortunately the wills of major families tended to be proved in the Prerogative Court of Canterbury and are therefore kept in the Public Record Office, where virtually all the inventories and other documents have been discarded long ago, leaving only book copies of wills. The Vaughan wills are largely uninteresting as compared with the early wills of the Joneses of Nanteos and the Powells of Llechwedd-dyrys, although the 1683 will of Edward Vaughan, son of Sir John Vaughan, refers to the two bags of gold in his study, one containing nine hundred pieces and the other two hundred; he was the last of the Vaughans to die solvent. Apart from family wills, the probate records of farmers may include references to their landlords; in the seventeenth century a heriot of the second-best beast had to be paid on the succession of a son to his father's tenancy. Other men invoked their landlord as guardian for their children, hoping to ease their widows' difficulties. Fortunately these wills are preserved in the National Library.

Thus in 1632 a minor local gentleman, Edward Lloyd of Llanfihangel-y-Creuddyn, named John Vaughan of Trawsgoed and his brother Henry Vaughan of Cilcennin as co-executors, but did not fail to note that Henry owed him £15. The will of Anne Vaughan, second wife and widow of the Edward Vaughan who died in 1635, was witnessed in 1650 at Maenarthur (Pont-rhyd-y-groes) by her son (Sir) John Vaughan and his wife Jane, who was the daughter of Anne by her first marriage, to John Stedman of Ystrad Fflur. To the will is appended a letter from Edward, John Vaughan's cousin and son to Edward and Anne Vaughan, seeking to chivvy the probate office at Carmarthen to act more swiftly. In 1656 a Llanfihangel-y-Creuddyn yeoman, Lewis ap Rees, bequeathed to John Vaughan his best yoke of oxen in lieu of a heriot.

Other useful records for identifying the wealth and status of gentry families can be found in the Public Record Office in the form of the lay subsidy and hearth tax records. Other tax records such as those for the eighteenth century window tax are missing for Cardiganshire, but lay subsidy and hearth tax returns survive. Some years are much fuller than others; some seem so brief as to be almost worthless. Nevertheless they offer a crude standard of comparison; thus for example in 1613 Richard Pryse of Gogerddan paid 53s 3d lay subsidy, and Morgan Herbert of Cwmystwyth 32s, but Edward Vaughan of Trawsgoed, like John Stedman of Ystrad Fflur, paid only 20s.

I have referred several times to the advent of good fortune in the unexpected discovery of sources. Who knows what else I may have missed? Late in 1996 I had completed the book and the disk was ready for the press. I began another project entirely, reading the coroners' inquest reports in the Cardiganshire Great Sessions Gaol Files records, in which I discovered that Ieuan Lloyd ap Lewis of Llanychaearn, a justice of the peace, had gone on 28 May 1565 to Llanafan, in an attempt to restore peace in a conflict between subjects and their liege lords. Ieuan was attacked and killed by

Richard ap Morris Fychan of Llanafan, gentleman, who thereupon fled. This man can be none other than the father of Morris ap Richard, who married in 1548, although by 1565 Morris the son was largely managing the estate. Even in unruly Cardiganshire the murder of a JP must have been a shocking event, but unfortunately no further records exist to reveal what happened. As a result of this discovery I was able to insert an additional paragraph into the book, in the nick of time.

It is vital that estate historians should have a grasp of more general history than that of the locality alone, so as to be aware to what extent their subjects are following general trends of the times. There is a limit to what one can include by way of comparative material without swamping the reader. What is most essential is an awareness of the extent to which the owners of the estate, largely unbeknown to themselves, responded to the pressures of their times. The Vaughans of Trawsgoed were part of the great movements of Welsh and British history. When Crown offices were available, they filled them. When heiresses were on the market, they married them. When it was *de rigueur* to marry English wives, they did so. When the Welsh upper gentry abandoned the Welsh language, the Vaughans did so. When the legal profession flourished, the Vaughans became lawyers for three generations. When monastic lands were for sale, they bought them. When conspicuous consumption was the order of the day, they overspent. When lands were sold, the Vaughans sold, and when so many Welsh estates finally broke up, Trawsgoed was broken up. What is almost unique about the Vaughans is that the present Earl of Lisburne is the direct descendant, from father to son, of that Adda ap Llywelyn Fychan who first occupied Trawsgoed in right of his wife, six and a half centuries ago.

SELECT BIBLIOGRAPHY

There is a useful introductory bibliography in Philip Jenkins, *A History of Modern Wales 1536-1990* (Longman, 1992).

Beckett, J.V., *The Aristocracy in England 1660-1914* (Blackwell, 1986).

Cannadine, D., *The Decline and Fall of the British Aristocracy* (London, 1990).

Clay, C., *Rural society: landowners, peasants and labourers 1500-1750* (Cambridge, 1990).

Dinely, Thomas, *The Account of the Official Progress of His Grace Henry the First Duke of Beaufort Through Wales in 1684* (ed. R.W. Banks, London, 1888).

Griffiths, R.A. *The Principality of Wales in the Later Middle Ages* (Cardiff, 1972).

Heal, F. & Holmes, C., *The Gentry in England and Wales 1500-1700* (Macmillan, 1994).

Howell, D.W., *Patriarchs and Parasites: the gentry of south-west Wales in the eighteenth century*, (Cardiff, 1986).

— *Land and People in Nineteenth-century Wales*, (London, 1985).

Hughes, J., *A history of the parliamentary representation of the county of Cardigan* (Aberystwyth, 1849).

Lloyd, H.A., *The Gentry of South-West Wales* (Cardiff, 1968).

Mills, D.R., *Lord and Peasant in Nineteenth Century Britain* (London, 1980).

Mingay, G.E. *English Landed Society in the Eighteenth Century* (London, 1963).

— *The Gentry: the Rise and Fall of a Ruling Class* (London, 1976).

— *Land and Society in England 1750-1980* (London, 1994).

Morgan, Gerald, *A Welsh House and its Family: the Vaughans of Trawsgoed* (Llandysul, 1997).

Phillips, Bethan, *Peterwell* (Llandysul, 1983).

Phillips, J.R., *A List of the Sheriffs of Cardiganshire* (1868).

— *Memoirs of the Civil War in Wales and the Marches* (London, 1874).

Phillips, J.R.S., *The Justices of the Peace in Wales and Monmouthshire 1541 to 1689* (Cardiff, 1975).

Roberts, Glyn, *Aspects of Welsh History* (Cardiff, 1969).

Royal Commission on Land in Wales and Monmouthshire, Evidence, vol. III (London, 1896).

Stone, L. *The Crisis of the Aristocracy* (London, 1967).

— *The Road to Divorce: England 1530-1987* (Oxford, 1990).

Stone, L. & J.C.F., *An Open Elite? England 1540-1880* (Oxford, 1984).

Thompson, F.M.L., *English Landed Society in the Nineteenth Century* (London, 1963).

NOTES TO CHAPTER 16

[1] *Tyddyn* now means a smallholding, but it originally simply meant 'farm'; in place-names it is usually abbreviated to *Ty'n-*.

[2] S.R. Meyrick, *History of Cardiganshire* (3rd edition, 1907).

17. THE RISE OF A NATIVE MIDDLE CLASS: THE PUGH FAMILY OF LLANFAIR AND LLANBEDR, 1775-1900

Lewis W. Lloyd

This chapter relates to a rather neglected aspect of Welsh rural history, to the emergence of a bilingual native middle class in the eighteenth and nineteenth centuries.* Whilst the perspective is essentially local the story of the Pugh family in Llanfair parish and other parts of Ardudwy does, I think, provide evidence of a widespread trend in rural Wales and, besides, their story is certainly not unique in Ardudwy as other documentary collections indicate. In other words, this chapter is concerned with a period of significant social change in rural society which culminated in the various institutional and other reforms of the second half of the nineteenth century.

As the new native middle class evolved it began to challenge the established order of squire and parson which had dominated the rural scene in the eighteenth century and earlier. The documents in this collection, the 'Pugh Family Papers', as I have called them, also relate to the largely submerged or subordinated strata of rural society in the nineteenth century, i.e. to the farm workers, labourers and domestic servants of a mainly pastoral society. It should be stressed, however, that the pastoral character of local society was significantly affected by the growth of mining and quarrying in the district and by the closely connected expansion of maritime trade. These economic developments accelerated the processes of social change in that they provided clear opportunities for the emergent middle class (and for some to join its ranks) and also, though rather more gradually, such developments influenced the social and political awareness of the working people of the district. Here, again, similar influences were at work in many other parts of Wales so that the local perspective of this study tends to broaden out at certain points.

---

* This chapter is based on a talk given to the Second Stages Course, 'People, Places and Pedigrees', in September 1996. See also the Foreword to this book.

The main constituents of the new middle class in rural Wales included the lesser freeholders, the more substantial tenant farmers, successful shopkeepers and tradesmen, cattle dealers and some cattle drovers, master mariners and, more generally, those who were able to accumulate modest amounts of capital. Economic advancement led quite commonly to entry into the professions of law, medicine and the nonconformist ministry, the seals of real 'respectability'. They were able to measure their social and economic status against that of the greater and lesser gentry, on the one hand, and the landless rural workers, miners, quarriers, seamen and poor, on the other. The former were commonly though not invariably English-speaking (by the nineteenth century) and Conservative, whilst the latter were generally Welsh-speaking, nonconformist and Liberal, though some of the poor remained Anglican and Conservative, since they looked to the gentry and the clergy principally for the alleviation of their misery. In general, members of the new middle class were bilingual, nonconformist and Liberal. They commonly provided the leaders of nonconformity and Liberalism in their localities. Social or class differences are seldom if ever clear-cut but there can be little doubt that distinctions were drawn and increasingly recognised in the course of the nineteenth century, even though the Welsh language served to unite middle and working classes in common endeavours, as did nonconformity. However, the notion of an undifferentiated Welsh rural society cannot be sustained. It was a myth utilised by middle-class leaders in their contest with the gentry; it was used in aid of Liberal-National causes.

During the 1970s three truly remarkable collections of documents were deposited in the Area Record Office at Dolgellau. All three relate primarily to the western part of Ardudwy.[1] Together they provide invaluable insights into the farming, commercial and social life of the district in the eighteenth and nineteenth centuries and their survival owes a great deal to the foresight of the three families to which they relate: the Joneses of Tŷ Cerrig (and Morrises of Gwrachynys) in Llanfihangel-y-traethau parish; the Richardses of Pensarn, Llanfair; and the Pugh family of Argoed and Caenêst in Llanfair and Llanbedr parishes respectively. This account is designed to place the Pugh Family Papers in their immediate familial and local historical context and the documentary illustrations will serve to demonstrate the value of this collection with regard to the history of rural Wales over the last two centuries. The value of the other two collections can only be asserted here. All three families engaged in pastoral farming and trade and their commercial interests involved investment in local shipping. There were several similar families in Ardudwy in the eighteenth and nineteenth centuries but, in most cases, their activities are rather poorly documented.

The Revd William Pugh (1750-1845) of Llanfair

William Pugh, the founder of the Pugh family in Llanfair, came from that vital though neglected stratum of Welsh rural society composed of freeholders who were described in local records as 'gentlemen', but who were somewhat less than gentry (petty gentry). William Pugh was the son and heir of Hugh Prichard or Richard of Llwyn-y-ffynnon in the ancient township of Brithdir Uchaf and parish of Dolgellau. Hugh Prichard was, in turn, the son and heir of Richard William (Pugh) of Llwyn-y-ffynnon, gent., who died in 1743, so it is likely that the family's association with Llwyn-y-ffynnon and Dolgellau parish was well-founded by the commencement of the eighteenth century. Hence William Pugh, the central character here, was the son and grandson of modest freeholders and Llwyn-y-ffynnon passed on his death in 1845 to his grandson, William Pugh, the eldest son and heir of Hugh Pugh of Hendre-fawr, Trawsfynydd, who had predeceased his father by some twenty-eight years. Unlike many such freeholders, William Pugh's family remained Anglicans during the early years of nonconformist advance and William Pugh was destined to become a clergyman, though none of his descendants followed his example.

After perhaps a local education, William Pugh entered Jesus College, Oxford, in 1770 and graduated BA in 1774. On Sunday 29 May 1774, he was ordained deacon by Bishop Shute of Bangor at Christ Church, Oxford. He was ordained priest also by Shute at Bangor Cathedral on Sunday 22 September 1776. When did he first come to Llanfair? According to his books of sermons, which he carefully wrote out in Welsh, he preached at Llandanwg and Llanfair as early as March and April 1775 and, thereafter, he wisely recorded the occasions on which he delivered the various sermons to avoid too frequent repetitions. William Pugh married, shortly after becoming priest, at Dolgellau, by licence, on 18 April 1777; his wife Mary (née Jones) bore him a son, Hugh Pugh, who was baptised at Llanfair on 23 May 1778. Mary bore him ten more children but before saying something about them I should like to concentrate upon the role assumed by the young cleric in Llanfair during the last two decades of the eighteenth century.

When the Revd William Pugh came to Llanfair in 1775-6 the parish possessed no vicarage or rectory, though the incumbents may sometimes have resided at Tŷ Mawr (otherwise known as 'Llanfair Ganol') near the church. Yet a few acres of glebe land lay on the sloping ground to the north-east of the village and it was here that William Pugh built 'Bryneglwys'(later called 'The Rectory') in the early nineteenth century.

The Revd William Pugh became tenant of Argoed farm which was then a tenement of the modest Caenêst estate, centred upon Llanbedr village. It was here that he remained for the greater part of his long life. His son William, and grandson of the same name, were to be tenants of Argoed for much of the remainder of the nineteenth century. The Caenêst estate was the property of the Poole family who were petty or lesser gentry owning a modest and rather scattered estate, many of whom were obliged to enter the professions as clergymen, lawyers (attorneys) and medical men (surgeons and apothecaries), since their income from land was quite limited. One of them, Revd Anthony Poole (1710-83), was both a fellow clergyman and William Pugh's first landlord at Argoed.

Certain documents in the collection indicate that the annual rental for Argoed at this time was £30, though William Pugh's tenancy also comprised the neighbouring and much smaller tenement of Ty'n Llidiart. By 1839, Argoed was a mixed farm of some 65 acres and included two Morfa marsh allotments which had been added in the early nineteenth century.

The old farm house at Argoed is an ancient structure though a new and larger house was added on the western or seaward side during William Pugh's lengthy tenure. Just one further point concerning Argoed needs to be made here: the farmyard contained a small tannery which was operated, in the late eighteenth century, by one Humphrey Ellis, tanner, to whom the Revd William Pugh apprenticed his eldest son, Hugh, in 1794. Hugh Pugh later moved to Trawsfynydd parish but his brother, John Richard Pugh (1785-1837), was tanner at Argoed for many years and he was succeeded by his brother-in-law, John Griffith, who operated the tannery until 1852.

It may be said, therefore, that the Revd William Pugh was much more than a clergyman for he was, as tenant of Argoed, a pastoral farmer with an interest in a tannery. Besides these secular interests, as a clergyman he would have played a full part in the religious and secular life of the parish since, in Wales as in England, the parish was the basic unit of administration. In this period, however, the Revd William Pugh experienced the steady reduction of his congregation at Llanfair as parishioners joined the Calvinistic Methodists or Baptists. Unfortunately, his feelings in this regard were not recorded.

A letter from Griffith Rowlands of Llanfair-isaf, dated January 1782, written in London and addressed to the Revd William Pugh, shows how William Pugh's activities were extended from time to time. The letter reveals that William Pugh had undertaken to look after Griffith Rowlands's affairs in Llanfair during his absence. Rowlands's main concern in this letter was the rebuilding of the village inn, Ty'n Llan, which was then occupied by Thomas Lewis (1724-1801), a former master mariner and native of Llanaber parish. The young Griffith Rowlands seems to have been quite content to leave this matter to William Pugh:

> The men who are to be employed in the Building of Thos. Lewis's House, are those whom to your judgement appear honest – Griffith William as joiner meets with my entire approbation.
>
> The kind of House you mention in your letter I think will best suit Llanfair; but indeed I will not pretend to dictate to you any thing about these things. But I leave every thing to your better judgement. I would wish you to consult my good Friend, Uncle J. Parry, if you think it right; and whatever assistance he may render you shall be most gratefully acknowledged.
>
> It will give me pleasure to know when you begin, and how you proceed, as often as you can conveniently oblige me with a Line.

William Pugh clearly found such work congenial since he also supervised the building of the new farm house at Argoed and of Bryneglwys, the Rectory. So the Revd William Pugh appears to have settled quite happily in Llanfair where he was leading a varied and full life.

Historians have tended to concentrate on the material and spiritual decay of the Anglican Church in Wales from the Reformation onwards and on the generally poor quality of country parsons in rural Wales. However, Llanfair seems to have been served rather better than many parishes by a succession of able and dedicated men. The incumbents of Llanfair included, in the sixteenth century, Theodore Price or Prys (1570?-1631), who became master of Hart Hall (later Hertford College), Oxford, and, in the seventeenth century, Owen Rowlands and Humphrey Lloyd, MA. The Revd Ellis Wynne (1670/1-1734), perhaps the finest exponent of Welsh prose, was rector of Llanfair from 1710/11 to his death in 1734 and his son, William Wynn (1704-61), succeeded him as rector from 1734 until 1760. So William Pugh was heir to a proud tradition and his books of Welsh sermons suggest that he took his pastoral duties as seriously as his pastoral farming at Argoed! He would also have been one of the very few residents of the parish and district who were literate in English and Welsh.

It seemed, in the 1780s, as if the Revd William Pugh's life was settled on an even course and that he would live out his days as a simple country clergyman who farmed in order to supplement his modest income from tithes. This was not to be, however, for, in the 1790s, he became curate of Llanfihangel-y-Pennant, a secluded parish in southern Merioneth, and it was here that an incident occurred which was to upset the even tenor of his life.

The story is told in Hugh J. Owens's *From Merioneth to Botany Bay* (1952) where, in Chapter VIII, entitled 'The Fiery Cleric', it is recorded that the Revd William Pugh BA, when curate of Llanfihangel-y-Pennant and Talyllyn, shot William Lewis Owen, one of his parishioners, on 17 March 1796. Owen died three days later and William Pugh was arrested and charged with manslaughter at the Merioneth Great Sessions at Bala. According to the brief report of the trial, William Pugh had charged his gun with gunpowder and a little brown paper and this charge struck Owen in the shoulder with what were to prove fatal results. The jury returned a verdict of 'Not Guilty' and the case must have possessed exceptional features if the verdict was justified by the facts. Owen, who added that William Pugh was allowed to remain in his living and become curate of Llanfair in 1801, was clearly unaware that he had been curate of Llanfair for many years prior to this incident in the churchyard of Llanfihangel-y-Pennant; but William Pugh of Llanfair and William Pugh of Llanfihangel-y-Pennant were clearly one and the same person.

Why he went to southern Merioneth in this period is part of the mystery that surrounds this fatal incident, for there can be little doubt that his family remained in Llanfair. His son David was baptised at Llanfair on 12 July and buried there on 14 July 1795, and his daughter Sara was baptised there on 17 June 1797 and buried there on 25 January 1798. Thus, apart from the mystery surrounding the incident itself, the Revd William Pugh's own circumstances at this time are obscure. Thereafter, however, the situation becomes much clearer. The Pugh Family Papers record that William Pugh was formally appointed curate of Llanfair in 1801 and rector of the parish in 1816. He remained rector there until his death in 1845 at the age of ninety-five years. His tomb lies near the church door close to the slate tombs of various members of his family.

William Pugh was curate and rector of Llanfair during the period when nonconformity became dominant throughout Ardudwy, Merioneth and the greater part of Wales. His dwindling congregation in the nineteenth century was a cross which he had to bear in common with numerous contemporary Welsh clergymen. The decline in his congregation probably owed little to any personal failing on his part and his curate, the Revd Rees Evans, can probably be absolved from direct responsibility as well. One public action worthy of note in this period was William Pugh's contribution to the building fund for Llanbedr school some time after 1817.

Llanfair parish was less fortunate, for a school was not built there until about 1868. The freeholders and tenant farmers of Llanfair might have supported a school prior to 1868 and such a school could have been a memorial to the Revd William Pugh, BA, as a long-serving incumbent of the parish, but sectarianism probably precluded this.

William Pugh's memorials in Llanfair, apart from his descendants, were his houses: Bryneglwys (the Rectory), the new farm-house at Argoed, (though this would have been paid for, one assumes, by the Pooles of Caenêst as landlords) and Ty'n Llan, the village inn, which was later called 'The Crown', rebuilt in 1782 at the behest of Griffith Rowlands of Llanfair-isaf.

The documents allow us to glimpse at various aspects of the Revd William Pugh's full and active life in Llanfair which spanned over two decades of the eighteenth and over four decades of the nineteenth century – significant decades in the life of the parish and of Wales in general. Towards the close of his days, William Pugh made his will, which was witnessed by Richard Humphrey Richards (1798-1847) of Llanfair-isaf, the village squire; John Owen (b. 1788) of Llanfair (Tŷ Mawr), a native of Trawsfynydd parish and a cattle drover in his younger days; and Owen Richards (1785-1852), the landlord of Ty'n Llan inn and a former shoemaker. He left Llwyn-y-ffynnon farm, which was subject to a mortgage agreement, to his grandson William Pugh, the son and heir of Hugh Pugh of Hendre-fawr, Trawsfynydd. He left his farm Gwerncneuddion in Llanenddwyn parish (Dyffryn Ardudwy) to his son William Pugh (1791-1858) of Caenêst and Argoed, the residuary legatee and sole executor of the will. He left his daughter, Elizabeth Pugh, £20 and the following bequests to his grandchildren: to Mary Morgans 'the clock in the kitchen at Argoed and Beaureau [bureau] up stairs'; to Mary Griffith £100 and 'the clock up stairs and beaureau in the parlour at Argoed'; and to Ellen, Jane, Catherine and William Morris Griffith £50 each.

An estate duty document in the collection provides a more detailed picture of the Revd Williams Pugh's material circumstances at the time of his death. His personal estate grossed £960 5s 0d, and of this £15 was 'Cash in the House'; the 'Furniture, Plate, Linen &c', at Argoed was valued at £47 10s 0d; the value of his 'Farming Stock, Implements and Husbandry &c' was assessed at £244 15s 0d; 'Rents due' amounted to just £10; 'Bonds, Bills, Notes and Interest due at the Death' amounted to £522 10s 0d and his 'Book and Other Debts' totalled £120 10s 0d. His funeral cost £25 10s 0d and the legacies listed above amounted to £320. William Pugh's net personal estate amounted to the not inconsiderable sum, having regard to time and place, of £688 5s 0d. To this may be added the unknown value of his two farms, which were both subject to mortgages. Apart from his private income, the Revd William Pugh had previously received tithes in kind as rector of the parish from 1816 to 1839 and, after 1839, he had received £150 a year as commuted tithes, a sum payable by the parish's hard-pressed and mainly nonconformist farmers and smallholders. Pluralism, or the holding of more than one ecclesiastical 'living', was no longer acceptable and the modesty of William Pugh's parochial income (a fortune for local working men) helps to explain his various commercial activities at Argoed and elsewhere.

We may now turn to the Revd William Pugh's family which has been reconstructed from the parish registers, gravestones, 'The Pugh Family Papers' and other sources.

William Pugh I and his wife Mary

The children of William and Mary Pugh (1758-1816) were eleven in number though some died young (see also Fig. 17-1):

Hugh Pugh of Argoed and Hendre-fawr, Trawsfynydd, was baptised on 23 May 1778 (Llanfair); and buried on 15 March 1817 (Llanfair). He married Eleanor Roberts.

He was apprenticed to Humphrey Ellis, tanner, at Argoed in 1794 and was probably working there as a tanner in 1809 when his daughter Jane was born. Some time after 1809 he left Argoed to become tenant of Hendre-fawr, Trawsfynydd, a farm of almost 124 acres where, after his death, his wife 'Ellin' remained the tenant until 1839.

In 1845, Hugh's eldest son, William, succeeded his grandfather as owner of Llwyn-y-ffynnon farm in Dolgellau parish. This property may well have been settled in 'fee tail male'.

Jane Pugh of Argoed was baptised at Llanfair on 18 April 1780, and died unmarried on 26 April 1825, aged forty-five (her gravestone gives her age as forty-seven). She seems to have been her father's housekeeper at Argoed after her mother's death in 1816 and, perhaps, for some years before that.

Catherine Pugh was baptised on 8 November 1782 and died, aged sixteen, in May 1798.

John Richard Pugh of Argoed, tanner, was baptised at Llanfair on 6 April 1785 and married Elizabeth Edwards (1789-1858) of Pensarn at Llanfair, by licence, on 7 December 1832. There were no children of this marriage as Elizabeth was a bride of forty-three.

Elizabeth was a daughter of Evan Edwards of Pensarn, farmer and timber merchant, who had been a master mariner during the American War of Independence. He had a life estate in Maes-y-clawdd, Llanaber, though his eldest son, also Evan, had taken possession of the freehold some years before his father's death in 1829. Another son, Lewis of Pantgolau, near Pensarn, was master of the brigantine *Dauntless* of Pwllheli and later a

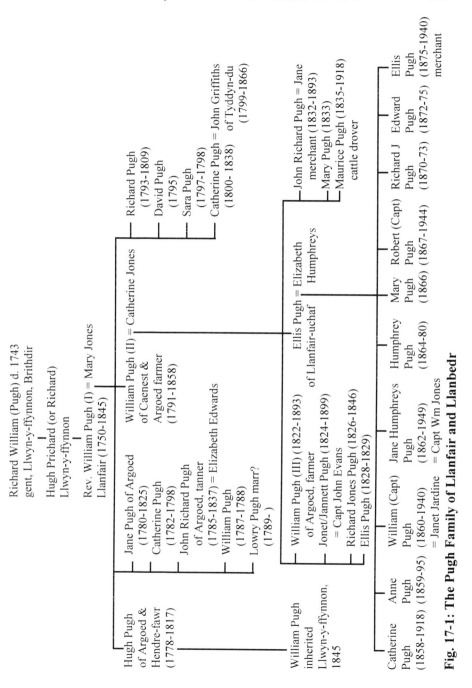

Fig. 17-1: The Pugh Family of Llanfair and Llanbedr

merchant at Pensarn. Lewis's descendants were shopkeepers at Llanfair and Harlech.

William Pugh was baptised at Llanfair on 11 November 1787 and buried there 14 July 1788.

Lowry Pugh was baptised on 22 March 1789. She probably married and the Mary Morgans, who was mentioned in her grandfather's will in 1845, may well have been her daughter.

William Pugh of Caenêst and Argoed, farmer, was baptised on 23 October 1791. He married Catherine Jones on 28 October 1822 at Llanfihangel-y-traethau.

Catherine was a daughter of Richard Jones of Tŷ Cerrig, near Ynys Llanfihangel, farmer and merchant, who was a son of ?Ellis Jones of Pentre Mawr, Dyffryn Ardudwy, gent., and his wife Catherine. Richard's eldest brother, John, was a customs officer.

The local middle class was consolidated by such marriages as this (a matter of effect rather than, perhaps, of intention). The children of William and Catherine Pugh will be considered later.

Richard Pugh was baptised on 9 August 1793. He was buried at Llanfair on 20 March 1809.

David Pugh was baptised on 12 July 1795 and buried two days later.

Sara Pugh was baptised on 17 June 1797 and buried at Llanfair on 25 January 1798. Infant mortality appears to have been unusually high during the early years of the Napoleonic Wars.

Catherine Pugh was baptised at Llanfair on 17 January 1801. As 'Catherine Pugh of Bryneglwys' (the new Rectory), she married John Griffith of Tyddyn Du Uwch Artro at Llanfair, on 15 March 1829.

John Griffith was a son of Morris Griffith of Tyddyn Du, farmer and prominent investor in local shipping, who owned a number of shares in Barmouth square-riggers. John and Catherine had four children: Ellinor who was baptised at Llanfair on 12 December 1830 and married to become a Mrs Lloyd; Jane Griffith; Catherine Griffith; and Capt. William Morris Griffith of Erw Fair, Beddgelert. When Ellinor was baptised in 1830 her father was a shopkeeper at Castellfryn, Llanfair, but by 1851, he, was living, as a widower, at Cae (Llidiart) Gwyn, Llanfair. He was a tanner and seems to have taken over the tannery at Argoed after John Richard Pugh's death in 1837.

One of the most interesting documents in the Pugh Papers is a deed of sale (dated 6 March 1852) whereby John Griffith sold his interest in the tannery to his brother-in-law, William Pugh. It appears that John owed William Pugh £500 (as executor of his father's will) and that he had not been able to keep up with the interest payments on the loan. When he surrendered the tenancy he sold his hides and other effects for £320, and this sum was 'abated and deducted' from the debt of £500.

On a happier note, John Griffith was a prominent and popular member and office holder of the Harlech Ivorites (*Gwir Iforiaid Caer Collwyn*), the principal local friendly society or benefit club. He was an accomplished public speaker and a singer of some note (the pun is accidental!).

Some time after 1852, the tannery at Argoed ceased to operate and this was a matter of concern to the landlord of Argoed, William Thearsby Poole of Caenêst and Gwynfa, Caernarfonshire, attorney-at-law. On 29 October 1867 he wrote to William Pugh (III), then farming at Argoed, in these terms:

> Dear Sir,
> What are you doing about the Tanhouse at Argoed – I understand it is now unoccupied and I have applications from several parties to take it – Let me hear from you – Your brother Ellis has never paid me for the bark [oak bark for use in the tannery] he had last year.
> Yours truly
> W. T. Poole

Ellis Pugh, brother of the recipient of this curt letter, may have taken over the running of the tannery in 1852. The census of 1861 gives his occupation as 'tanner' and the letter suggests that he was still involved in the business in 1866. According to the census of 1871, Ellis Pugh was described as a 'Retired Farmer' so it seems unlikely that he resumed operations at Argoed. Whether another tenant was found for the tannery, following W.T. Poole's letter, is unclear but even after the Second World War the slate-lined tan pits were still intact at Argoed, though they have since been filled in.

These, then, were the children of the Revd William Pugh (I) and his wife Mary. Not surprisingly, William Pugh (I) outlived them all save his fourth son, also William (II), who died in 1858 aged sixty-seven.

In turn, this William and his wife, Catherine, had eight children between 1822 and 1835. (Incidentally, Catherine's uncle, Maurice Jones of Criccieth, a member of the Tŷ Cerrig family, left her £100 in his will dated 21 January 1837, a most acceptable windfall from across Tremadog Bay.) Those eight children were:

William Pugh (III), farmer, was farming at Argoed in 1851 when the census was taken. He was then twenty-eight years old and single but he married some years later and his wife Ellen bore him at least one child: Richard Jones Pugh born in 1864.

William Pugh died at Argoed on 15 November 1893 aged seventy-one, just twelve days before his landlord, William Thearsby Poole. The social distance between these two contemporaries is patent, as the letter of 1867 confirms.

A little more will be said about this William Pugh III and his son in a moment.

Jonet/Jannett Pugh was born at Tŷ Cerrig, her mother's home, but she was baptised at Llanbedr on 1 August 1824. She was married in 1854 (a Valentine card to 'Miss Pugh', dated 1853, is retained by members of the family in Llanbedr), on 18 February at Llanfair, to Capt. John Evans of the schooner *Salem*. Their marriage was recorded in a notebook by William Pugh of Caenêst, Jonet's grandfather, who referred to her as Jonnett Pugh of Argoed. Prior to her marriage, Jonet had kept house for her brother William at Argoed.

Capt. John Evans was a son of Capt. Evan Evans of Barmouth who was lost at sea in 1820, when John was four years old. Jonet or Jannett Evans lived at Tanrhiw, Llanfair, before moving to the larger house, Bryngolau, which became the family home. In 1860, the schooner *Jannett Evans* (97 tons) was launched from Eben Robert's shipyard at Porthmadog. Capt. John Evans was the vessel's master and principal shareholder until the *Jannett Evans* was lost off Cornwall on 3 May 1875. In the same year, he acquired sixty shares (60/64ths) of the brigantine *Keturah* (140 tons register) and his mariner son, John Evans, then acquired the remaining four.

Built at Bridport in Dorset in 1855 the *Keturah* was registered anew at Caernarfon on 14 February 1880 after Capt. John Evans had concluded a mortgage agreement for £450 with his brother-in-law, William Pugh of Argoed. With interest at 5% per annum, William Pugh's loan was secured by thirty-two shares (32/64ths) in the vessel. The relevant documents are included in the Pugh Family Papers. The *Keturah* was lost in 1885 and the register was closed on 4 May 1885. Capt. John Evans, senior, had died some three years earlier on 22 April 1882 aged sixty-six. His widow Jannett died on 30 April 1899 aged seventy-five.

There were at least six children of this marriage: Capt. John Evans, junior, who appears to have commanded the *Keturah;* Richard Jones Evans, a mariner, died in Cardiff on 1 August 1874 aged nineteen and was buried there; Catherine Evans, their eldest daughter, who died on 31 October 1888 aged thirty-two; Jennett Evans, who was six when she died on 27 January 1873; Anne, who married Capt. Griffith Owen Jones; and Margaret, who married Walter Bevers, a schoolmaster from Yorkshire, on 30 July 1892.

Mrs Bevers was for many years a teacher in Harlech. Her son, Lieutenant Isaac Gwilym Bevers, was killed in the First World War.

Thus the maritime associations of the (extended) Pugh family were strengthened steadily in the course of the nineteenth century. This was true of many similar families in Ardudwy.

Richard Jones Pugh was named after his grandfather, Richard Jones of Tŷ Cerrig, and was baptised at Llanbedr on 22 March 1826. He died on 8 March 1846, in his twentieth year.

Ellis Pugh was baptised at Llanbedr on 18 January 1828 and died on 28 June 1829.

Ellis Pugh of Llanfair-uchaf, farmer, was born at Argoed on 19 October 1829 and was baptised at Llanfair on 1 November. He died on 27 October 1875 aged forty-six.

Ellis achieved much during his brief life, as the *englynion* on his tombstone at Llanfair attest. He farmed at Llanfair-uchaf and, as noted above, he operated the tannery at Argoed for a number of years. He was also a local historian, an active member and office-holder of the Harlech Ivorites and a leading supporter of Samuel Holland, quarry-owner, the successful Liberal candidate in the Merioneth by-election of 1870.

With his brother-in-law, Edward Humphreys, Ellis Pugh formed and conducted the Llanfair Church Choir for some years towards the end of his brief yet full and useful life.

Ellis Pugh married Elizabeth Humphreys the only daughter of Capt. Humphrey Humphreys of Llanfair Hill and his wife Jane. Jane was one of the eight daughters of Robert Humphreys of Llanfair-uchaf, gent., a freeholder and one of the district's earliest Baptist converts. Robert Humphreys provided the land for the first Baptist chapel (Capel Bethel or 'Capel-y-Dwr') in Harlech in 1786.

The children of Ellis and Elizabeth Pugh will be considered later. Their homes in Llanfair were: Llanfair-uchaf, Bronfair and Llanfair Hill (where, in the census of 1871, Ellis Pugh was described as a 'Retired Farmer').

John Richard Pugh of Gwern-Canyddion (*sic*), Llanenddwyn, and Britannia House, Harlech, merchant. He was baptised at Llanbedr on 11 June 1832 and died on 12 October 1893 aged sixty-one. His wife Jane bore him at least four children: William, John Ll., John and Rees Ll. Pugh, the last three of whom died in the three year period 1864-66 which leaves us with a moving list of bereavements in Llanfair churchyard. The middle initials of the first John and Rees (Ll.) indicate that their mother, Jane, was a daughter of Rees Lloyd (1801-69) of Llechwedd Du Bach, Harlech, gent., and his wife Margaret (née Roberts).

According to *Slater's Directory* for 1880, John Richard Pugh of Britannia House, Harlech, was a grocer and draper, a common combination of trades in rural Wales in the last century. A document in the Pugh Family Papers shows that J.R. Pugh was also a coal merchant.

Like his brother Ellis, John Richard Pugh was an office-holder in the Harlech Ivorites. It appears that he moved from the farm of Gwerncanyddion, Llanenddwyn, to Britannia House, Harlech, at some point between 1863 and 1869. How the Revd William Pugh came to own Gwerncanyddion is still a mystery – the solution might help to explain why the young clergyman came to settle in Ardudwy in the 1770s.

Mary Pugh was baptised at Llanbedr on 8 December 1833 and she died three weeks later on 28 December.

Maurice (Morris) Pugh was baptised at Llanbedr on 25 October 1835, the youngest child of William and Catherine Pugh, and was probably named after his mother's brother, Maurice Jones.

Maurice Pugh became a cattle drover (or drover's helper) and seems to have followed his father in this time-honoured occupation. The completion of the railway links in the 1860s meant the effective demise of long-distance cattle droving so that he was probably one of the last surviving drovers in Ardudwy towards the end of his days. Various references in the Pugh Family Papers suggest that he remained a cattle dealer after ceasing to be a drover. In his later years he lived in one of the cottages at Tan-y-buarth, Llanfair, and he died unmarried in 1918 aged eighty-two.

Since the Pugh Family Papers relate primarily to the Revd William Pugh I (1750-1845), his son William Pugh II (1791-1858) of Caenêst and Argoed, and to William Pugh III (1822-93) of Argoed, the clergyman's grandson, I should like to concentrate upon William II and William III in order to illustrate the value of the collection for the light it throws on farming in the district in the nineteenth century. Then finally, I should like to say something about the family of Ellis Pugh (1829-75) of Llanfairuchaf, Bronfair and Llanfair Hill.

William Pugh II (1791-1858) of Caenêst and Argoed
As we have seen, William Pugh was the only member of the clergyman's large family to outlive his father. He was baptised at Llanfair on 23 October 1791 and he clearly received an education, perhaps from his father, which was superior to that of most of his contemporaries in Ardudwy.

He became tenant (probably a 'tenant at will') of Caenêst, Llanbedr, the 'home farm' or nucleus of the Caenêst estate, and also tenant of Argoed, Llanfair, at least after his father's death in 1845. He was, in short, a substantial tenant farmer. Various documents in the Pugh Family Papers relate to his farming activities. Of particular interest are those that concern the sale of pigs and cattle and the payment of wages to his employees, both regular 'farm servants' engaged for six months at a time or short-term workers employed in the harvesting of hay and corn and so on. This William Pugh was certainly a cattle dealer and there is reason to believe that he was also a cattle drover for a number of years, an occupation pursued by several tenant farmers in Ardudwy.

Two of the servants on the farm were William Davies and Hugh Davies and documents show that, in 1854, they were earning about £1 per month. As servants they would have lived in a *llofft stabal* (stable loft) in the farm yard. (My late father, Lewis Pugh Lloyd, slept in the same loft at Argoed when he was a farm servant there in 1913 – his first employment after leaving Llanfair School at thirteen years old.)

In 1845, William Pugh II succeeded his late father as owner of Gwerncanyddion, but he remained tenant of Caenêst until his death some thirteen years later. He bought out his brother-in-law, John Griffith, in 1852, so far as the tannery at Argoed was concerned and thereby recouped £320 of his loan to John of £500. The documents tell us virtually nothing about the man but they provide a good deal of evidence concerning the farmer, dealer and employer, i.e. his more public persona.

William Pugh's predecessors as tenants at Caenêst were Edmund Lloyd and his son Evan Lloyd, a son and grandson of Evan Lloyd of Cwm Bychan, gent. William Pugh certainly became tenant prior to Evan Lloyd's death in 1844 since he signed an account book as 'William Pugh Caenêst' in September 1838. This is confirmed by the following letter to him from the landlord, Richard Anthony Poole, dated 3 June 1840:

> Dear Sir,
>
> I am glad to find Humphrey Evans is commencing at Caenêst – He wrote to me saying that he thought the large Parlour would not be sufficiently light, and that another window might easily be cut but I will thank you to tell him *not to delay* on that account, as I can easily decide upon that when I come over: and I have no objection to rooms that are rather dark – Does he know when the Plaisterers (*sic*) intend to come; if so, please drop me a line – I hope to come over very soon but I cannot yet fix a day ...
>
> I am dear Sir
> Yours truly
> Richd. A. Poole

This suggests that a good deal of work was being done on Caenêst house (or 'mansion') at the time.

The Caenêst estate was very much centred on the village of Llanbedr and totalled about 1,450 acres spread over six parishes, namely: Llanbedr (341 acres), Llanfair (196 acres), Llandanwg (211 acres), Llanfihangel-y-traethau (28 acres), Llandecwyn (505 acres – mainly upland) and Llanenddwyn (167 acres). It was, then, a fairly typical lesser gentry estate and beyond Llanbedr village, the tenements lay, like buffers, in the interstices of the major estates of Corsygedol (over 15,000 acres), Glyn Cywarch and Maesyneuadd.

The annual rent charge, in lieu of tithes in kind, for Caenêst home farm was £10 11s 7¾d, an indication of the relative value of the farm of which William Pugh was tenant for some twenty years. In William Pugh, Richard Anthony Poole had a tenant who was a man of some substance, a fellow-Anglican, and one whose social status was not generally inferior to his own. The extract from the letter quoted above suggests that landlord and tenant, in this instance, were on fairly easy terms with each other. General evidence indicates that R.A. Poole and his son, William Thearsby, were fair and considerate landlords, with regard to both time and place.

William Pugh III (1822-93) of Argoed

As we have seen, this William Pugh was the eldest son of William and Catherine Pugh. He succeeded his father as tenant of Argoed and some of the documents in the collection relate to his tenure of the farm. Like his father, he dealt in cattle and sold hay, straw, potatoes and other items. These records will amply repay detailed examination since they provide evidence of the cattle trade at the beginning of the railway age in Ardudwy. Cattle were no longer sold to dealers and drovers in the fairs at Harlech (near the new St Tanwg's Church built in 1839-40) but to dealers at the mart near Harlech railway station, below the town.

William Pugh recorded on 10 October 1867, the 'Opening [of] the Railway from Barmouth to Pwllheli' (to Abererch, in fact). This was, of course, a noteworthy event in the history of Ardudwy and, for William Pugh, the line cut through the lower section of his farm and it divided the farm proper from two enclosure allotments on Morfa Dyffryn (near the present airfield) which had been allocated to Argoed soon after 1806.

Yet William Pugh, like other farmers, probably expected great things of the railway and its adverse effects upon local shipping and cattle droving (he may have participated in the latter as a young man) were matters which would not have concerned him greatly. Here was a new form of transport which would link Ardudwy to distant markets much more effectively than sailing ships or cattle drives. It would also convey many more visitors to the district than the stage-coaches, thus increasing, seasonally, the local market for farm produce. Welsh farmers were no more romantic than their English,

Scottish or Irish counterparts. It is commonly urban romantics who invest sailing and droving with a mystique which their practitioners seldom if ever felt or experienced. This is not to say, of course, that we should not study these and other activities to enhance our knowledge of the realities, often the grim realities, of the past.

Finally, I should like to refer to a few entries which William Pugh made in a Welsh diary for 1886. He noted, on 25 October, that his mariner-cousin, the younger Capt. John Evans of Bryngolau, Llanfair, had returned home from Pwllheli. They were gathering potatoes (*Tyny tatws*) at Argoed on 25, 26 and 27 October and finished this task on 28 October (*Gorphen tyny tatws Argoed*). On 2 November, William Pugh noted that his nephew William Pugh, son of Ellis Pugh, who was then twenty-six years old, 'sailed from Lpool for Charleston'. It was raining on 3 November but they began to gather potatoes at Caenêst on the following day. These and other homely entries fill out the basic content of William Pugh's life. The reference to Caenêst suggests that, like his father, William Pugh was tenant of Argoed and Caenêst. As noted earlier, he died in the same month and year as his landlord William Thearsby Poole (1825-93) and, as with the Poole family's long association with Caenêst, we are now approaching the end of this story.

William's son, Richard Jones Pugh (1864-1939), farmed Argoed and Caenêst for some years after his father's death and it was at Caenêst that his son, W. Eric Pugh, was born in the early years of this century. Richard Jones Pugh then moved to the Half Way Hotel, Bontddu, where he died, though he was buried in the family plot in Llanfair churchyard. Most of the family seem to have developed strong attachments to Llanfair.

It now remains to consider briefly the children of Ellis Pugh (1829-75), farmer and tanner, by his wife Elizabeth (née Humphreys, 1833-91), the only daughter of Capt. Humphrey Humphreys, merchant, by his wife, Jane, of Llanfair-uchaf.

Ellis Pugh (1829-75) of Llanfair and his Family

Ellis Pugh makes but few appearances in the documents but his story is certainly worth recording here to amplify the earlier sketch of his life.

He was born at Argoed on 19 October 1829, the fifth child of William Pugh by his wife Catherine (née Jones). Although he died aged forty-six in 1875 he was a leading figure in Llanfair and the neighbouring parishes. He was the local agent of the victorious Liberal candidate, David Williams of Castell Deudraeth, in the Merioneth election of 1868. He also acted in the same capacity for Samuel Holland (1803-92), Williams's successor as MP, in the by-election of 1870.

Ellis Pugh served as president of the Harlech Ivorites, the 'Harlech Club', which three members of the Pugh family had joined in 1841, a year after the friendly society's establishment. He was also something of a local historian for, under the pen name of 'Elis ap Huw', he submitted an essay on the history of Harlech to one of the Eisteddfodau Castell Harlech which the Ivorites sponsored in this period. The preservation and promotion of the Welsh language was an important aspect of the Ivorites throughout Wales. Ellis Pugh's essay on Harlech was later published by his son Capt. Robert Pugh.

As noted above, Ellis Pugh and his brother-in-law, Edward Humphreys, founded and conducted the popular Llanfair Church Choir. In about 1857, he married Elizabeth, the only daughter of Capt. H. Humphreys of Llanfair Hill. Elizabeth bore him ten children between 1858 and 1875-6 and it is to this interesting family that we now turn to conclude this background to and survey of the Pugh Family Papers. The ten children were:

Catherine Pugh She died on 11 May 1918 aged sixty. Like so many women she left but little trace in public records.

Anne Pugh A spinster, Anne died on 23 March 1895, aged thirty-nine.

Capt. William Pugh The seafaring life must have been a fairly natural choice of career for the young William Pugh, with a retired mariner grandfather at Llanfair Hill and several other seafaring relatives.

Like so many of his generation William Pugh went to Porthmadog to begin his career at sea. There was to be no formal apprenticeship for, when he was fourteen, he signed on as 'Boy' aboard the brig *W.W. Lloyd* (243 tons) of Porthmadog at £1 a month and his keep – ship's biscuit or 'hard tack', salt beef and salt pork, 'duff' with a few currants in it (if you were lucky, weevils if you were not), i.e. the standard fare of ships' crews the world over. The *W.W. Lloyd* was then commanded by Capt. Thomas Parry of Llaniestyn, and included two other members of the crew, from Merioneth.

The Crew Lists and Agreements (Articles) of the *W.W. Lloyd*, and later for the brig *Palestine,* give a very full picture of his sea-faring life until he retired in 1918 as Marine Superintendent with Rankin, Gilmour & Co. of Liverpool.

Captain William Pugh's nephew, Mr Gwilym Artro Pugh, recalls some of his uncle's exploits as a master mariner, exploits which the old mariner recounted to him in his retirement in Llanfair. During the Boer War he carried horses from Holland to South Africa at the behest of the British Government. William Pugh also, it seems, conveyed Kitchener to South Africa (incognito) in about 1899-1900, but this story is unconfirmed. Capt. Pugh also recalled that, on a voyage from New York to Fremantle, Western

Australia, in the early 1900s, he and his crew salvaged a vessel which was on fire by towing her about 1,000 miles to Fremantle. The salvage money was in the region of £7,000.

In 1908, Capt. William Pugh married Janet Patterson Jardine (1868-1937). His wife was Scottish though she had emigrated with her family to St. John's, Newfoundland. Janet was a Scots Presbyterian and William Pugh, was, by this time, a Calvinistic Methodist, despite the predominant Anglicanism of his family.

On his retirement, Capt. and Mrs. Pugh left Liverpool to live in Llanfair, at Bryn Mor, a large house with a southern aspect commanding a fine 'view' of Cardigan Bay. He became a Parish and County Councillor and, with his cousin Capt. John Evans, junior, of Bryngolau, he initiated the Llyn Fedw water supply scheme, a great boon to local inhabitants. Mrs Janet Pugh was killed by a car on Rhiw Caecethin, Llanfair, in 1937 and Capt. William Pugh, after many years of willing service to his native community, died in 1940, aged eighty.

Jane Humphreys Pugh She married Capt. William Jones (1858-1911) who died at Valparaiso, Chile, in 1911. On what proved to be his final voyage Capt. Jones was accompanied by his son Alun, who was then about twelve, as it was thought that an ocean voyage would be good for his health. Alun Jones of Llanllyfni died in 1989. He was a keen local historian and visitors from Llanfair to his home at Llanllyfni were always assured of a warm welcome. The family home was Bryntirion, Llanfair.

Humphrey Pugh Humphrey Humphreys Pugh left the Harlech Board School (opened in 1874) in 1879 at the age of fifteen. He went to sea and died in Bahia, South America, on 22 August 1880, aged sixteen.

Mary Pugh Mary was born on 4 June and died 23 June 1866.

Capt. Robert Pugh After leaving school, Robert Pugh was apprenticed to the local general practitioner, Dr. R.O.H. Jones of Penygarth, Harlech, but the sea's call proved strong. He went to sea and served for over forty years in the Merchant Service, retiring about 1932 as a very experienced master in the service of T. & I. Harrison, Liverpool. One of his vessels was the *s.s. Tactician.* He lived, when at home and in retirement, at Bryneithin, Llanfair. His wife Evelyn Maud (1881-1967) survived him by over twenty years. There were no children of the marriage.

Richard Jones Pugh Richard died on 28 June 1873 aged three years and five months.

Edward Pugh Edward died on 13 November 1875 aged three years and seven months.

Ellis Pugh Ellis Pugh, junior, spent much of his early adult life in business in China. He died, on 18 March 1940, at Plas Gwyn, Pentre'r-felin, near Criccieth, aged sixty-four. According to his death certificate, Ellis Pugh of Bryn Mor, Llanfair, was a 'Cotton Goods Merchant'. His wife was Mary Elizabeth (1878-1952).

Conclusion

It is still common in many quarters to regard rural Wales in the eighteenth and nineteenth centuries as a backwater where pastoral farming was practised according to age-old customs and in which the people were virtually isolated from the wider world, at least until the advent of the railways in the 1860s. I hope that this chapter and the documents to which it relates will encourage a general re-examination of the myths that still surround and distort the relatively recent history of Wales in its more rural parts. The farmers of Ardudwy were not, in the light of this evidence, an ignorant peasantry for, like the Pugh family of Llanfair, many of them engaged in trade and commerce which, even in the local fairs and markets at Harlech and elsewhere, brought them into contact with people from many other parts of Wales and Britain. Some, like William Pugh II of Caenêst and Argoed and his son, Maurice, were cattle dealers and drovers. The latter occupation took them commonly to the English Midlands (Leicester and Northampton, in particular) and on to London, to such cattle fairs as those at Romford and Barnet.

Then, again, there were the mariners of Ardudwy and the shareholders in local shipping, many of whom were farmers, which operated from Barmouth and Porthmadog. Many of the local vessels were coastwise traders to London and elsewhere throughout the British Isles, but others crossed and re-crossed the Atlantic. Many local mariners sailed from the port of Liverpool to all quarters of the globe, as did William and Robert Pugh and several of their contemporaries, as well as members of earlier generations of Ardudwy seamen.

The myth of rural seclusion begins to recede in the face of such evidence as is contained in this collection of documents and in supplementary sources. The wonder is, in fact, that the myth has persisted so long and has been accepted by so many historians. This does not mean to say, of course, that many of Ardudwy's inhabitants did not lead secluded lives, but they were scarcely typical – certainly of the male inhabitants. Farm and domestic servants commonly changed their places of work within their home districts and a number moved well beyond their home districts to gain employment. Besides, a significant number of people migrated from Ardudwy to England and many emigrated to the United States, Australia and Canada in the course of the nineteenth century and later. On the other hand, inward migration to Ardudwy, from England, was not very significant until after 1945.

Ardudwy remained a stronghold of the Welsh language and of Welsh popular culture until the post-Second World War period. Farming methods and practices were improved from the 1840s onwards following the establishment of the Merioneth County Agricultural Society. Thrashing machines and tractors were introduced in due course, yet this writer well remembers horses being shod by 'Bob Gof' at the smithy at Pentre'r-efail, Harlech, in the late 1940s. Much that was old, familiar and valued lived on in such a society; the real onslaught occurred from the 1950s onwards, under the banner of 'modernity'. The changes then effected were both good and bad. Decent housing and health provision were amongst the beneficial effects. The adverse effects of 'modernity' in Ardudwy, as elsewhere in Wales, are too obvious and painful for words, i.e. even for those who, like this writer, have no more than childhood memories of the recent past.

Admittedly, the Pugh family of Llanfair was not in all respects typical of the new native middle class in Ardudwy, mainly because of their clerical ancestor and the fact that many members remained Anglicans in an increasingly nonconformist community and country, but they were fairly typical in most other important respects, apart from the fact that few if any of them emigrated. They formed part of a significant stratum of local society and their papers illuminate many aspects of their relationships and activities.

Some of the accounts in the collection go further in that they reveal to us something of the lives led by their employees in the mid-nineteenth century, i.e. farmworkers, both servants and labourers, and female domestic and farm servants. These are much neglected people and yet, for many of us, they are our ancestors, the landless poor, the vulnerable and the subordinated. The Pughs at Argoed (Llanfair) and Caenêst (Llanbedr) appear to have been considerate masters but masters they were. Employees are often referred to in these records by their first names, but no farm servant or labourer or domestic servant would have been on first name terms with their employers in the nineteenth century. There were divisions in Welsh rural society apart from the widening gap between the gentry, grand or petty, and the rest, and it is important that we recognise this fact.

The value of these documents lies primarily in their rich variety and they deserve to be studied with every bit as much care as those documents which relate to the gentry of Wales since, if for no other reason, they penetrate through the middle stratum of rural society to those who actually worked the land for a few pounds a year or for a daily 7d and 1s 6d in the harvest fields. The lives of such people were hard and insecure; their hearts and voices were regularly uplifted in their simple but yet vibrant chapels but they toiled and sang on a diet of oatmeal (*uwd*), potatoes, diluted butter milk (*glasdwr*), stewed tea and precious little else save on high days and holidays. Conditions varied, of course, between farm and farm and employer and employer, but few farmers erred on the side of generosity in providing for their employees. Frugality was generally considered a virtue. This attitude was reinforced when a severe depression set in towards the end of the 1870s.

Finally, it is worth emphasising that most of these documents are in English, the language of a tiny minority in nineteenth century Ardudwy. In fact, most financial records of farmers, shopkeepers, master mariners and others were kept in English, for Welsh was reserved, as in the case of the Revd William Pugh's sermons, for higher things. The most notable exception in this locality were the records kept by the Ivorites of Harlech for they were exclusively in Welsh in accordance with a principal objective of the society.

Members of the Pugh family were able to operate on two levels – through the medium of English with their equals, to some extent, and their superiors, almost invariably, and through the medium of Welsh with their subordinates, whether employees or others. Their landlords in the period covered by these records, a clergyman and two attorneys, could certainly speak Welsh but they probably confined it to their dealings with those who could not speak English. The spread of the English language into Wales in the nineteenth century has yet to be properly examined because historians have tended to concentrate on the effects of schooling, notably pursuant to the Education Act of 1870, and the use of the 'Welsh Not', whereas the English language was fostered in Wales much earlier by master mariners, cattle dealers and drovers, merchants, shopkeepers and others, i.e. by members of the emergent native middle class. However, such people, including the Pughs of Llanfair, kept a foot in both linguistic camps until some chose or were constrained to abandon this pose for fear of rupturing themselves! Many proclaimed the commercial advantages of the English language whilst recognising the counter-advantages in terms of social control exercisable by a bilingual middle class in a context of popular monoglot Welshness.

In other words, those who were virtually innocent of the English language could be, and in fact were, protected and guided in what they read and much of what they heard through the agency of the Welsh language. However, on the limited evidence provided in this collection of documents members of the Pugh family do not seem to have regarded the Welsh language as an instrument of social control. On the contrary, these records suggest that leading members of the family, and many other members of the emergent middle class in Ardudwy, valued the language for itself as their natural and regular means of discourse and as the medium of a distinctive, a unique literary heritage. This view is supported by the prominent part which several members of the family played in the local Ivorites Friendly Society (*Gwir Iforiaid Caer Collwyn*), a benefit club dedicated, as no other similar societies or clubs were, to the use and promotion of the Welsh language. In short, they did what they could to sustain Welshness in the fastness of Ardudwy as the early signs of danger were manifested. Yet they kept their own accounts mainly in English. There is a clear ambivalence, but the issue is a complex one and cannot be examined further here.

[1] Editorial note: For the general geography of this area see also Fig. 22-2.

18. THE WELSH IN THE PROFESSIONS

Sheila Rowlands

Welsh people in the professions have no special characteristics distinguishing them from others in these islands – they qualify in the same way and the records of their achievements are registered together. Nevertheless, we may usefully study their background to understand them better, and we can seek further genealogical and family information about them in subsidiary sources which are often conveniently found in Wales. For the most part we shall be considering the eighteenth and nineteenth centuries, though many of the records considered come down to the present day.[*]

The Professions

A profession is variously defined: 'an employment not mechanical and requiring some degree of learning; the collective body of persons engaged in any profession'; 'a vocation or calling, esp. one that involves some branch of advanced learning or science'.[1] Before nineteenth-century advances in science, the title profession was confined to the 'classical professions' of the Church, the Law and Medicine (though even Medicine was a matter of inherited knowledge and technique for much of the period). Churchmen and their records have been covered elsewhere, so will have only passing mention here.[2] There are also the largely nineteenth-century new professions which arose as a result of the expansion of scientific knowledge and the need to organise and formulate practice. To a great degree, it is not relevant to treat their Welsh members as different from anyone else, but a short section considers some of these and gives pointers to research.

When Welshmen entered the professions, in any century, they also entered an English world. By this I mean, first, that they had to be English-speaking, so that their education often followed the English pattern even if it took place in Wales; and second, that they often had to leave Wales to

---

[*] This chapter is based on part of a talk given to the Second Stages Course, 'Occupations and the Records Relating to them', held in September 1995.

qualify in their chosen field and, in many cases, did not return – this sounds self-evident but it affected many areas of the professional man's life.

Background

There was a steady growth in numbers of Welsh in the professions from Tudor times. Many Welsh people had followed in the train of Henry Tudor and settled in London; they were well placed to take advantage of the expansion which took place in government at this time. As the effects of the Acts of Union between England and Wales began to be felt in Wales, the need for administrators grew, and there was a demand for academic education to fulfil this need. At the same time, Welsh parents, especially those wishing to be accepted as gentlemen, began to seek education and a career for their sons. Professor Glanmor Williams has written:

> ... the founders of new gentry families were successful lawyers, clergymen, physicians, and others who had purchased landed estates by deploying those steady profits ... made out of their professions.[3]

Below them in the hierarchy were the small parish gentry, whose social ambitions were also developing and who increasingly looked towards the professions for their sons.

Education

The history of education in Wales has been covered elsewhere,[4] but we should recall that before the great educational changes of the nineteenth century, choices were limited. Nevertheless, those who became professional men received some formal education at least, and the search for information about that is worthwhile.

Within Wales, boys of good family were most often educated at the grammar schools. The following schools existed from Tudor times: Abergavenny, Bangor, Beaumaris, Brecon, Carmarthen, Cowbridge, Ruthin; seventeenth and eighteenth century additions were Haverfordwest (1614), Cardigan (1653) and Ystrad Meurig (1770). It is important to realise that even Anglicans made use of the academies set up by the dissenters, especially the one at Carmarthen, and Castell Hywel, Cardiganshire, kept by the Unitarian, David Davies.

A great deal has been written about individual Welsh schools. To locate this you should consult the *Bibliography of the History of Wales*.[5] This is a random list of Welsh schools about which something appears in print: Anglesey schools, Abergavenny (Henry VIII's Grammar School), Bala Grammar School, Friars School, Bangor, Queen Elizabeth School, Carmarthen, Llandovery College, Presteigne Grammar School, Ruabon Grammar School, Ystrad Meurig. Charity schools mentioned include

Llanfyllin Charity School, Lewis School, Pengam, the Welsh Cathedral Schools, and the Welsh Charity School at Ashford. Schools of all types are usually listed in directories throughout the nineteenth century.

Many professional men of Welsh origin would have received their schooling in England. It is well worth consulting the published registers of English public schools.[6] The names of Welsh boys from better-off families can be found in many, and not only in those near the border, such as Shrewsbury.[7] Most registers provide details of date of birth and parentage, and often indicate relationships with other pupils, for example, where brothers or fathers were also pupils. Details of earlier schooling and of the date of leaving are frequently given, as are careers and dates of death.

Lists have also been compiled (from *Alumni*) of Welshmen at Oxford and Cambridge.[8]

Basic Sources

Records of men who entered the professions are likely to be found in the standard sources, where they have survived. Most will be represented in parish registers, having needed proof of age and/or baptism to enter a profession, and most will have married by licence and left a will. As time went on and dissenters were able to enter the professions, nonconformist registers come into the reckoning. Such familiar sources will provide the main part of biographical information about professional people, just as they do for humbler folk, but should be found more consistently.

Lawyers

The law was a profession which appealed very much to the emerging new Welsh middle class, but Welsh lawyers did not have a good press. Throughout the seventeenth century it was observed that the Welsh had a passion for 'lawying' and indeed that they were 'cantankerous, crabbed, cunning in the law'.[9] One writer said that Wales, instead of breeding cattle, was now breeding two-legged asses good for nothing but braying in the courts.[10] The Welsh gentry were renowned for their litigious nature, while the law as a profession was equally attractive as a means of providing for younger sons; it became attractive also to the smaller gentry, the freeholding class. Successful Welsh lawyers practising in London were, it is said, besieged with offers of likely lads from home to be apprenticed as clerks.[11] It has been estimated that in some years Welshmen formed 20% of those admitted to the Inns of Court – this from an area which contained about 7% of the population of England and Wales.

When Robert Wynn wrote in 1611, 'If he would seek after worldly honour, the law is the only way', he pointed the way ahead for many Welsh families. Success was achieved often at the cost of smaller people who stood in the way, and lawyers acquired a reputation for rapacity and disdain for their neighbours, taking advantage of their position to buy up land.

Sons of wealthier families were likely to be steered towards the Bar. Barristers are allowed to act as advocates in court after qualifying through one of the Inns of Court – Lincoln's Inn, Middle Temple, Inner Temple, Gray's Inn. The Inns of Court, however, gave a general education besides, often acting as 'a finishing school for the young man about town'.[12] Over 1,000 Welshmen attended the Inns in the seventeenth century, the largest proportion being at Gray's Inn, which has kept Welsh links to the present. Many admissions registers have been published and, as time went on, include details of the student's age, father's address and occupation.[13] Frequently they appear in University *Alumni*.[14] Joseph Foster's *Men-at-the-Bar* is a biographical handlist, giving details of education and qualifications, but also of birth and marriage.

Although incidental references to lawyers may be found in various documents, the first lists to be kept were the result of the Attorneys and Solicitors Act of 1728. This provided that attorneys and solicitors should serve under articles as clerks, should take an oath, and their names should be enrolled. Articles were for five years, and affidavits attesting to their completion had to be registered as a result of an Act of 1749. The names of parents and guardians may be found with the affidavits or articles. Indexed registers are at the Public Record Office. *Tracing Your Ancestors in the Public Record Office* is an excellent summary of what is available there.[15]

There has been an annual *Law List* since 1775 and this contains details of barristers, as well as of solicitors and attorneys. Most searches should start with the *Law List*, which is available in long runs in large libraries, although it has deficiencies in the early period.[16,17]

The *Law List* of 1812 has a list of Judges, including those who sat in the Court of Great Sessions, King's Counsel, Counsel, certificated Conveyancers, Special Pleaders, Public Notaries, etc, while certificated attorneys are divided into those practising in London and in the country. There are many people with Welsh names, in the London section of which these are typical examples:

> Jones, John, 2 Size lane, Bucklersbury, Vestry clerk of Bromley St Leonard's, Middlesex, and Secretary to the London Hospital ...

> Lewellin, Daniel, Great College street, Westminster [18]

Names are alphabetical and the address is of the practice; posts are named where applicable.

The list of Country Attorneys groups them geographically. For example, [No.] 2. Aberystwyth, Card[iganshire] is 211 miles from London (a fact necessary to calculate postage). Practising in the town were Dan. Williams, Tho. P. Hopley, Comm. for Affidavits in Great Session, Solic. to Trustees of Aberystwyth Harb[our] and Turnpike for co. Cardigan, and Henry Lewis. Letter-codes refer to their London agents, also listed.

In the same list [No.] 471. Llandovery, Carmarthenshire (191 miles) had three also: T. Bishop, Edward Jones and Edward Jones, junior.

The alphabetical index to names which follows is by surname only, followed by the index number of the place – e.g., among the many Jones entries listed is a reference to 471 (Llandovery).

So the *Law List* is a means to locating lawyers, but does not provide biographical information. Although individuals may be followed up in the PRO records, such information is highly likely to be found in local sources for birth/baptism, marriage and death/burial. Other sources should always be checked: *The Aberystwyth Guide* (1816) gives the names and addresses of five 'attornies or solicitors', including Thomas Pelham Hopley, Bridge Street, Henry Lewis, King Street, and Daniel Williams, Long Acre.

As time went on, the *Law List* became easier to read and information relating to addresses somewhat fuller. In 1851 Robert Owen Jones was of 24 Southampton Buildings, Chancery Lane, and of Black Fen, near Eltham, Kent.[19] In the same year, fourteen country attorneys were listed in Carmarthen. No addresses are given but this was a census year and most Welsh towns were small enough for a census search to be feasible – Carmarthen, like many other towns, has been indexed for 1851. In addition, local directories became more numerous as the nineteenth century went on and lawyers featured in the classified lists of occupations.

As time went on, lawyers became very respected members of Welsh society, and often appear in biographical works. In a useful biographical index compiled by W.W. Price,[20] there are four handwritten cards and a newspaper cutting about William Jones Canton (1883-1960), a solicitor in Merthyr Tydfil for fifty years: these give his education, professional qualifications, his honours (OBE, DL), his parentage, his marriage to a woman from the Welsh enclave in Hughesoffka, south Russia, his daughters and their marriages, his brothers and their callings, his addresses, clubs and hobbies.

Medical Practitioners

The practice of medicine was in the hands of the Church in mediaeval times and its evolution towards the modern system was slow and not always well-defined. Forerunners of modern medical practitioners were the apothecaries, who prepared and dispensed medicines, the physicians, who dealt with internal ailments, and the surgeons, who carried out operations. Their roles often overlapped and distinctions were blurred. The background history is fully described in Bourne & Chicken (1994) and in Herber (1997).

Apothecaries were incorporated with the Grocers' Company in 1607 (the connection being the use of spices, etc) and became a separate body in 1617. Formal licences were granted in England and Wales from 1815, and a five-year apprenticeship was required. Early records (from 1670) are at the Guildhall Library; apprenticeship details include the date of baptism, the father's name and abode, the date of apprenticeship and the master's name.

The history of physicians and surgeons are intertwined even though the London College of Physicians (now the Royal College of Physicians of London) was founded in 1518, with advantages for its members. Licences to practise as physicians and surgeons were granted by bishops from 1511 until this fell into abeyance in the late eighteenth century; the actual licences were given to the individuals but were to be recorded in the bishop's register. In Wales, these records vary in quantity in different dioceses and never seem as numerous as one hopes. They are often tucked between long lists of ordinations and appointments to benefices, and the occasional licence to teach or conduct a school, and read, for example:

> 3 Oct[r] 1765 A Licence was granted to David Thomas of Rossilly in the County of Glamorgan Surgeon to Practice the Art of Surgery in and throughout the whole Diocese of St Davids.[21]

Other records relating to licences may survive, usually in the form of petitions, testimonials and oaths.[22] Sometimes, as in the case of Eugene Daly of Llantrisant in Glamorgan, churchwardens and other parishioners vouched for the candidate's fitness 'to practice Physick and Surgery'.[23] More convincingly to the modern mind, the testimonial of David Davis of Caerphilly in the parish of Eglwysilan, Glamorgan, was signed 'by those whose names are here underwritten being examined Surgeons', though, sadly, in this case only one of the signatures has survived the ravages of time, that of Thomas Rees.[24]

Surgeons had less prestige than physicians. Their history was bound up with that of the Barbers' Company, though surgeons broke away and founded a separate Company in 1745, which received its charter in 1800 as the College of Surgeons (now the Royal College of Surgeons). Early records of the Barber Surgeons are at the Guildhall Library, London, later ones at the College. New entrants were apprenticed, and their records may be in hospital records. Details of Fellows of the College are well recorded, whilst all have been listed in the *Medical Directory* since 1845.

By the eighteenth century many physicians became graduates in medicine – such degrees could be bought – and are to be found in the

Alumni of Oxford and Cambridge. Many qualified at Trinity College, Dublin, or in Edinburgh, St Andrews, Aberdeen or Glasgow; others qualified abroad, e.g. at Leiden, Holland. Occasional medical directories were compiled in the late eighteenth century, but they give very little information about the individuals listed.[25]

However, for that period, much of the groundwork for locating medical ancestors has been done in *Eighteenth Century Medics* by P.J. and R.V. Wallis.[26] This lists 35,000 medical practitioners, from such sources as subscriptions, licences and apprenticeships; they are of all categories. (apothecaries, chemists, druggists, surgeons, etc), alphabetically, with (variously) dates of indenture and qualifications, details of apprenticeship, address, parent and master. The key to each item of information allows the researcher to go to the original source.

Although the situation in Wales was relatively poor – there was 'a dearth of qualified medical men'[27] – there were by the mid-eighteenth century physicians of some sort in most Welsh towns. By 1790 Brecon had four surgeons and a druggist, Carmarthen had ten surgeons and apothecaries, and even Llandovery had four apothecaries by 1761, something which prompted Lewis Morris to exclaim, 'London come almost to our doors'.[28] However, most qualified men had to go to London to practise or to join the Royal Navy.[29] It is very noticeable that many late eighteenth and nineteenth century medical men in the printed sources, bearing names typical in some way of Wales, are found to have fathers who practised in, for example, Bristol or other English cities, so that they are certainly at least second-generation representatives of the Welsh in England.

Biographies of Fellows and Licentiates of the College of Physicians were compiled by Dr William Munk in four volumes (the last being of Fellows only).[30] The years covered by Munk's *Roll* are: Volume 1, 1518-1700; Volume 2, 1701-1800; Volume 3, 1801-1825; Volume 4 1826-1925. These extracts show the amount of biographical information one may hope to find:

> HUGH OWEN M.D., was educated at Leyden, where on the 26th September, 1730, in the rectorship of Boerhaave, he was entered on the physic line, being then twenty-three years of age. He graduated doctor of medicine at Rheims 17th October, 1733, and was admitted an Extra-Licentiate of the College of Physicians 27th February, 1733-4. He practised in Merionethshire.[31]

> THOMAS JONES M.D., of the university of St. Andrew's, of 31st March, 1810, was admitted a Licentiate of the College of Physicians 25th June, 1810. One Thomas Jones, M.D., presumably our Licentiate, died 26th May, 1848, aged sixty-eight, at John's Town, near Carmarthen.[32]

George Rees, MD, with an entry in the third volume, was a Pembrokeshire man, the son of a clergyman. Details are given of his main qualifications and their dates, and of his published works. He founded the Pembroke House Lunatic Asylum in Hackney and later became superintendent of a similar establishment in Bodmin, Cornwall; he died in 1846 at his London address. George Rees also merited entries in the *Dictionary of National Biography* and *A Dictionary of Eminent Welshmen*, both of which give references to other sources, such as the *Gentleman's Magazine.*

This last example makes the point that, as the nineteenth century progressed, supplementary information is more generally available in other published works. In addition more formal attempts were made to list practitioners: in 1845 the *Medical Directory* began and has appeared annually ever since. This was followed in 1859 by the official *Medical Register,* the result of the recent legal requirement of registration of doctors. In the early years, the lists include those in practice before 1815.

Taking the 1859 *Medical Register* as an example, sections include a London Medical Directory with a Street List, giving the Residences of Medical Practitioners in London and the suburbs, and a general alphabetical list of names, addresses, qualifications, appointments, and published works. This covers Physicians, Surgeons and General Practitioners; details of universities, colleges, schools of medicine, metropolitan hospitals, etc. The Provincial Medical Directory has a similar list of towns where doctors reside, then an alphabetical list of practitioners. At the end is a list of Registered Non-residents and an Obituary section.

From the Provincial List one can find, for example, that Aberystwyth had the following medical practitioners: H. Bell, MD; R. Gilbertson; T. James; J.W. Jones; J. Morgan; J. Roberts; J. Rowlands, with this sort of extra detail:

ROWLANDS, JOHN, Portland-st. Aberystwyth, Cardigansh. – MRCS, Eng., and LM, 1855; Surg. to several mines.

The *Medical Directory* of 1861 lists these medical men practising in Pembroke Dock – much of their work related to the working population of the Royal Naval Dockyard:

BENNETT, CHARLES V.S. Bush-st. Pembroke Dock – MRCS and LSA Eng. 1858; (Guy's).

SUMPTER, J., 7 Queen-st. West, Pembroke Dock, Pembrokesh. – MRCS, Eng. 1836; LSA 1835.

THOMAS, WILLIAM, 8 Queen-st. West, Pembroke Dock, S. Wales – LRCP. Edin. 1859; FRCS Eng. 1853; MRCS 1823; LSA 1822; (Boro' Sch.); Dep.-Lieut. for Co. and JP; Dist. Insp. Agencies; Gen. Superint. and Confid. Med.

Ref. Scott. Union Ins. Co.; late Surg. to Troops in Garrison, and to Guard-ship and Roy. Marines in Pembroke.

Once more, other details can be obtained from directories and the census, and the lives of Doctors Sumpter and Thomas are recounted in a local history.[33]

The Obituary section can be useful. In the same volume:

> JONES, Thomas C., Deputy Inspector of Hospitals and Fleets, on October 19 [1860], at Pembroke, aged 80.[34]

> LEWIS, Frederick Owen Butt, MRCS. Eng. and LSA, on January 27, at Cwmaman, Llanelly, Wales, aged 48.

Biographical works should always be consulted.[35] *Who's Who in Wales* (1920) has for example an entry for Naunton Wingfield Davies, the bare details of whose name and address were located in a directory. *Who's Who* provides many family details with minimum effort (but check them against other sources for accuracy), together with an insight into his personal opinions:

> DAVIES, Naunton Wingfield, FRCS, etc, Edin., Phys. (Gold Medallist, silver Medallist); *b.* 1852, Newport, Mon; *s.* Late D.W. Davies, MD, Llantrisant, Glam; *ed.* Edinburgh, Dublin and Irish University and Coll. Surgeons; *m.* Mary, *dau.* late Daniel Owen, JP, Ash Hall, Cowbridge; three *s.* one *dau.* Publ. Author of various professional Works, Dramas, and other books. *Rel.* Belief in all creeds sincerely held; *Pol.* Hopes for the day when Party politics will give way to statesmanship. *Recr.* Hunting, Fishing. *Club:* Home. *Address:* The Laurels, Llantrisant, Glam, *Tel.* 14; also 6 Windsor Pl., Cardiff, *Tel.* 3261. M.C. FO 630.

As with any profession or trade, medicine often ran in the family and one source may lead to another, with obituaries in newspapers and wills providing pointers to the lives and careers of relations.

Published works

Published works, other than the specialised professional directories, will cover most Welsh professional people: among those for or including Welsh people are the University *Alumni,* the *Dictionary of Welsh Biography,* the *Dictionary of Eminent Welshmen, Enwogion Môn, Eminent Men of Denbighshire, Enwogion Sir Aberteifi, Enwogion Ceredigion.*[36]

Other Professions

With the advent of new professions many modern professional bodies have annual **membership lists**, of which the following are examples: accountants, architects, bankers, chemists, civil engineers, civil servants, colonial officials, dentists, geologists, mining engineers, pharmacists, veterinary surgeons.

There are **biographical dictionaries** for many professions and occupations, including the following: actors (and other theatricals), artists (painters, sculptors, etc), authors, bookbinders, booksellers, engravers, inventors, librarians, members of parliament, musicians, publishers, railway engineers, scientists, teachers. [37]

Among the professions regularly listed in nineteenth-century commercial and social **directories** are artists, auctioneers and valuers, estate agents, photographers, surveyors, teachers who ran schools and academies, veterinary surgeons.

BIBLIOGRAPHY TO CHAPTER 18

References are made to:

Jones, P.H., *A Bibliography of the History of Wales* (Cardiff, 1989), referred to in the Notes as *BHW.*

See also *Welsh Family History: A Guide to Research* (2nd ed., FFHS, 1998), referred to in the Notes as *WFH;* especially Chapter 23, 'Select Bibliography'.

General

Bevan, A. (ed.), *Tracing Your Ancestors in the Public Record Office* (5th ed., PRO, 1999).

Dodd, A.H., *Stuart Wales: The Social Order* (Clwyd CC/WEA, 1991), reprinted from *Studies in Stuart Wales* (UW Press, 1951, repr. 1971).

Jenkins, G.H., *The Foundations of Modern Wales 1642-1780* (Oxford and Cardiff, 1987).

Williams, G., *Recovery, Reorientation and Reformation: Wales c.1415-1642* (Oxford and Cardiff, 1987).

Biographical Works

Jenkins, R.T. (ed.), *The Dictionary of Welsh Biography down to 1940* (London, 1959).

Who's Who in Wales (1920, 1933, 1937).

The Gentleman's Magazine – see for example: *Index to Biographical and Obituary Notices in The Gentleman's Magazine 1731-1780* (British Record Society, 1891).

Education

Foster J., *Alumni Oxonienses 1500-1714* (Oxford & London 1891-2).

Foster J., *Alumni Oxonienses 1715-1886* (Oxford & London 1887-8).

Jacobs, P.M., *Registers of the Universities, Colleges and Schools of Great Britain and Ireland* (1964).

School, University and College Registers and Histories in the Library of the Society of Genealogists (Society of Genealogists, 1988).

Seaborne, M., *Schools in Wales 1500-1900: A Social and Architectural History* (Denbigh, 1992).

Venn, J. & J.A., *Alumni Cantabrigienses, from the Earliest Times to 1900* (Cambridge, 1922-54).

Occupations – General

The Book of Trades or Library of Useful Arts. 3 volumes, 1811-18. (Republished by Wiltshire FHS, 1993).

Christmas, B.W., *Sources for One-Name Studies and for other Family Historians* (Guild of One-Name Studies, 1992).

Culling, J., *Occupations: A Preliminary List* (FFHS, 1994).

Herber, M.D., *Ancestral Trails* (Sutton & Society of Genealogists, 1997). Chapter 21 has a very full reading-list on the professions and occupations.

Raymond, S., *Occupational Sources for Genealogists: a Bibliography* (FFHS, 1992).

Saul, P., *Family Historian's Enquire Within* (FFHS, 5th ed., 1995) has addresses of professional bodies which keep registers.

Lawyers

Records of the Registrar of Attorneys and Solicitors from 1843, held by: The Law Society, Ipsley, Redditch.

Registers of the Inns of Court.

Foster, J., *Men at the Bar: a biographical handlist of the members of the various Inns of Court* (London, 1885).

Williams, W.R., *The History of the Great Sessions in Wales 1642-1830 together with the Lives of the Welsh Judges* (Brecknock, 1899).

Medical Practitioners

The Medical Directory (1845 to date; obituaries to 1914).

The Medical Register (1858 to date).

Cule, J., *Wales and Medicine: a source-list for printed books and papers showing the history of medicine in relation to Wales and Welshmen* (Aberystwyth, 1980).

Munk, W., *The Roll of the Royal College of Physicians of London, 1518-1825* (London, 1861-1878).

Plarr's Lives of the Fellows of the Royal College of Surgeons.

Wallis, P.J. & R.V., *Eighteenth Century Medics* (2nd ed., 1988).

The Dentists' Register (1879 to date).

Bourne, S. & Chicken, A.H., *Records of the Medical Profession* (1994).

Hilton, C., 'Citadel on the Euston Road: The Wellcome Institute for the History of Medicine' in *Genealogists' Magazine,* 26, 4 (Dec 1998).

Pelling, M., 'The Patient's Choice: Identifying Medical Practitioners', *English Genealogical Congress: Selected Papers given at the Congresses of 1978 and 1984* (London, 1986).

Raymond (see Bibliography: Occupations – General) lists the publications of the various medical colleges and institutions.

Thornton, J., *A Select Bibliography of Medical Biography* (1970).

Directories and Lists on microfiche:

The Society of Genealogists has published on microfiche: Law List 1812, Apothecaries 1815-1840, Medical directory 1847, Medical register 1779; also trade, commercial and post office directories on fiche.

ADDRESSES

Public Record Office, Ruskin Ave, Kew, Richmond, Surrey TW9 4DU.
Website:

Society of Genealogists, 14 Charterhouse Buildings, Goswell Road, London EC1M 7BA. Tel: 0171 251 8799.
Website:

Wellcome Institute for the History of Medicine, 183 Euston Road, London NW1 2BE. Tel. 0171 611 8582.
Website: <www.wellcome.ac.uk/institute/library>

For those who have access to the Internet, a website on medical ancestors exists at <http:/user.itl.net/~glen/doctors.html>, with links to other useful sites, such as libraries, the Royal Colleges, etc.

NOTES TO CHAPTER 18

[1] Chambers' *Twentieth Century Dictionary; Concise Oxford Dictionary.*

[2] Chapter 3 in the present work deals with records of the clergy. As there is so much overlap between the topics, readers should refer to that chapter's bibliography and references also.

[3] Williams (1987).

[4] Seabourne (1992). See also D.A. Pretty, 'Education Records', Chapter 14 in *WFH.*

[5] *BHW*: 1536-1780: EGJ1-521780-1870: 4GHF1-4GHH2.

[6] The best collection I know of is at the Society of Genealogists – see notes to Chapter 3. Welsh schools do not have a good record of publishing lists of their pupils.

[7] For example, I have found details of members of one family of Welsh descent in the registers of Aldenham Grammar School, Brighton College, Cheltenham College, Elizabeth College, Guernsey, Rugby School, St John's Leatherhead, Tonbridge School, Wellington College and Westminster School.

[8] *BHW*: Welshmen at Oxford in 3GJ62; Welshmen at Cambridge in 3GJ623. Some entries are about individuals, some are lists abstracted from *Alumni* and other sources.

[9] Quoted in Dodd (1971).

[10] W. Vaughan, *The Golden Fleece* (1626).

[11] Dodd (1971).

[12] Emrys Jones, 'The Welsh in London in the Seventeenth and Eighteenth Centuries' in *Welsh History Review* X, 4 (1981).

[13] A good collection is at the Society of Genealogists; NLW has few.

[14] See Bibliography.

[15] Bevan (1999); there is also a PRO information leaflet, 'Records of Attorneys and Solicitors', free to readers, or downloaded from the PRO website.

[16] Between 1775 and 1789 they contain names of men who were never actually admitted to a court; until 1861 they do not give the admission date (PRO leaflet).

[17] Published professional directories, etc, may be seen at the National Library of Wales, though there are rarely complete runs.

[18] We cannot, of course, tell if they were Welshmen from the information provided.

[19] Punctuation and use of capital letters modernised.

[20] W.W. Price, Aberdâr, *Biographical Index* [NLW 1981].

[21] NLW: Church in Wales Records SD/BR/5 (Bishop's Register 1761-1825). This register, like some others, is indexed in a separate manuscript volume but the names of physicians and surgeons are not generally included in the index.

[22] There are lists in the schedules of Church in Wales records, arranged by diocese.

[23] NLW: Church in Wales Records LL/SM/4.

[24] NLW: Church in Wales Records LL/SM/7.

[25] The 1779 *Medical Register* has been published on microfiche by the Society of Genealogists. The headings of its lists of names are: 1. Physicians 2. Surgeons 3. Surgeons and Apothecaries 4. Apothecaries.

[26] See Bibliography.

[27] Jenkins (1987).

[28] Quoted in Jenkins (1987), p. 274.

[29] Surgeons of the Royal Navy kept Medical Journals, which are now at the Public Record Office in class ADM 101.

[30] See Bibliography.

[31] Volume 2, 1734.

[32] Volume 3, 1810.

[33] Elizabeth E. Peters, *A History of Pembroke Dock* (1904).

[34] As with trade directories, the year of the title represents information collected up to twelve months earlier.

[35] See Bibliography to this chapter and to Chapter 3 (on the clergy); see also the Bibliography (Chapter 23) in *WFH*.

[36] *Enwogion*: 'famous men of ...'

[37] Raymond (1992) has full titles, dates, etc.

19. THE LLOYDS OF TY NEWYDD: A STUDY OF A NORTH WALES FAMILY

John Dilwyn Williams

The aims of the family historian, as the name implies, are not merely to produce a family tree, but to find out as much as possible about the actual history of each individual, to try and breathe some life into a bare list of names.* The following chapter is a case study that aims to show the extensive range of sources that can be utilised to enable one to build up as full a picture as possible, although it must be admitted that it was fortunate in this case that so many family records had survived.

Tŷ Newydd, located in the parish of Llannor in Llŷn in the former county of Caernarfon, has been described as a 'house of two storeys and attic, with added wing at back, probably of the late 17th century and 18th century respectively' (see Fig. 19-1).[1] However, it may be slightly earlier. Receipts for Hearth Tax survive which show that there were two fire-hearths in 1675 whereas by 1686 there were three.[2] An end wall of the main block was rebuilt some years ago and amongst the rubble was found a stone inscribed 'O.Ll. [for Owen Lloyd] 1682'. The first reference to the name 'Y Ty Newydd', which means 'the new house', comes from 1648, although the actual name does not necessarily have to refer to the present building.[3]

For the location of Tŷ Newydd and other places named in this chapter, see Fig. 19-2.

The Lloyds ranked amongst the comparatively large body of minor gentry who, though not amongst the county élite, held sway in their own localities. The history of this class in general was one of steady decline during the seventeenth and eighteenth centuries as mounting debts forced many to sell their lands to the larger, more prosperous estates. Tŷ Newydd, however, managed to survive a little longer. Its owners were styled 'gentleman' and even 'esquire'. One member did, in fact, become High

---

* This chapter is based on talks given to the Family History in Wales Course in several years from 1991 to 1998.

Sheriff of the county. As well as farming their own land and receiving rents for other tenements, they supplemented their income by acting as stewards for neighbouring larger estates. They also featured prominently in the local Customs service. Although the estate did eventually fall foul, in the mid-nineteenth century, to pressing mortgage debts, the main house itself has never been sold – though it too has had a chequered history.

Fig. 19-1: Tŷ Newydd in 1998

More often than not, the records of these minor gentry families have been lost along with the families themselves. Those that have survived, amongst the archives of the larger estates into which the lands were swallowed, are more often than not confined to legal deeds and documents. Luckily, in the case of Tŷ Newydd, it is a different matter for, as well as legal documents, some business and personal records have also survived. These have been dispersed over the years but they are to be found in four main collections. A collection of papers that survived at Tŷ Newydd itself – some 1,247 items in all – has been deposited at Gwynedd Record Office.[4] These consist of a few deeds and nineteenth-century rentals, but mainly nineteenth-century business and personal correspondence, bills, invoices and miscellanea. There is also a fragment of an early eighteenth-century Letter Book containing draft correspondence for the years from 1706 to 1708, which is of especial interest. Two other collections in the Gwynedd Record Office specifically concern the Tŷ Newydd estate, consisting of deeds and personal papers from the sixteenth to the early nineteenth centuries.[5] A further bound volume of personal and business correspondence, inventories and draft deeds, dating from the late seventeenth and eighteenth centuries, is located at the University Library at Bangor.[6] There are other valuable records too, outside the specific 'family archives' and these will be referred to in the course of the chapter.

The first Lloyd of whom any details are known is John Lloyd, in whose marriage settlement of 1648 is found the earliest reference to Tŷ Newydd.[7] He had been married for some six or more years prior to drawing up the settlement, for we know that his son and heir, Owen Lloyd, died in 1729 aged eighty-seven, having therefore been born around 1642. This deed of 1648 refers to *Y Tuy Newydd* and its demense lands, together with other specified properties in the parish of Llannor which made up the estate of *John Lloyd of Llannor, gent*.[8] Not all the names from the seventeenth century have survived, but from knowledge of the estate in later centuries it is estimated that it was at the time approximately 180 acres in all. The settlement provided a jointure for his wife Jonett for her lifetime, and entailed the estate on his son and heir, Owen Lloyd, and his heirs for ever. John Lloyd had obviously inherited the estate from his own father, for there is a reference to the dower or thirds of his mother, Elizabeth. A later deed of 1668/9 gives her full name as Elizabeth v[er]ch Hugh, and that of 'her late husband' as Owen Lloyd.[9]

She had been born around 1580 for she is presumably the same 'Elizabeth vch Hugh wydow aged 66 yeares or thereabouts' who gave testimony in the court of Quarter Sessions at Caernarfon in 1646 following an attack upon her three sons, William, John and Henry Lloyd. It was the Civil War period and a local Catholic family, Gruffith and Dorothy Wynne of Brynhunog and their three sons, John, Robert and Charles, stood accused, together with some six royalist officers, that they

> upon the last day of march last at Llannor ... did make and beginne an assault and affray upon the said Wm lloid, John lloid and Henry lloid being then peaceably in the church yard of Llannor aforesaid and unweaponed to defend themselves and with swordes pistols and staves did beate and wound the said Willm John and Henry lloid and followed them into the ryver there hardby.

> And that the said Dorothy tooke the said Henry lloid by the hayre of his head twise. And that the said Henry recd. two woundes thone being a thurst [*sic*] in his thigh and thother a thurst in his breast which was done by the said John Wynne whereby the said Henry lloid is languishing in great daunger of his lief.[10]

The counter-claim was 'that Captain Wm. Edwards receaved a hurt upon the brow by a ston flung out of the handes of John Lloyd of Llanor'.[11] No records survive to show the outcome of the case but there are further references to John Lloyd of Llannor among the Caernarfonshire Quarter Sessions records.

An earlier file, of 1643, contains a letter signed by Richard Gruffith, probably of Llanfair-is-gaer, asking the Justices to release John Lloyd of Llannor from two recognisances to appear at Quarter Sessions as 'the sd John Lloyd is in his Maj.'s service and formerly under my command but now under Capt John Madryn's command'.[12] Richard Griffith of Llanfair-is-gaer was captain of the trained bands of Eifionydd and Uwchgwyrfai and in 1643 was in charge of a Caernarfonshire contingent which formed part of the Chester garrison when that city was under siege from parliamentary forces in the early stages of the Civil War.[13] Whether John Lloyd had left his command prior to this is impossible to tell.

It is difficult to reconcile the fact that John Lloyd was a royalist with the subsequent attack on him and his brothers three years later by the royalist officers in Llannor churchyard, unless John Lloyd had already by then changed or trimmed his allegiance. In the 1654 Quarter Sessions file, the year following Oliver Cromwell's installation as Lord Protector, there is an undated petition from John Lloyd of Llannor asking to be granted a pension from the maimed soldiers' mize as he had 'served in the service of the parliament of England this long tyme and hath lost the use of his arm in that service and is run farre in debt and decaied in his estate'.[14] His request was unsuccessful, however, for the footnote added to the petition states 'this read but nothing done'.

He would have been about forty-eight years of age at the time, for two years previously 'John Lloyd of Llannor, aged about xlvi years, gent.' had complained to the justices that Anne verch Richard, the wife of Richard Roberts of Carnguwch, clerk, had assaulted him; he had 'been hurled att and beaten with stones to the bruising of his body' and she had threatened to 'find out a man that should beat him worse than ever he was before'.[15] The reason for her animosity is not known, nor is the outcome of the complaint. It is possible that religious differences might have been the cause for, following the restoration of Charles II in May 1660, 'John Lloide Llannor' was one of nineteen Dissenters and republicans imprisoned in Caernarfon in January 1661. Scribbled in the margin by his name, however, is the word 'discharged'.[16]

The next reference to John Lloyd does not come until 1668/9 at the time of his son's marriage. Owen Lloyd married Mary Griffith, daughter of

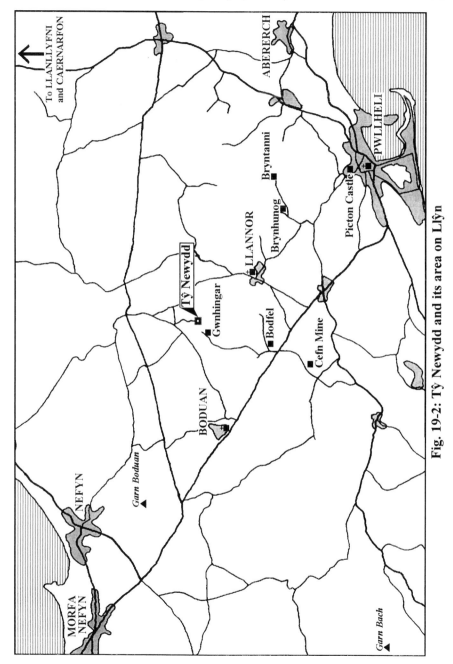

Fig. 19-2: Tŷ Newydd and its area on Llŷn

Griffith Jones, gent., of Bryn-tanni in the neighbouring parish of Abererch, and by the terms of the marriage settlement the whole estate, apart from one house and lands called *Tuy yn y Llan* (later called Cae'r Ficar), was to be to the use of Owen Lloyd and Mary for their lifetimes, thus providing her with a jointure.[17] As for *Tuy yn y Llan*, it was in the occupation of John Lloyd's mother, Elizabeth verch Hugh, who was, therefore, still alive aged eighty-eight or eighty-nine. After her death, John Lloyd was to have the use of *Tuy yn y Llan* for himself. For details of the children and later descendants of Owen Lloyd and Mary Griffith, see Fig. 19-3.

In return for 'the preferment of the said Mary to marriage as aforesaid' and thus safeguarding his daughter's future, Griffith Jones committed himself to several obligations. The marriage settlement states that Griffith Jones was to provide Owen Lloyd and Mary with 'meat Drinke & Lodging' with him at his own house for three, four or five years after their marriage, as they so wished, and he was to provide maintenance for any children they might have for as long as they chose to stay with him. When they were to leave his house, Griffith Jones was to give Owen Lloyd £40 towards stocking his land and £5 or its worth 'in household stuffe towards furnishing their house or chamber'. Furthermore, Griffith Jones bound himself to paying 'several great debts' owed by John Lloyd, amounting to £90 8s 9d. As far back as 1654 John Lloyd had complained of having 'run farre in debt and decaied in his estate'.[18]

Griffith Jones and Owen Lloyd committed themselves to pay John Lloyd further sums of £5 per quarter during the lifetime of Elizabeth verch Hugh and then £8 per quarter during the lifetime of John Lloyd himself. It is not known when Elizabeth verch Hugh died but John Lloyd was dead within three years, for on 24 November 1671 Owen Lloyd was given a receipt for ten shillings paid as relief to the king on entering his estate following his father's death.[19]

Griffith Jones, a tenant himself at Bryn-tanni, must have thought it a lucrative enough investment to bail out John Lloyd in order to provide his daughter and her descendants with landed property. Bryn-tanni was part of the large Bodfel estate, of which Griffith Jones was steward, the mansion house and demesne of which estate bordered onto Tŷ Newydd.[20]

Following his father's death, Owen Lloyd and Mary must have moved from her father's house to Tŷ Newydd. In 1674 Owen Lloyd added to the estate by purchasing a small farm called *Tu yn y Cae* otherwise known as *Pentre*, in the parish of Llannor.[21] Owen Lloyd, however, also became indebted himself. Credit would have been widely available through a network of kin and neighbours. His son and heir, Owen Lloyd, junior, drew

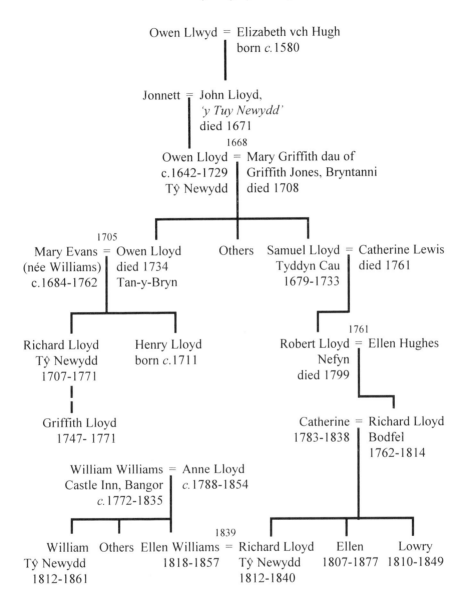

Fig. 19-3: Three hundred years at Tŷ Newydd

up a list of his father's debts 'due at my first going to London 1690'.[22] They amounted to £94 10s 0d. They had been reduced to £60 within eight years, for a subsequent list was drawn up on the back of the same sheet, of 'Debts owing by Owen Lloyd as given me by my mother this 1st March 1697/8'.

Owen Lloyd, junior, was the eldest to survive of at least nine children born to Owen Lloyd and Mary Griffith. The record of baptism of two has survived in the bishop's transcripts for Llannor; Samuel was baptised in 1678/9 and Griffith in 1686. Griffith did not outlive his father but Samuel is among the seven listed in his father's will in 1724 – Owen, Hugh, Samuel, Robert, Lowry, Sarah and Ann.[23] There was another son called Richard who died at sea in 1706 whilst serving on board the frigate *The Streatham* with the East India fleet. Reference to his death is found in the early eighteenth-century Letter Book, mentioned above as having come from Tŷ Newydd, kept in the neat and easily recognisable hand of his eldest brother.[24]

Owen Lloyd, junior, had obviously received a classical education, for a book list has survived in his hand – 'Henway llyfre a adewais i gartre wrth fynd i Lundan y waith gynta' ('the names of the books I left at home when I first went to London') – and among the 'Llyfraŷ yscol' (school books) are Greek and Latin texts and grammars.[25] At the top of the list of his other books are the Bible and the Book of Common Prayer, but the list is also testimony to the diversity of his interests, with books such as 'Austen of Fruits' (Ralph Austen, *A Treatise of Fruit Trees*, first published 1653) and 'Ro. Records Urine Book' (Robert Recorde, *The Urinal of Physick*, first published 1547). He also had five Welsh books. These included three theological books, together with a dictionary, 'Geirlufr Thomas Jones' (*Y Gymraeg yn ei Disgleirdeb*, 1688), and the famous 'Llyfr y fickar', the Revd Rhys Prichard's collection of didactic verses, *Canwyll y Cymru*, which first appeared in print in 1658 but of which a more comprehensive edition had been published in 1681.

When Owen Lloyd compiled this list in 1690 he was about to begin a period of seven years in the service of Sir William Cranmer of London whose testimonial to him has survived:

> I, Sir William Cranmer of London Knt, doe hereby certifie that Owen Lloyd hath dwealt with mee as my servant neare seven yeares, & hath behaved himselfe soberly, diligently, & honestly during that time for any thing I know to the contrary, wittnesse my hand this 12th day of June 1697.   William Cranmer.[26]

Sir William Cranmer lived in 'the precincts of Savoy' and there are references in his will to his managing estates and drawing up accounts.[27] It is probable, therefore, that Owen Lloyd spent his time with Sir William Cranmer gaining practical experience in estate management and book-keeping. He then returned to Tŷ Newydd, but before finding employment he put his experience to good use at home. The list he received from his mother of his father's debts has already been noted. He also catalogued the estate deeds and documents – 'A Schedule of writings I have delivered to my mother to be kept this 10th March 1697/8'.[28] Almost all of those deeds have survived. It is interesting to note that it was his mother whom he entrusted with their care. The reason is probably found in a letter written by Owen Lloyd, junior, almost ten years later, in September 1707, to his uncle William Jones, 'a minister at London', his mother's brother. He writes, 'My mother can look after nothing as she did and you know my father never could do it'.[29]

Having spent the year at home, Owen Lloyd wrote from Tŷ Newydd on 20 July 1698 that he was 'this day to go to my Ld. of Bangor's and to be in his Lordship's family for some time'.[30] The Bishop of Bangor since 1689 was Humphrey Humphreys (1642-1712), who was translated to Hereford in 1701.[31] There are references in the Letter Book alluded to which suggest that Owen Lloyd may have followed him in his service.

On 15 October 1705, however, Owen Lloyd signed the following oath:

> Owen Lloyd of the Parish of Llannor maketh oath that Marie Evans of the Parish of Llanllyfni is a widow and that himselfe is a Batchellour, and that there is no pre Contract between either of them and anybody else to the best of his knowledge, and that there is no Consanguinity & Affinity between them but that they may Lawfully marry.[32]

They were married the following day at Abererch church. Mary was the young widow of Andrew Evans of Neigwl Plas, in Llŷn, and the daughter of Ellen Williams, then of Tan-y-bryn, Llanllyfni, widow of Henry Williams, apothecary, of Clynnog. Mary Evans had a baby daughter by her first husband and following her marriage to Owen Lloyd they all lived at Tan-y-bryn, together with Mary's mother, grandmother, and younger sister. Mary was the heiress of Tan-y-bryn and the addition of her property was to more than double the Tŷ Newydd estate. Mary Lloyd also provided ready cash – over £2,000 she herself claimed when a disagreement arose between her and her son in later years over her right of dower – and during the following years Owen Lloyd was able to purchase properties in his own native parish as well as in the nearby county town of Caernarfon.[33]

Fairly detailed cameos exist for the years between 1706 and 1708, in Owen Lloyd's Letter Book, shedding light on various aspects of their life, both professional and personal, both ups and downs.

In February 1706 we read that his 'wife's only sister, a singlewoman abt 18 yrs old was buried 3 instant after about a fortnight's illness.' In August of the same year their first child was born. 'On Tuesday the 6th August abt 9 in the morning my wife was brott to bed of a son whom we had christened Owen the Satturday following by Mr Price Vicar of Clynnog at Llanllyfni.' Nothing is known of this child and he did not survive into adulthood. The letters in fact refer to the harshness of the times both for man and beast. In March 1707 he writes that 'Children die often here of the ague & smallpox. We have had a mighty wet winter …The fodder especially straw being bad many cattle die.'

On the last day of September of the previous year, Owen Lloyd and his family had had to move to Pwllheli 'so as to be nearer my business'. He worked within the Customs service and as part of his duties he had to attend to a shipwreck that occurred at Porth Neigwl (Hell's Mouth) one Sunday night in late November 1706. The episode also shows an indirect effect of the War of the Spanish Succession on Llŷn, for it was 'a French prize taken lately by the Dover on the Banks of Newfoundland a Fishing [which] came unfortunately in to Hells Mouth where she perished. She was about 2/3d full of Codd & had about 15 to 20 tons of bay salt in bulk, some wine & oyl but nothing of all this saved. The men got all safe being 12 of the Dover's crew & 3 Fr. prisoners.'

In November 1707 their second son, and eventual heir, was born. Mary Lloyd had apparently returned home to her mother during the pregnancy for Owen Lloyd wrote from Tan-y-bryn on 15 December that 'my wife was brott to bed abt a month agoe of a boy whome is named Richard so that I have been forced for a long while to come hither a Satturday night & to go off generally on Mondays.'

By then Owen Lloyd had acquired an additional post to supplement his income, for the previous August he had followed in the footsteps of his maternal grandfather and had been appointed steward of the property of Sarah, Countess of Radnor, daughter of Colonel John Bodvel. Technically it was by then no longer the Bodfel estate for a large portion, which included Bodfel itself, had been sold off. In his letter of acceptance of the '20£ per annum for receiving, returning etc. your Hon.'s rents', Owen Lloyd explains that he was 'Griffith Jones your old servant's only daughter's son & she now lives at Tu Newydd (near Bodvell)'.

A use was soon found for the increased income. Whilst making arrangements for the delivery of an order of tobacco from London on behalf of an acquaintance, Owen Lloyd wrote on 9 April 1708 to Mr Robert Evans, a London tobacconist, stating that 'my wife complains the pewter spoons grow dull and is not pleased without silver ones so pray send me in the same box six silver spoons that are fashionable sizable and substantial wch I suppose you may have for about 15/= a spoon.' The spoons were to be marked with their initials:

LL
O M

One of the last letters in the Letter Book was also directed to London a month later, but it had the doleful purpose of informing the uncle, William Jones the minister, that his sister, Owen Lloyd's mother, had died on 13 May 1708. Her daughter Ann was apparently in London as well and the uncle had written to Owen Lloyd to acquaint him 'with the troublesome haste Sister Ann made to leave London.' But in his reply Owen Lloyd was 'forced to inform [him]':

> that she is come I am afraid too late to see my poor mother dead much more alive for she was taken ill at Pwllheli yesterday was fortnight and could hardly get home but linger it out to this day about one in the afternoon when uncles R & S and all her children except sister Ann and all her Brothers but yourself were present at her parting. The funeral is appointed to be a Sunday as she desired. She was (like her mother) sensible to the last and as my grandmother got up out of bed a little before she died to take her leave (as she expressed it) *ar hen gwpwrdd ar hen fwrdd* [of the old cupboard and the old table] so my mother got this morning out of bed and went to the butry ... and took a loaf and butter and brott to the hearth in the house for a relation and old friend of hers but it being another woman that sat by the fire she hurried back to put the victual in the cupboard and went to bed.

Mary Griffith predeceased her husband by some twenty years.

Owen Lloyd, junior, and his wife were soon able to settle permanently at Tan-y-bryn. His initial capacity in the Customs service is uncertain but a certificate of oath has survived, dated 23 August 1708, on his appointment as Riding Surveyor of the Salt Duties in Wales West.[34] This was a supervisory position over the riding officers, who were part of the land guard which patrolled the coast to detect and prevent the smuggling of salt. This post probably made it no longer necessary for him to reside at Pwllheli. He also continued as steward for the former Bodfel estate. Although the original family were to sell off all their property, rentals survive to show that Owen Lloyd remained as the local steward for the new owners.

In 1729 Owen Lloyd, senior, died at Tŷ Newydd aged eighty-seven. The family remained at Tan-y-bryn, however. Owen Lloyd himself died within six years and was buried at Llanllyfni on 11 February 1734/5. Apart from his landed property he left a personal estate valued at £794.[35]

There were two surviving sons, both of whom were Cambridge graduates. Richard, the eldest, graduated from Queens' College in 1729, and

Henry graduated from St John's in 1733.[36] Owen Lloyd entailed his estate on his heir-at-law and so Richard, as the eldest son, inherited. However, a dispute arose between Mary and Richard Lloyd over her right of dower out of the estate, which led to litigation. An agreement was drawn up in August 1735 whereby Richard Lloyd agreed that his mother was to keep the lands she was entitled to in her own right – either as heir-at-law or as having a life interest in some of the properties purchased by her late husband – while he was to give his mother one-third of the rents of the remainder of his father's estate. The following March he sold his share of the 'stock, goods and chattels' at Tan-y-bryn to his mother and it was at Tŷ Newydd that Richard Lloyd was to settle, while his widowed mother lived on at Tan-y-bryn until her own death in 1762. She held her lands for almost twenty years 'without hindrance or molestation' until 1756 when, for some reason, Richard Lloyd took over from his mother the rents of those properties which his father had purchased. As he also held the title deeds to these properties Mary Lloyd had to resort to further litigation at Great Sessions to try and resolve the matter, which was eventually achieved through referral to arbitration, the agreement between the two being signed in May 1760.[37]

Richard Lloyd, Esq., of Tŷ Newydd, as he was by then referred to, was in fact Sheriff of the county in 1760 for the second time. As Richard Lloyd of Tan-y-bryn he had been appointed Sheriff in 1755 as well. Like his father and great-grandfather before him, he acted as steward of part of the former Bodfel estate. He also became steward of the Madryn estate and also steward to Mrs Salusbury, widow of John Salusbury of Bachegraig, who owned the tithes of two Llŷn parishes, Llangwnnadl and Tudweiliog. The Salusburys, natives of the vale of Clwyd, had lived for a few years at Bodfel as neighbours to Richard Lloyd. Their daughter, Hester Lynch Salusbury, was born there in 1741 and spent her first six years there. In later years she became Mrs Thrale, the renowned bluestocking and friend of Dr Samuel Johnson and would remember with affection her 'poor old friend Dick Lloyd … who played many a game of romps with me, and at draughts with my father before I was seven years old'.[38]

Richard Lloyd also features, indirectly, in the early history of Methodism in Llŷn, following Howell Harris's first visit to the peninsula in 1741. The Revd John Owen, vicar of Llannor at the time and also Chancellor of the Diocese, was a stern opponent of Methodism and Robert Jones of Rhos-lan, in his history of the revival, *Drych yr Amseroedd*, first published in 1820, refers to him and his followers persecuting the early Methodists in Llannor parish. But, he continues, there was also a gentleman living in the parish, one Mr Lloyd, esquire, of Tŷ Newydd, who was an excellent scholar; but there was great animosity between Mr Chancellor and him. When the Chancellor and his party came to persecute, the gentleman was sure to be there by the door to meet him. They would first converse in Welsh, then English, then Latin and finally Greek, but the Chancellor was not very proficient in Greek and the gentleman derided him by stating that he had allowed himself to forget more Greek than John Owen had ever learnt. And so the congregation received their blessing within the house while the two gentlemen argued outside.[39]

The oral tradition behind this story had lived on for almost eighty years before being written down by Robert Jones but there is certainly contemporary evidence of animosity between the two concerned. As Chancellor of the diocese, John Owen would have presided over the Bishop's consistory court and in 1750 a case was brought against Richard Lloyd for 'irreverent and indecent behaviour in Church at the time of divine service'. The case dragged on for two years before Richard Lloyd was pronounced guilty. He appealed to the Court of Arches and in the Process Book of that court is recorded a summary of the original case which gives the circumstances behind the charge. Andrew Hughes, parish clerk of Denïo, the parish which contains the town of Pwllheli, maintained that on the Tuesday of either Easter week or Whitsun week 1749 Richard Lloyd had disturbed the congregation at Denïo so much 'by playing with one Jane Hughes of Pwllheli' that Andrew Hughes, as parish clerk, had been obliged to approach them and ask Jane Hughes to sit elsewhere, 'that the congregation might have quietness to attend to divine service'. The charge referred to occurrences at Llannor and Abererch churches as well but the testimony of witnesses from Abererch states that they had not seen anything untoward. The appeal at the Court of Arches failed at first but the sentence was subsequently reversed and costs of £20 levied against the Revd John Owen and David Williams, the proctor. One of the questions asked in court on Richard Lloyd's behalf was 'at whose instance and request' did Andrew Hughes appear as a witness? The expected reply 'Mr Chancellor' was received, which suggests that Richard Lloyd might have viewed the case as personal vindictiveness on the Chancellor's behalf.[40]

Not that Richard Lloyd was entirely irreproachable in such matters of the flesh. Although he never married, an entry appears in the register of the neighbouring parish of Boduan which records the baptism in 1747 of 'Griffith a base son as supposed of Richard Lloyd of Tŷ Newydd, gent. & Jane Griffith Spinster'. Richard Lloyd, however, unlike many others of his class in a similar situation, did not shirk his responsibility. Letters have survived written by Richard Lloyd to Mrs Salusbury, the mother of Mrs

Thrale, one of which, dated 27 July 1764, refers to Mrs Thrale speaking kindly of his 'sins at Croydon'. The next letter, of 29 August, mentions 'the poor unfortunate boy at Croydon'. It transpires, through subsequent letters, that Griffith was the boy referred to at Croydon, where he was being trained by a certain Mr Harper to be eventually 'put out to a lawyer'. Richard Lloyd writes to Mrs Salusbury that her 'kindness to the poor fatherless boy at Croydon has been such that it is past my capacity to return proper thanks. I am sorry Mrs Thrale gave him money and she must not give him books. I have ordered his mother to buy everything he wants.' By 1766, however, problems are evident, both financial and personal. Richard Lloyd had thought 'that Attorneys used to take their Clerks into their houses and that after paying the money I should be at no farther expense than for cloaths and pocket money but since it is not so I soon came to a final resolution not to settle him in London for I knew my spark was not to be trusted out of his master's family'. It seems that excessive drinking was proving a problem for Griffith and he had swaggered Mr Harper. By early April, Griffith Jones the drover would be in London to pay Mrs Salusbury the money she had 'advanced for the lad and to bring him home'.

Griffith Lloyd does appear in the letters once more, for it seems that he had written to Mrs Salusbury in 1769 asking for her help to get him put under instructions in the Excise. Richard Lloyd was doubtful of Griffith's 'sobriety, application and temper to manage his business', but was willing to make one trial of him. 'My heart aches when I think of him and I can't help thinking of him too often.' The worry caused him by his son, in conjunction with the bouts of gout he himself suffered, led to a rather poignant postscript to this letter:

> I have neither heat, affection, limb nor spirit to make my riches pleasant nor anybody worth anything to come after me.[41]

Mrs Salusbury's influence in obtaining a post must have proved successful, for in his will written on 18 February 1771 Richard Lloyd refers to his 'Natural son Griffith Lloyd, now an expectant in the Office of Excise'.[42] He was bequeathed an annuity of £20 but a codicil of 7 May states that Griffith Lloyd had died.

Richard Lloyd himself died at Tŷ Newydd on 29 May 1771 aged sixty-three and was buried at Llannor. His next-of-kin was a first cousin, Robert Lloyd, customs officer at Nefyn, but Richard Lloyd had found an alternative answer to his quandary as mentioned in the postscript of 1769 quoted above, that he did not have 'anybody worth anything to come after me'. He bequeathed his estate to his housekeeper, Martha Prichard and her husband John, a shoemaker. They received a few of the properties permanently but the major part of the estate was bequeathed to them for their lifetimes and then for a further twenty-one years to whoever they willed before finally reverting to his 'own right heirs'. Despite the fact that the cousins had not been on friendly terms for some years, Robert Lloyd had thought the estate to have been entailed and that he would naturally inherit as heir-at-law. He must have received a tremendous shock when the will was published and would very much resent seeing a shoemaker and his wife occupying an estate he considered to be rightfully his.

In August a complaint was filed on his behalf at the Court of Great Sessions charging John and Martha Prichard with attempting to defraud him of his inheritance. He accused Martha Prichard of plying Richard Lloyd with drink 'for some years in order to compleat and bring about her long concerted and iniquitous scheme of making and executing the said pretended will.' There is no room here to look at the case in great detail but the volume of paper connected with the case is full of valuable background information, including a very detailed inventory of Tŷ Newydd's contents. The case continued for over two years but John and Martha Prichard eventually won and the will was proved in their favour on 21 October 1773.

It seems that Richard Lloyd had, in fact, barred the entail on the estate and could therefore bequeath it as he wished. He had considered leaving the estate in its entirety to Griffith Lloyd but his frequent drinking had caused ill-feeling between them. Griffith Lloyd had left Tŷ Newydd without telling his father, taking a mare with him and selling her at Holyhead before embarking for Ireland. That was why his bequest had then merely been an annuity of £20. Richard Lloyd had suffered from gout for some twenty years but towards the end of 1769 had suffered a severe attack 'and he never afterwards perfectly enjoyed the use of his limbs'. In his final years he had led a reclusive life, with only his close neighbours coming to sit with him. They did not drink to excess. In fact, for many years before his death Richard Lloyd had been 'very abstemious'. Martha Prichard had worked for him for some twenty years but her sole responsibility had been 'the management of household affairs'. She held no influence over him and 'he formed a good opinion of Martha from his long experience of her honesty and fidelity in his service and of her attention to his interest.'[43]

And so it was that, when Mrs Thrale visited her birthplace at Bodfel in 1774 in the company of her husband, her daughter 'Queeney' and Dr Samuel Johnson, John and Martha Prichard owned and lived at Tŷ Newydd. They borrowed horses at Bodfel and rode over to Tŷ Newydd where they 'found Poor Mr Lloyd's mistress or maid to whom he left his little all'.[44]

The Prichard family held Tŷ Newydd for a total of forty-four years. Martha Prichard died first, in 1782, and when her husband died on 24 July 1793 and left the estate to his son Evan Prichard, the countdown had begun. Twenty-one years to the day the estate reverted to the Lloyd family. Robert Lloyd of Nefyn had died in 1799 and so on 24 July 1814 his eldest son, Richard Lloyd, succeeded to the estate. He was steward of the Bodfel estate and actually resided at Bodfel, just across the fields from Tŷ Newydd. He was to enjoy his inheritance for a mere six weeks, however, but the fact that he had succeeded is carved onto his gravestone in the churchyard at Llannor. He is buried with his great-grandfather. 'Here also lie/ the Remains of Richard Lloyd/ Late of Bodvel Esq. Great Grandson/ of the above named Owen Lloyd/ and second Cousin and Heir/ at Law of Richard Lloyd late of/ Tŷ Newydd Esq. to which/ Estate he succeeded on the/ 24th July/ and died on the/ 6th Octr 1814/ Aged 52'.

The land tax assessments show that Evan Prichard had not in fact occupied Tŷ Newydd for longer than a year or two; by 1795 it was let to a tenant and so when Edmund Hyde Hall visited Caernarfonshire between 1809 and 1811 Tŷ Newydd and other former gentry houses in the parish are described as being 'reduced to the rank and condition of farmhouses'.[45] It was still let to tenants when Richard Lloyd inherited. His widow remarried and lived on at Bodfel, moving some years later, when widowed a second time, to neighbouring Gwnhingar. The heir, another Richard Lloyd, was not yet two years old when his father died and during his minority the estate was run by trustees appointed in his father's will. There were two elder sisters also and by the terms of the will the estate was to provide them with portions of £1,000 each when they were twenty-one or married with the consent of the trustees. Ellen married in 1827 and Lowry in 1832. Their brother came of age on Christmas Day 1833 but he lived on at Gwnhingar with his mother – his sister Lowry and her husband John Lewis living at Tŷ Newydd until Michaelmas 1836 when Richard Lloyd finally moved in.

In order to clear the debts of Richard Lloyd of Bodfel and to provide the portions for his two daughters, Robert Thomas Carreg of Cefn Mine, the final surviving trustee, had, at the request of Richard Lloyd the heir, raised £4,600 by mortgaging the estate. The 4 per cent interest rate swallowed up almost half the annual rental which amounted to a little under £450.[46] In letters and bills from the period that had survived at Tŷ Newydd there are references to racing at Chester, to owning greyhounds, to fishing parties and to purchases of brandy, gin and other spirits. Financing the lifestyle of a landed gentleman, however, became increasingly difficult without encumbering the estate even further and in June 1838 Richard Lloyd raised a further £2,000 upon mortgage, increasing it by another £500 in the December of the same year.[47]

On 24 May 1839, at Llanbeblig church, Richard Lloyd of Tŷ Newydd married Ellen Williams of the Goat Hotel, Caernarfon. Aged twenty, she and her widowed mother were then living with her mother's cousin at the Goat Hotel but she was, according to the Marriages column in the *Carnarvon & Denbigh Herald*, 'daughter of the late Mr Williams of the Castle Inn, Bangor'.[48] In his letter of congratulations on 'the happy event just happened', Thomas Ellis of Pwllheli, Richard Lloyd's solicitor, writes thus: 'I trust you will both long live in peace and be blessed with every happiness and prosperity that this world of trouble can possibly afford you'.[49] Unfortunately, however, it was not to be. Within the following eighteen months a major part of the estate would have to have been sold off and Richard Lloyd would be in his grave.

The frontispiece shows the portrait of Mrs Ellen Lloyd of Tŷ Newydd, Llannor, which was painted by Hugh Hughes in 1845.

Pressing financial problems become increasingly evident in the letters that survive which refer to Richard Lloyd's bank bills being dishonoured. A list of her husband's liabilities which Mrs Lloyd had asked the solicitor to provide in January 1840 amounted to £8,785 18s 6d.[50] By then the decision had already been taken to sell all the outlying portions of the estate at Llanllyfni (which included Tan-y-bryn), Clynnog, Caernarfon, Pwllheli and Nefyn. The auction was to be held in March at Ellen Lloyd's former home, the Goat Hotel, Caernarfon. Interestingly, the Sale Particulars are headed 'To Capitalists',[51] for it was still a period when collapsed estates were being sold off to neighbouring large landowners or members of the new rising gentry rather than to the tenants themselves, as became the case towards the end of the century. The bulk of the Tŷ Newydd lands then sold went to the Gwynfryn, Coed Helen and Plas Coch estates.

Towards October of that year letters from Dr O.O. Roberts[52] indicate that Richard Lloyd was suffering from ill health.[53] He died at Tŷ Newydd on 12 December 1840, a fortnight short of his twenty-eighth birthday, leaving a widow of twenty-two. According to his death certificate the cause of death was 'Disease of the liver'. The Deaths column of the *Carnarvon & Denbigh Herald* records that he was 'deeply lamented by his numerous connections and friends'.[54] A tablet to his memory is to be seen inside Llannor church, 'erected as a small Tribute / of her affection by his mourning widow.'

Although his will has not survived, references to it in later documents show that Richard Lloyd bequeathed all that remained of the Tŷ Newydd estate to his wife. The sale, however, had not covered all of the money owed and there was a deficiency of £1,800[55] and so Ellen Lloyd herself had cause to raise a further £2,000 by mortgage. This she paid off in 1848 by selling one further property, Rhyllech, to Benjamin Thomas Ellis, her solicitor's nephew. It is ironical that the Ellis family of Rhyllech appears in J.E. Griffith's tome, *Pedigrees of Anglesey and Carnarvonshire Families*, whereas the Tŷ Newydd family does not.

Her mother lived with Ellen Lloyd at Tŷ Newydd and might, in fact, have lived there prior to Richard Lloyd's death as well. In 1845 they were visited by Wales's most prolific nineteenth-century artist, Hugh Hughes, who painted both their portraits. The receipted bill has survived to show that Ellen Lloyd paid £5 each for the portraits and £2 5s 0d for each frame.[56]

In 1852 Ellen Lloyd decided to let Tŷ Newydd and move to Pwllheli. She rented Picton Castle, overlooking the town, for her mother and herself. The agreement for letting Tŷ Newydd, however, shows that she held on to 'the parlour next to the garden and the bedroom above it and the upper part of the garden' so that it would be possible for her to visit if she so wished.[57]

Mrs Ann Williams died at Picton Castle in 1854 and Ellen Lloyd was to survive her mother by a mere three years. She died in April 1857 aged thirty-eight of 'Acute Bronchitis'. The *Carnarvon & Denbigh Herald* records the death 'On the 4th inst. highly respected aged 36 [*sic*] at her residence Picton Castle, Pwllheli, Mrs Lloyd, relict of the late Richard Lloyd, esq. of Tŷ Newydd and formerly of Bodvel in this county'.

She bequeathed the Tŷ Newydd estate to her brother, William Williams. Over the years, however, Ellen Lloyd herself had had cause to borrow further sums of money, from her solicitor, in amounts ranging from £700 to £50, but totalling £2,900.[58] As a result, her brother was faced with having another auction. It was held at the Crown Hotel in Pwllheli on 24 October 1860 and the estate was subsequently reduced to Tŷ Newydd itself and two neighbouring small-holdings.[59] Those two were also sold off during the present century but Tŷ Newydd itself remained in the hands of William Williams's descendants and does so to this day. The name also continues, for William and Ellen's mother had, by coincidence, herself been born a Lloyd.

Apart therefore from the usual resources of the family historian, such as parish registers, civil registration, wills and gravestone inscriptions, the above study has made use of a variety of other sources. Estate records – title deeds, rentals and accounts – provide the physical background, whereas personal records, mainly correspondence, provide a more intimate view. Much information has also been gleaned from public records, particularly the records of the courts of Quarter Sessions, Great Sessions and Arches, as well as the land tax assessments. Printed sources have also been made use of, such as University lists and sheriffs lists, and including those of a more literary nature referred to in the body of the article.

NOTES TO CHAPTER 19

[1] RCAM, *An Inventory of the Ancient Monuments in Caernarvonshire*, Volume III (HMSO, 1964).

[2] Gwynedd R(ecord) O(ffice), XM/436/39.

[3] Gwynedd RO, XD/59/39.

[4] XD/50.

[5] XM/436 and XD/59.

[6] Bangor 1218.

[7] As note 3.

[8] The settlement refers to: *Y Tuy Newydd, kay(r)werne, Tyddyn David Moel, yr hendir, Gweyn Iago,* two little closes near *Llwyn Newburgh, y kae kerrig, Pen cau(r)chwith,* and all the lands from thence down to the river called *Avon gwahallwy,* the close called *Goytre, Tyddyn gwladyn, y Tuy n y Llan* and *kae yr viccar.*

[9] Gwynedd RO, XM/436/29.

[10] Gwynedd RO, XQS/1646/91; Norman Tucker, 'Wartime Brawl in Llannor Churchyard', *Caernarvonshire Historical Society Transactions*, Vol. 26 (1965), pp. 50-52.

[11] Gwynedd RO, XQS/1646/89.

[12] Gwynedd RO, XQS/1643/52.

[13] Norman Tucker, 'Richard Griffith at the siege of Chester', *NLW Journal*, vol. XIII, no. 1, 1963, p. 57-66; B.E. Howells, *A Calendar of Letters relating to North Wales* (Cardiff, 1967), pp. 10-11.

[14] Gwynedd RO, XQS/1654/11.

[15] Gwynedd RO, XQS/1652/125.

[16] NLW 3071E, f. 73.

[17] Gwynedd RO, XD/59/45-46 (Jan. 26 & 28, 1668[/9]).

[18] See note 14 above.

[19] Gwynedd RO, XD/59/51. Relief was a customary payment to the lord of the manor by an incoming freeholder.

[20] A letter giving instructions to Griffith Jones re estate matters is in Bangor 1218, f.3. Internal evidence indicates that the author was Elizabeth Bodvel, widow of Sir John Bodvel.

[21] Gwynedd RO, XD/59/53; subsequently called Cae'r Pentre.

[22] Gwynedd RO, XM/436/42.

[23] NLW Probate, B/1729/155.

[24] Gwynedd RO, XD/50/1.

[25] Bangor 1218, f.17.

[26] Bangor 1218, f.16.

[27] PRO, PROB 11/442, f.306.

[28] Gwynedd RO, XM/436/9.

[29] Gwynedd RO, XD/50/1.

[30] Bangor 1218, f.8.

[31] *Dictionary of Welsh Biography* (*DWB*).

[32] Bangor 1218, f.19.

[33] Details in Gwynedd RO, XM/436 and XD/59.

[34] Gwynedd RO, XM/436/47.

[35] NLW Probate, B/1734/134.

[36] J. & J.A. Venn, *Alumni Cantabrigienses*.

[37] Bangor 1218, *passim.*

[38] A.M. Broadley, *Doctor Johnson and Mrs Thrale* (Bodley Head, 1909); see also Adrian Bristow, *Dr Johnson & Mrs Thrale's Tour in North Wales 1774* (Wrexham, 1995).

[39] G.M. Ashton (ed.), *Drych yr Amseroedd, Robert Jones, Rhos-lan* (Cardiff, 1958).

[40] Lambeth Palace Library, B16/249, B17/213, D1295. I am grateful to Mr Dewi Williams, Penmorfa, for these references.

[41] John Rylands Mss, John Rylands Library, Manchester.

[42] Gwynedd RO, XM/436/19.

[43] NLW, Records of the Court of Great Sessions.

[44] See note 38 above.

[45] Edmund Hyde Hall, *A Description of Caernarvonshire (1809-1811)* (Caernarfon, 1952).

[46] Gwynedd RO, XD/50/709.

[47] Gwynedd RO, XD/50 *passim.*

[48] *C&DH*, 25.5.1839.

[49] Gwynedd RO, XD/50/92.

[50] Gwynedd RO, XD/50/106.

[51] Gwynedd RO, XD/50/1113.

[52] A well-known political activist and social reformer. *Vide DWB.*

[53] Gwynedd RO, XD/50/150&151.

[54] 19 December 1840.

[55] Gwynedd RO, XD/50/140.

[56] Gwynedd RO, XD/50/896. See also Peter Lord, *Hugh Hughes, Arlunydd Gwlad* (Gomer, 1995).

[57] Gwynedd RO, XD/50/702.

[58] Gwynedd RO, XD/50/706.

[59] Gwynedd RO, XD/50/1113; *C&DH,* 20 Oct 1860.

20. MORIS REIGNALD, GENTLEMAN, 1606-1678: SHEEP FARMER IN NORTH CARDIGANSHIRE

Helen M. Kaznowski

Moris Reignald, born in about 1606, lived all his life in the mountains of Llanfihangel Geneu'r Glyn and Llangynfelyn.[*] His father, Rinallde William[1] brought up five more children, John, David, Evan, Howell and Elizabeth and, later on, at least eleven hill farms in the same area belonged to his male descendants.[2] For a location plan of this area, see Fig. 20-1.

In 1626/31, Rinallde (Reignald) William of Llanfihangel Geneu'r Glyn, yeoman, bought Tyddyn yr Helig, Cwm Clettwr, Llangynfelyn, with some extra land, for £60, for his son, Moris.[3] Yr Helig was a typical little sheep farm, 800 feet up, with a few small fields[4] below the house, other little farms nearby and rough moorland on the slopes above.

Tre'r-ddol, and the lowland road from Machynlleth to Aberystwyth, lay a mile to the west and an important north-south trackway ran along the hilltops not far off. Tal-y-bont, where cattle and sheep fairs were held, drovers gathered and there were blacksmiths and other essential craftsmen, was only a couple of miles away. Machynlleth, Llanbadarn Fawr and Aberystwyth were a morning's ride away. Travel was only by horseback or on foot and was difficult because the 'roads' in the valleys often became clogged with mud churned up by herds of cattle passing along. The hill tracks, though rough and tiring because of their steep gradients, were well-used and criss-crossed the region, but there were numerous streams to be crossed, peat bogs often meant long detours, and the fog, which can descend suddenly, made them dangerous.

Moris completed the purchase on his own in 1631, so his father may have died before then.[5] I cannot tell how long he and his wife[6] stayed in Helig. They brought up a large family – five sons and three daughters. The majority of parents in west Wales actually reared only small families in this

---

[*] This chapter is based on a post-course assignment for the Second Stages Course, 'Occupations and the Records Relating to them', held in September 1995.

period.[7] The fact that Reignald and his son, Moris, brought up large families is proof that they had a higher standard of living than most at that time. Peasants and poorer farmers reared only a few children because their physique was usually damaged by the malnutrition or hunger which followed the recurrent natural disasters of harvest or hay-crop failure and diseases among the animals, and they were the chief victims of the many epidemics of smallpox, typhus, diphtheria and measles.

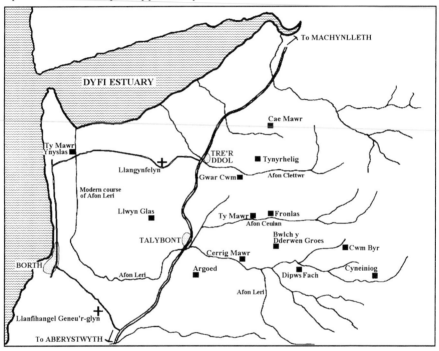

Fig. 20-1: The farms associated with Moris Reignald and his descendants

Sometime before 1658,[8] perhaps as early as the 1630s, Moris and his family moved south to Cyneiniog, a large farm[9] on a south-facing slope at the far end of Cwm Tynant. The building was probably in the traditional style.[10] At that time the hill farms were stone-built and reed-thatched, the thatch roped down with ropes weighted with stones, and most were of the ancient longhouse type with the animals housed in a byre beyond a partition wall at one end of the dwelling, and the family living at the other, but there must have been many variations of accommodation. Sometimes there was a low room above the byre, often a long, narrow room ran the length of the farmhouse on one side; part of this would be the dairy and the other sometimes had a long table for meals where servants and family ate together; sometimes it was simply a scullery. In the living quarters, which usually consisted of one large high 'room' with open rafters above, there were usually one or two big beds with doors that enclosed them. By the mid-1600s the wealthier farmers had improved on this style and in the better farms there was a bedroom upstairs as well as a sleeping loft for menservants over the cattle stalls. There was even a parlour in some, added on to the end, and perhaps Moris had such a home, which may account for the entry *'1 et 1'* which it had in the Hearth Tax list.

Families seem to have worked the farms themselves, using the labour of their bigger children, farm servants, poor relations and neighbours when necessary. The wealthier farms – and I think Moris Reignallt's home was very prosperous – would have had farm servants living in, especially when the farmer's children were small. Usually there was an extended family group in one farmstead, consisting of three or four generations. Wealthier farmers bought or gave properties to their elder sons on their marriages but the youngest son often stayed at home after his marriage, helping his father more and more as time went by and eventually inheriting that home.[11] Moris Reignallt and his eldest son were literate,[12] though two other sons could only make their mark. In 1694, one of them, Evan Moris of Fron Las, made provision in his will for the schooling of one of his sons, probably with David Evans who was the schoolmaster in Tal-y-bont.

The farming economy of hill farms like Cyneiniog was based on herds of cattle and flocks of sheep and goats, with oats, barley and rye being grown and oxen kept for ploughing. At the start of the 1600s the wealth of a family was usually mainly in the small black Welsh cattle, which throve on sparse pasture and were almost agile as goats and very hardy. However, it was impossible to feed many beasts through the winter and most were sent with drovers to English markets in summer, mainly for fattening, though some for slaughter for meat and leather.

Flocks of sheep were the other mainstay of the farms, and the value of wool sales from the flock grew towards the end of the century and the size of flocks increased. In certain wills[13] each member of the family, including those who were very young indeed, was given 'as many sheep as he has upon his own earmark', indicating the custom of giving lambs as gifts within the family. There were also goats on the hills, both wild and domesticated, and the latter usually ran with the sheep in the flock. The wool, carded and spun by the women at home, was dyed and woven by the men, often in lean-to sheds, or at Tre'r-ddol and Tal-y-bont. Our area specialised in flannel which, though not a fine cloth, being uneven and coarse, was hard-wearing and always in demand. It was taken by packmen to Shrewsbury or Oswestry for the English markets but the cattle drovers also took cloth to the Midlands or southern England, and large quantities of knitted stockings and caps produced on the farms went to the stocking market at Farnham in Kent. When Morris died he had 52 stone of wool in store and owned nearly 400 sheep. As Welsh sheep fleeces weighed two to four pounds, that represented his entire flock's product, taking the lower figure. It was April and the shearing was not done till May, so the wool was from the past season and he may have been waiting for prices to rise, though few farmers could have afforded to wait like that.

Farm households rose very early indeed and, for the greater part of the year, unless the weather was very bad, most members spent the daylight hours out of the house, children over seven included. Our family had miles of open moorland pastures above the farms where flocks and cattle would have been taken in spring. Shepherds and a stockman would have been up with the flocks but not alone, because there was plenty of work to be done in the hills. Sheep, goats and cattle had to be milked and cheeses made. In May the wool had to be washed on the sheep, and then sheared. Peat had to be cut in the spring and stacked in late summer, bog hay was cut in June – a tedious job as the hay grew in scattered clumps – and both hay and peat were carried down in September. Rushes for candle dips had to be gathered into bundles, lichen collected by children for dyes and bracken for burning to make ashes which were sent to England for soap-making.

Most of those who worked on the farm, whether farm servants or family, probably worked up in the hills for days at a time. A type of transhumance system, dating from earliest times, still persisted only a few miles away in Merioneth during the seventeenth century. In that system, the entire farm household, with their flocks and herds, moved to temporary shelters up on the high pastures for the summer. However, the custom was beginning to die out in the seventeenth century and I think it probable that only the young working people from a prosperous farm such as Moris Reignald's would have stayed up on the hill-pastures in the summer, and not he or his wife, however hard-working they were.

The techniques of cereal crop-growing in our area lagged well behind those in England. The language barrier and the remoteness of the area were mainly to blame for this, both cutting us off from agricultural developments in England. The primitive ox-drawn wooden ploughs and harrows were inefficient and heavy loads had to be moved by wooden sleds. Soil exhaustion was common because crop rotation and the use of fertilisers was unknown. In our area, between 1600 and 1750, grain crops were grown mainly for use in cooking, with very little to spare for winter feed for any animal. The grain was broadcast by hand, reaped using sickles, threshed with flails on the field and dried on woollen blankets in drying kilns fired with straw, built in the corners of the fields.

The people in the valleys had developed a powerful community spirit. Much farm work was organised communally and neighbours gathered to help each other at the busy times such as sheep-shearing and harvests. In the lower valleys everyone able to work gathered at one farm on being summoned and then moved on to another farm when the work was done. The visiting of the farms followed a long-established order of precedence, food being provided by each farm being visited. In the high remote areas like Cyneiniog all the flocks were gathered at a central point for shearing.

Most of the inventories of the family hill-farms at that time listed one yoke of oxen, a wooden plough and harrow, wooden hurdles, three or four horses with their young, a cow and calf, three or four heifers and a few bullocks, a flock of barren sheep and yearling lambs and a flock of milking sheep and goats. Moris Reignald himself had a bigger establishment than most and, in particular, more horses than the average farmer. The household stuff and implements were more than usually valuable. There is a contrast between a typical small farm, like his brother Evan's, a typical prosperous lowland farm, Llwyn Glas, belonging to Moris's son-in-law, and Dypws Fach, shown by these inventories taken when each owner died.

February 1664: Fron Las, Evan Reignald	£	s	d
4 bullocks 6 cows 8 heifers	5	0	0
47 sheep, 10 lambs	4	6	0
1 horses 2 mares 3 colts	2	0	0
3 pans 1 box		15	0
household stuff & farm implements	1	5	0
Total	£13	6	0
April 1678: Llwyn Glas, Hugh Richards	£	s	d
4 cows, 4 calves, 3 barren cows, 8 bullocks			
2 heifers, 5 yearling beasts 1 bull	55	0	0
2 horses, 2 mares, 2 fillies	10	0	0
76 sheep, 27 lambs, 9 goats, 3 kids	16	0	0
corn in ground and store	30	0	0
household stuff and implements of husbandry	8	0	0
Total	£119	0	0
April 1678: Dypws Fach, Moris Reignald	£	s	d
134 wethers, 30 ewes & lambs, 135 ewes,			
89 yearling lambs	80	0	0

14 cows with calves, 12 bullocks, 7 heifers, 12 yearling cattle	54	0	0
1 yoke of oxen, 2 horses, 3 mares, 7 colts	20	0	0
20 goats, 3 sows	2	0	0
52 stone of wool	23	0	0
corn & grain in store	9	0	0
household stuff & farm implements	9	0	0
Total	£197	0	0

In the seventeenth century food eaten on the farms was almost entirely their own produce, and oats and dairy products predominated. Meat from the cattle, sheep and goats would be eaten so long as the farmer was prospering but poorer farmers often had to forgo eating meat and rely on fish. Oats, used as oatcakes and in many kinds of gruel, jelly and porridge, rye bread, together with milk, buttermilk, cheeses of different kinds, together with cabbage, beans, carrots, onions and leeks, formed by far the greater part of each meal. Cabbage and leeks seem to have been the only winter source of vitamin C. I have found pigs in the inventories of the wills of hill farmers in only two cases, both well-off farmers, and I believe they were not always kept on the smaller hill farms. Hens were either not thought worth mentioning, or only a very few were kept, and geese are not mentioned either.

Cooking methods had not, apparently, changed for generations and were dictated by the use of open peat fires. Bread and large scones were baked on bakestones or in lidded iron pots set in the hot ashes. I have even found a bakestone, pot-hook, chain and bellows in an inventory,[14] showing that they were considered to have intrinsic value. Most cooking took place in cauldrons suspended over the fire, though a spit was used for meat when there was occasion. The inventories of well-off farmers mentioned copper pans, bedsteads and feather beds, sheets and coverlets, 'table-boards', cupboards, coffers, chests and 'boxes', pewter ware and dairy pans.

Most necessities were made on the farm, iron implements, kitchen ware and furniture being the exceptions. Payments were often by services or farm products – a stack of corn in return for the blacksmith sharpening and repairing all the farm implements, one sheaf in ten or more as a payment for the man who threshed the harvest with a flail, the right to graze one or two sheep in the pasture as part of the wages of a farm worker. However, legal documents required cash, as did fines and penalties during and after the Civil War.

The small lead and silver mines west of Tal-y-bont were important during the Civil War but Moris died before the 'boom' years of the local mines, 1690-1715.

When the Civil War broke out, Moris was probably a Royalist supporter, in view of his close social contacts with Thomas and Richard Pryse of Glanfread, two of the most active loyal Royalists.[15] Though he may have paid fines as a Royalist, heavy taxes, epidemics and bad harvests, would probably have affected him more than the change from King to Lord Protector and back again.

Moris had five sons. Two, Reignald and Hugh, died before 1678. Reignald left a daughter named 'Britchert' who married John Jenkin.[16] Hugh left a son, Simon Hugh, who seems to have lived with his grandfather and was probably sent to school.[17] For details of the family of Moris Reignald and their descendants, see Fig. 20-2.

Moris's heir was Richard Moris Reignald, who lived at Cyneiniog. His first wife was Jane Lewis Evan.[18] Richard was literate and a man of some standing and responsibility, assessor for the will of Richard John Phillipps in 1688,[19] party to his sister's marriage settlement, together with the wealthy Rowland Lloyd of Henllys and Richard Pryse of Glanfraed, and witness for property deeds such as those between Evan John Moris, his brother-in-law, and Evan Moris Reignald, his brother, in 1679.[20] He died intestate in 1699, probably still aged under sixty, at Cae Mawr, Llanfihangel Geneu'r Glyn, and his eldest son, Moris took over Cyneiniog. This branch of the family eventually used the surname Moris. There was also a younger son called William.

Another son of Moris Reignald was Evan Moris Reignald, who died in 1694. He owned Tythin y Fron Las,[21] Tythin y Ddol and Tythin y Fron, all in Cwm Ceulan (these were his wife's dower), and in his later years he bought Tythin Brin y Garn and Y Cerrig Mawr, in Cwm Leri. Together with his brothers, Richard Moris and a Mr Penny, he dealt with tithes, taking defaulters to court on behalf of the owner of the tithe rights. Evan had three sons, Simon, Moris and Meredith and four daughters, Elizabeth, Mary, Catherine and Jane.[22]

Moris Reignald's daughter, Mary, married Evan John Moris in 1663,[23] and Cerrig Mawr was her dower. Their son, Symon, was born in 1671. In 1658, another daughter, Elizabeth, married Hugh Richard ap Rowland David Lloyd,[24] of Llwyn Glas. This family began to use the surname Hughes in the mid-eighteenth century and H. Harold Hughes, FRS, was a descendant. In 1669, the youngest daughter, Britchert Morris, married Hugh John ap Jenkin Howell Jenkin of Allt Goch.[25]

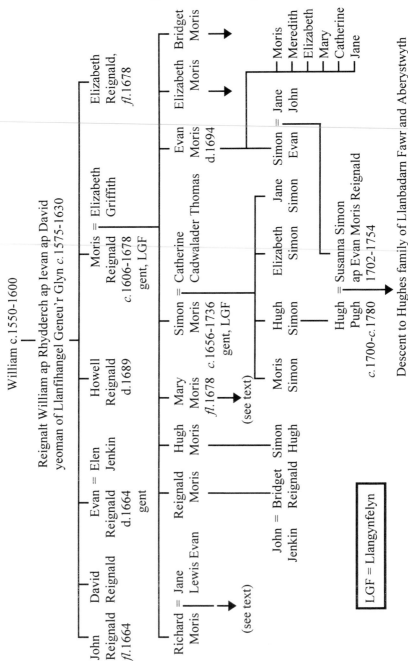

Fig. 20-2: The descent from Reignalt William of Llanfihangel Geneu'r Glyn

The youngest son was Simon Morris, my six-times-great-grandfather, born probably between 1640 and 1659 and, like his brother, Evan, illiterate.[26] In 1677, Simon married Catherine Cadwalader Thomas, and old Moris gave him Tyddyn yr Helig, Llangynfelyn, as a marriage settlement.[27] His father only made his mark on this document so, presumably, his eyesight was already failing in his old age.

Moris's sister, Elizabeth, and his brother, Howell, outlived him but Howell's name was among those too poor to have to pay Hearth Tax in 1670. Another of Moris's brothers, Evan, died in 1664,[28] leaving a widow, Elen Jenkin. They had two farms, 'Tyddyn y Bron Las' which was, apparently, their home, and 'Bwlch y blaydd & maynyr dol y yro', and he was relatively old when he died. He left his farms to his wife and, after her death, to Morris. The amounts of money and stock in his will seem shockingly low if one is accustomed to the standards of England at the time. However it is a typical local 'small farming gentry' will, so far as I have observed, showing how simple and modest were the standards of the area.

Moris died in March 1678 at Dypws Fach, two miles from Cyneiniog. He left Dypws Fach, with 'her third' (part of his possessions), to his 'now-wedded wife, Elizabeth Griffith' and after her death it was to go to his 'three sons'. He gave small gifts of money to several relatives, £10, two kine and thirty sheep and 'his own marked sheep' to Simon Hugh, his grandson, and £3 and two stone of wool each, to his daughters Bridget and Elizabeth, and he asked to be buried 'in the church of Llanfihangel Geneu'r Glyn'.

BIBLIOGRAPHY
Davies, John, *A History of Wales* (Penguin, 1993).
Dodd, A. H., *A Short History of Wales* (Batsford, 1977).
Godwin, F. & Toulson, S., *The Drovers' Roads of Wales* (London, 1977).
Jenkins, Geraint H., *The Foundations of Modern Wales 1642-1780* (Oxford, 1987).
Jones, J. Graham, *The History of Wales* (University of Wales Press, 1990).
Lewis, W. J., *An Illustrated History of Dyfed* (Dyfed County Council, n.d.).
— *Born on a Perilous Rock* (Aberystwyth, 1980).
— *Lead Mining in Wales* (University of Wales Press, 1967).
Owen, Trefor M., *The Customs and Traditions of Wales* (University of Wales Press, 1991).
— *Welsh Folk Customs* (Gomer Press, 1959).
Parry-Jones, D., *Welsh Country Upbringing* (Batsford, 1948; repr. Ffynnon Press, 1974).
Peate, I. C. *The Welsh House* (Liverpool, 1944).
Williams, D.J. *The Old Farmhouse* (Golden Grove Editions, 1961).

NOTES TO CHAPTER 20

[1] Rinallde William ap Rhydderch ap Ievan ap David of Geneu'r Glyn.

[2] Cyneiniog, Cwm Byr, Dipws Fach, Cerrig Mawr, Brin Fedwen Fawr, Cae Mawr, Fron Las, y Fron, y ddol, Bwlch y blaydd and yr Helig in Cwm Clettwr.

[3] NLW: Ithel W. Jones deeds 1 & 3.

[4] Field acreage under 30 acres in the 1845 Tithe Schedule.

[5] £40-60 seems to have been the usual price for one of the small hill farms in the mid- and late-1600s. £60 was quite a lot for 1631.

[6] In his will in 1678 he refers to 'Elizabeth Griffith, my now-wedded wife' so I presume she was a second wife. There is circumstantial evidence for Margaret Phillipps being the wife of his youth.

[7] Health details are from G.H. Jenkins, *The Foundations of Modern Wales*, 91, 258.

[8] 'Kyninog' was named in connection with Moris Reignald and his heir, Richard, in a 1658 marriage settlement. NLW: H. Harold Hughes 51-2.

[9] In the 1845 tithe schedule it had still 100 acres as fields/meadows and 414 acres of 'sheepwalk'.

[10] It had only one hearth (or rather, '*I et I*') in the 1670 Hearth Tax returns.

[11] This did happen in our family in the nineteenth century. Thomas Hughes, youngest son of John Hughes of Cefnhendre, Llanbadarn Fawr, in 1842 inherited the farm he had been helping to run.

[12] Moris signed the dower bond of his daughter in 1663. (NLW: W.I. Williams deed 30) and Richard, his eldest son, signed the marriage settlement of another sister in 1658 (NLW: H. Harold Hughes, 50-1).

[13] NLW: St David's Probate, 1678/106, Moris Reignald; 1727/121, Moris Richard.

[14] NLW: St David's Probate, Richard Morrys of Cae Mawr, Llangynfelin, 1699/118.

[15] NLW: H. Harold Hughes deeds 51-2, 60. Richard Pryse was party to the marriage settlements of Moris Reignald's daughters. In his will, Moris Reignald left Simon Pryse (his godson?) 20s.

[16] She was named as the wife of a John Jenkin, in her grandfather's will in 1678.

[17] Named in his grandfather's will. Simon was able to sign his name as a witness.

[18] Very probably the daughter of Lewis Evan Moris of Brin y Fedwen Fawr (NLW: St David's Probate, 1704/93).

[19] NLW: W.I. Williams deeds 16, 17 & 48.

[20] NLW: W.I. Williams deed 31.

[21] Moris Reignald had received it as a legacy from his brother, Evan, in 1664 and had obviously given it to his son, Evan.

[22] NLW: St David's Probate, 1694/102, Evan Moris Reignald.

[23] W.I. Williams deeds 29/30 & 32/33, NLW.

[24] NLW: H. Harold Hughes, deeds 51-2.

[25] NLW: H. Harold Hughes deed 60.

[26] In 1678 he put his mark, only, to his father's will.

[27] NLW: H. Harold Hughes deeds 51-2.

[28] NLW: St David's Probate, Evani Reignald 1664/136.

21. TITUS JONES OF LLANFIHANGEL-AR-ARTH

Marion Martin

My great-great-great-grandfather, Titus Jones, was born in the parish of Llanfihangel-ar-arth, Carmarthenshire,[1] circa 1827/8.[*] The river Teifi flows just to the north of the parish of Llanfihangel-ar-arth and is the natural boundary between Cardiganshire and Carmarthenshire. During the nineteenth century the woollen industry was steadily growing. Along the banks of the river there were many woollen mills. The mill owners were producing, amongst other things, flannel which was made into rough hard-wearing shirts for the coal miners and steel workers of the coastal industrial towns.

It was some time before 1851 that Titus Jones travelled from this rural area in order to work in the prosperous and growing town of Llanelli, Carmarthenshire. It is possible that he joined a wagon, journeying to the industrial towns of the south, where the mill owners were transporting their goods to the fairs in places such as Llangyfelach near Swansea.[2] He might have travelled with his father Evan Jones in search of work, before the other members of the family joined them.

Titus Jones was a mason by trade at this time, and his skills would have been welcome in the building of the new tinplate works. This was the era of the great tinplate industry in Llanelli: in 1847 the Dafen Tin Works was opened, followed by the Morfa Tin Works in 1852 and, in 1853, the Old Lodge Iron Works.[3] Many other industries were springing up. These included Buckley's Brewery, the South Wales Pottery, glass-making near Loughor, as well as the manufacture of Welsh hats and candles. The expansion in the industries drew more people from the rural areas to Llanelli. These were prosperous times for the town and employment was in abundance. The population in 1801 was 2,000 and had increased to more than 20,000 by 1870. Apart from industrial buildings, houses were needed for the work force.

---

[*] This chapter is based on a post-course assignment for the Second Stages Course, 'Occupations and the Records Relating to them', held in September 1995.

than 20,000 by 1870. Apart from industrial buildings, houses were needed for the work force.

> A large number of dwelling houses for the rapidly increasing population (supplying a want severely felt in the neighbourhood) have also been recently erected; in fact the town is comparatively modern, as many of the old inhabitants have watched its progress from a small straggling village to its present importance.[4]

In 1845 the parish church was restored, roads were widened, two schools were built and in 1848 the Chamber of Trade was founded.[5] Indeed a great deal was changing.

Cwmfelin, in Berwick hamlet, three miles south-east of Llanelli, is the place where Titus Jones settled. Here there seem to have been three quarries, the largest being Genwen, to the north of the main road. It is not clear whether Titus had served a seven-year apprenticeship, or whether he was merely a mason's labourer, which seems likely. Labourers in about 1830 were earning from 2s 6d to 3s per day, but the more skilled craftsmen could earn double that sum.[6] The mason's work required both skill and strength. The stone, after it was quarried, was squared and cut to the correct size for building. The stones were frequently extremely large and levers and pulleys were needed to manoeuvre them on and off the carts. There were a variety of tools used by the mason. These included the square, level, plumb-line, bevel, compass, chisel, mallet and trowel. The mason also used a saw which had no teeth. It was moved backwards and forwards by one man and cut the stone by its own weight.

On 28 February 1851 Titus Jones married Margaret James at Capel Als Independent Chapel in Llanelli.[7] The minister at that time was Revd David Rees, known as 'Rees Capel Als', whose ministry spanned the years 1829-1869. Margaret was the daughter of John and Ann James of Dinas, Pembrokeshire. From the marriage certificate it can be seen that Titus Jones was able to sign his name. The couple began their married life in Cwmfelin, lodging with William Roberts, his wife and young family. William Roberts had in fact been a witness at the marriage of Titus and Margaret. At this time, according to the 1851 census, Titus had now become a collier. Coal had been mined in the Llanelli area for hundreds of years:

> At Llanelthle a village of Kidwelli Lordship a vi miles from Kidwelli, the Inhabitans digge Coles, elles scant in Kidwelli land.[8]

The area of Llwynhendy and Cwmfelin had many coal pits. An old map of the Spitty district dated 1771 shows a large number of 'old pits and Old coal works'. The coal mining community had adapted and accepted the difficulties and dangers they faced in order to earn a living. Most colliers had allotments or kept pigs and grew vegetables, a much-needed diversion from the backbreaking nine-hour shifts and also a necessity for the self-sufficiency of the family.

The miners worked on a system known as the longwall. A main roadway was made some distance into the coal seam, leaving an unworked pillar of coal around the shaft to give support. On each side smaller roadways were driven at intervals and working faces were opened out on either side of them. After about 1850, roadways were made high enough for men to walk along them without bending. This also allowed pit ponies to be used to transport the coal. The first process at the coal face was to undercut the coal using a pick. This work was very tiring as the miner had to work while bending down. The method was called holing or curving. The holer placed props under the cut to prevent the coal from falling while he was cutting. He would cut inwards for four feet, crawling under the seam as he cut. This was a very dangerous job. The props were then knocked out and removed, allowing the weight of the coal to drop downwards. Wedges were then hammered into the coal face so that the coal could be levered out. After about 1830 gunpowder was sometimes used, except when larger lumps of coal were needed. The coal was then loaded into baskets or trams and transported out of the mine. The depth of the shafts varied considerably and sometimes young boys dragged the baskets to the main roadways where they were loaded onto long wheeled carriages running on rails. Rails were first introduced underground as early as 1760 and were laid only on the main roadways in the mines.

Later when shafts were sunk, winding devices were introduced. As the shafts were driven deeper, the horse-drawn windlass was used. To cope with the increasing depth of the shafts, more and more ingenious winding mechanisms were devised, culminating in the 'whim gin'. A rope was wound around a horizontal drum which passed over a pulley wheel and down the shaft. A horizontal bar was attached to the drum and the horse was harnessed to this and walked around in circles. The rope with the basket attached could be lowered and raised. As the shafts were driven deeper into the ground, up to eight horses were used. Only towards the end of the century were steam engines (designed to pump water out of the mines) adapted and used as winding engines. The cage was invented in 1835 and this type of haulage became used in the 1840s. The coal could now be loaded directly into wheeled wagons at the coal face and brought on rails to the pit bottom where the carts were pushed onto the cage which, held steady by guide rods, ascended to the pit top. This new system quadrupled the amount of coal raised to the surface and also meant that the men could ride in the cage, a vast improvement on the previous method of ascending and descending by clinging to a loop in a rope. So, in this dangerous occupation, Titus Jones began his married life.

Margaret Jones was a formidable lady, and had plans for her husband. She was doubtless aware that wealth meant prosperity and status. She persuaded Titus to buy two lambs for slaughter and sent him off to sell the resulting meat to the villagers.[9]

> Men who bought on the hoof, killing and dressing their own meat, had dominated the Victorian butchery trade ... they operated from fixed shop premises too ... Fixed premises were, of course necessary for the slaughtering. Some butchers must have possessed considerable capital since they feature in the lists of parliamentary electors after 1832 as £10 householders ...[10]

Gradually Titus earned enough money to build himself a house and to start a grocery business. By 1861 Titus Jones, now aged thirty-two, his wife Margaret and five daughters, Hannah (my great-great-grandmother) aged ten, Ann aged eight, Mary aged five, Elizabeth aged two and Margaret aged six months, were living at 9 Cwmfelin Row (see Fig. 21-1). Titus was a grocer; Hannah, Ann and Mary were scholars.[11] It is not clear where they went to school as Llwynhendy school was not opened until 1870.[12] Most of the villagers living in Cwmfelin Row were coal miners, and so the grocery shop would have been very convenient for them.

By the 1860s the village shop was an integral part of village life. It was now possible for even the poorest villager to buy a few items such as tea, sugar, black leading and soap. More people were coming to the village shop and the shopkeeper was not solely dependent on the wealthy customers. The nineteenth century grocer sold items of drapery, as well as household goods and groceries. Improvements in transport meant that a greater supply of goods was reaching the rural areas. Better roads and railways brought produce from further afield. The South Wales Railway line was opened from London to Reading in 1840. In 1852 the section from Swansea to Carmarthen was opened, which improved supplies considerably.[13] Tea, which had been a luxury item, had nearly halved in price and cost 3s and 4s a pound by the 1850s.[14] A range of new products appeared: biscuits, chocolates and soap, which were sold at lower prices so that they were accessible to a wider range of people. The cottagers, who at the beginning of the nineteenth century had relied on the pedlars and fairs, now found affordable items in the village shops. By this time the itinerants were unable to compete with the shopkeepers, who were able to receive regular deliveries of goods all the year round.

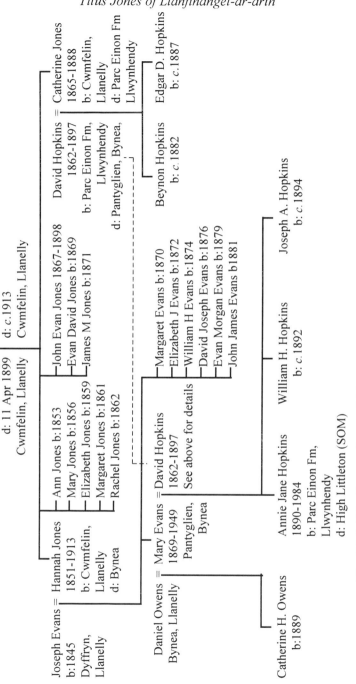

Fig. 21-1: The Descendants of Titus Jones of Llanfihangel-ar-Arth and Llanelly

The town of Llanelli had a large market at its centre which covered an area of between three to four acres. There were four entrance gates, and a large outdoor area. One side was lined with butchers' stalls, while the other side was a covered area for sellers of farm produce. Woollen goods were also sold at the market. The market remained virtually unchanged well into the 1950s. The villagers of Llwynhendy and Cwmfelin doubtless travelled to the market once a week on market day, but nevertheless relied tremendously on the village shop, particularly since, even in the 1870s, villagers had become less self-sufficient.

The wealthier classes still patronised the local shopkeeper, which meant that the shopkeeper was able to keep large stocks of goods including the high quality items, which made him more accommodating towards his less well off customers. My grandmother told the story of Margaret and Titus often giving loaves of bread to those who had fallen on hard times. The shopkeepers were extremely business-like; their hours of opening were regular and long. Many shops stayed open until 7 or 8 o'clock and on Saturday, when they had a great deal of business, they would frequently remain open until 11 o'clock. I believe Margaret Jones was the driving force behind the grocery business and worked extremely hard. The family was growing: two more daughters, Rachel and Catherine, were born in 1862 and 1865; and at last three sons: John Evan born in 1867, Evan David born in 1869, and finally James Morgan born in 1871.

In 1867 their eldest daughter Hannah was married.[15] She had just had her sixteenth birthday. She married Joseph Evans, a twenty-three-year-old miner, on 12 July 1867 at Sion Baptist Chapel, and the couple settled at Pantyglien, Bynea, about a quarter of a mile from Titus and Margaret Jones. By this time the grocery business had expanded and Titus Jones is described as a Shopkeeper on the marriage certificate. Times were good for the Jones family; they now built a public house next to the shop which they called the Butchers Arms and Titus obtained a licence to sell beer and spirits (see Fig. 21-2). Public houses were brought under stricter control by legislation in 1869 and 1872, as were controls on street traders and fairs. On 14 October 1874 there is a record that Titus Jones was convicted of selling beer at illegal hours.[16] This seems to have happened occasionally to various landlords in the town.

The grocery business continued, the public house prospered and Titus built two more houses where two of his daughters lived with their husbands and families. In 1876 John Ungoed and his wife Elizabeth (Titus's daughter) were now living at the Butchers Arms and there is documentation to show that John Ungoed was licensed to sell alcohol.[17] Meanwhile Titus and

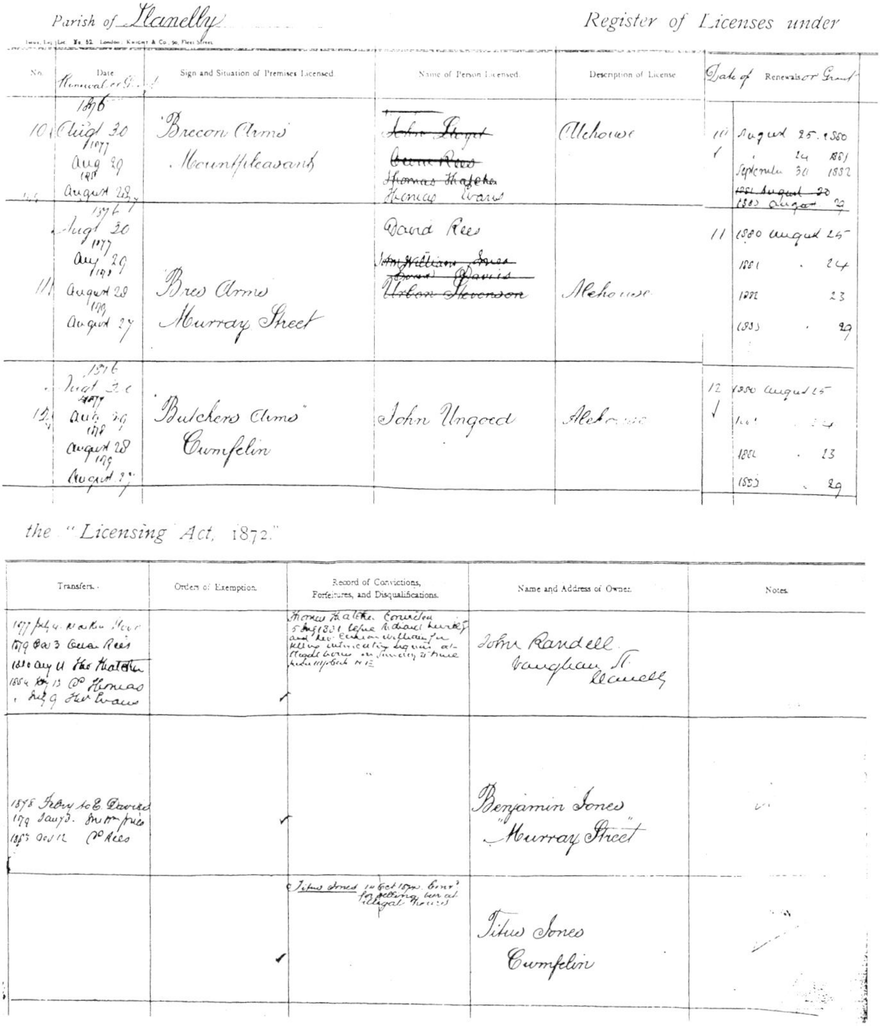

Parish of *Llanelly*   Register of Licenses under

the "Licensing Act, 1872."

Fig. 21-2: Register of Licenses for the Butchers Arms

Margaret continued to run the grocery shop. They bought more land and they also had some land where they kept a horse and a pony. They had one large open carriage and a smaller carriage. The large carriage must have been extremely useful, not only for the business but also for transporting the large family. By 1881, Titus is described in the census as being a farmer of 30 acres. This would have been considered as a smallholding and probably was sufficient to sustain the growing family.

Sundays were very special in the Jones household. After chapel, the whole family, which included nine children, their wives, husbands and numerous grandchildren, gathered in the large room above the Butchers Arms. After lunch the women and girls sat around the edge of the room gossiping and chatting. The men would remain around the table discussing the family business and sorting out any family problems.[18] One such problem concerned two young members of the family. On 4 June 1881 Catherine Jones, youngest daughter of Titus and Margaret, married David Hopkins of Parc Eynon farm, Llwynhendy.[19] Two sons were born: James Henry Beynon Hopkins in 1882 and Edgar David Hopkins in 1887. Sadly Catherine died in 1888.[20] She was twenty-three years old. Meanwhile, Hannah and Joseph Evans's eldest daughter Mary had married Daniel Owens, a railwayman. They had a daughter, Catherine Hannah. Daniel Owens was tragically killed by a train when he was walking home along the railway line; Catherine Hannah was six weeks old. The family now arranged a marriage between widower David Hopkins and widow Mary Owens (née Evans). The couple were married on 13 August 1889.[21] They had three more children, Annie Jane (my grandmother), William Henry and Joseph Aneurin. David Hopkins died on 16 December 1897, leaving his wife Mary with Beynon aged fifteen, Edgar aged ten, Catherine Hannah aged eight, Annie Jane aged six, William Henry aged four and Joseph aged two. Family ties were strong, and responsibilities shouldered willingly: Titus and Margaret took the eldest two boys into their home, Catherine Hannah went to live with the Owens family and Joseph and Hannah Evans helped their daughter Mary with the three youngest children.

By the 1890s Titus had retired from the grocery trade. He had enough land to maintain a smallholding while others in the family looked after the Butchers Arms and the shop. His sons had been well educated. John Evan was training to be a teacher, Evan David worked at the town hall[22] and later became a harbour master and James Morgan was also a teacher, later to become headmaster of Five Roads School[23] (affectionately known as Uncle Jim Five Roads). Of his grandchildren, two became clergymen, two solicitors, one a surgeon; and one granddaughter became the chief harpist of Wales and wrote poetry – her bardic name was Mair Elli.

Titus Jones died on 11 April 1898.[24] He had begun his life as a humble mason's labourer, and with hard work and a resourceful wife he had improved his standing both financially and socially and had made it possible for his children and grandchildren to be well educated and find their places in society.

There have been and still are successful village entrepreneurs who can always make a living if not a fortune and who will view the next decade or so with modest optimism.[25]

BIBLIOGRAPHY

The Book of Trades or Library of Useful Arts Vol. 1 (Wiltshire FHS, 1995).
Brown, Jonathan & Ward, Sadie, *The Village Shop* (Cameron Books, 1990).
Davies, John, *A History of Wales* (Penguin, 1993).
Griffin, A.R. *The Collier* (Shire Publications, 1982).
Innes, John, *Old Llanelly* (Cardiff, 1902).
Jenkins, J.G. *Life and Tradition in Rural Wales* (London, 1976).
Jenkins, Philip, *A History of Modern Wales* (Longmans, 1992).
Parry Jones, D., *Welsh Country Upbringing* (Batsford, 1948; repr. Ffynnon Press, 1974).
Winstanley, M.J., *The Shopkeeper's World 1830-1914* (Manchester, 1983).

NOTES TO CHAPTER 21

[1] 1861 Census RG 9/4110, fol. 76, p. 24.
[2] Jenkins (1976).
[3] Innes (1902).
[4] Moral's *Directory of South Wales* 1875.
[5] Innes (1902).
[6] *Book of Trades or Library of Useful Arts.*
[7] Capel Als, Llanelli: Marriage Certificate No. 17.
[8] Leland's Itinerary about 1540 (from Innes, *Old Llanelly*).
[9] *Ex inf.* Dr E.H.B. Hopkins, Llangennech (great-great-grandson).
[10] Winstanley (1983).
[11] 1861 Census RG 9/4110, fol. 76, p. 24.
[12] Innes (1902).
[13] Jenkins (1992).
[14] Brown & Ward (1990).
[15] Sion Chapel, Llanelli: Marriage Certificate No. 85.
[16] Register of Licences, 1876. Record of Convictions (*ex inf.* G. Thomas, Llanelli).
[17] Ibid.
[18] *Ex inf.* Miss I.G. Prosser (great-great-granddaughter).
[19] Sion Chapel Llanelli: Marriage Certificate No. 133.
[20] Soar Baptist Chapel, Llwynhendy: Monumental Inscriptions
[21] Llanelli Register Office: Marriage Certificate No. 32.
[22] *Kelly's Directory for South Wales* (1923).
[23] *Star* Newspaper: Obituary 10 June 1939.
[24] Principal Probate Registry, London: Will of Titus Jones, 11 April 1899.
[25] Brown & Ward (1990)

Parliament House of Owen Glyndwr, Dolgelley

Fig. 22-1: Cwrt Plas-yn-dre

22. 'BARON' LEWIS OWEN OF DOLGELLAU AND HIS DESCENDANTS

E. Mary Hartley

This account of Lewis Owen and some of his descendants describes the part they played in the affairs of the communities in which they lived.* Dates in the sixteenth century are hard to estimate; I have based the dates for the births of the sons and daughters of Lewis Owen on the date of the second son's matriculation at Oxford and the ages given by the third and fifth sons when they were deponents in a Star Chamber case in 1602.

Dolgellau, a town at the confluence of two rivers, each with tributaries rushing down from the surrounding mountains, lies under the highest of these, Cader Idris. At the period of the Acts of Union of England and Wales (1536-43) it was the home of one of the then leaders in Merioneth, Lewis ab Owen. His house, Cwrt Plas-yn-dre, survived in the centre of Dolgellau until the 1880s when it was – unfortunately inexpertly – moved to Newtown and in consequence lost its character.[1] A copy of a nineteenth-century engraving, in the possession of the National Library of Wales, can be seen in Fig. 22-1. A reference to the reputation of the house as it existed in earlier days comes in a recent article:[2]

> Tri pheth sydd fawr eu lonydd,
> Ty Tudor Goch ap Ednyfed,
> Y Neuadd Wen is-law moel Onthwrm,
> Ac yscubor fawr y Barwn.

The third of these 'three things giving great fullness' (hospitality, perhaps) is described as 'the great barn of the Baron', that is, Cwrt Plas-yn-dre. The site left vacant in about 1885 is now occupied by an ironmonger's shop, but a street at the rear perpetuates the name.

---

* This chapter is based on a post-course assignment for the Second Stages Course, 'People, Places and Pedigrees', held in September 1996.

Lewis Owen was born around 1500.[3] He married Margaret Puleston, a niece of Sir John Puleston,[4] of Hafod y Wern, to whom Lewis Owen was a deputy in 1540,[5] and in his will in 1551 Sir John left land to Lewis Owen 'who has had the same heretofore these twenty years' and also 'all my goats in Merionethshire to Margaret Puleston, wife of Lewis Owen'.[6] Some of the descent from this union through four of the sons and one of the daughters (in all they had seven sons and four daughters) is given in Figs. 22-3 and 22-4. An account of the whole family is given by Robert Vaughan of Hengwrt (himself a great-grandson of Lewis Owen).[7] The second son, Hugh Owen, was a graduate of Oxford and later trained in the Inns of Court; he founded the family associated with Caerberllan, Llanfihangel-y-Pennant.[8] The fifth son was Robert Owen of Dolserau, (ancestor of Quaker emigrants to Pennsylvania in the following century); the seventh son, Ellis, is dismissed by Robert Vaughan with the phrase 'he had but daughters'.

To become a leading administrator in the Wales of 1535-55 must have been a challenging experience. The twenty-two Acts of Parliament passed between 1536 and 1543, collectively described as the 'Acts of Union', are summarised in the book *Union to Reform*.[9] Some of the Acts were economic, others political measures, involving substantial changes in local administration. Under Henry VIII, Lewis Owen was appointed deputy chamberlain of North Wales and baron of the exchequer at Caernarvon (the position which resulted in his description as 'Y Barwn'). He was Sheriff of Merioneth in 1545-6 and 1554-5, and represented Merionethshire in four parliaments between 1547 and 1554.

The convulsions in the realm in the later years of the reign of Henry VIII and in the next two reigns affected Lewis Owen in at least three ways. In Merioneth, the Dissolution of the Monasteries (1536-40) resulted in new owners for lands formerly belonging to Cymer Abbey. Owen acquired lands in Nannau, Llanegryn and Talyllyn, and in 1552 he took a twenty-one-year lease of the township of Dolgellau, so that before his death he had built up a considerable (if scattered) estate.[10] For the location of the places named in this chapter, see Fig. 22-2.

Lewis Owen represented Merioneth in the two parliaments in the reign of Edward VI (November 1547 to April 1552, and the brief one of March 1553). The first of these saw the passing of the two Acts of Uniformity (January 1549 and April 1552) and the introduction of the two versions of the English Prayer Book.[11] At the same time sweeping changes in religious practice were imposed, with the removal of images, pictures and frescoes from parish churches; many mediaeval customs were abrogated. The introduction of an English Book of Common Prayer, replacing the Latin, did

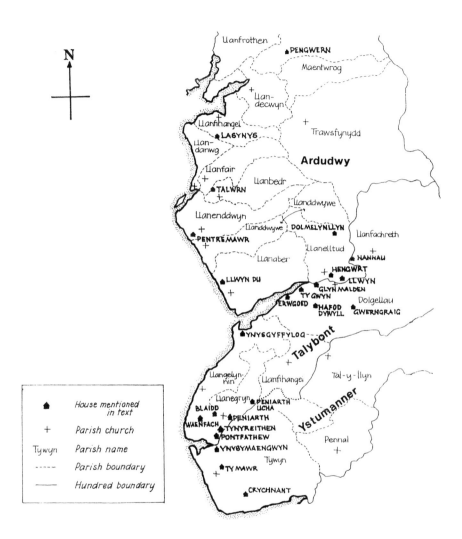

Fig. 22-2: The Merionethshire of 'Baron' Lewis Owen

not provide a service more generally comprehensible in Wales. We do not know how Lewis Owen reacted to these changes, nor to the still more dramatic ones in the next reign. He was not in the first parliament of the reign of Mary I (October to December 1553) but he served in both in 1554, in April (shortly before Mary's marriage to Philip of Spain) and in November to December at the time when it was believed she was pregnant. Lewis Owen may well have been in Parliament when, on 30 November, Pole – the papal legate – addressed the Lords and Commons and the clergy, and 'all knelt to ask forgiveness for their error in breaking away from the Holy See'.[12] The country then, according to Philip, returned to the Catholic faith; within three weeks the former heresy laws were re-enacted and open Protestants could be, and were, burned at the stake.

Lewis Owen did not live to experience the Elizabethan settlement which eventually restored some measure of religious balance. He was Sheriff for Merioneth from 1554 until his death, and with Sir John Wynn of Gwydir attempted to bring greater order into the commote of Mawddwy, which had only been incorporated in Merionethshire in 1543. Whether or not the unrest was actually caused by a gang of red-haired brigands, this became the accepted story.[13] The capture and execution of some leaders in late 1554 led the rest to look for revenge. Robert Vaughan describes the outcome.[14] Lewis Owen was returning from the Montgomeryshire Assizes (when he had been treating with Richard Mytton about the intended marriage of his eldest son) when he was 'met by a damned crew of thieves and outlaws who in the thick woods of Mawddwy lay in wait for his coming, and had cut down long trees to cross the way and to hinder his passage'. The ambush (at the place on the road, about three miles from the junction at Mallwyd, still called 'Llydiart y Barwn') resulted in Lewis's death, on Friday 11 October 1555. The event passed into local folk history, in its way as well known in Merioneth as the martyrdom in Oxford – only five days later – of Latimer and Ridley, the 'lighting of a candle that was not easily put out'. Certainly Robert Vaughan considered that his great-grandfather's murder had been a turning point, when many of the gang were captured and were either executed or fled the country. His account finishes: 'And so with the loss of his life he purchased peace and quietness to his country, the which God be praised we enjoy even to our days'.

John Lewis Owen, eldest son of Baron Owen, married Ursula, a daughter of Richard Mytton of Shrewsbury and Dinas Mawddwy.[15] Initially he is described as 'of Dolgellau', but in his middle years he built a new house, Llwyn, about a mile outside the mediaeval town and north of the river Wnion. In 1574 (*jure* his father-in-law, one assumes) he became a Burgess of Shrewsbury, the Admissions Roll showing that he had then four sons and six daughters. The eldest three, Lewis (born about 1561), John (1564) and Henry (1570) played a prominent (if, as we shall see, sometimes lawless) part in Dolgellau life in the last years of the century.

John Lewis Owen followed his father, and brother Hugh, as MP for Merioneth, in his case holding the position in 1572-83, though he seems to have taken little part in national politics. Locally he was more active, serving as JP from 1563, Sheriff on three occasions, and latterly as Deputy Lieutenant. Unfortunately rivalry dogged his career and in 1597 an ally of the Salisburys of Rûg brought a Star Chamber action against Owen and his co-deputy lieutenant, Cadwaladr Price of Rhiwlâs, accusing them of embezzlement, false imprisonment, bribery, extortion and intimidation.[16] The upshot was that in 1600 both of them lost their positions as deputy lieutenants and on the Commission of the Peace. Glanmor Williams refers to them as 'prize rogues', an appellation richly deserved if one were sure the allegations were in fact substantiated.[17]

Towards the end of his life John Lewis Owen, with his three sons and joined later by several Owen nephews, became involved in more local rivalry.[18] The dispute was at first a conflict over control of the town of Dolgellau, which had been in the province of the Nanneys in the fifteenth century; as we have seen, Baron Owen and his sons became powerful in the area in the next century. The feud, spreading to involve the inhabitants of Dolgellau and Llanfachreth parishes, continued even into the eighteenth century.

In 1592 Griffith Nanney became MP for Merioneth. This seems to have triggered a series of disputes; for example, Griffith's father, Hugh Nanney 'Hên', enclosed a piece of common land, and the three sons of John Lewis Owen with their cousin Robert Owen of Hengwrt knocked down the wall. A series of court cases followed. There were incidents when the pew in St Mary's church in Dolgellau belonging to one family was broken down by members of the opposition, with evident retaliation; there is even a story of a challenge to a secret dual to take place at dawn 'on the sea shore directly under the Church of Llanddwywe'.

One event is well documented, though some of the Great Sessions papers are missing. Edward ap David, a servant of Hugh Nanney, was alleged to have seduced a cousin of Robert Owen of Hengwrt. Wednesday 24 June 1601 was the last day of the Midsummer Fair at Dolgellau, held on the Marian, an open space between the town and the river Wnion. Edward ap David was playing bowls with Edward Nanney when he was attacked by a group of young men, including Robert Owen of Hengwrt and two of his cousins, Lewis Simon Owen and Robert Simon Owen (then aged about eighteen and seventeen); in the ensuing melée Edward ap David died. There followed a coroner's jury, and then two separate trials at the Great Sessions at Bala. On at least one occasion Robert Simon Owen was found guilty, but he was finally acquitted. The 'losing' side then started a Star Chamber case, alleging that the juries had been rigged; the statements by the many deponents are vivid, if not lurid.[19] One is left with the impression that, by chance, no one had been around at the Fair when the victim was stabbed.

As a sequel to this case, in 1636 we find Robert Simon Owen, by then married with six children and living at Ty Gwyn, serving as a sub-collector for Talybont Uwch Cregennan (that is, the parishes of Dolgellau and Llanfachreth) for a Subsidy collected that year. The list of contributors in Merionethshire was, in 1831, in the possession of Ellis Owen of Pant Phylip (a direct descendent of Robert Simon Owen) and was printed, with useful notes, in the *Cambrian Quarterly Magazine*.[20]

Llwyn remained the home of the Owens after the death of John Lewis Owen in 1606/7. The eldest son, Lewis, died there in about 1635, leaving no children, and after that Llwyn was bought by the Anwyls. The second son John married an heiress of the important family of Ynysmaengwyn (near Towyn), and lived at Erwgoed, the home for several generations; they were later at Waenfach (Llanegryn).[21]

In the seventeenth century two great grandsons of Baron Owen came to the fore. The first was Robert Vaughan of Hengwrt, later known as 'The Antiquary'.[22] He was born about 1592, the only legitimate son of Hywel Vaughan of Gwerngraig and his wife Margaret, a daughter of Edward Owen of Hengwrt. We met Margaret's brother Robert Owen in the 'Marian murder' incident. It seems that, later, Hengwrt passed by mortgage to Hywel Vaughan, and Robert Vaughan probably moved there after his marriage to Catherine, a daughter of Griffith Nanney (also prominent in the Owen-Nanney feuds). Robert had matriculated at Oriel College, Oxford, in 1610 but after a short time there he returned to Wales. He took a normal part in local affairs, for instance, serving as a JP,[23] but for the next fifty years his main interest was his study of Welsh antiquities. He amassed a vast collection of manuscripts, unparalleled in the whole of Wales, obtaining books where he could and transcribing what he could not keep. The manuscripts now form the major part of the Peniarth Mss in the National Library of Wales. His only original work, *British Antiquities Revived* (published in 1662), did not show his real genius.[24] It is for the painstaking collecting and preserving the contents of his huge library that he is remembered and revered.

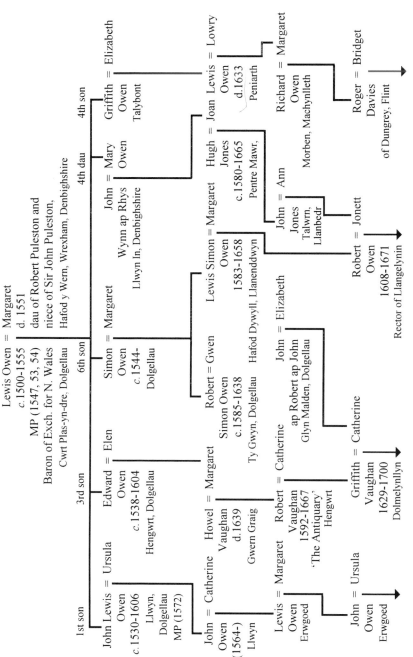

Fig. 22-3: Descent from 'Baron' Lewis Owen, 1500-1720 (continued on Fig. 22-4)

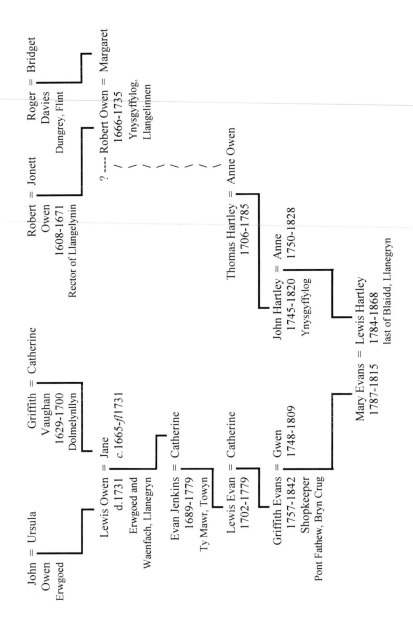

Fig. 22-4: Descent from 'Baron' Lewis Owen, 1608-1868 (continued from Fig. 22-3)

Robert Vaughan's fourth son, Griffith Vaughan of Dolmelynllyn (1628-1700), shared his enthusiasms, and it is thought that the collection in Peniarth 288 was copied, if not all compiled, by him. Griffith Vaughan married the eldest daughter of Robert Simon Owen;[25] one of their daughters, Jane, married Lewis Owen of Erwgoed.

The other great-grandson of Baron Owen to contribute, though in quite a different way, to Merioneth, particularly in the period of the Commonwealth and Restoration, was yet another Robert Owen (1608-71).[26] He was the third son of Lewis Simon Owen of Hafod Dywyll (again, met in the Marian murder episode). Lewis and his brother Robert both went to Shrewsbury School, and each in turn sent his sons there.[27] Lewis's three eldest sons entered together in June 1618 when Robert was ten. Robert, with his elder brother Simon, went to Hart Hall, Oxford, where they both matriculated in March 1625/6. Simon spent ten years at Oxford, completing a degree in medicine in July 1636; Robert graduated MA in 1630. Unfortunately the Hart Hall records did not survive its later take-over by Hertford College, and Robert disappears from view for the next twenty years. He was presumably ordained somewhere but his activities in the period of the Civil War are unknown. By 1649 he had become Rector of Llangelynnin, and there throughout the Commonwealth period (when so many parochial details disappear) he served his parish and kept his registers meticulously. In 1659 he married a widow, Jonett Edwards (née Jones), a daughter of one of Robert's second cousins, (descended from Mary, wife of John Wynn of Llwyn In). She already had three daughters, and six more children were born before Robert's death in 1671. He left a careful and comprehensive will, with Jonett as guardian of her young family.

Sadly, disaster followed in the next generation. The only son to survive into adult life was Robert, who was not quite five years old when his father died. Eighteen months later his mother was re-married, this time to the young curate of Dolgellau, fifteen years her junior, Rowland Price. He was granted administration of the Revd Robert Owen's will, and for about twenty years did nothing about it.

In 1686 Robert Owen married Margaret Davies, a descendant of Griffith, the fourth son of Baron Lewis Owen. At first all went well; by 1692 Robert had obtained a copy of his father's will, and documents in the Bryn-y-gwin archive at Dolgellau Record Office show that he was trying, if belatedly, to carry out some of his father's wishes. But from 1686 he had been trying to get possession of the estate which, under the clear terms of the will, should have been his; after Jonett's death early in 1687 his stepfather resisted every attempt to yield possession. Unfortunately for Robert, Rowland Price had two younger brothers, both lawyers. The whole family features in an article about Llanuwchllyn,[28] in which, *inter alia*, Rowland Price is mentioned as 'begetting at least nine bastards', a description which is authenticated in the Dolgellau parish register of the period. With the aid of Thomas Price, a lawyer in London, and Edward Price, a lawyer in Dolgellau, Rowland continued to hold on to the estate that he claimed was 'appropriately' his, as Jonett's third husband. The processes of the law failed Robert; he was three times in prison in Dolgellau for debt; he was sentenced to outlawry; he lived in hiding in London; and after Rowland Price's death in 1713 the case was revived, first by Thomas Price and then by Edward Price. It was not until 1725 after Edward's death, that Robert Owen, by then nearly sixty, reappears at Ynysgyffylog.

At some point in this sorry tale Margaret Davies had disappeared. By 1725 Robert had just one (natural) daughter Ann, born in London about 1705, as well as one nephew, Thomas Williams, living in Barmouth and his heir-at-law. In 1727 Ann married Thomas Hartley in London and, at the invitation of her father, she and her husband came to live at Ynysgyffylog, where Robert Owen survived to see the first three of a family of grandchildren. When he died in 1735 he left the estate in trust for his two-year-old grandson, who took the name Robert Hartley Owen.

Immediately trouble flared again, this time with Thomas Williams, and it took nine years before Thomas Hartley was authorised to administer the estate on behalf of his son. Thomas Hartley was described as a 'warehouseman' when he married, but after 1744 he appears in the Merioneth Quarter Sessions Rolls as 'gentleman'.[29] He seems to have been accepted into local society.

The end of the story must be reached. Griffith Evans, a shopkeeper at Bryn Crug (great-grandson of Lewis Owen and Jane Vaughan) was of the family of Evan Jenkins of Tŷ Mawr, Towyn,[30] and his daughter Mary married a grandson, Lewis Hartley, of Thomas Hartley and Ann. Lewis farmed in Llanegryn, being churchwarden and later parish clerk there. Though a tenant farmer, Lewis wrote a *cywydd* to his landlord which showed his pride in the ancestry of himself and his wife.

BIBLIOGRAPHY

Books

Cheney, C.R. (ed), *Handbook of Dates* (Royal Historical Society Guides and Handbooks No. 4, 1978).

Davies, G., *Noddwyr Beirdd ym Meirion* (Dolgellau, Archifdy Sir Feirionnydd, 1974).

Dwnn, L. (ed Meyrick, S.R.), *Heraldic Visitations of Wales* (Llandovery, 1846).

Foster, J., *Alumni Oxonienses*, 1500-1714 (Oxford and London, 1891-2).

Griffith, J.E., *Pedigrees of Anglesey and Carnarvonshire Families* (Horncastle, 1914; reprinted Wrexham, 1985).

James, A.J. and Thomas, J.E., *Union to Reform* (Gomer Press, 1986).

Jenkin, R.T. (ed), *The Dictionary of Welsh Biography down to 1940* (Honourable Society of Cymmrodorion, 1959).

Lloyd, J.Y.W., *History of Powys Fadog*, (6 vols) (London, 1881-7).

Rowlands, J. *et al.* (ed), *Welsh Family History, a Guide to Research* (1993). See now J. & S. Rowlands (ed.), *Welsh Family History, a Guide to Research* (2nd ed., FFHS, 1998), published since the author's death.

Siddons, M.P., *The Development of Welsh Heraldry*, (Aberystwyth, vol. i 1991, vols ii & iii 1993).

Sylvester, D., *A History of Gwynedd* (Phillimore, 1983).

Venn, J. and J.A., *Alumni Cantabrigienses, from the Earliest Times to 1900*, (Cambridge, 1922-54).

Williams, G., *Recovery, Reorientation and Reformation, Wales, c. 1415-1642*, (Oxford, 1987).

Journals

Archaeologia Cambrensis (Arch. Camb.).

Journal of the Merioneth Historical and Record Society (JMHRS).

NOTES TO CHAPTER 22

[1] Hugh J. Owen, 'Owen Glyn Dŵr's Old Parliament House at Dolgelley', *JMHRS* ii, 81-8. (In the final paragraph the author states that this building – which may or may not have had associations with Owen Glyn Dŵr – was certainly the residence of Baron Lewis Owen.)

[2] Peter Smith and Richard Suggett, 'Dolgun-uchaf, a late mediaeval hall-house', *JMHRS*, xii, 98.

[3] S.T. Bindoff, *The House of Commons 1509-1558* (Secker & Warburg, 1982), 289; *Dictionary of National Biography*, xlii, 431-2; *Dictionary of Welsh Biography (DWB)*, 715.

[4] S.T. Bindoff, op. cit, 160-1.

[5] University College of North Wales, Bangor, Nannau MSS 3716.

[6] PRO, PCC 7 Bucke.

[7] Robert Vaughan: quoted in J.Y.W. Lloyd, *History of Powys Fadog*, vi, 409-12.

[8] P.W. Hasler, *The House of Commons, 1558-1603* (HMSO, 1981), 160. J.E. Griffiths, *Pedigrees of Anglesey and Carnarvonshire Families*, 363.

[9] A.J. James and J.E. Thomas, *Union to Reform* (Gomer Press, 1986), 78-83.

[10] E.A. Lewis and J.C. Davies, *Records of the Court of Augmentations relating to Wales and Monmouthshire*. Board of Celtic Studies History and Law Series no. 13 (Cardiff, 1954), 427-8.

[11] E.C. Ratcliffe, *Historical and bibliographical note as a preface to an edition of the first and second Prayer Book of Edward VI* (Dent, 1910).

[12] Maria Parry, *Elizabeth I, A Life from Contemporary Documents* (The Folio Society: 1990), 105-6.

[13] J. Gwynfor Jones, 'Lewis Owen, Sheriff of Merioneth and the "Gwylliaid Cochion" of Mawddwy in 1554-5, *JMHRS* xii, 221-36. This article was published after the work for the present chapter was complete. It analyses in particular the circumstances of Lewis Owen's assassination and the judicial records which ensued.

[14] Robert Vaughan, op cit.

[15] P.W. Hasler, op cit, 181-2.

[16] *Star Chamber* (ed Edwards), University of Wales Board of Celtic Studies, History and Law Series no. 2, 91.

[17] Glanmor Williams, *Recovery, Reorientation and Reformation, Wales, c.1415-1642*, (OUP, 1987) 343.

[18] Bryn R. Parry, 'Hugh Nanney Hên (c.1546-1623), Squire of Nannau'. *JMHRS* iii, 185-206. This long article gives full details and references for the many incidents at this period.

[19] PRO: STAC 5/N/12/21.

[20] *Cambrian Quarterly Magazine*, 1831, 449-60.

[21] W.W.E. Wynne, 'History of the Parish of Llanegryn' (*Arch. Camb.*, 1879) 114-139. PF iv, 291-2.

[22] *DWB*, 1005-6; *JMHRS* I, 21-30 and viii, 397-408.

[23] J.R.S. Phillips, *The Justices of the Peace in Wales and Monmouthshire, 1541 to 1689* (University of Wales Press, 1975) 50.

[24] Francis Jones, 'An approach to Welsh Genealogy' (*Transactions of the Honourable Society of Cymmrodorion*, 1948), 407. A critic remarked that 'he (i.e. Robert Vaughan) has shown that it is possible to write a book on an important subject without contributing anything profound or original to it'.

[25] NLW: Bangor Probate: Robert Symon Owen, Dolgellau, 2 Feb 1637/8.

[26] E.M. Hartley, 'Jonett Jones of Pentre Mawr,' *JMHRS* xi, 169-81. This article contains much detail for which there is no room here.

[27] E. Calvert, *Regestum Scholarium, 1562-1635*. (This is the first available register of Shrewsbury School.)

[28] E.D. Evans, 'A Llanuwchllyn Ecclesiastical Dispute', *JMHRS*, xi, 414-32.

[29] Keith Williams-Jones, *A Calendar of the Merioneth Quarter Sessions Rolls* (Merioneth County Council, 1965).

[30] Jean Wave and Hugh Hunt, *The Several Lives of a Victorian Vet*, (Bachman and Turner, 1979). The schedule of Dr Griffith Evans' papers in NLW contains full references to his pedigree.

INDEX

Place-names of towns, villages, hundreds, etc, but not houses or estates, have had pre-1974 county codes provided (in brackets) in this index, except where the place and county share a name.

Llangunnog (Mgy) 108, 112
Llangynfelyn (Cgn) 112, 309
Llanidloes (Mgy) 67, 101
Llannerchaeron (Cgn) 40
Llannor (Cae) 289-307
Llanon (Cgn) 35
Llansantffraid (Cgn) 32-41
Llanuwchllyn (Mer) 338
Llanwenog (Cgn) 38
Llanymynech (Mgy) 104
Lledrod (Cgn) 38
Lloyd family, Tŷ Newydd 289-307
Llŷn 289, 298, 300
local history journals 244
Lost Houses of Wales 240
Loughor (Gla) 83
Machynlleth (Mgy) 59, 60, 101
Mackworth, Sir Humphrey 64
Madryn estate 300
manorial records, *see* estate records
maps 210-225, 229, 233, 236-7
    enclosure 212, 214, 218-9
    estate 219-20
    manuscript 212, 214-20
    Ordnance Survey 211-2, 221-3
    tithe 212, 214-6
    Valuation 220
maritime 262, 268, 270
    Crew Lists and Agreements 270
    East India fleet 296
    expansion of trade 253
    master mariners 254, 260, 270, 272-4
    shareholders in ships 264, 272
markets and fairs 61, 319, 324, 333
marriage by licence 48, 53
masons 319-20
Mawddwy (Mer) 332
Medical Directory 281, 283
Medical Register 283
Members of Parliament 247, 330, 333
Men at the Bar 279
Merioneth County Agricultural Society 273
Merthyr Tydfil (Gla) 3, 5, 11, 58, 62, 67-77
    Abercannaid 65

Caedraw 74
China 5, 74 -5
Cyfarthfa 68
Dowlais 68
Penydarren 11, 68
Plymouth 68
Ynysgau 74-5
metal-working 81-93
middle class 6-7, 253-75
migration 166, 272
    from rural areas 76, 319
Miles, John 50
Minera (Den) 105, 107, 108
Mines Act (1842) 65
mining 81-93, 253
    coal-mining and miners 320-1
    domestic economy 321
    manufacturing and 10
missionary societies 1
monasteries, dissolution of 247, 330
Monmouth 20
monumental inscriptions 110, 265, 304, 305
Moris Reignald 309-17
Mountain Ash (Gla) 42
Munster (Irl) 172
muster rolls 153, 179, 185
Myddleton family (Chirk) 105
names, personal
    given
      see also surnames
      15th century 152
      ancient Welsh origin 171
      Anglo-Norman 152
      Old Testament 54-5, 166, 170
      profile of 148
      lists of 16, 17, 106, 109, 151, 153, 162, 164-165, 172, 173-4, 191-3, 282-4
Nanney family 333-4
Nanteos estate 242, 243, 249, 250
National Library of Wales 33, 140, 155, 175, 199, 212, 216, 240, 245-6, 248, 329, 334
National Monuments Record of Wales (NMRW) 229-38
    air photographs 235-6